THE INTELLIGENT MR KINGHORNE

A BIOGRAPHY OF ALEXANDER KINGHORNE (1770-1846)

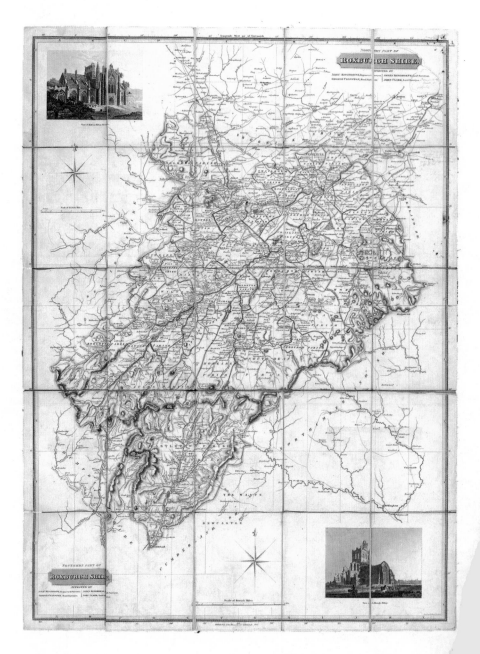

Plan of The County of Roxburgh; attested by Alexr Kinghorne, James Kinghorne, George
Cranston and John Clark; engraved by N.R. Hewitt; Edinburgh: John Thomson & Co., 1822
[Author's collection]

THE INTELLIGENT MR KINGHORNE

A BIOGRAPHY OF ALEXANDER KINGHORNE (1770-1846)

CHIS MAXWELL & ALEX PUGH

AUSTRALIAN SCHOLARLY

By the Same Authors

The Merchant of Sydney, James Chisholm 1772–1837
The Master of Hell's Gates, William Kinghorne 1796–1878

First published 2023 by
Australian Scholarly Publishing Pty Ltd

7 Lt Lothian St Nth, North Melbourne, Vic 3051

Tel: 03 9329 6963

enquiry@scholarly.info / www.scholarly.info

ISBN 978-1-922952-05-9

Front cover photo: Humphry Repton surveying with a theodolite, unknown artist, circa 1800. [Heritage Image Partnership Ltd / Alamy Stock Photo].

Back cover photo: Leith Pier and Harbour, 1798. [Grant, James, *Old and New Edinburgh*, Edinburgh: Cassell, 1880, Vol VI, 273].

Cover design: Lucia Sankovic

Dedicated to

Brian Hinton Fletcher OAM FRAHS FAHA, 1931–2018

Contents

List of Figures

14. Georgian frontage of Kippilaw Mansion House [author's photograph, 2014].

15. Scott's View [author's photograph, 2016].

16. Gledswood House, Berwickshire [RCAHMS, SC 1382685, ©Crown Copyright: HES.].

17. Plan of Netherton and Muirside (Melgrund Estate) by Alexander Kinghorne, 1806 [NRAS RHP 03634-00001].

18. David Steuart Erskine, 11th Earl of Buchan, by John Finlayson (after Sir Joshua Reynolds, 1764), mezzotint published 1765 [National Portrait Gallery, London D893].

19. Maxton Kirk [author's photograph, 2016].

20. Alexander Kinghorne's coat of arms, from Kinghorne Family Bible, Nowra Museum [author's photograph, 2022].

21. Plan of the farm of Faugh-hill, 1813, by Alexander Kinghorne [courtesy of the Duke of Roxburghe].

22. Plan of the Estate of Linthill, 1820, by Alexander Kinghorne [NRAS SC1524405].

23. Plan of Selkirkshire; attested by Rt. Hon. Lord Napier, Thomas Mitchell, road surveyor, Alexander Kinghorne, civil engineer and James Kinghorne, land surveyor, Edinburgh: engraved by William Johnstone; Edinburgh: John Thomson & Co., 1824 [author's collection].

24. Lord Buchan to Alexander Kinghorne, 28 December 1822 [author's collection].

25. Ebenezer Faichney, on behalf of Lord Buchan, to Elizabeth Kinghorne, 29 July 1823 [author's collection].

26. Map of Emu Plains Convict Farm by Alexander Kinghorne, 1826 [NSW State Archives, map 2660, Crown Plan E-277A].

27. Map of Emu Plains Convict Farm by Alexander Kinghorne, 1826. The letters on the map indicate the approximate positions of (A) 'Government House', (B) convict huts, (C) Sydney-Bathurst Road, (D) Sydney-Bathurst Road zig-zag, (E) Alexander Kinghorne Jnr's Mill, (F) Old Bathurst Road [NSW State Archives, map 2661, Crown Plan E-277B].

28. View of the Colonial Secretary's Residence, Sydney, by Conrad Martens, 1839 [State Library of NSW ML1618].

29. Letter from Alexander Kinghorne to Archdeacon Thomas Hobbes Scott, 20 May 1826 [NSW State Archives, 4/346, 101. 11].

30. Bonnyrigg House, Male Orphan School [author's photograph, 2015].

31. Copies of Plans for Male Orphan School buildings, Bonnyrigg, 1831, by Lieutenant Richard Sadlier [Thorp, *Bonnyrigg House*, Plans 1 & 2: 148–9].

32. Drummond House, Terminus Street, Liverpool, ca 1960 [Op den Brouw, Glen, *Town's First Fleet Power Couple, Liverpool City Champion*, 1 April 2019].

33. Cartoon of neck collar and irons worn by Privates Sudds and Thompson, 1826 [Hall, *Refutation of Lieutenant-General Darling*].

34. Large Cavern in the Wellington Valley. Engraving showing James Kinghorne and Thomas Mitchell in Cathedral Cavern, Wellington Caves, 1830 [Oldroyd, *In the Footsteps of Thomas Livingstone Mitchell*, 357].

35. Map of the Parish of Beecroft, County of St Vincent, 1936. The boundary of Portion 1, Alexander Kinghorne's property Mount Jervis, is outlined in red [State Library of NSW].

36. Montagu Point, adjacent to Mount Jervis, Jervis Bay, NSW [author's photograph, 2013].

37. View across Wollondilly River to Kippilaw, Goulburn, NSW [author's photograph, 2017].

I caused it to be surveyed by the intelligent Mr. Kinghorn, in November 1803, when the real track was again ascertained

George Chalmers, *Caledonia*

Foreword

This is the third book from the fruitful collaboration of the two authors. It is well up to the high standard they set in the first two. It has been meticulously researched over a period of several years, well written and very readable. To discover so much information and to set it in context about an obscure man who tried to make his mark but ultimately failed is quite remarkable. The search has involved careful explanation of the social, political and economic milieu of Alexander Kinghorne's life in the Scottish Borders in the early nineteenth century before at the age of fifty-four he left to make a fresh start on the far side of the world. That intriguing fact in itself justifies this biography.

There follows the challenge of finding out how Kinghorne fared in his courageous endeavour. Here too diligent research with a completely separate set of sources has enabled the story to be told skilfully and with real empathy. The reader wants Kinghorne to succeed and is disappointed when he does not. That in itself is the result of the authors' ability to tell the tale. What then? Was there any point in going any further?

Certainly, because this excellent book shows what can be done when skilled, painstaking historians working at a high level of scholarship, tackle a difficult challenge. It is an encouragement to others to do likewise. The subjects of a biography do not have to be famous and successful. Courageous battlers who never gave up, like Alexander Kinghorne, deserve to be remembered, and their lives recorded with sympathy.

Stuart Braga
August 2022

Introduction

Antiquities may be looked upon as the planks of a shipwreck, which industrious and wise men gather and preserve from the deluge of time.

Francis Bacon, *The Advancement of Learning*, 1605

In our previous books, *The Merchant of Sydney* and *The Master of Hell's Gates*, we considered the lives of two members of the extended Chisholm family in Australia: its founder, James Chisholm, and Captain William Kinghorne. The other important founder was Alexander Kinghorne, William's father and the subject of this biography, who arrived in 1824. His daughter Elizabeth married James Chisholm Jnr, and her brothers, along with her sons began a large pastoral empire.

Alexander Kinghorne was born in 1770, emerging from a humble background – at least two generations of tailors in the border counties of Berwickshire and Roxburghshire – to rise to some prominence in Scotland. He shared with many Scots, in the aftermath of the Civil War and Jacobite Rebellions, a romantic belief that he had noble ancestors, but that his family had fallen on hard times. In this book we have delved into his history, with some surprising results.

Like other scientific figures of the industrial revolution, his advancement in life was driven by ambitions and aspirations encouraged by important patrons. These started fortuitously, with his education alongside Sir Walter Scott, who became the stellar exponent of romanticism in 19th century Scotland. Alexander began his working life as a schoolteacher, but soon found opportunities beyond that amidst the agricultural and engineering fervour gripping Scotland during and after the Napoleonic Wars. He lived in a society in which economic and social advancement was impossible without patronage. We examine his connections with the prominent landholders, engineers and antiquarians of his day, and whether he was able to maintain his self-respect through this.

His life in Scotland, the first part of this book, was a story of some glories and disappointment. In the middle of life he charted a different course, a 'sea change' it would be called nowadays, and the second part follows him and his family as they shipped themselves off to New South Wales, and what befell them there. It is a story of courage and hope, with turns of achievement and twists of adversity few would have foreseen, and some most unexpected legacies in the life of the burgeoning nation, which became Australia. It was a pattern among Scots to go to the colonies and make their fortunes, and then return 'home' to show what they had made of themselves. The third and final part of this book describes Alexander's return to his native Scotland, where he was hit by hard times, again unexpectedly, and was to die in obscurity in Galashiels in 1846.

As we researched this biography, we became increasingly fascinated with this humane individual. We hope you will enjoy reading, as much as we did writing, the story of the interesting life and extraordinary legacy of *the intelligent Mr Kinghorne.*

Chis Maxwell and Alex Pugh
November, 2022

PART I

SCOTLAND

Chapter 1

Origins and Prospects (1550–1770)

'Tut! man,' said Bolton, 'make the best of it, thy mother's father was but a tailor,
old Overstitch of Holderness – Why, what! because thou art a misproud bird, and
despiseth thine own natural lineage, and rufflest in unpaid silks and velvets, and
keepest company with gallants and cutters, must we lost our memory for that?'[1]

Sir Walter Scott, *The Monastery*, 1820

The port of Leith was a bustle of activity that afternoon, as their carriage made its way onto the docks, its wheels clattering over cobblestones, worn by centuries of use, and assuredly not designed for comfort. As they alighted on the waterfront, the hubbub surrounded them, as stevedores ran to and fro with handcarts over the stones, laden with goods and sea chests, and calling one to another in a language intelligible only to themselves. Seagulls added their cries to the cacophony, as they squabbled about the dock, or wheeled over it in arcs. Beyond that, lining the waterfront on one side, were offices, and the warehouses, their doors thrown open for their day's trade. On the other, the ships' masts swayed before the sky, those that were moored close, ill-at-ease upon the low tide. Others lay at anchor further out upon the Firth, among them what remained of the North Sea Fleet, which but a few years earlier had defended Britain from Napoleon. The smell of the wharfs was singular, the ropes and burlap, the smoke of tobacco, charcoal from the braziers, and somewhere tar, the ooze of exposed seaweeds, muds and sands, and wafting in from beyond all that, the scent of the open waters, for which they were bound.

He had been here before. It was just shy of twelve years to the day since he had brought his son William to this place, at the height of the wars with Napoleon, to board H.M.S. *Nightingale* as a ship's boy and begin his naval career. Now it was his turn, in different circumstances, but no less an adventure. So it was that Alexander Kinghorne, accompanied by two sons and three daughters, boarded the *Portland* at Leith to commence the voyage to New South Wales. They were to set sail upon the flood tide the following morning, 1 April 1824, the captain wanting everything loaded and his passengers bunked by the previous evening, so that there would be no delay.

Alexander had very mixed feelings for the venture. Many times over the following months he would ask himself what had possessed him, aged now in his fifties, to abandon his home in Scotland. Doubtless, as the *Portland* sailed from the Firth of Forth into the North Sea, steering first north for Orkney and then south-west into the Atlantic, rarely comfortable waters, and then, at the southern extremity of their course, to pick up the Roaring Forties and mount the waves of those latitudes bordering the Indian and Southern Oceans. He carried letters of introduction from his most important connections, people of nobility and influence he had cultivated over decades. He was confident that when he presented himself to the Governor of the Colony, Sir Thomas Brisbane, he would secure a favourable position, and grants of land. But letters afforded no protection from the discomforts and dangers of such a sea voyage.

How could he? His boys were enthusiastic enough. Their older brothers had gone on two years before and wrote favourably of the place; but his other son had refused to go. And his girls, well Isabella at least was pining for her romantic notions of a life in Roxburghshire society, but she was but a child, and embarked out of obedience to the patriarch, and because she had no choice. For his own part, Alexander was leaving because he had exhausted his prospects in Scotland and he was sliding into poverty. Emigration represented his only hope to secure the future of his family.

Oh, but he had dreams!...He wanted to rise above the social restrictions, which inhibited advancement in his homeland, and had made him struggle for what he had achieved, even with his many obvious talents. He wanted to become a landed gentleman, like those who had been his employers and patrons. Indeed, he wanted to restore what he saw as the lost nobility of his family, represented by his distinguished name. To do this he needed land and money, in large quantities, and like many Scots for centuries before him, he knew the place to find them was in the colonies. He had been encouraged by his childhood friend, Sir Walter Scott, whose romantic novels he read avidly, and which he had discussed with their author in his sprawling estate at Abbotsford. His was a world where social mobility could be achieved through opportunity, through imagination, through industry, through alliances with the right people, through valour…Would Alexander succeed? Would he rescue his children, and restore them to the prominence in society he was sure was enjoyed by his shadowy forbears?

The Ancestors of Alexander Kinghorne

> *The past is a foreign country.*
> Lord David Cecil, a lecture of 1949[2]

The Kinghorne family originated from Kinghorn in Fife, north-east of Edinburgh. *Kinghorne* was a regional surname given to people, most often after they moved to another area from that town. Different spellings of the name can be found in Alexander's family, the earliest known being 'Kingorne'. Alexander himself was baptised 'Kinghorn' and changed it to 'Kinghorne' in 1799. For convenience this book uses Alexander's chosen spelling, 'Kinghorne', as a general use, but maintains the spellings for individuals as they appeared in the source documents.

Alexander's family has been traced to Dunfermline in Fife in the early 16th century, with its origin clearly from the town of Kinghorn in the preceding centuries. From Dunfermline a branch of the family moved to Edinburgh, and then Berwickshire in the 17th century. Alexander knew little to nothing about this family history. A study of Alexander's forbears is in Appendix 3 to this book. The following provides the context relevant to Alexander's life, and his ideas of lost nobility.

The Kinghornes of Dunfermline and Edinburgh

Alexander Kinghorne's family has been traced to Adam Kingorne (1490s– c.1563), who was Chamberlain of Dunfermline Abbey, and held various Vicarages including Kinglassie in Fife, and Linton in Peeblesshire (now West Linton). The Abbey owned the Tower of Kingorne-Waster, which is in Burntisland, three miles to the south-west of the town of Kinghorn. The tower had been for some centuries in the keeping of the Durie family as custodians or tenants for the Abbey. Adam personally enjoyed the patronage of two successive Abbots of Dunfermline from that family: James Beaton, and his nephew George Durie.

Adam's parents have not been identified with certainty, but he was either the son or a close relative of David Kingorne, who was a Chaplain of Dunfermline Abbey at the end of the 15th century, and later Abbot of Crossraguel Abbey in South Ayrshire. Dunfermline Abbey was a royal foundation, and Dunfermline had been the seat of the royal government for some centuries, with the Royal Palaces near the Abbey gates. There are records of clerks and priests named 'Kyngorne' since the early 13th century, and this might have represented a family or a small number of families providing young men for the royal and ecclesiastical services. As Chamberlain of Dunfermline Abbey, Adam was well-known in the Royal Palace, where the Abbot had his apartments. He also had a significant role regarding the Abbey's relationship with the Burgh (or 'Regality') of Dunfermline, of which the Abbot was overlord.

Adam's allegiance was to his patrons, James Beaton and George Durie. Both were opposed to the Reformation, with judicial involvements in the martyrdom of reformers. While Adam seems to have taken a back seat in the affairs of the Church in the last decade of his life (1552–63), he did not break with his patrons, and continued to enjoy the benefits he had gained.

Adam Kingorne was a monastic priest, who had taken vows of poverty, chastity, obedience and stability under the Rule of Saint Benedict. However, he broke his vows, fathering children, and owning property in Dunfermline, at least thirty years before the Reformation led to the Abbey being 'cleansed' and pillaged in 1559–60, and the monastic community dissolved.

In 1552 Adam Kingorne undertook a legal process to 'legitimize' his three natural sons: David, William and Henry.[3] His eldest son, David Kingorne, became a notary, and 'Clerk of the Regality of Dunfermline', a prominent position, responsible for the administration of the Burgh of Dunfermline, its civil and legal records. Thereafter, the position seems to have been heritable, passed down in the family. David was succeeded in the position by his probable son, James, and James' son, David, would hold this position a few years after his father's death in 1631, as would another son, Patrick.

James Kingorne had nine children, of whom Thomas, born in 1606, is significant to the story of Alexander Kinghorne. Thomas left Dunfermline, perhaps after an extramarital affair was discovered by the birth of a child in 1629. It appears that he moved to Fetteresso in Kincardineshire, where he married in 1632 and had three children. He then moved with his surviving family to Greenlaw in Berwickshire, where he married Joane Johnstone in 1652. While Thomas' employment is not known, his family's profession as Clerks of the Burgh and notaries in Dunfermline suggests he might have taken a similar role in the administrative and legal professions in Greenlaw.

Adam's other grandson of interest, Robert Kingorne, was a schoolteacher in Edinburgh, first recorded there in 1605. He produced a family of ten children, the youngest of whom was another Adam Kingorne, baptized in Edinburgh in 1632. Robert died not long after Adam's birth. His Will, probated in 1635, had particular concern for his son Adam being a 'minor', although he was unable to make much provision for him. School teachers were not highly paid, and Robert's large family were left to their own devices, and the support of family. Adam's cousin, Thomas Kingorne, appears to have been part of this support, and Adam had moved to live in Greenlaw, Berwickshire, by 1649.

The Kinghornes of Greenlaw, Gordon and Kelso

Old Greenlaw was a pretty town, then situated atop a hill, the Green Law, in the foothills of Lammermuir on Blackadder Water. It had become the County Town and later head Burgh of Berwickshire, a trade centre, and a barony by the late 17th century, when it moved a mile north of its original position on the hill.

It was there, in Greenlaw, that a young Adam Kingorne married Issobell Pringle, on 29 November 1649.[4] He was seventeen at his marriage, and his relationship with Issobell has the hallmarks of a love-match. There was no wealth either side. The death of Adam's father, Robert, in Edinburgh while Adam was an infant, was an event with a serious impact on him. There was no inheritance, and what followed was a story of decline, with knowledge of his forbears in Dunfermline being lost by the generation of his grandchildren.

Sometime after Adam and Issobell married, they moved to nearby Hume (Issobell's origins appear to have been in Hume and East Gordon). It was in Hume that their son Alexander was born on 16 January 1653, the great grandfather of Alexander Kinghorne, the subject of this biography. The distance from Greenlaw to East Gordon and to Hume forms a triangle

The Family Tree of the Kinghornes of Greenlaw, Gordon, Hume and Kelso

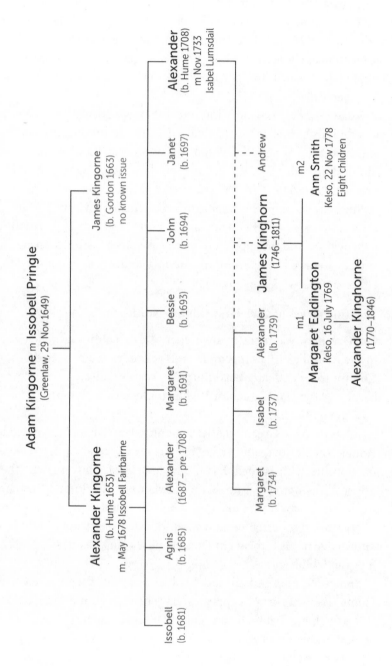

Adam Kingorne m Issobell Pringle
(Greenlaw, 29 Nov 1649)

James Kingorne
(b. Gordon 1663)
no known issue

Alexander Kingorne
(b. Hume 1653)
m. May 1678 Issobell Fairbairne

Issobell
(b. 1681)

Agnis
(b. 1685)

Alexander
(1687 – pre 1708)

Margaret
(b. 1691)

Bessie
(b. 1693)

John
(b. 1694)

Janet
(b. 1697)

Alexander
(b. Hume 1708)
m Nov 1733
Isabel Lumsdail

Margaret
(b. 1734)

Isabel
(b. 1737)

Alexander
(b. 1739)

James Kinghorn
(1746–1811)

Andrew

m1
Margaret Eddington
Kelso, 16 July 1769

m2
Ann Smith
Kelso, 22 Nov 1778
Eight children

Alexander Kinghorne
(1770–1846)

of approximately three miles each side, and the descendants of Adam and his cousin Thomas would remain thereabouts for the next century and a half.

Adam's son Alexander married Issobell Fairbairne on 26 May 1678.[5] They had eight known children, of which the youngest, Alexander, was baptised in Stichill and Hume on 2 November 1708.[6] He was the grandfather of Alexander Kinghorne, the subject of this book.

Alexander Kinghorn (the grandfather) married Isabel Lumsdail on 17 November 1733,[7] and had five children. The following entry in the parish registers in 1746 identifies that Alexander Kinghorn was resident and employed in Gordon, but that he was in trouble with the church authorities:

> 1746…July 27…After prayer Sedrt the minister William Shaw John Brown Wm Hope & Jon Murray Eldrs this day is being laid before the session that John Walker had given scandal offence in procuring and allowing his measure to be taken upon a Lords day about ye end of May last by Alexander Kinghorn Taylor. the minister represented yt he (ye sd John) had expressed his sorrow to him for the same and was willing to satisfie the session in whatever they should appoint & yt he would attend this day. The session were of opinion that he should be called in & be rebuked for ye sd scandal & offence and he being called in it was accordingly done… Ye Sedrt closed with prayer.[8]

Alexander did not appear before the session at the Kirk to answer the charge against him. This was most likely because he was a dissenter, or worse, and had placed himself beyond the authority of the kirk. Two of his sons, James and Andrew, would not be baptized in the kirk. This is not surprising, as attested by Christopher Douglas in his 1791 analysis of the birth and baptism records of Kelso. Douglas concluded they were much understated and, 'owing to the number of dissenters from the established church, and others who neglect to register their baptisms, it is impossible to ascertain the number'.[9]

Nevertheless, this matter establishes that Alexander Kinghorn was a 'Taylor', a profession he was to pass on to his son, James. To that extent, this had become a family profession, although this should not be assumed for the previous generations.[10] Master Tailors were burgesses (merchants) under the system in Scotland since the Middle Ages. The Industrial Revolution was to lower the status of the profession, although less so in

Scotland than in England.[11]

Alexander and Isabel's fourth child, James Kinghorn (1746–1811) was born in East Gordon in Berwickshire on 10 March 1746. His birth was recorded in his son's Family Bible.[12] James married Margaret Eddington (sometimes 'Idington'), with the bans read at Gordon and Kelso on 6 July 1769.[13] The marriage was held 10 days later in Kelso when the following record was made:

> James Kinghorn of this and Margaret Eddington of Gordon parish are to be proclaimed on the 16th of July 1769. Witnesses Alexander Kinghorn and Robert Crosby. [14]

The ceremony was conducted by Rev'd Cornelius Lundie (1716–1800), Minister of the established Presbyterian Church,[15] in the makeshift church built into what remained of the west end of the old Kelso Abbey. James was by this time a resident of Kelso, eight miles from his birthplace in East Gordon, where he had established himself as a Master Tailor. The Alexander Kinghorn witnessing the marriage was either James' father or elder brother. James and Margaret produced only one child: Alexander Kinghorn (later Kinghorne), the subject of this biography, born at Kelso 15 May 1770, and baptised there on 20 May 1770.[16]

Noble Ancestors

It was a blithe time in Wight Wallace's day, or good King Robert's, when the pock-puddings gat naething here but hard straiks and bloody crowns. But we will see how it will a' end.

Sir Walter Scott, *The Monastery*, 1820[17]

Alexander Kinghorne believed his family had a noble past but had fallen to a lowlier status in terms of the ranking of Scottish society. A story in the Kinghorne family in Australia was that they were descended from King Robert the Bruce, the Scottish hero-king who defeated the army of King Edward II of England at Bannockburn. This story has been traced to Alexander's daughter, Elizabeth Kinghorne, who would have had it from Alexander himself.[18]

Alexander's ancestor, Adam Kingorne, had a significant profile in the Abbey and the Regality of Dunfermline, and would have passed in and out of the Royal Palace on his duties. His descendants also had prominent roles as Clerks of the Regality in Dunfermline and other places.

Adam Kingorne's patronage links were to the high-ranking families of Kinghorn, the Duries, and possibly the Lyon family. The Lyon family, who later became Earls of Kinghorne, *were* descended from King Robert the Bruce. But their family name remained Lyon, and they got the title of their Earldom from the Burgh, much as Alexander's family had gotten its surname. Alexander's reveries were encouraged by this association with his name, as shall be seen in Chapter 15 and his commissioning of a coat of arms. However, there is no evidence that Alexander had a blood relationship with the Lyons, the Duries or any other noble family. Nor were the marriages in his family suggestive of a noble connection.

Alexander had little or no idea about his actual forbears, or much further back than his tailoring grandfather. There might have been family stories about past greatness, followed by hard times. These were common enough in the years following the Civil War and the Jacobite Rebellions. Alexander would try to make something from that, but never to his satisfaction. The idea of lost nobility will recur in this book, inflamed by Alexander's reading of the works of his friend, Sir Walter Scott. But apart from the feeling that something was there, Alexander did not know what it was.

The irony is that Alexander did have prominent ancestors, although they were not 'nobles'. In the St Clair Museum and Archives in Goulburn, New South Wales, is Alexander's copy of Sir Walter Scott's *The Monastery*. Of all the works of his friend, this one is known to have been carried with him into his new life in the colony, and pored over, and upon which he made notes. It is a romance, loosely based on Melrose Abbey at the time of the dissolution of the Monasteries. The Abbot was fearful of the Scottish noblemen who were pillaging the Church's properties and stealing or destroying their valuables and relics. Alexander's ancestor, Adam Kingorne, was a canon of Dunfermline Abbey, the royal abbey where King Robert the Bruce was buried, with Adam embroiled in the very conflicts about which Scott wrote. A legend of Melrose Abbey was that the *heart* of Robert the Bruce was buried there. This would have been well-known to Alexander, who visited Melrose many times, and where Sir Walter Scott had commenced a restoration project in 1822, during the period of their conversations about *The Monastery*.[19]

Alexander's father, James Kinghorn, moved from Gordon to live in Kelso, some time before the summer of 1769. Kelso was a steadily growing market town, with a population of 2,781 in 1755, rising to 4,324 by 1793. During this period, there was considerable land amalgamation, forming large estates from the small farms, which drove much of the rural population away from the villages, into the town. Nevertheless, the prosperity of the gentry on these estates brought productivity and retail trade. Thus, 18th century Kelso owed its wealth not to industry, nor manufacturing, but rather to agricultural development and, surprisingly, intellectual pursuits with an emphasis on education.[20]

The primary reason for James Kinghorn's relocation from Gordon to Kelso must have been to improve his economic situation and establish the family business on a surer footing. He was twenty-three years old in 1769, an age at which he might be expected to make an independent move, and about to marry. He might have felt constrained by the character and rebelliousness noted above in his father, limiting the opportunities available to him in his home town. This is speculative, but both James and his elder brother Alexander were to leave Gordon, and build their lives in other towns, separate, but not too distant.

Despite the decline of the guilds throughout rural Britain, the local economy in Kelso was 'on the move', with the trade corporations remaining strong throughout the 18th century.[21] In 1791, Kelso employed 47 tailors, one of the largest trades in the town, exceeded only by weavers and shoemakers (60 of each), serving 826 families living in 376 houses. According to 19th century historian Rev'd J.M. McCulloch, the records of the Tailor's Guild in Kelso went back to 1619, but they were lost in 1794, so the location of James Kinghorn's premises cannot be confirmed.[22] Nevertheless, the thriving economy of Kelso drove the demand for the making of apparel:

> The weekly market day is Friday...the concourse of people being great, and beyond what is known on the like occasions in any part of Scotland, it is productive of immense profits to the shopkeepers, milliners, tailors, etc. among whom they lay out incredible sums of money, principally for wearing apparel...[23]

If your trade was tailoring, Kelso was the place to be in the 18th century.

There was money to be made from the well-to-do populace and there were opportunities for social advancement.

James Kinghorn's father, Alexander, had passed on to him the skills of the trade, and this was certainly his profession when he moved to Kelso, as shown in the records of apprentices for tailors in that town, which are extant from 1710 to 1811. James likely set up the family business in the Horse Market,[24] training eight apprentices between 1772 and 1792.[25]

Table 1. Apprentices of James Kinghorn, Master Tailor of Kelso

Date of Record	Apprentice	Reference: Piece & Page
28 May 1772	Wm Stewart	Piece 58 (p. 90)
13 May 1774	Jno Lourie	Piece 59 (p. 51)
2 Sep 1778	Jno Kirk	Piece 61 (p. 61)
12 May 1780	Alex Stewart	Piece 61 (p. 147)
1 Aug 1782	Rob Wood	Piece 62 (p. 150)
13 Oct 1785	Wm Smith	Piece 63 (p. 181)
12 Mar 1790	Thos Black	Piece 65 (p. 156)
29 Sep 1792	Walter Scott	Piece 66 (p. 143)

James' business was comparatively small, as other master tailors mentioned in the records employed several apprentices at the same time. Nevertheless, by 1782, he was successful enough to be one of the subscribers to the dissertations of Rev'd John Muirhead, a self-declared 'Minister of the Gospel' in Kelso.[26] While it seems he did not own the property that housed his tailoring shop,[27] it was one of the businesses and trade corporations then thriving in Kelso.[28]

Since the Reformation, Kelso had become 'the chief resort of the gentry in the district' and 'a place of considerable reputation as a seat of learning'. The Kelso schools, including a grammar school and nine others, were of a very high standard and were frequented by the sons of the nobility. In the 1780s, a 'school of industry' was founded for the employment of poor girls 'who have stated hours for sewing, knitting, and tambouring, for learning to read and write, and for inculcating moral duties'.[29] McCulloch wrote that, in the late 18th century, the Rectorship of Kelso Grammar School was considered a more prestigious appointment than the Chair of Humanity at the University of St Andrews. There were, indeed, plentiful economic and social reasons for the Kinghorns to relocate to Kelso, a move that would lead one of their children to aspire to excellence.[30]

James Kinghorn and Margaret Eddington had one child, Alexander, the subject of this history, born in 1770 as detailed above.[31] Margaret died when Alexander was about five. There is no burial record for her. James remarried to Ann Smith, and they had eight children, all born between 1779 and 1792 at Kelso.[32] James would die at Kelso on 25 October 1811, aged 65 years.[33] Ann died at Kelso a little over a year later, on 25 February 1813.[34]

A sure foundation had been laid for the young Alexander Kinghorne by his father's move to Kelso and the establishment of a successful business. He was about to build on this through the acquisition of an education.

Chapter 2

The Early Life of Alexander Kinghorne
(1770–1799)

*From this time the love of natural beauty, more especially when combined with
ancient ruins, or remains of our fathers' piety or splendour, became with me an
insatiable passion, which, if circumstances had permitted, I would willingly have
gratified by travelling over half the globe.*

Sir Walter Scott, *Memoirs*

The Town of Kelso and its Powerful Border Families

Alexander Kinghorne spent his early life in and around Kelso, located at
the confluence of the Tweed and Teviot Rivers, about 45 miles southeast of
Edinburgh (Figure 1). The town sat in the centre-right of the old Scottish
Border counties of Roxburgh, Berwick and Selkirk. From the 16th century,
two families dominated the region: the Kers (various spellings) and the
Scotts, both of which would become Alexander's patrons, and some of
them his friends.

Kelso owed its existence to the founding of Kelso Abbey in 1128,
which remained its main support until the dissolution of the monasteries
during the Reformation. As the power and wealth of the Abbey declined,
it shifted to the Ker family, who took over many of the Abbey's properties
after Robert Ker of Cessford became the first Earl of Roxburgh in 1599.

Melrose Abbey, some fourteen miles to the west, became central to
the wealth and status of the Scott family. By the early 18th century this
Border clan had acquired all the land formerly belonging to the Abbey.
They had many branches, of which the Earl (later Duke) of Buccleuch was
perhaps the most prominent, and the Scotts of Harden and Raeburn of
most importance to this history.

There was feuding among the landed families in Roxburghshire from
the 16th century, including between the Kers and the Scotts, a catalogue
of warfare and deaths compounding the bitterness. However, by the time

15

the Kinghorns were living in Kelso, peace had broken forth, and the two families were fully reconciled. Besides the Duke of Roxburghe in Kelso and the Duke of Buccleuch in Selkirk, prominent members of these families also held adjoining properties near the town of St Boswells, known as Kippilaw, Mertoun, Maxton, Maxpoffle, and Lessudden (Figure 7).

Alexander Kinghorne's links with the Kers and Scotts, would be key pillars of his life. The names of the 'seats' adopted by these families also give important clues to the origins of the names of Kinghorne and Chisholm family properties in Australia. Further details are provided in Appendices 4, 5 and 6.

By the time of Alexander's birth, after years of local family feuding and national religious wars, all was peaceful and protestant in Kelso. The influence of the monasteries was long gone, and the last hurrah of the Catholics crushed with the '45 Jacobite rebellion, 'for the Duke of Roxburghe, who is ... a true protestant, has razed them to the very foundation, and swept them off, with the besom of destruction, from that part of his estate.'[1] With the peace, Kelso became, by the late 18th century, a thriving market town and trade centre, and it was here that Alexander Kinghorne grew up and received his education.

The Young Alexander Kinghorne of Kelso

Alexander was just 5 years old when his mother died in 1775.[2] It would have been traumatic for the boy and have had a long-term effect on his outlook. His father also would have been sorely affected, the two clinging together in their grief, before James took stock of his domestic circumstances, and the welfare of his son.

Alexander was eligible to commence schooling at the age of seven (in 1777). James Kinghorn re-married in 1778, providing Alexander with a stepmother and, in due course, seven siblings. However, it was necessary for someone to care for the boy during the interim years, between his mother's death and school, while James was busy with his tailoring. The possibilities are his grandparents, Alexander Kinghorn the tailor at Gordon; or John and Jean Idington near Gordon, where John was a farm worker; or his uncle and aunt, Alexander and Margaret Kinghorn; or that he remained in Kelso in the care of a nanny, housekeeper or another of his relatives, and helping James about the shop. James might have availed himself of some or all of these for short periods of time.

Alexander, being the eldest son of James Kinghorn, represented the great hope for the future of his family. The child had an inquiring mind, was quick to pick up the measuring and numerate skills of his father, became interested in a wide range of subjects and showed promise of better things. James Kinghorn encouraged him to improve himself through education, a widely held conviction in 18th century Scotland, which was strongly supported by the Presbyterian kirk. In this they benefited from Kelso being the seat of a Grammar School, one of the most prestigious in Scotland, which served as the parochial school for boys. The fees were steep (more than 15s and 6d a quarter). Without evidence of how he achieved it – by thrift, a scholarship or connections – James made sure his eldest son obtained the best education available at the time. It is possible that he was assisted in this through the town's unique system of trade governance.

In the late 18th century, Kelso was governed by a baron bailie, appointed by the Duke of Roxburghe, assisted by councillors ('deacons' or 'stent-masters') elected annually by the Duke and by a number of mercantile groupings. These included the Merchant Company of Kelso, the butchers, and the five 'incorporated' trades of the town, namely the tailors, weavers, shoemakers, skinners and hammermen. James Kinghorn, as a prominent tailor, would have been a member of this local 'trade corporation' structure. He might have served as a 'deacon' in the council. This would have provided him with opportunities for financial concessions or a scholarship to fund the education of his son.[3]

Whatever the wherewithal, James ensured that Alexander was enrolled in Kelso Grammar School, the first of his family to achieve a grammar school education, and to develop aspirations far above the station of his birth.

Alexander's Education at Kelso Grammar School

Alexander's grammar school education would open career paths for him beyond his family's trade background. Moreover, it provided connections with the most influential families, who sent their sons there, and this would be advantageous for social advancement.

There had been a school at Kelso since the 12th century, then run by the monks of Kelso Abbey, which was accounted one of the four principal schools of Scotland. After the Reformation, this developed into a boys' Grammar School run under the auspices of the kirk.[4] Alexander recorded having been there in 1783,[5] aged thirteen. The school accepted students from the age of seven, and it is likely he had studied there for some years prior, given his abilities, the subjects he later taught as a teacher, and the depth of his education.

There was also a parish school in Kelso, apart from the Grammar School. This was established in 1780, when Alexander was ten, and was similar in nature to the schools in all towns and most villages in Scotland, where boys and girls were given a fundamental education. These, together with the grammar schools, were part of a well-established system by the end of the 18th century and were monitored through returns to the House of Lords at Westminster. In 1841 the fees at the parish school in Kelso were around a third of those in the Grammar, with far less subjects on offer, and less depth in the curriculum.[6] There is no record of Alexander having attended the parish school. While it is a possibility, he likely began his education before the date given for the school's foundation and was enrolled from the beginning at Kelso Grammar.

Lancelot Whale, Rector of Kelso Grammar School from 1780 to 1791, had an impressive reputation and seems to have been the archetypal 18th century headmaster. Under his administration the school was rebuilt (1781)[7] and the heritors separated the Latin and English schools under different masters: Whale, as Rector, taught Latin, French and Greek, while the English schoolmaster, James Forbes, taught 'writing, compting, and a little of the French language.' The fees stated in the heritors' Minute for 31 January 1781 were '4/- per quarter for the Latin language, 6/- for the Greek, 2/6 for Do. and writing, 2/- for English, 3/6 for reading, writing and common arithmetic.' The Merchant Company and the Incorporated Trades of Kelso, who contributed to the funding of the school, agreed that the teaching of French, and any other modern language, was 'to be left open for such terms as can be agreed betwixt the teacher and parents … and leaving it always to the schoolmaster to make such agreement with strangers for education of their children as they think fit.'[8] While there is no record of the courses Alexander studied, he later taught as a schoolmaster: English, writing, arithmetic, mathematics, French, Latin, Greek, geography, and book keeping.[9] So, he must have received his own education in most of these at Kelso Grammar School.

Mathematics was sometimes described as 'Practical Mathematics' and at the Grammar School included the study of Euclid, as well as the application of mathematics to everyday life. Alexander was interested in and adept at measurement and arithmetic, from his childhood experience in his father's tailoring establishment, and would find in mathematics and bookkeeping essential knowledge for his later careers as a farm factor and surveyor. He later demonstrated knowledge of Latin in his correspondence and could write and converse in French.[10]

Kelso was equipped with well-stocked circulating and subscription libraries.[11] These cultivated a love of literature, poetry and antiquities in the young Alexander Kinghorne, which was evidenced throughout his life.

Sir Walter Scott: A Key Influence on Alexander Kinghorne's Life

Alexander recorded his presence at Kelso Grammar School, in his personal copy of Sir Walter Scott's novel, *The Monastery*, where he describes Scott as a 'classmate' and 'close friend'.[12] Significantly, Scott, the future poet, novelist and exponent of Scottish romanticism, also attended school there in 1783 (Figure 2).

Scott was staying with his aunt Miss Janet Scott who lived in a cottage, now called Waverley Lodge, within gardens adjacent to the churchyard in Kelso and extending down to the banks of the Tweed. The young Walter suffered from lameness, likely resulting from childhood poliomyelitis, and was sent to the country as a means of 'building up his constitution' before tackling classics at the University of Edinburgh. Scott attended Kelso Grammar for six months in 1783, at the same time as Alexander Kinghorne. Scott's later publisher, James Ballantyne, like Alexander the son of a local merchant, also attended.[13]

Alexander and Walter likely knew each other before attending Kelso Grammar School. Scott had been visiting the town, spending much of his summer leisure time in and around Kelso, since 1781, and the adjacent kirk provided a setting where children would meet regardless of social class. Moreover, Scott continued a long association with the town until

19

1827: his uncle, Captain Robert Scott, owned the thirty-acre Rosebank estate, also in the town, where Walter often stayed, and which he eventually inherited.[14]

Scott also stayed, on at least two occasions in his childhood, with his grandfather Robert Scott at Sandyknowe Farm, next to Smailholm Tower. A well-known painting by Sir Henry Raeburn shows an infant Sir Walter in Highland dress, accompanied by his Aunt Jenny and a stout little walking stick, in the dramatic setting of Smailholm.

In the mid–17th century, Auld Watt Scott of Harden had bought this forbidding Border Peel Tower, and the family retained it and the surrounding Sandyknowe Farm until the 19th century. It was here at the age of three that the 'wee, sick laddie' was sent from the dingy confines of Edinburgh, to stay with his paternal grandparents, Robert and Barbara Scott, in an attempt to elicit a recovery from his crippling ailment.[15] Walter came to Sandyknowe and Kelso for several summers, absorbing the stories told by his grandmother and aunt, and dreaming the adventures of his ancestral past. He spent his waking hours, and doubtless some of his sleep, with Bold Buccleuch, Auld Watt of Harden and the other reivers, and heard the romantic tales that had developed around them,[16] as he gazed up at the looming presence of Smailholm Tower (Figure 3).[17]

The co-attendance of Alexander Kinghorne and Walter Scott at Kelso Grammar School provided the foundation for their friendship, and the fuel for Alexander's romanticism. According to Scott's biographer, Lockhart, the young Walter entranced all his fellow-pupils at Kelso with his story-telling ability, so much so that it 'overwhelmed his school-fellows and it would, doubtless, so excite many of them, that in the exuberance of their glee, they might call Scott 'daft'.'[18]

Walter was fifteen months younger than Alexander.[19] The year 1783 was probably Alexander's last at Kelso Grammar School, as students usually completed Grammar School at age twelve or thirteen.[20] Accordingly Alexander's name does not appear on a hand-written list of classmates (1784 to 1788), recorded in the papers of Walter Scott's cousin, William Scott of Raeburn, in 1838. Walter Scott and Ballantyne, both born in 1771, were nevertheless included, as was the author of the list, who was born in 1773. It seems that William Scott felt it necessary to include his famous cousin, even though he was not there that year, but exclude Alexander who was.[21] Other notable long-term friends of Alexander Kinghorne recorded on the list were Willie's younger brothers Robert and Hugh Scott, and Robert Lundie, the son and successor of Rev'd Cornelius Lundie, minister of the parish of Kelso.[22]

Sir Walter Scott described Whale as 'an excellent classical scholar, a humourist, and a worthy man…In point of knowledge and taste he was far too good for the situation he held, which only required that he should give his scholars a rough foundation in the Latin language.'[23] Despite his youth, Scott was the only known teaching assistant to Mr Whale, writing that he acted as usher and 'heard the inferior classes'.[24] In turn, Whale lavished considerable extra time on the short education of Walter Scott at Kelso. Scott is reported to have 'discovered' the 18th century novel there, delighting in the works of Richardson, Fielding, Smollett and Mackenzie, and Bishop Percy's ballad-collection, *Reliques of Ancient English Poetry*. Much has been written about the influence of Kelso Grammar School on Walter Scott. Rev'd W.S. Crockett, in *The Scott Country*, wrote:

> He [Sir Walter] made considerable progress in his studies, and became daily more fit for the higher position of a university student…One can scarcely estimate the influence of the Kelso years on the life of Scott…It was here that Scott began to gather up his intellectual gains, and make his friendly conquests.[25]

Scott's own description of the influence of his early years in Kelso, might well reflect its effect on Alexander…

> To this period I can trace distinctly the awaking of that delightful feeling of the beauties of natural objects which has never since deserted me. The neighbourhood of Kelso, the most beautiful if not the most romantic village in Scotland, is eminently calculated to awaken these ideas. It presents objects, not only grand in themselves, but venerable from their association. The meeting of two superb rivers, the Tweed and the Teviot, both renowned in song – the ruins of an ancient Abbey – the most distant vestiges of Roxburgh Castle – the modern mansion of Fleurs [Floors Castle], which is so situated as to combine the ideas of ancient baronial grandeur with those of modern taste – are in themselves objects of the first class; yet are so mixed, united, and melted among a thousand other beauties of a less prominent description, that they harmonize into one general picture, and please rather by unison than by concord. I believe I have written

unintelligibly upon this subject, but it is fitter for the pencil than the pen. The romantic feelings which I have described as predominating in my mind, naturally rested upon and associated themselves with these grand features of the landscape around me; and the historical incidents, or traditional legends connected with many of them, gave to my admiration a sort of intense impression of reverence, which at times made my heart feel too big for its bosom. From this time the love of natural beauty, more especially when combined with ancient ruins, or remains of our fathers' piety or splendour, became with me an insatiable passion, which, if circumstances had permitted, I would willingly have gratified by travelling over half the globe.[26]

As will be seen later in this history, Alexander, who was ever seeking the romantic ideal, could have written these words himself.

Were Alexander's view of the closeness of their friendship shared by Scott, or did he later imagine it? Alexander is not mentioned in Scott's published papers.[27] This might be thought to support the latter proposition. On the other hand, the textual notes in Alexander's copy of *The Monastery* are quite clear and concise and have the appearance of a truthful account of Alexander's recollections at the time they were made (1832).[28] Whatever was the case, it is clearly Scott who influenced Alexander, and any influence in the other direction was less remarkable.

Scott's friendly and generous manner has been attested by his biographers. According to Herbert Grierson, Scott was loath to give up old friends regardless of their social class. He made many friends in Kelso, described by him as 'apprentices', whom he remembered and acknowledged for the rest of his life. Maria Edgeworth wrote of him, 'I was particularly struck with his unaffected, gracious, simple and dignified manner of receiving all the complimentary visits and speeches made to him'. Robert Chalmers wrote, 'Sir Walter speaks to every man as if they were blood relations'.[29] Scott's earliest and most intimately knowledgeable biographer, his son-in-law J.G. Lockhart, in describing Scott's character, praised 'his readiness to interrupt his own tasks by any drudgery by which he could assist those of a friend; his steady and determined watchfulness over the struggling fortunes of genius and worth'.[30] It is clear, from their earliest acquaintance in 1783, that Walter Scott saw some *worth* in Alexander Kinghorne that deserved his encouragement.

22

Even placing the relationship with Scott in this perspective, that is, a kind of romantic attachment on Alexander's part, and a generous nature to people from all stations of life on the part of Scott, it will nevertheless become apparent that Sir Walter Scott assisted and mentored Alexander until he left Scotland many years later. This he did by cultivating connections for him with important people, helping him to gain commissions to perform survey work and assisting him to emigrate and find a situation in the colonies.[31]

Alexander Kinghorne: Schoolteacher

Little information has been found on the life and further education of Alexander Kinghorne for the years between 1784, when he presumably left Kelso Grammar School, and 1791 when he was appointed as the schoolmaster at Bowden. His movements can only be inferred from his later correspondence and from what is known of his first professional appointment.

Alexander's employment and subsequent marriage in Bowden near St Boswells, meant that he left his childhood home of Kelso. Before that his permanent home was in that town with his parents, in an increasingly crowded house. He might have stayed at school beyond the age of thirteen. The previously mentioned records of Whale's students at Kelso Grammar suggest otherwise, unless he remained at that school as a tutor, which would explain his absence from William Scott's list of students from 1784–1788. Continued studies at the same school under a different master, or at another school specialising in mathematics and geometry, are further possibilities. These subjects would have been the interest that led to his later professions: surveyor, architect and civil engineer.[32] Alternatively, he might have worked as a private tutor, as a preliminary to his first known employment as a schoolmaster.[33]

Despite the lack of a record on his further education, Alexander must have attained educational excellence, as he was appointed in 1791 as schoolmaster at the Bowden Parish School. The appointment came at the behest of Rev'd James Hume, whom Alexander, in his later correspondence, claimed to have known.[34] Hume, the Minister at Bowden from 1742 to 1792, was in his 80th year when he died in 1792. He had been licensed (1735) and ordained in Kelso (April 1742). As Parish Minister he was responsible for the Parish School, and, in the absence of a schoolteacher, would have run the school directly, and given lessons himself, doubtless with the assistance of able parishioners. This would have been a greater burden as his age increased and health declined, requiring the services of a fulltime schoolteacher.

A key parishioner at Bowden was Andrew Blaikie, the feu tenant of the Holydean estate, which he had held from the Duke of Roxburghe since 1757.[35] Blaikie will emerge in this narrative as a friend and active mentor of Alexander. He was a former student of Kelso Grammar, which he had attended from the age of twelve, riding there fourteen miles a day from his childhood home of Faughill near Bowden, and fourteen miles back.[36] Again the gaze of those involved would turn towards Kelso Grammar.

They would have inquired about likely candidates for the role of schoolmaster from their contacts at Kelso: notably from the Rector of Kelso Grammar School (either Lancelot Whale or Dr John Dymock, who replaced Whale in 1791) and the Kelso minister Cornelius Lundie, father of Alexander's schoolmate Robert.[37] The Rector of the Grammar School was also Session Clerk of the Kelso kirk, so there was a natural progression from the knowledge of former pupils, to the appointment of schoolmasters.[38]

An involvement by the young Walter Scott is quite possible. Scott visited Bowden parish and stayed at Kippilaw in September 1790, a few months before the period of Alexander's appointment, and might well have mentioned him to Rev'd Hume and others. Moreover, Scott's relatives across the river at Mertoun House were within Blaikie's social circle.[39] So, there were several influences which might have brought Alexander to Bowden, where his life would be changed for ever, together with those of the subsequent generations of his family.

The appointment was in the gift of the Duke of Roxburghe, who was the principal heritor for Bowden Parish. Through this process Alexander Kinghorne *got the nod* and was presented to the Bowden kirk session by John, Duke of Roxburghe, as the successful candidate. The appointment could have been in the summer of 1791 or even earlier, as Hume died in January 1792.[40]

The Bowden Parish Statistical Account

The Scotland of the 1790s saw itself as a reformed society, based on science and reason, underpinned by a faithful following of the word of God. This was an illusion, as the pillars of the Scottish economy were the plantations of the Americas and slavery, as well as Scotland's contribution to the British colonial endeavour: certainly not the whole, but significant enough to contribute the gloss of national prosperity. However, the morality of this did not form part of the society's accounts of its own enlightenment. While still controlled at Parish level by the kirk, the local landholders and ultimately the aristocracy, there was much interest in economic geography. This was rooted in improved agricultural practice and diverse urban life. A phenomenon arising from this was the preparation and publication of the *Statistical Accounts of Scotland*, treated by its authors as a means for promoting civil utility, but in fact performing a wider purpose.

One such endeavour was proposed in 1781, by Alexander's later mentor and friend, David Erskine, 11th Earl of Buchan, founder of the Society of Antiquaries in Scotland. He undertook a general parochial survey of Scotland to further historical understanding, and, as he put it, advance 'national improvement'. Only a few parishes were surveyed in Buchan's scheme. By the time the limited results were published in 1792, it had been overtaken by Sir John Sinclair's wider *Statistical Account*.[41]

There were other proposals and attempts, earlier than Buchan's. These, together with the Ordnance Survey Maps, fulfilled a purpose for the rulers of Scotland in the years following the Civil War and Jacobite Rebellions: they defined the geography of Scotland for military and civil government, including land ownership and the rights of the aristocracy who were in control following the wars. In the latter sense, the *Statistical Account* fulfilled a similar function to the *Domesday Book*, compiled seven hundred years earlier to cement Norman control over England.

The *Statistical Account of Scotland* was laboriously undertaken by the politician and author Sir John Sinclair (1754–1835), supposedly the first to use the word 'statistics' in the English language.[42] It ran to twenty-one volumes and was printed between 1791 and 1799. No such widespread description of the country had been produced before. The research required was vast and daunting.

For Sinclair, compiling statistics meant collecting facts, which were not necessarily numerical. Every Parish in Scotland was to be described, measured, have its history recorded and its population counted. Such knowledge resided with the minister of each parish church, particularly those who had been incumbent for many years, as had James Hume in Bowden for some 47 years. However, Hume was ailing by the time the request for information came in 1791. His successor, Thomas Kirkpatrick, was not appointed until September 1792. Kirkpatrick hailed from Dumfriesshire and had only recently been ordained in Kelso, and so had no prior knowledge of the Parish of Bowden.[43] Therefore, the task of compiling the local information fell to two local people, one named in *The Statistical Account*, and the other unnamed:

> Drawn up by a Friend to Statistical Inquiries, from Materials chiefly furnished by Mr Andrew Blaikie, Tenant in Holydean, who has resided 35 years in that Parish.[44]

Andrew Blaikie, whose Holydean tenancy had a boundary with the Kippilaw estate, was to become a close mentor and friend to Alexander. He advised him on all manner of things from surveying to scientific agriculture.[45] Recourse to a 'Friend to Statistical Inquiries' occurred elsewhere, in each case the minister being unable to undertake the work.[46] The 'Friend' was someone in the middle, between Sinclair and Blaikie, and almost certainly was not Alexander.[47] Nevertheless, Alexander was involved. In the case of Bowden, there is detailed information about the parochial school, its courses and costs, which at that point would only have come from its schoolmaster, Alexander. The remainder of the entry runs the gamut of both Blaikie's and Alexander's interests: boundaries, areas and their measurements; soil and climate; farms, rents and inheritance; cultivation, farm produce and fertilizer; livestock; population and trade statistics; the employment and cost of labour... There is even a description of the 'remains of a military road', which Alexander was to investigate in 1802 as part of his survey of the antiquities of Roxburghshire for George Chalmers.[48]

The Statistical Account became the foundation for Blaikie's and Alexander's friendship and co-operation.[49]

Marriage – The Brockies of Dryburgh

> *Tide, Tide, what'er betide,*
> *There'll aye be Haigs at Bemersyde*
>
> Thomas the Rhymer [50]

On 31 December 1793, at the age of 23, Alexander Kinghorne married the 24-year-old Elizabeth (Betty) Brockie. The ceremony took place in the kirk at Mertoun and was conducted by Rev'd James Duncan who was then incumbent.[51] Among other gifts, the wedding was marked by the presentation of a magnificent eight-piece silver service to the couple, presumably by James Kinghorn.[52] The handles of the cutlery pieces were engraved with an ornate 'K' – an auspicious beginning to what would be a loving and fruitful marriage, but one fraught with challenges and tragedy (Figure 4).

Betty Brockie was born at Bemersyde, near St Boswells, in May 1769. Her parents, William (1740–1814) and Elizabeth Brockie, were feu tenant farmers on the estate, owned by the Haig family of Bemersyde, near Mertoun.[53] It was a love match, but also a step up the social ladder for Alexander. The family was said to have been Flemish in origins, and to have settled in Fala and Soutra, Midlothian around the turn of the 1700's. Betty's grandfather, Thomas Brockie, moved to Mertoun, Berwickshire, just across the River Tweed from Bowden in Roxburghshire.

William Brockie's tenancy included 'a comfortable farm house with extensive outhouses, offices and attached'.[54] He occupied a significant area, farming on a large scale.[55] According to Alexander Kinghorne, by virtue of their father's tenancy at Bemersyde, the 'Dryburg Brockies' earned the privilege of being buried in Dryburgh Abbey alongside their masters, the Haigs of Bemersyde.[56] This is confirmed by the survival of many of their gravestones in the grounds of Dryburgh Abbey today (2014; Figure 5).

William Brockie would provide Alexander with valuable connections, including the Haigs, and James Maitland 8th Earl of Lauderdale. Betty's uncle Thomas provided a connection with Gilbert Elliot, Lord Minto. Such connections were important for Alexander in his career, as well as there being agricultural interchanges with both William and uncle Thomas as farmers.[57]

There was another link between the Brockies and Sir Walter Scott. At least one, if not all William Brockie's daughters had inherited the gift of ballad singing. By the time James Hogg was writing poetry in the late 18th century, the pagan traditions of the Borders, which had coexisted with Christianity for centuries, began to reach public notice as they were incorporated from memorised and sung ballads into published poetic works. In 1801, Hogg wrote to Scott about the rich sources of such traditions: 'Till this present age, the poor illiterate people in these glens, knew of no other entertainment, in the long winter nights, than repeating, and listening to, the feats of their ancestors, recorded in songs, which I believe to be handed down, from father to son, for many generations...'[58]

As the Scottish historian Alistair Moffat has pointed out, it was neither the fathers nor the sons, but rather the women, who were the custodians of these tales, and the new collectors of folk songs and stories were very much dependent on the memories of these women for their material.[59] James Hogg's own mother, Meg Laidlaw, was a major source for Scott's *Minstrelsey of the Scottish Border*. Made famous by Scott in the early 19th century, most traditional ballads were transmitted, usually in song, from generation to generation by women such as Janet Scott (Sir Walter's aunt), Meg Laidlaw, and one Nancy Brockie of Bemersyde. While women were the custodians of these ballads, they themselves remained very much hidden within historical records, which highlight mainly male escapades.[60]

One of these songs, *The Twa Sisters*, tells of a girl drowned by her jealous sister. It exists in versions from England, Scotland and the Continent, mainly from women's recitation, but the version favoured by Sir Walter Scott was from a manuscript of Thomas Wilkie, which was incorporated into Scott's *Scotch Ballads, Materials for Border Minstrelsy*. Wilkie had taken down this poem, among several others, 'from a Miss Nancy Brockie, Bemerside, who learned it from an old woman called Maron Miller, Threepwood.'[61] This was Betty's sister, Nancy (Agnes) Brockie, born in 1780.[62]

Gone are the days when families made their own entertainment of an evening, with music, poetry and masques. Instrumental music was more particularly seen as a female accomplishment, while the possession of a fine voice was prized, but not always achieved, amongst the men. The other two Brockie sisters are likely to have joined in Nancy's interest in the memorization and singing of folk ballads and passed these on to their female offspring. The tradition was retained by future generations, both men and women, of the Kinghorne and Chisholm families in Australia.[63]

The Family of Alexander Kinghorne and Betty Brockie

How Alexander and Betty met is not known. They attended different churches, but relatively close (Bowden and Mertoun kirks are five miles apart by road). Betty's younger siblings were of school age when Alexander took up his appointment at Bowden. Something involving the parochial schools, a contact between Alexander at Bowden and the teacher at Mertoun, might have led to an encounter with Betty.[64] Another possibility is some agricultural connection between Alexander and the farming community of Mertoun, such as surveying land for a member of her family.

The social environment might have presented further opportunities. They might have met at some gathering in the house of a mutual connection, such as described in the novels of the day, like Jane Austin's *Pride and Prejudice* (1813). There are no clues in Alexander's later correspondence, except that people like Blaikie and Buchan were friends of both Alexander and Betty. Alexander probably met Buchan when the peer visited Kelso Grammar in 1782.[65] William Scott of Raeburn also was a regular visitor to the Kinghornes' home. There would be others as the years progressed, but such of their visits as were documented were later than this point of time. It is a natural line of thought that their mutual acquaintances brought them together.

The best opportunity was that for a brief period, somewhere between 1788 and 1792, Betty's uncle Alexander Brockie and his wife Alison were resident in the Bowden parish, where their second son Archbald was born in 1792. One could well imagine Betty visiting, perhaps attending church and meeting the young teacher.[66]

After their marriage, Alexander and Betty lived in the schoolhouse at Bowden, where Alexander was the schoolmaster, from 1791 until July 1801 (Figure 6).[67] Bowden was a small but thriving community with a population of 860, of which 223 were under the age of ten.[68]

In appearance, Bowden remains much as it was when Alexander and Betty lived there. It was centred on one long street, leading past a village

Family of Alexander Kinghorne and Betty Brockie

Alexander Kinghorne (1770–1846) m. 1793 Betty Brockie (1769–1816)

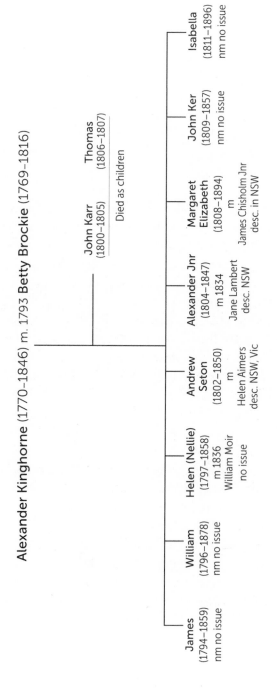

James
(1794–1859)
nm no issue

William
(1796–1878)
nm no issue

Helen (Nellie)
(1797–1858)
m 1836
William Moir
no issue

Andrew
Seton
(1802–1850)
m
Helen Aimers
desc. NSW, Vic

Alexander Jnr
(1804–1847)
m 1834
Jane Lambert
desc. NSW

Margaret
Elizabeth
(1808–1894)
m
James Chisholm Jnr
desc. in NSW

John Ker
(1809–1857)
nm no issue

Isabella
(1811–1896)
nm no issue

John Karr
(1800–1805)

Thomas
(1806–1807)

Died as children

green, lined with single and double-storey cottages, now of exposed stone or white-washed. Situated among the southern slopes of the Eildon Hills, the surrounding countryside was lush and undulating, displaying plentiful blooms of spring wildflowers, including small flowering stone-fern, yellow sulphur-wort and cowslip. There was a market cross in the centre of the village, erected in 1531, and to the north of the town the ruins of Holydean could be seen, the original home of the Ker family demolished in 1760.

Towards the east end of the main street was the parish schoolhouse where the Kinghornes lived. This remains in existence as a house but has been replaced as a school by a new structure built in 1831. There was a single schoolroom in Alexander's old schoolhouse, the rest of which provided accommodation for him and his family. From the schoolhouse, a narrow lane passed southwards down a steep hill, over the narrow-bridged Bowden Burn and up a short rise to the ancient Bowden kirk. This church was built in 1128, shortly after the establishment of the Parish, as part of King David I's foundation charter of Selkirk. It has been renovated many times. [69]

There were two schools in the parish in the late 18th century, both on the parochial establishment,[70] and Alexander was located at the central village school in Bowden. Here he taught all the secular subjects: 'English, writing, and arithmetic, practical mathematics, French, Latin, Greek, geography, &c.'

As the 'principal schoolmaster', he received a salary of £8.6.8d per year, £5 more than the teacher at the other school at Midlem. The statistical record published 1795 shows there were seventy pupils at Bowden; 'of these 30 read English at 1 s. per quarter, 25 both read and write at 1 s. 6 d. and about 15 commonly are taught arithmetic, book-keeping, and mathematics, on such terms as can be agreed upon'. Being a parochial school, 'the children of paupers [were] taught gratis'. However, Alexander received an extra £3 for teaching the poor, and his family were provided with food, a house and garden, making their total annual income about £30. They were supported by a strong educational ethic among the local population, because 'the people have been always so much alive to the benefits of education, that there are none in the parish above six years of age who cannot read, and very few above that age who cannot write also.'[71]

Alexander's teaching subjects of 'arithmetic, practical mathematics... geography...[and] bookkeeping' provide clues to the skills to be applied to his developing profession as a surveyor.

Alexander and Betty had ten children, the first three born at Bowden and the others at the nearby Kippilaw estate. The first child, James, was born on 8 November 1794 and baptized at Bowden by Rev'd James Duncan, Minister of Mertoun, on 24 November. [72] Their next child, William, born 12 August 1796, was baptized by Rev'd William Balfour before the congregation at Bowden on 28 August.[73] Helen (Nellie) followed on 12 August 1798, with her baptism on 27 August, also at Bowden.[74]

Alexander's situation during this period was, therefore, child-focused, looking to the education of the children of Bowden Parish, and to his own growing family. All indications suggest an attentive parent, if later very much the patriarch, and mostly at ease with *common folk* of all age groups. However, he had in view more serious interests than the hurly-burly of the classroom, and the contents of young minds. There was a firm desire for social advancement. His next move would put him progressively and more firmly associated with the society of the wealthy and ranked families of the district. He was not one of them, but was well known to them, and of use to them – providing him with further influential connections to assist his progress.

Chapter 3

The Factor of Kippilaw (1799)

This is no doubt a new line of life to me, ... but I have very good friends to advise with on every occasion, and though they do not altogether agree on the step which I have taken, they are still ready to assist me, and I hope it will turn out to the advantage of both you and me.

Alexander Kinghorne, January 1800

In 1799, after Alexander had been employed as the schoolmaster at Bowden for some eight years, he made a complete change of direction. He took up an appointment as factor, or estate manager, for John Seton Karr of Kippilaw, a nearby estate. This would allow him to pursue professionally his interests in agriculture and surveying and provide a bigger house and better life for his increasing family. His 'very good friends' were influential in this move, as he acknowledged in the above-quoted letter. Alexander's connections were always crucial to his outlook and development, and his new appointment represented a shift in balance, from a compliant recipient of patronage, towards the society of his employer and the wealthy families of the district. This in turn provided access to the patronage of the next echelon up the social ladder – the aristocracy.

The Kippilaw Estate and Mansion

So, who were these people? The countryside surrounding the village of Bowden was a patchwork of large farming estates. The following table shows they were occupied by aristocratic families, or their tenants (Table 2).

The Kippilaw estate of the Karr family, which was to be in Alexander's charge, lay between Bowden and Clarilaw, three miles southwest of the town of St Boswells. It was an integral part of this local network. It covered about eight hundred acres of high ground between the River Tweed, in the north, and the Water of Ayle (or Ale), in the south.

In the late 18th century, it comprised three separate farms: Kippilaw

Mains (sometimes referred to as St Boswells Farm), Bowden Moor (or Muir) and Bowden Mill Farm (with its adjacent mill) (Figure 7).[1]

Table 2. Estates adjacent to Bowden, Roxburghshire, 1799–1810[2]

Name of Estate	Direction from Bowden	Occupant/tenant or owner
Whiterigg	North	Lieutenant-Colonel William Sibbald, 15th Regt of Foot
Faughhill	West	Duke of Roxburghe, tenanted by Mr John Murray
Holydean	West	Duke of Roxburghe, tenanted by Andrew Blaikie
Camieston	East	Thomas, and later William, Riddell
Maxpoffle	South East	William ('Willie') Scott of Raeburn
Kippilaw	South & West	Karr family [Alexander's charge]
Clarilaw	South & West	Duke of Roxburgh, tenanted by Mr Murray and later Mr Brodie
Newhall	South	Robert Shortreed
Cavers Carre	South	John Carre of Cavers
Linthill	South	Lieutenant Colonel Richard Edgar Hunter (until 1807), then William Riddell of Camieston, tenanted by John Harvie

The Moor and Mill, some distance north of the Mains farm, might be considered wild and romantic. The Mill was mentioned as the 'wind-mill of Kippilaw' in Sir Walter Scott's novel, *Waverley*, haunted by more witches than any other place in Scotland:

> One moonlight night, as he rode over Bowden Moor, on the west side of the Eildon Hills, the scene of Thomas the Rhymer's prophecies, and often mentioned in his story…'You may see my dwelling if you will,' said the stranger; 'but if you lose courage at what you see there, you will rue it all your life.'…At the foot of this eminence, which is almost as famous for witch meetings as the neighbouring wind-mill of Kippilaw.[3]

Scott might have discussed the mill and moor on his visits to the earlier tenants of Kippilaw, or with Alexander when the properties were in his charge. When Alexander eventually read it, years later, he can only have been struck by the text which followed:

> 'He that shall sound that horn and draw that sword,' said the stranger,

who now intimated that he was the famous Thomas of Hersildoune, 'shall, if his heart fail him not, be king over all broad Britain. So speaks the tongue that cannot lie.'[4]

This reference to the sound of the King's Horn was an echo of Alexander's name. Whether intentional or subconscious on Scott's behalf, it suggests their conversations, and can only have excited Alexander's ideas of nobility. It shows how the landscape affected both Alexander's and Scott's imaginations.

The Kippilaw Mains farm was the most fertile of the three, containing the mansion, stables and farm buildings, the factor's house, and other accommodations. A number of these would be designed, built and/or renovated by Alexander, as part of his management of the overall estate.

The mansion (Kippilaw House) was located at the southern corner of Kippilaw Mains farm and adjacent to the Clarilaw Estate. According to David Christison, in his book on the ancient fortifications of Scotland, the earliest parts of the house were built in the 15th century near a 'Pictish' stronghold, captured by the 'Scots' and later became a 'Roman' fort called Rowchester. This so-called fort is still located in a field at Kippilaw Mains, about 120 metres west of Alexander's back door.[5] Traces of what Alexander was convinced had been a Roman road were visible near the old house and are shown on contemporary ordinance survey maps as 'Military Road'.[6]

A modern archaeological survey, compiled by the Royal Commission on the Ancient and Historical Monuments of Scotland (RCAHM), described Kippilaw House as a composite of medieval 16th, 18th and 19th century components. Up to the beginning of the 19th century, the approach to the mansion had been through the Clarilaw Estate, through an avenue of trees. The house was in the form of an ancient Peel Tower with some two-storey additions. The south side of the old Tower was very substantial, and the walls were said to be so thick as to be 'bomb-proof'.[7]

To the imaginative Alexander, Kippilaw had everything, all within a few miles' radius: from the mists of prehistory, to the Romans, to the medieval, two ruined Abbeys and the heart of Robert the Bruce a few miles distant, to the dark days of James VI and his puritan followers' persecution of 'witches', to the reivers and Scotland's bloody civil wars, to his own far more enlightened times.

Scott's exposure to Kippilaw had been earlier than Alexander's. In 1790, Scott's friend James Ramsay, who later made a fortune in the East India Company, tenanted Kippilaw House while David Ramsay Karr, then Laird, was absent in Portsmouth and his brother Andrew Ramsay, the next Laird, was Governor of Bombay.[8] James Ramsay was the son of the architect of the same name and served an apprenticeship with Scott's father, becoming a Writer to the Signet (WS).[9] As a consequence of their close acquaintance, Scott visited on 3 September 1790, and wrote to his friend William Clerk in Edinburgh:

> ... from the country habitation of our friend Ramsay, where I have been spending a week as pleasantly as ever I spent one in my life. Imagine a commodious old house, pleasantly situated amongst a knot of venerable elms, in a fine sporting, open country, and only two miles from an excellent water for trouts, inhabited by two of the best old ladies [Ramsay's aunts], and three as pleasant young ones [Scott's sisters] as any person would wish to converse with – and you will have some idea of Kippilaw. James and I wander about, fish, or look for hares, the whole day, and at night laugh, chat, and play round games at cards. Such is the fatherland in which I have been living for some days past, and which I leave to-night or to-morrow.[10]

Some ten years later this estate, described in idyllic terms by Scott, would be subject to a succession process, which led to John Seton Karr becoming Laird of Kippilaw, and his employing Alexander Kinghorne to be his steward.

The Kippilaw estate was, in the late 18th century, in the hands of another branch of the family, the Ramsay Karrs. John Seton (1741–1815) succeeded in 1799, through his mother Jean Ramsay (1719–1766), the sister of the former lairds, David and Andrew Ramsay Karr of Kippilaw, mentioned above.[11] John, her eldest, son became heir to Kippilaw as affirmed in the will of David Ramsay Karr.[12] As a result he was granted, by Royal License, the additional surname of 'Karr of Kippilaw'. Thereafter, the Seton Karr family held Kippilaw until sold in 1914.[13]

John Seton was educated at United College, St Andrews (1757–1760) and studied law at the University of Edinburgh (1762–1763).[14] He practiced as a WS in Edinburgh, where he was a colleague of the Kelso-born journalist William Jerdan and his friend (Sir) Walter Scott. Before his accession to Kippilaw John Seton became a parliamentary agent after his move from Edinburgh to his London residence at 29 Golden Square.[15] On 17 February 1783 he married Elizabeth Tucker at St James' Church Piccadilly.[16] He represented many Scottish gentlemen and peers, as an advocate or witness, in the Houses of Commons and Lords. His clients included the Duke of Argyll, the 3rd Duke of Roxburghe and later the Bellenden-Ker branch of the Duke's family. In 1805, he was appointed Commissioner and Auditor to William Bellenden-Ker, the short-lived 4th Duke of Roxburghe, who died in the same year.[17] Seton Karr then worked with the English Barrister Henry Gawler, notably on the cause celebre of his later life, their unsuccessful appeal to the House of Lords regarding the accession to the Dukedom of Roxburghe, discussed in Chapter 10.

John Seton also represented several major Scottish and Irish companies and development projects. He acted as secretary to the Commissioners for the Crinan Canal Company, the Forth and Clyde Navigation Company, and the Midleton Irish Distillery in Cork.[18] These responsibilities kept him in London for most of the year. He therefore required the assistance of a capable and well-qualified steward to manage his estate in Scotland.

John Seton knew Alexander Kinghorne before he acceded to Kippilaw. Alexander wrote in 1812, 'I keep all your Letters and can produce you everyone I have received since the year 1798 and several before that time.'[19] As the eldest nephew and heir, Seton was responsible for the affairs of his uncles in their absence. He would have been a regular visitor to Kippilaw – annual visits during the summer months were his habit after his accession to the estate. It is likely they met in Bowden and got on well. When Seton was looking for someone to conduct an inventory and survey of the Kippilaw Estate on the death of his uncle Andrew Ramsay Karr, he approached the nearest available person, whom he trusted, who had the appropriate skills to complete the job.[20]

The earliest surviving contact documented occurred after the death of Andrew Ramsay Karr on 6 January 1799. In March of that year Alexander was employed, ostensibly by Ramsay Karr's executors, to compile and analyse the 'State of Accounts Respecting the Estate of Kippilaw, from 14 November 1798 to 15 March 1799' and to undertake a survey of 'Contents of the Estate of Kippilaw Belonging to John Seton Karr Esqr, 1799'. The analysis, which could be described as a 'quantity survey', took detailed account of various bills paid, sales income from '13 ½ Bolls Barley, 2 Swine, a foal, an old mare's skin, etc.' Income and expenses were balanced at £109-19-10½, for the period.[21] Alexander also prepared a detailed description of the area of land available for farming (a 'land survey'). Every grass park, arable field, muir (moor), moss bog, tree planting, road, ditch, hedge and garden area, comprising sixty-two separate land components, was defined in both Scots and English units of area. The survey, not including Bowden Moor which had an unnamed long-term tenant, indicated a total area of grass, arable land, avenues and plantings belonging to the estate of '233 ac, 3 rods, 2 F Scots or 322 acres, 1 rod, 17 perches English.'[22] The addition of Bowden Moor and North Bowden brought the total area of the estate to some eight hundred acres, which was sizeable for the times and district, but less productive than some neighbouring estates. Faughhill, Linthill and Clarilaw Estates, for example, each contained similar acreages of arable land, but carried significantly more livestock than Kippilaw.[23]

The land survey of Kippilaw is the earliest record found of Alexander's professional work as a surveyor. It confirms that by 1799 he had developed these skills and, based on the comprehensive nature of the detail in the *Seton Karr of Kippilaw Papers*, was proficient at it. The implication is that Alexander had trained and received instruction in land measurement and surveying. His mentoring by Andrew Blaikie for the *Statistical Accounts* provides a convincing proving ground for these skills, which would form essential basics for the profession of factor.

On completion of this work, Alexander settled with Francis Napier, an Edinburgh based WS, who was acting for John Seton in London. The purpose for conducting an inventory, then the land survey, becomes clear when it is considered that Kippilaw had been occupied by tenants since the accession of David Ramsay Karr in 1746, the first of two absentee landlords.

John Seton noted the thoroughness of Alexander's meticulous analysis. In consequence, it is not surprising that he was subsequently commissioned to undertake further work in relation to the management of the estate. Alexander then produced a series of designs for various items of furniture for the Kippilaw house: washstands, fire fenders, curtains and blinds, carpets, window fittings, wallpaper and furniture plans.[24] In May 1799, he organised an auction of livestock from Kippilaw, presumably because the new laird wished to replace them with younger animals or to reduce the size of the livestock enterprise. The auction, called a *roup* in Scottish parlance, was advertised in the newspapers:

> Articles of a Roup of Cattle and Horses to be sold this day, by Alexander Kinghorne Schoolmaster of Bowden for behalf of the Executor of the deceased And^ew Ramsay Karr Esqr, as a specified in a Commission from John Seton Esqr dated at London the 5th April 1799. The rules for the auction are set out and the auctioneer 'David Ross licensed auctioneer of Lessudden Green', signed by Alexander Kinghorne and James Dickson Merchant of Bowden.[25]

So began a working relationship between Alexander Kinghorne and John Seton Karr that was to last some thirteen years.

The precise nature of Alexander's initial employment is complex. He retained his position as Schoolmaster at Bowden until 1 June 1800. This was a formal appointment in the gift of the Duke of Roxburghe, and Alexander needed to fulfil his obligations, if he was to maintain his reputation. His arrangements with John Seton Karr were sufficiently flexible to permit him to continue for a period as schoolmaster, undertake the duties of factor, and undertake private surveying commissions while in Seton Karr's employ. An early example of this was in March 1800, when Alexander was away for two weeks on a private commission, measuring land at Jedburgh. In 1800 there is a record of Alexander holding yet another position as County Fiscal and Road Surveyor for Roxburghshire.[26] Such *outside work* was to increase over the succeeding years of his employment as factor, becoming less parergon and more profession as time went on.

Nevertheless, in early 1800 he was doing four jobs at the same time, a situation that could not continue. He began by making plans for a successor at the Bowden school, firming up his commitment to move his family to one of the old steadings at Kippilaw Mains and, with reservations, devote himself to the service of the Estate. At the end of January 1800, he wrote to John Seton Karr:

> I have a fine lad as assistant to my school till Whitsunday[27] So that I am quite at liberty to go back and forward to Kippilaw as often as I please – I have done little this winter in the surveying line, the weather being much against me. I have several good jobs in view – the Heretors are busy advertising for a successor aft Whitsunday when I must remove to the Mains – There will be some little repairs needed on the house at that time, as the thatching is very bad...I hope every thing will go smoothly

on after Whitsunday, as you may depend on my whole attention being fixed on carrying every thing forward according to your orders – Accidents may happen with the most careful management – This is no doubt a new line of life to me, & I know I will have the eyes of many people to look after me, but I have very good friends to advise with on every occasion, and though they do not altogether agree on the step which I have taken, they are still ready to assist me, and I hope it will turn out to the advantage of both you and me.[28]

How Alexander fulfilled his commitment to his 'whole attention being fixed on carrying every thing forward' will become clear in the next section of this history. At this stage of his career, his formal position as County Fiscal and Road Surveyor gave him responsibility for roads, bridges and buildings. Informally it was a step in his career to make important connections throughout the county and establish his reputation as an honest surveyor of independent judgement.

Alexander was still the Schoolmaster at Bowden when Betty gave birth to their daughter Helen (Nellie), in 1797. However, when John Karr Kinghorne was born on 11 July 1800, his father's occupation was described as 'Factor to Mr Karr of Kippilaw'. Thus, John Karr's baptism was conducted 'before a Meeting at Kippilaw House [on] 25th July 1800.'[29] Andrew Seton, born 30 July 1802, was baptized on 13 August, also before a meeting at Kippilaw. It says something of the close but respectful relationship between the Kinghornes and John Seton Karr that Alexander and Betty named their two first sons born at Kippilaw, John Karr and Andrew Seton, after their laird. These names, Seton and Karr (or Kerr) were later perpetuated through several generations of the Chisholm and Kinghorne families in Australia.

Improvement and Utility

Alexander's change in direction and the attitudes he expressed were much in harmony with the 'new ideas' forming during his times. Scotland was undergoing a transformation stimulated by a combination of agricultural innovation, urban and industrial development, and population growth and displacement. The thinking of what is now termed 'the Scottish Enlightenment', in the wake of the Jacobite catastrophe, was to transform society based on science and reason. An early proponent was Scottish philosopher David Hume, who in 1751 proposed a new morality based on 'public utility'.[30] This was not only a political and philosophical movement but also a geographical one, aimed at improving land management, soil quality, and agricultural productivity, as well as aspects of urban life. When the *Statistical Account of Scotland* was published between 1791 and 1799, the new science of geography was being used as a means for promoting political and social cohesion. Amid this, the plights of the urban poor and the highland crofters became visible and widely known.

In the lowlands of Scotland, and in Roxburghshire in particular, there was dramatic agricultural change, typified by enclosure – the movement from open land to closed fields with stone march dykes or hedges. The old run-rig ploughing system, which allocated a fixed number of furrows (runs) and ridges (rigs) to each tenant farmer, was replaced by newer methods of land management. These included the tenancy of fixed areas of enclosed land, the use of rotational cropping and grazing, and the application of fertiliser. Cultivation shifted from wooden ploughs drawn by oxen to better designed ones with metal tynes, such as James Smith's revolutionary sub-soil plough, drawn by horses and requiring less labour than the old systems. Tenancy agreements were extended with written leases and the ownership of land was concentrated in fewer hands. The rhetoric of *improvement* informed both the landowners' views of their life mission and the State's view of the agrarian economy. Farm labour, previously paid for in kind, now demanded payment in cash along with additional conditions of employment. The idea of making a profit in a competitive marketplace, as opposed to the old ideal of stewardship, was gradually penetrating Scottish farming.[31]

The Scottish Borders, specifically, benefited from an increase in cereal cropping, advances in rotations, and new farming technologies. The science of agriculture was at the forefront of these changes, and Alexander Kinghorne was emotionally and practically in the thick of them. He became friendly with two influential agricultural improvers, the aforementioned feu tenant at Holydean, the eccentric but gifted agricultural innovator Andrew Blaikie, and Lord Buchan of Dryburgh Abbey.[32] Blaikie provided Alexander with many ideas that he was able to apply to improve the cultural and husbandry operations at Kippilaw.

In the spring of 1802, 'Old Blaikie', as Alexander called him (he was then 64 years of age), took a 'study tour' through England, travelling by himself on horseback, staying with the Seton Karrs during his visit to London, and discussing his ideas with King George III at Windsor, an indication of the old man's extraordinary status! Blaikie's son Francis was then factor to the Earl of Chesterfield at Bradley Hall in Derbyshire.[33] Lord Chesterfield gave Blaikie a letter of introduction to the 'King's factor at Windsor', Mr Frost. He met the King, in the company of Mr Frost and Lord Somerville at 'the Great Ox Byre', where His Majesty sought Blaikie's 'opinion of [the] weight, value etc.' of his fat oxen. Both Somerville and the King had read Blaikie's contribution to the statistical account of Bowden, so the King chatted with him for some time on agricultural matters in Roxburghshire. Blaikie kept a daily journal of his travels, which survives today as a thirty-two-page booklet, compiled by his grand-daughter Jeanie Lang (née Blaikie). The journal provides a fascinating commentary on the agricultural practices of early 19th century England and makes interesting observations about the King, then of sound mind. He describes His Majesty favourably 'as plain as any country gentleman, or even a farmer', speaking 'good broad English, and distinct, yet from repeating so fast one is apt to lost him in part.'[34]

Blaikie was excited by his visit to Windsor. In remembering himself to 'that family: Mr and Mrs Kinghorne, and [wishing] them all well' he wrote to his wife from Windsor: 'Tell Mr Kinghorn I regret his loss in not getting with me. He might come twenty times before he had such opportunitys as the present.'[35] Andrew Blaikie was well aware of Alexander's desire for patronage, and there could be no higher potential patron than the King.

Alexander reported Blaikie's findings on his return home in the spring of 1802:

> Mr Blaikie is arrived in grand spirits from London – He was at Windsor and had a good deal of conversation with the King, principally about farming – He gives a dismal account of the farming in England, & says he never saw a bit of land properly managed from the time he left Hawick till he arrived on Tweedside at Kelso – When he began to convince some of the English farmers of the impropriety of yoking four or five Horses a-Head in the plow, & told them he could make 2 Horses a-Breast do more than their five – Yes, says they, we understand you are a Scotchman, but the Devele a word of that we believe.[36]

Despite the hyperbole in this statement, it reflects Alexander's belief in

42

the Scottish Borders as a cradle of agricultural innovation at the turn of the 19th century. A judgement that would have been cultivated by Blaikie himself.

Under Blaikie's influence, Alexander was able to improve the efficiency of his operations at Kippilaw by the introduction of draught horses in the place of oxen and by rotational culture, improved pasture species of clover and rye grass, and the application of fertiliser. Blaikie, as a highly respected local agrarian authority and livestock breeder, also assisted Alexander to realign boundaries and exchange land in Bowden Moor with some of the Duke of Roxburghe's Clarilaw Estate, providing considerable advantage to both His Grace and John Seton Karr in the operation of their farming enterprises.[37]

Given the foregoing, and the ideas that were developing in Alexander Kinghorne's mind, it is clear that John Seton Karr *chose* him for the position of factor at Kippilaw, with the advice of the same people who encouraged Alexander to take it. The new role was entirely in keeping with Alexander's outlook. He perceived his future at the forefront of the new wave of scientific innovators. He wanted to take the next step from teaching. To apply his knowledge of mathematics and measurement on a larger scale and contribute to the movement for improvement in both agricultural and industrial development. The best way to do this was to continue contract surveying, seeking bigger and better projects, and develop his interests in agriculture in a real situation: the development of a country estate. Moreover, John Seton Karr was well connected amongst the Scottish aristocracy and London elite. Alexander would have realised that the position of factor on a prestigious country estate would enhance his status and provide new opportunities for patronage through friends in high places.

The Relationship Between John Seton Karr and Alexander Kinghorne

Alexander's letters to John Seton Karr remain in the keeping of the latter's family, annexed to the National Archives of Scotland, the *Seton Karr of Kippilaw Papers*.[38] While generally about estate matters, the letters also show the closeness of his relationship with his employer. His writing style is somewhat orotund, possibly mirroring his manner of speech, but this was the fashion of the time and an indication of his level of education.

Uninformed readers could mistake these letters as correspondence between close friends. This is because Alexander emulated the loyal but opinionated relationship, typical between Scottish retainer and master, best known from the stories of Queen Victoria and her Gillie John Brown. Sir Walter Scott frequently elucidated this kind of 'obedience with rapport' in the *Waverley* novels, much loved by Alexander Kinghorne:

> The idea of the master or mistress of the mansion feeding or living apart from their domestics, was at this period never entertained. The highest end of the board, the most commodious settle by the fire – these were the only marks of distinction; and the servants mingled, with deference indeed, but unreproved and with freedom, in whatever conversation was going forward.[39]

Alexander's relationship with his employer was equally informal and jocular, despite their long separations, as the Karrs only visited their Scottish estate for two to three months each year in summer and autumn. In a letter to Seton Karr in January 1806, for example, Alexander quipped romantically about local concerns and preparations for a possible invasion by the French:

> I have been twice marked as a leader of the pike men but have luckily got off – I would willingly take a musket or broadsword but a pike I hate. In case of an invasion I have offered to serve as a guide which I think I could well do as I know almost all the roads and fords in this and the two adjoining counties…[40]

Alexander clearly admired Seton Karr, who was an antiquarian and interested in the genealogy and history of his own family, having prepared extensive documentation and a family tree on his ancient lineage.[41] Alexander also displayed in the above letter some pride in the profession for which he had been trained: land surveying. At times, his correspondence was obsequious and rather fawning, but this also reflected the attitudes of the time:

> I shall never forget your Kindness in recommending me so warmly to the Duke, & for which I return you my most hearty thanks –[42]

Other letters demonstrated a closeness and trust, redolent of friendship rather than subservience, although his tendency to the hypochondriac must have irritated his employer:

I have got a very bad Cold with a Hoarsness & pain at my breast which I am a little afraid of, I wish you could give me your advice what to get for it – A.K.[43]

All the other Creatures on the Estate are thriving except myself I have been very ill of the Influenza these eight days and my Old complaint of a Bleeding at the nose is I fear going to return this year. I have been quite stupid these two days.[44]

I am under Spences hands at present as I have completely lost the use of the little Finger of each hand by a Rheumatism the effects of cold caught on Tiviotside about a month ago when on a survey – He orders me to wrap them with Hannel and I have got a Linement to rub them with, the pain in the night is excessive.[45]

John Seton Karr believed himself to be both a mentor and strong counsellor to Alexander, who was still in his twenties when he became his factor. At times Karr could be strongly directive and blunt, sending long lists of jobs 'to be done', with pedantic deadlines, without the usual niceties of a greeting or cordiality.[46] Such directions and instructions were focused on the mansion house and garden at Kippilaw, and rarely concerned the farming operations, unless these were costing too much or failed to produce a financial return. Alexander's letters, on the other hand, were full of detailed reportage on the wider estate. Seton Karr's rare instructions regarding farm work were sometimes misguided or untimely, as Alexander would politely point out: 'I observe what you say respecting pruning & boxing up the young Thorns, which shall be duly attended to in the spring, as if done at this season our frosts which are already set in would make all the Earth crumble sown again on account of its being so loose & open.'[47] To all directives regarding the mansion house, however, Alexander gave his 'promise that every thing mentioned in your Long list of particulars shall be got done in proper time, and I have this day noted down Every Article in my pocket memorandum Book lest any of them should escape me...'[48]

A typical communication from Seton Karr would draw attention to the need for certain vegetables to be sown in time for the arrival of the family in August, or for beer to be brewed, hams to be cured, or suckling pigs produced ready for roasting. There was always concern for the welfare and condition of the riding hacks, especially the grey mare Charlotte.[49] The Seton Karrs also left several dogs at Kippilaw, a combination of hunting hounds and pets. These dogs were a major focus of the letters arriving from London, and woe betide the staff if they failed to care for them.[50]

Most of the minor menagerie of dogs and fowls at Kippilaw were in the care of the housekeeper Molly Joy Wilson, who wrote regular but simplistic letters, according to her level of education, to Seton Karr. These were generally repetitive and entirely focused on her animal care and house duties.[51] She firmly believed these were more important, and deserved a higher priority, than the farming activities of the estate.[52]

For their part, the Seton Karrs viewed Kippilaw as their annual escape to the country, where they expected to be able to relax, entertain their friends and enjoy what luxuries the estate could provide. Everything had to be 'just so' for their arrival. John Seton Karr was an aficionado of good beer, and from 1809 onwards, Alexander was encouraged to employ a local brewer, and later his son James, to prepare copious quantities of 'Ale' and 'Table Beer' for the Kippilaw dining table during the annual visits. The quantities involved suggests that they must have entertained lavishly during their summer on the estate.[53]

There was a flurry of maintenance as the date for the Laird's and Mistress' arrival drew near, with Alexander trying to do 'every thing in [his] power to render every thing comfortable for the reception of you & Mrs Karr.' This involved white washing the mansion house, milking parlour and laundry, beautifying the poultry sheds and pigeon house, painting and repairing the carriage that would carry them from Berwick-upon-Tweed to Kippilaw, and ensuring that everything in the garden was flowering and beautiful.[54]

The focus of all this activity was the comfort and provision for the Seton Karrs during their annual summer holiday in Scotland.[55] Nevertheless, the staff at Kippilaw, and Alexander and Betty in particular, genuinely looked forward to the arrival of the laird and his family each year, and there is little doubt that they felt real loyalty and affection towards them.

Chapter 4

Improvement (1799–1805)

a Scottish country gentleman may be a scholar without the pedantry of our friend the Baron, a sportsman without the low habits of Mr. Falconer, and a judicious improver of his property without becoming a boorish two-legged steer like Kil-lancureit.

Sir Walter Scott, *Waverley*, Ch. XXIII

The Kippilaw estate had fallen into disrepair during the second half of the 18th century under the absentee lairdships of John Seton Karr's uncles.[1] The deterioration of the estate was widespread, affecting farming practice, staff management, buildings including the mansion house, enclosures, land tenure and tenancies. John Seton Karr was determined to return the estate to aesthetic splendour but with the financial returns to support his lifestyle. He expected this to be implemented by his enthusiastic new factor. Alexander's ambition was for Kippilaw to be at the forefront of agrarian improvement based on 'agricultural science', a blank canvas upon which he could paint his ideal. Would their two objectives be compatible, or would this lead to conflict with his master?

Agriculture and Farm Structure

Alexander's early years at Kippilaw coincided with harsh weather conditions, as well as upheavals in Scotland and Europe. Between 1798 and 1801 there was a series of warm, dry summers followed by severe, cold winters, which he documented in a Journal of the Weather, and in his letters to John Seton Karr.[2] Further afield, crop failures in 1799 brought a famine that continued until 1801. Food shortages, high taxes and unemployment culminated with public riots in Glasgow and Edinburgh, and the anarchy soon spread to the major Borders towns. There were shortages of grain, both for sale and animal fodder.[3] Alexander was determined to update Kippilaw to cope with the challenges presented there.

Critical to modernisation were the interrelationships between local estates with respect to crops and animals. Kippilaw obtained new varieties of seed potato for the spring plantings from Lord Buchan of Dryburgh Abbey.[4] Alexander considered the improvement of the vegetable and flower gardens, and tree forestry, to be part of his mission. He planted new varieties of fruit trees and other ornamental species, which were ordered from England by Mr Archibald Dickson, the Nurseryman in Hawick.[5]

The built infrastructure at Kippilaw was considerably upgraded and enlarged during Alexander's stewardship. What modern commentaries about Kippilaw fail to reveal,[6] but is clear from the correspondence in the *Seton Karr of Kippilaw Papers*, is that these works were conceived, designed and implemented entirely by Alexander Kinghorne, largely in Seton Karr's absence although with his approbation.

Some agricultural works, such as the draining of the Marle Moss, required considerable persuasion on Alexander's part to convince his employer of their future benefit. Seton Karr was concerned about the high costs and very slow returns from agricultural improvement.

Nevertheless, in the middle of 1800, Alexander set in train a series of structural works that delighted his employer. These included a new carriage-way approach, with a tree-lined avenue leading from the mansion house to the main road, complete with gate-lodge and elaborate gates (Figure 8); a new coach-house and stables incorporating accommodation for farm workers (Figures 9 & 10);[7] the renovation of the farm building at Bowden Moor; and plans for the re-building of the main farmhouse at Kippilaw Mains, where Alexander and his growing family were to reside (Figure 12). The time was fast approaching when the mansion house itself, then a two-storey pile built around the original medieval peel tower, would need to be expanded, as befitted both Alexander's idea of the status of his employer, and John Seton Karr's own views on the same subject. The plans drawn for these improvements reveal Alexander's growing interest and ability in architectural design, which was to become a feature of his future work.[8]

The method for constructing buildings in the early 19th century was dependent in part on the availability of raw materials. One of the newly available products was straight-sawn timber, as mechanical saws began to replace the old technique of splitting tree trunks with wedges into uneven beams; squared-off joists were also available, all cut to the same length and width. Two-storied farmhouses did not appear in Scotland until the 1770s and slates replaced thatch as straight purlins were fitted to accommodate the sarking needed to seal roofs and hold the slates in place. The main building materials required for walls were stone or bricks and lime mortar, replacing the old dry-stone or stone rubble construction methods.

The main bedrock in the Borders was 'whinstone', a hard rock of volcanic origin. Above this bedrock was often a layer of a more tractable rock called 'marle' or 'marlestone'. Marle was rich in carbonate minerals, similar to but softer than limestone and less fissile than shale. The marle was a raw material for building, being used on its own or readily turned into bricks and producing lime for mortar. In August 1800, Alexander conducted a survey on Kippilaw for this material, using cores bored in the Moss Park at various locations and depths. What he found was to excite him, and engage his mind, and the bank account of John Seton Karr, for some years to come.[9]

The Division of Labour on the Estate

Most of the early building work at Kippilaw used the existing farm workforce, supplemented by occasional hired labourers. Alexander himself participated in the more esoteric tasks, such as tree planting. In 1800 the estate had a permanent staff of five: John Bichet (overseer or assistant manager), Thomas [Old Tom], George Sibbald, John Spiden and Walter Lithhead. A specialist gardener was also employed to look after the grounds at the mansion house.

Annually employed *hynds* supplemented these servants. The hynding system, a typically Scottish approach to the employment of farm labour, continued in the Borders until the middle of the 20th century. By the end of the 18th century, the *plooman* had become the aristocrat of the farm labour force, and ploughing was a specialty of the hynds. These sought-after *experts* usually resided on the estate in a cottage with a smallholding, along with their spouse, and, often, a *bondager* – a female labourer hired and paid for by the hynd. The intensity of the arable farming system, particularly at harvest time, necessitated a large female labour force, but they were also used to weed and shore up crops, milk cows, make butter and cheese, cure hams and a variety of other back-breaking jobs.[10]

In the Borders, hynds would offer themselves for hire by 'roup' (auction) or negotiation at the major town fairs (often called hiring fairs), held each year at Kelso, Melrose, St Boswells, Hawick and Jedburgh. The best hynds went to the highest bidders for whom he, his family and his bondager if he had one, would work for a year in exchange for the sum determined plus accommodation, provisions, pasture for a cow and a few sheep and other negotiated benefits. Housing figured large in these contracts, and the tenancy of an unfurnished cottage was usually included. There was considerable competition to get the best hynds, and knowledge of their prowess spread rapidly through the farming grapevine, so that the best ones were snapped up early in the season.[11]

In June 1800, the specialist ploughman Thomas Henderson was the first new hynd hired by Alexander Kinghorne at St Boswells Fair. Henderson commanded a high fee, but Alexander was able to entice him to Kippilaw with the promise of high-quality housing and a variety of fringe benefits.[12] In March 1801, Alexander hired more hynds, including Alexander Grierson. Grierson proved an asset although his wife, originally bonded to work, became ill in 1803 and was unable to continue. To secure skilled hynds, Alexander had to accept some of their demands for special conditions of employment, such as higher pay, freedom of their wives from bondage and special provisions of food.[13]

Apart from assistance with the renovation programme and general maintenance, each of the Kippilaw staff had particular skills around the estate: Old Tom was a ploughman, as were the hynds Henderson and, later, Grierson. Walter Lithhead tended the many hedgerows, which required regular maintenance called 'switching', and his son spent much time 'scouring [the] ditches', which formed the main boundaries of the estate before Alexander converted them to stone march dykes. George Sibbald's main responsibilities were in animal husbandry and 'waiting on the cattle'.[14] All work was made difficult by the harshness of the winter of 1799–1800, and by mid-January the roads had become blocked with snow so that 'there [was] no passage betwixt Bowden and Kippilaw'.[15]

As the winter chill intensified, the oldest member of the estate staff, 'Old Tom', had considerable difficulty ploughing the hard ground, delaying the planting of the summer crops. Alexander faced a dilemma, as a new servant was needed and Tom would have to be laid off.[16] To remove the livelihood of the main family breadwinner in a time of famine was, to a man of Alexander's morality, harsh in the extreme, and must have played heavily on his mind. His elegant solution was to provide the family with both an alternative income, by employing Tom's son as a hynd, and renting the family an estate cottage made available by the recent death of a tenant.[17] Unfortunately, Alexander's opinion of the son of Old Tom was to change dramatically the following year, when he dismissed him for 'dishonesty, discontentment and greed.' Nevertheless, Old Tom was allowed to live out his remaining few years in the estate cottage.[18]

The need for the annual review of hynds was a constant problem for Alexander. However, by 1807 the staff were tending to make their arrangements with him well in advance of the hiring fairs, saving him from attending the annual roup.[19] This is a positive reflection on his ability to recruit, train and retain farm staff on the estate. However, his relationship with the domestic staff at the Kippilaw mansion house was a very different matter.

Disputes with the Domestic Staff

Kippilaw House was run separately from the main farming enterprises of the estate. Alexander had to work closely with the housekeeper, Molly Wilson, and her daughter Mary, as he was their administrative superior. Consequently, he often included reports on household management in his letters to John Seton Karr.[20] His relationship with them was generally cordial during the first two years of his administration, but it gradually soured, declining dramatically after 1810. The genesis of this disharmony was a lack of agreement over minor household arrangements that Molly, a stubborn and strong-willed character, considered to be strictly under her purview.

A particular source of disagreement arose in 1801, when Alexander purchased a 'Milch cow' from his father-in-law, William Brockie, for the use of the main house. He failed to consult Molly Wilson about this animal, subsequently named 'Brockie' by the household staff, and its perceived productivity, or lack of it, became a serious bone of contention.[21] Molly complained of the low butterfat yield from the cow, but Alexander defended his purchase with valiant, but meaningless, hyperbole: 'With regard to the new cow, Molly says that she gives plenty of Milk, but yields only 5 English pounds w^t of Butter per week, which I am very much surprised at, as I know her to be one of the best breed in Berwickshire; she is exactly 4 years old, and is the prettiest Cow within 10 miles of where she stands.'[22]

Alexander's forays into domestic management at the mansion house continued to lack success. There were numerous squabbles resulting in a growing lack of consultation by both parties. This was reflected in the combatants' separate letters to John Seton Karr, regarding cooking and the preparation of food for the laird's table,[23] the provision of a suitable milking cow,[24] and the reluctance of Mary Wilson to operate a newly acquired horse-powered threshing machine or do any work in the barn, which was usually expected of female servants.[25]

The heart of the dispute lay in the separate lines of accountability for house and estate staff. Molly was accountable to Mrs Elizabeth Karr, as manager of her household, and Alexander to John Seton Karr. John Seton Karr failed to clarify these separate responsibilities in his correspondence, nor did he support his factor in house-related matters where he clearly had jurisdiction. Molly and her daughter often misunderstood, or deliberately ignored, Mrs Karr's directions.[26] This also reflects badly on Alexander's leadership style. A skilful manager would have resolved tensions early and amicably, not needing to request a letter from his master to solve petty domestic problems. Alexander lacked the experience to relate with the domestic staff, a situation that later became apparent with some of the farm staff. The ongoing disputes engendered Mrs Karr's strong displeasure, further undermining Alexander's authority, and his reputation with John Seton Karr.[27]

God Bless the Duke of Argyll

As part of his scientific approach to agricultural improvement, Alexander fancied himself as a breeder of fine livestock, particularly cattle. His capacity to express this proclivity was limited at Kippilaw, as the small number of animals on the estate were used mainly to produce meat for home consumption, and for aesthetics. Yet, these limited opportunities, and the associated connections he made with livestock breeders, were to prove valuable for his formation as a landed gentleman and future *grazier*.

52

Horses were the most important component of the Kippilaw stock, as they were essential to farm work. The estate kept riding hacks and several cart or draught horses. In the period from 1797 to 1798, for which farm horse tax records are available, Kippilaw had nine farm horses, comprising the three riding hacks and six draught or cart animals.[28] The latter were in constant use gathering in farm produce, such as turnips and hay, and for 'leading out' dung, moss and marle to the pastures. The draught horses were dedicated to the use of the ploughman throughout the winter months for cultivation of the fields.

The focus of John Seton Karr's attention was his riding hacks, which obviously held a special place in his heart. One of them was a fine grey mare, named Charlotte, whom he rode when at Kippilaw. She was often sent down to Kelso, either to Fleurs Castle for some special attention from His Grace's Groom, or to Mellerstain to be mated by Mr Baillie's prize stallion. The mare and her foals were given the best and closest attention, and Alexander provided regular reports on their condition. In 1805 Charlotte had a male foal, named George, who also claimed considerable favour. Alexander gilded the lily using the opinion of Colonel Hunter, a neighbour whom Seton Karr considered to have a good eye for horse flesh: he 'called here yesterday and says he is the best Colt of his age he ever saw.'[29] It was soon clear that George would be kept as a stallion for breeding at Kippilaw. He was given the utmost care and attention, visiting the Mellerstain stables the following year for breaking and shoeing.[30]

The foals of Charlotte accumulated, as none was ever sold, and included George, and the Countess and Baps. The Countess, a fine looking mare, turned out to be infertile. She constantly deceived Alexander that she was 'in foal' when she was just displaying the effects of good spring feed. The repeated enthusiasm expressed in Alexander's letters concerning the Countess' prospective parturitions was more a reflection of his capacity for wishful thinking, than any skill at pregnancy diagnosis.[31]

Apart from the horses, Kippilaw ran a small number of cattle. Some of these were the aforementioned 'milch cows', usually two for the mansion house and one or two belonging to the farm workers and hynds who lived on site. The remainder, about a dozen cows and heifers (*Queys* in old Scots), along with their calves in season, were beef animals. They were a

53

mixed bunch before Alexander came to Kippilaw, but principally of the Highland Breed, familiar today as the short, red-coated, long-haired and long-horned cattle seen in the Scottish Highlands, known as *Kyloes* in old Scots.

Alexander's neighbour and friend, Andrew Blaikie of Holydean, was a breeder of Devon cattle, then one of the most improved and popular beef breeds in Britain. Originating, as the name suggests, in southwest England, they were red in colour, but were not generally described in the literature until the late 18th century. The Devon Cattle Breeders' Society claim them as an ancient breed from which many modern types, including the Hereford and Teeswater (or Shorthorn), were said to have been derived.[32]

Alexander was interested in the Teeswater, suggesting he was au fait with current trends in cattle breeding, and saw the introduction of this breed to Kippilaw as a way of developing friendly competition with Andrew Blaikie. Although not detailed in his correspondence, he purchased a Teeswater bull named 'the Bishop' for Kippilaw in 1803 or 1804, and the progeny began to appear in 1805.

In one of his letters to Seton Karr, Alexander referred to 'Mr Robson… [getting] a prize at Lord Somerville's Shew.'[33] John, 15th Lord Somerville – the same Lord Somerville met by Andrew Blaikie at Windsor in 1802, he also became a friend of Sir Walter Scott – distinguished himself by the attention he paid to agriculture, and transmitted his name to posterity by the introduction of Merino sheep from Lisbon into Great Britain.

The 'Mr Robson', who won a prize at Lord Somerville's Show, was likely the Teeswater breeder William Robson. His name appears in the first volume of *The English Herd Book of the Shorthorn Breed*, published in 1822, as the breeder of a famous bull, referred to only as '538', born in 1780. While no other information has been found on William Robson – apart from the comment by Alvin Sanders, in his history *Shorthorn Cattle*, that he was an 'eminent breeder' – it is reasonable to assume that Alexander purchased The Bishop from him.[34]

It is a picture of Alexander in his element, nobbing with the foremost breeders and agriculturalists, all bringing with them a network or pedigree of connections. It was also a circle in which a more frugal Scotsman might describe the best as being 'pricey'.

John Seton Karr, unlike Alexander, was not a progressive livestock breeder, nor did he see himself as one. He was more interested in having animals on his estate that were both aesthetically pleasing to look at and sourced from the best pedigrees of aristocratic society. In the early 19th century, this meant the Duke of Argyll's Highland Cattle. His Grace's Inveraray estate was reputed to have the finest cattle in the West Highlands at the time, which were used, principally by the Campbell Lairds, to improve the West Highland breed.[35] Seton Karr purchased seven West Highland heifers from the Duke in 1805. Rather than criticising his employer's choice of female stock, Alexander was delighted that there would be more females on tap to mate with his prestigious Bishop:

> It gives me much pleasure to hear of your getting the Heifers from the Duke of Argyll – A Cross from the Bishop & them will astonish Roxburghshire – The sooner they arrive after the 1st of May the better, that they may meet with <u>His Reverence</u> in order to have calves in due season ...[36]

Alexander favoured the West Highland cattle over the local Kyloes, which were sold 'if possible at St Boswell's fair & rear & feed your own stock – The Inveraray Heifers with your own stock are now sufficient for wintering.' The other problem was that none of the original Kyloes had been 'bulled by the Bishop' during the summer mating period, and so would be a feeding burden to no purpose in the coming winter months.[37]

Gradually, Alexander bred the small herd towards the Teeswater type. Common to his enthusiasm for all forms of agricultural improvement, he was not above hyperbole regarding livestock. At the end of July 1805, he reported confidently to John Seton Karr that one of the bull calves born in the spring had grown into '<u>a young Bishop</u> still prettier than his father, and is esteemed by all judges who have seen him, to be one of the finest calves ever reared in Roxburghshire.'[38] Moreover, he remained fulsome in his praise for the West Highland cattle purchased by his employer; 'I never saw any thing so much improved as the Inveraray Heifers are since they have get home to feed and rest.'[39] The heifers all calved in April 1806, so that the small herd now comprised seven Inveraray cows, and five others, all with calves at foot, and two bulls.[40] Alexander had kept 'the young Bishop' and decided, purely by subjective judgement, that the old Bishop would have to be sold at St Boswells fair: 'The young Bishop will exceed his Father both in size and Beauty.'[41] Yet, within 2 years, the 'young Bishop' himself had been supplanted in Alexander's mental ranking of bull superiority, probably because he suffered from poor libido: there were few calves on the ground due to his lack of attention to the cows. However, his replacement, 'Young Argyll', seemed to be doing his duty, sealing The Bishop's fate – 'God Bless the Duke of Argyll'.[42]

In this period, one of the status symbols and marks of success was to have one's horse, or bull, or cow portrayed by a skilled painter, the likes of George Stubbs – much more prestigious than having one's ruined pile painted by Mr Turner. Alas, while Turner was to visit Scott at Abbotsford years later, with many works coming out of their collaboration, no painting has been found of Messrs Karr or Kinghorne standing proudly by The Bishop, Young Argyll, or any of their creations, bovine or equine. A deficiency in regard for posterity, one should think.

Alexander continued selecting and breeding amongst the small herd of Argyllshire cattle at Kippilaw and learned much about the husbandry and care of the stock. He even developed some skills in animal medicine: he wrote of one sick heifer that 'we are giving her boiled Barley Chaff and Hay Tea – I hope she will come round in a few days – I am sorry anything should ail her she has been so good a Creature.'[43] His management of the herd during the harsh winter months had been considerably improved by his construction of a 'byre' (cowshed) in which they were hand-fed and his improvement of the grass parks for spring and summer feeding.

The prices he was able to obtain for the cattle he sold at the local roups, butchers and the spring fairs were excellent by contemporary standards, even in the early years of the Napoleonic wars. Those recorded in his correspondence ranged from fifteen to thirty guineas,[44] which compare favourably with limited contemporary data for fat cattle prices.[45]

The livestock skills Alexander developed at Kippilaw, guided by his helpful mentor Andrew Blaikie, were to serve him and his descendants well into the future. They were to become cattle breeders in New South Wales, on a scale far more considerable than in Scotland, and were to achieve this using Alexander's original breed of interest, the Teeswater, which by the 19th century had been renamed the Beef Shorthorn.

The Laird's Annual Visit

The rearrangement of accommodation at Kippilaw, including Alexander moving his family from Bowden to one of the farmhouses, a steading at Kippilaw Mains, occurred on 26 March 1800.[46] As the summer of 1800 approached, the workforce at Kippilaw prepared for the expected arrival of the Seton Karrs who, accompanied by two of their servants from London, would be in residence during August. The new lodge and front gates were nearing completion and Alexander 'dug as much peat in the wester moss as will keep you in Fire for a considerable time.'[47] It is not certain whether this was the new laird's first visit to Kippilaw since inheriting the Estate, but it was certainly the first since Alexander became factor.

The Seton Karr family travelled by sea from London to Berwick-on-Tweed in one of the many 'Berwick Smacks' that plied the salmon trade. The journey took three to four days at sea, depending on the weather, and a further day's carriage journey down Tweedside from Berwick to Kippilaw.[48] They broke the sea voyage at Stockton-on-Tees, County Durham, staying for several days with Karr's spinster sisters, Katherine, Helen and Jean Seton and, on this occasion his two brothers Daniel and James. Daniel had been absent for many years as Lieutenant-Governor of Surat in India, and James was also a parliamentary agent in London. The house at Stockton was part of the estate of David Ramsay Karr, and remained in dispute with the Ramsay family for some years after the Setons occupied it.[49] Mr and Mrs Seton Karr were at Stockton-on-Tees in July 1800 when Alexander received word that their baggage had arrived at Berwick-on-Tweed and was in the hands of his capable transport agent, Mr Graham.[50]

Alexander ensured that a warm welcome was prepared for them, as he 'rejoice[d] to hear that you and Mrs Karr are to be soon at Kippilaw. We have now most charming weather and every thing about the Estate looks blooming and delightful; and what contributes most of all to the happiness of every person in this country, is the near prospect of a plentiful crop of Corn of every kind.'[51] Unfortunately, Alexander's optimistic descriptions were not to be reflected in the coming season.

Continuing Hard Times

After the Seton Karrs left Kippilaw for London at the end of their summer holiday, the winter of 1800–01 struck with a vengeance. Alexander's work journal for February recorded strong wind and sleet. The strong wind lasted three days, the roof of the Byre was much damaged, the cattle had to be turned out, and the cart shed was ruined. This was followed by more snow and sleet. Tom began ploughing in the small field south from the Lady's park, but there was a hard frost. He tried to plough but found the ground too hard. After ploughing resumed, there was heavy rain, 'Tom is obliged to give up plowing in the wheat field it is so wet.' A fell winter for all, Alexander had considerable difficulty in the collection of 'park rents', with several the tenants remaining in arrears due to the failure of their crops.[52]

The poor state of the economy and continuing food shortages caused further public unrest and considerable civil disruption. Grain stores had been set up in the major towns as a buffer against famine, further increasing the price of grain and bread, and angering the poor who were already in desperate straits. The town of Kelso was twice set on fire in January 1801. The perpetrators had 'too well affected their purpose…', as in one fire nineteen houses and thousands of pounds worth of grain were destroyed, several cattle and horses were burned to death and two people lost their lives. There were continuing threats of civil unrest in Melrose, Lillisleaf and other nearby villages.[53]

The feed situation improved considerably in the spring of 1802 but was tempered by a severe drop in livestock prices:

> There never was a better appearance of Grass than this season and at the same time pasture Lands never let so ill – A great part of the Grass grounds in the Upland districts of Hawick & about Selkirk cannot be got let at any price – This is entirely owing to the young Cattle having been so effectually drained from the country by the tempting high prices given in the South for this long time past – this seems now to be over & Cattle of all kinds (particularly fat ones) are rapidly declining in price.[54]

The decline in stock prices reflected a short lull in demand between the wars with France (French Revolutionary, 1792–1802, and Napoleonic, 1803–1815). The value of livestock in Scotland, and in particular the price paid for beef compared with mutton or pork, was to rise considerably with the re-involvement of Britain in war with France. This was consequent partly on the increased demand for salted meat for the army and Royal Navy, but also because many farmers had switched from livestock to the production of wheat and other grain products.[55] Kippilaw was to obtain only minimal benefit from these economic changes, as it too had followed the trend to increased cropping in lieu of animals, and because the animals on the Estate were mainly devoted to the aesthetic satisfaction of, and the provision of special food for, the Seton Karrs during their annual summer holidays.

The House at Kippilaw Mains

Alexander's steading at Kippilaw Mains was converted into a small but well-designed two-storey farmhouse. The work began in early 1801. The lower level was 'plastered & nearly dry' by May of that year,[56] but work was then delayed by the intense farming activity that followed the hard winters of 1799–1801. It was not until the spring of 1803 that Alexander submitted rough plans for the main alterations to the house (Figure 12), which were approved by Seton Karr.

> In regard to the Alteration of the Farm House at the Mains, the saving of expense is obvious, when you consider that the present Hen house is to remain as it is only lacking a small passage of 3 feet from it to enter to the Kitchen – There will be no more Doors in front than at present, only the two doors on each end of the Farm house will be brought a little nearer the Middle of the wall as in the sketch…[57]

The foundations for the new parts of the house were laid in May 1803, but work was further delayed by a violent windstorm.[58]

Alexander planned to accommodate himself in rough digs in the wester granary during construction. However, after weathering the storm earlier in the month, Betty decided to take herself with the children to her uncle, John Brockie's farm at Lochton, and did not return until the end of July 1803. By then the house was, if not properly finished, water-tight and providing better accommodation than the building they had occupied since moving to Kippilaw.[59] Their reunion must have been blissful, as Alexander Kinghorne Jnr was born near nine months later. Nevertheless, the house remained unfinished when the winter snows and hard frost arrived in December, and it was mid–1805 before the final touches were completed, along with an attached dairy.[60]

Apart from the ravages of time, Alexander Kinghorne's house at Kippilaw Mains was, when the authors visited in 2014, much as it had been in 1803, an example of Georgian symmetry and utility (Figure 11). The internal room layout was the same as when Alexander designed it (shown in Figure 12). The upper floor, not detailed in Alexander's drawings, contained two large bedrooms, a twentieth century bathroom, and a small nursery designed for one or two infants. The occupant in 2014 was a descendant of a family prominent in the district in Alexander's time, but the house, farm buildings and surrounding land were no longer part of the Kippilaw Estate. The house was sold in 2019 and has been renovated by the new owner.

Coal Discovered!

One of Alexander's character flaws was his exaggeration of the benefits and financial returns from 'improvements'. He tended to go off half-cocked on schemes, without giving due consideration to his ability to carry them through to completion. An example of this, towards the middle of 1801, was his firm belief that he had discovered a valuable seam of coal on the Kippilaw Estate:

> I have now to mention a discovery which I made last week, which at present makes more noise in this County than any thing which has happened for many years – I mean the discovery of a Coal Mine in the neighbourhood of Huntly wood –[61]

He claimed that he had dug a trench at Bowden Moor and found a seam of coal fourteen feet thick, 'quite Black & clear in the Heart like Coal'...

> I brought some of it home in my pocket which I showed to several people in the neighbourhood who were all of opinion that it certainly was a kind of Coal – I returned along with Balfour the Minister and some of the Bowden people on the Saturday, & they came all home with pockets full of the stuff which we found to turn easily Red in the Fire...

Alexander showed the seam to a miner, who confirmed it as coal, the Rev'd Balfour and several members of his congregation from Bowden, and a long list of local dignitaries. He was clearly excited by his discovery and detailed the exact location of the coal to his employer, encouraging him to discuss the matter with the Duke of Roxburghe and the local member of parliament, Sir George Douglas, 'as it will be a universal blessing to every description of people for 20 miles around.' He then launched into a full description of his plan for raising funds by subscription to establish a mine, supervised by a committee of local landowners, and concluded with his 'earnest prayer that you shall be the proprietor of a Flourishing Colliery.'[62]

John Seton Karr was furious! Alexander had effectively spread the news of the discovery far and wide before consulting him or taking the proper steps to ensure that the discovery was genuine. Karr's written response has been lost but can be inferred by the tone of Alexander's next letter…

> [I] am sorry I should have done any thing respecting the Coals contrary to your wish – I assure you I had nothing but your Interest in view, and which I thought it my duty to endeavour to promote on every occasion – I shall say no more concerning them till you are on the spot and then you can judge for yourself what is most proper to be done.[63]

Seton Karr could see that all-and-sundry would want a piece of the action in any coal mining development. Alexander had let his imagination get the better of him, displaying considerable immaturity and naivety. His actions had been neither prudent nor conservative and were more than a little vain and impetuous. The presence of coal was never mentioned again in the Seton Karr of Kippilaw correspondence. In 1835, Bowden's supply of coal was still being brought from Mid-Lothian, as had been the case before Alexander came to Kippilaw.[64] One can only conclude that Alexander had thoroughly exaggerated his find.

Antiquities – 'the intelligent Mr Kinghorn'

Alexander Kinghorne's interest in literature and poetry stemmed from his education at Kelso Grammar, while his admiration for Scott led him in the direction of historical romanticism. He had a complete set of Scott's Waverley novels but was also a subscriber to earlier-published romantic literature. Like many young Scots of his time, he was an avid reader of poetry, and subscribed to magazines that published both poetry and romantic prose, such as the Whig *Edinburgh Review* and the Tory *Quarterly Review*, and he later read the radical Whig magazine, Cobbett's

Political Register. Arts and science have been characterised by some as antipathetic. But this has rarely been the case, and a love of literature, and in particular poetry, was central to Alexander's life. Furthermore, Betty's interest in balladry has been noted earlier, and this would have been her input to the family's evening entertainments.[65]

James Ballantyne, who knew Alexander from their school days at Kelso Grammar, began his career as a solicitor in Kelso. As his practice was not immediately successful, he started a printing business, launching the staunchly pro-Tory newspaper the *Kelso Mail*, which he both edited and printed.[66] He also made tentative steps towards publishing, by printing the work of local bards. It is likely that Alexander was influenced by the works printed by Ballantyne in Kelso, such as Walter Scott's *An Apology for Tales of Terror* (1799),[67] which contained his translation of Goethe's *Erl-King*, and the highly successful *Minstrelsy of the Scottish Border* (1802).[68] The ballads, thought to have arisen from Scottish antiquity, captured the imaginations of many across Scotland, a gentler well-spring from an otherwise bloody history.[69]

'Antiquities', as the term came to be used in the 16th century, were regarded as the evidence for history, whether physical or documentary. Among the first recognisable 'antiquaries' were topographers, cartographers and primitive archaeologists.[70] Given Alexander's avid reading of Scott, and his growing interest in surveying and cartography, it is not surprising that he became fascinated with the antiquities and ruins in and around the Kippilaw estate. These included an old 'Roman road' that, he thought, passed Kippilaw Mains on its path north across the Tweed and through the old Roman Camp of Newstead, near Melrose.[71]

By late 1802, John Seton Karr had provided an introduction for Alexander to the Scottish antiquarian and writer George Chalmers (1742–1825). Chalmers was Chief Clerk to the Committee of Privy Council on matters relating to trade. As this sinecure made few demands on his time, he devoted much of his attention to the antiquities, poetry and topography of his native Scotland. The author of many works, including biographies and political writings, his best known, *Caledonia*, investigated the people, language, civil and ecclesiastical history, as well as the agricultural and commercial state of Scotland during the thirteen centuries from Roman times.[72]

Chalmers had contacted Walter Scott in 1796, requesting the use of some of his poetry in *Caledonia*, [73] and they continued to trade poetic ballads and antiquarian materials. While Scott might have mentioned Alexander Kinghorne as a potentially useful local surveyor,[74] the connection was made through John Seton Karr. Chalmers was acquainted with Seton Karr in London, through his membership of the House of Commons Select Committee on the Caledonian and Crinan Canals, and other capacities, and wrote to him in September 1801 seeking details of the county of Berwickshire as part of his research for *Caledonia*:

> By consigning me a packet, your young man has put me in mind that you can help me a little where you quietly are. I have been writing a Sketch of the history of Berwickshire, for my great Topography of Scotland; and I want to know from you,
>
> 1. When Greenlaw was made the Shire Town?
>
> 2. When was Lauder made a royal borough?
>
> 3. Is Lauder Castle, and Thirlestone Castle, different places?
>
> 4. What is the name of the Water, whereon the district of Thirlstone lyes?
>
> 5. Pray is the [illegible] opened?
>
> I wish you, and yours, every pleasant enjoyment, brimming with infinite kindness.[75]

Seton Karr would have passed the enquiry on to *his* 'young man' (Alexander), who was familiar with these regions of Scotland by virtue of his ancestry. Whether or not this was their first point of contact, by early 1803 Chalmers was in regular correspondence with Alexander on matters of local antiquity. So, as part of his research for *Caledonia*, he used him as a local 'observer' for his studies…

> I have had a Letter from Mr Geo. Chalmers respecting his Roman Enquiries, but am not fully ready for him, as I have not had a Day to spare since you left us – but if you would be so good as let him know that as soon as we have fresh weather, & get quit of the snow, I will devote two or three days in making observations, & will then fill up the Map, & write him as particularly as I can in answer to all his queries.[76]

What Chalmers had in mind was an extensive survey of the area around Bowden, Maxton and St Boswells, of what were suspected to be numerous Roman sites, roads and other antiquities.

The level of interest for Alexander was intense, despite his protestations of busyness to Seton Karr, as his house at Kippilaw Mains was less than a hundred yards from the site of the old 'Roman Fort' of Rowchester, and which he would have undoubtedly carefully examined. Within a month, Alexander had 'filled up Mr Chalmers' plan as far as I can at this time & will write him Answers to his Queries by Mondays post.'[77] Several follow-up letters ensued, as Chalmers clarified matters; those on the record were addressed through John Seton Karr. Chalmers had made up his mind that the ruins at Kippilaw were Roman, as he had already 'written my account of Roman affairs, in general and I only want satisfaction on two or three points of local facts.' His leading questions to Alexander were designed to obtain evidence to back up his pre-conceived thesis.[78] Based on Alexander's observations, Chalmers outlined the course of the local roads and other antiquities in *Caledonia*:

> I have been writing the history of Roxburghshire, and have made a good deal of use of Mr Kinghorns notes, which he had the goodness to send me. I am thus led to say, that I would give the world for answers to my last queries, as they would enable me to settle some material points, as to the course of the Roman Road along the Leader. I hope your harvest is well in, and that you can now spare him for a day; and I will do as much for you.[79]

Chalmers' account embodied and made quotations from the survey report on the 'military road' that ran through Kippilaw prepared by 'Mr Kinghorn', who found the remains of the road and clearly described it...

> Mr Kinghorn, who surveyed this part of the Roman road for me in 1803, says that the remains of it are very distinct where it passes down the bank on the south side of Bowden-burn.[80]

He favourably contrasted Alexander's survey with previous descriptions of the road given in 1782 by Adam Milne,[81] in his monograph on the Parish of Melrose, and earlier by William Roy...

> ... General Roy in tracing its course, has completely mistaken its track towards Soutra-hill ... he was misled by the appearance of the *Girthgate*, which passes from the bridge end of Tweed up the valley of Allan-water, across the moors to Soutra-hospital on Soutra-hill. This footway, without any examination of its formation or materials, he mistook for the only remains of this Roman road ... He might have seen some

useful intimations in Milne's Melrose, who had thrown his curious eyes on this interesting remain in 1746. I caused it to be surveyed by the intelligent Mr. Kinghorn, in November 1803, when the real track was again ascertained.[82]

The Ordnance Survey of 1858–1860,[83] which records the old fort at Rowchester, also quotes Alexander's survey for Chalmers…

The smaller strengths of Row.chester at Kippilaw Mains & Blackchester Southward of Clarilaw, appeared also to have been converted from British Forts to Roman Forts. 'Rowchester is two miles, and Blackchester three and a half miles, Southward of Eildonhills – The past of Rowchester, which stands on a gentle eminence is in the form of a Parrallelogram, having the angles rounded, it was fortified by a strong rampart, and large fasse, including an area of two and a half acres – Rowchester is the name of a Roman Fort west Severus's wall[84] – Roechester is also the name of the Roman station in Reedsdale, and Rochester in Kent, derives its name from a Roman Fort' – Kinghorns MS Survey.[85]

The details provided to Chalmers in 'Kinghorns MS Survey', which is no longer extant, highlight Alexander's early interest in Scottish antiquities, particularly those that might have been considered mysterious. The content of the 'Survey MS' must have been detailed, extensive and widely respected, based on the fragments that survive in the Roxburghshire, Berwickshire and Selkirkshire Ordinance Survey Name Books (1856–1860).[86]

However, more modern surveys point to the origins of the 'Military Road' near Kippilaw as being uncertain. The main points of confusion were Chalmers' conclusions that the Rowchester site was Roman, and that the nearby ('400 yards') road was part of Dere Street, the northern extension of the main Roman artery from London known as Ermine Street. The Dere Street section of the road probably connected the forts at Corbridge (in Northumbria) and Newstead (Melrose) and was built by the Roman Governor Julius Agricola (ca 81 AD).[87] Chalmers concluded that it connected Coldshiels (Cauldshiels) Hill (to the north-west of Faughhill Moor) and Blackchester (near Lauder), both designated in the Ordnance Survey of 1858–60 as 'Roman Forts.'[88]

In recent times (2000), the Royal Commission on the Ancient and Historical Monuments of Scotland (RCAHM) and the Ordnance Survey have documented these ancient road excavations and re-examined the Rowchester site at Kippilaw. The analyses of Rowchester are equivocal, suggesting that Alexander's report that the fort was a parallelogram with rounded corners, 'fortified by a rampart and a fosse thirty feet wide and nearly twenty feet deep,' was hard to reconcile with the remains as they now appear. Archaeological test pits dug around the Rowchester site in 1961 were 'devoid of significant archaeological features.' However, this was based on a small number of test pits and one trench, and the considerable cultivation, control of rabbit infestations and removal of artefacts in the intervening period since 1803 might have removed or obscured the evidence.[89]

In relation to the road excavations, RCAHM concluded that the Kippilaw features were not part of Dere Street and might be medieval or even pre-Roman. If they ever existed as part of a Roman Road, they were unlikely to have branched from Dere Street, because it is located about three miles east of Kippilaw near the village of Maxton.[90] The conclusions from the RCAHM surveys compared with Alexander's of 1803,[91] were that the structures at Kippilaw, marked on the Ordnance Survey as 'military road' were an ancient 'defensive frontier earthwork', of considerable scale, which might have been associated with the fort on the northernmost of the three peaks of the Eildon Hills, which dominate the landscape of the Tweed Valley. Named Trimontium by the Romans, as was the fort they built at Newstead near Melrose, these hills were a focal point for both their fortifications and those of the Celtic civilization that preceded them. Whether the Kippilaw structures were Roman, or possible part of the extensive defensive excavations constructed around the year 1000 BC by their Celtic predecessors, remains unknown.[92]

The foregoing suggests Alexander was mistaken about what he found at Kippilaw. There was no science of archaeology then. The methods he employed are still part of archaeological procedure – the topographical survey, the interpretation of evidence – but the study has developed light years since. If Alexander did not have the expertise to test theories, nobody much did.

Not for the last time, Alexander threw himself into work which reinforced another person's preconceptions, in this case George Chalmers, sitting hundreds of miles away in London, who had very much made up his mind on the matter. For his part, Chalmers was full of praise for the work of 'the intelligent Mr. Kinghorn'.

Through this commission, Alexander was able to cultivate Chalmers as a useful patron in the upper echelons of the British Government, who was later to provide him with written support for his application to emigrate from Scotland.[93]

Thou Man of Wond'rous Ken

Amid the shortages of 1801, Alexander began an ambitious plan for improvement: the design and construction of drainage works for the reclamation of agricultural land in the Marle Moss.[94] The outcome was an engineering achievement, celebrated in verse; but it was also part of his undoing, as it became an unappreciated expense that weighed heavily on the finances of John Seton Karr. This was not helped by Alexander's over-optimistic predictions regarding the benefits of the work: 'I shall pledge myself that this improvement shall return your money with Interest in a few years...'.[95] While this promise *was* eventually fulfilled, it was not to be within his employer's lifetime.

An article in the *Gazeteer of Scotland* published in 1806 described the soil in the area west of Kippilaw as 'light and fertile. There is a moss containing marl, of great extent, and four small lakes'.[96] Such 'light' soils were known to benefit from the application of marle, which 'had the effect of binding the various soil fractions together into a more compact and consolidated soil'.[97] Alexander's aim was to bring unusable bog land into agricultural production by digging drainage tunnels. As a by-product, the extracted marle and moss would be utilised as fertiliser to improve the productivity of the soil on the estate, a practice since overtaken by industrial fertilisers in most parts of Scotland, but which would survive in Roxburghshire where marle continued to be plentiful until the mid–19th century. Alexander's objective was not new. There had been extensive mining and application of marle on the nearby lands of the Duke of Roxburghe's estate in the late 18th century, and Andrew Blaikie had already applied it extensively at Faughhill and Holydean. Notwithstanding, Alexander's approach to the drainage of the land prior to the extraction of the marle was unique, innovative and would result in the reclamation of unusable bog-land.[98]

Rev'd Thomas Jollie, minister of the Parish of Bowden (1830–1848), described the method used in some detail…

> Drains are cut from two to four or more feet deep, according to the nature of the soil and the situation, and are filled with broken stones to within twelve inches of the surface, the undermost being always carefully laid in by hand, and set on edge, or in the form of a conduit at the bottom; the rest are thrown in promiscuously above them, and are broken and levelled on the top; a slight covering of straw or turf is then put over them, and the earth is put above all…[99]

Alexander's drains were elaborate underground affairs described as 'a work of great labour, the drift being carried 300 yards through a solid whin-stone rock, 50 feet below the surface.'[100] The project needed the approval of the Duke of Roxburghe, upon whose property the water from the drains would flow.

Alexander began to provide details of the proposed work in letters to Seton Karr from March 1801. He devoted considerable time in consultation with John Murray, the tenant on the Duke of Roxburghe's Faughill estate, and asked Seton Karr to liaise directly with the Duke.[101] He also consulted local master mason, John Smith from Darnick, on the requirements for lining and shoring up his stone drains. Smith would later build the first phase of Sir Walter Scott's Abbotsford near Melrose.[102] The issue with the Duke of Roxburghe's land was settled to everyone's satisfaction by January 1802, and Alexander began the search for a contractor to complete the work. He chose John Gardner from Lothian, the brother of William Gardner, one of the contractors who worked on the Crinan Canal.[103] He also provided Seton Karr with a detailed financial analysis of the project, including a total costing of £150–19. He predicted the work would be 'finished before Harvest' and that 'this year will finish your expense on that account [purchase of lime fertilizer] & that we will get plenty of Marle at home with which I have not the least doubt of your doubling the Rental of your Estate in a few years – It is a small outlay at first but a sure return in the end.'[104] However optimistic Alexander's costing for the project, and foolish his guarantees regarding the increase in rental returns from the parks, they were sufficient to convince Seton Karr to approve the project, with work beginning at the end of February 1802.

The process began with a sixty-yard open-cut drain, lined with quarried flagstone, and was to continue with a 'mine' (tunnel drain) into the whinstone at a depth of twelve feet, which was to be blasted out with gunpowder.[105] The 'mining' was a most dangerous process. 'When he sets fire to the match [Gardner] tyes a Rope round one of his Thighs & two men haul him up by a windlass to the top before the shot goes off … but no accidents have yet happened!' To be employed by Alexander Kinghorne could be a life-changing experience.

It soon became apparent that progress would be much slower than originally predicted as 'Gardner still pushes on with the Drain – The Rock is now very hard – He has only advanced Four yards this last week.'[106] Alexander's praise for Gardner's abilities also became tempered by a concern over his drinking habits: '[he], like all the rest of the Colliers is a drunken dog, but he is one of the most active workmen I ever saw.'[107] He turned a blind eye as long as the work team made progress: 'Gardner was drunk for nine days successively after Melrose fair, but is now carrying on very briskly.'[108]

Alexander continued to report very slow progress throughout 1802 and into 1803, with respite only for Gardner's regular drinking binges.[109] Then, 'Gardner has been on the Ramble these 10 days I heard that he sold his Coat yesterday at Galashiels for sixteen pence to buy whisky.'[110] The following week, 'Gardner has never yet made his appearance – last accounts of him was from Langholm where he passes for an Architect from Argyleshire – I have wrote Mr Briggs to send me a man from Lothian.'[111] The project looked to be stretching well into the following year.

The 'man from Lothian', by the name of Douglass, duly arrived and by May 1803 the harvesting of both moss and marle began. After eight days, fifty cartloads of 'fine moss' had been extracted and piled up into heaps. Alexander hoped this would provide enough material for the whole farming operation at Kippilaw until the winter.[112]

What he failed to explain was that the effect of marle was slow, when compared with pure lime application, with little discernible change in soil productivity likely until 2 to 5 years after application. Moreover, the marle needed to be thoroughly mixed with the soil each year to achieve the desired effect. Once fully incorporated in the soil, however, the improvements tended to be permanent and long lasting.[113] John Seton

Karr would have seen little benefit from Alexander's efforts.

Another team of 'miners' was employed in early 1804 to complete the drains. The costs of the work continued to escalate, and he had to request more funds to pay out the mining team. This considerably displeased Seton Karr, who insisted that the work proceed with Kippilaw labour only.[114] He was able to personally implement this order in July 1805 when in residence at Kippilaw for the summer holiday.

Finally, in December 1805, Alexander reported that the water had 'quite gone from the Moss within these two days' and 'a very respectable Marle heap and worth fully one hundred pounds, besides a very large quantity of rich Moss to mix with our Winter's dung, with which I hope in another year to make the Dam-head park look as it ought to do.'[115] The marle and moss were put to full use to improve the pastures from the end of 1806 onwards, and by the middle of 1808 Alexander was able 'to sell Marle in June at Earleston fair.'[116] When he left Kippilaw, some four years later, the mining and sale of marle was just becoming a substantial component of the estate revenue.[117]

Others followed in Alexander's wake. In 1811, Adam Meldrum superintended reclamation work in the county, draining the Long Moss between Selkirk and Bowden.[118] Both Alexander and Meldrum were eulogised in a pastoral ode, *The Cotter's Moss-Day* by Andrew Scott (1757– 1826), a minor Borders poet who lived at Camieston, a neighbouring estate to Kippilaw:

> Success to thee, thou man of wond'rous ken,[119] [Alexander]
> Moss haunting spunkies tremble at thy lore ;
> The sedge crown'd sisters frae their watery den
> Thou skills to draw, an' points the mining bore…[120]

Among the many subscribers listed in the back of Andrew Scott's book were John Seton Karr, and a retinue of highly ranked patrons. Sir Walter Scott's name was notably absent.

Such accolades aside, the project was to represent a small sized entry by Alexander into engineering, which he would pursue as a profession in later years. What lessons had he learned from this foray?

Chapter 5

Tenancies and Inheritance (1800–1807)

...if he gets his Way I shall be infeft in Melrose Abbey with my Ancestors before I am infeft in Kippilaw

John Seton Karr, July 1801

Over the first seven years of his factorship, Alexander Kinghorne was to learn much about property and tenancy law. Utilising his experience as a land surveyor he was, within a short time, embroiled in complex negotiations concerning the tenants, estate boundaries and inheritance issues at Kippilaw. A series of troublesome long-term tenants, who continually defaulted on their rents, required management, a test also of Alexander's social skills.

The Park Rents

A significant proportion of the Kippilaw estate, between 600 and 650 acres each year, was leased to tenants. The leases were of two types: (1) long-term tenancies of up to twenty years, such as those over the Bowden Mill and Bowden Moor (separate parcels of land to the north of Kippilaw Mains), and (2) the so-called 'park rents'.

The latter, comprising enclosed 'parks', were rented to tenants on an annual basis. Ten to twelve of these parks, ranging in size from 20 to 25 acres,[1] were offered in April each year by a roup that determined their rental price for the year. Alexander advertised the date of the roup in the local papers and retained the right to withhold land on the day if the price offered or the attendance was too low, the latter sometimes being the consequence of bad weather. The parks were generally rented for between £10 and £25 each, forming an important component of the Estate income, some £150–250 per annum.[2]

An unplanned consequence of the famine in 1800 and 1801 was the failure of several tenants to pay their rents. These defaults were understandable, given that an entire year's crop had been lost and some of the tenants had no other sources of income. As estate manager, the unpleasant task of following up on these rental arrears fell to Alexander. He explained his leniency to Seton Karr …

> I do not wish to enforce payment by harsh measures, as they are all good people, and it might hurt the letting of the parks in the future – and I hope the little indulgence they have got this year, will lead them to be better tenants next season when I will look more strictly after them…[3]

This 'little indulgence' displayed Alexander's solicitous nature, in response to the genuine hardship of the tenants, even though it had to be justified in terms of economy. He was to display his genuine compassion for the oppressed and suffering in various situations throughout his life.

Troublesome Tenants

Despite the harsh conditions, Alexander had less sympathy for the long-term tenants who were late with their rents. Particularly difficult cases were those of Thomas Best, a miller with a tenancy over Bowden Mill and part of Restonrig Farm, and John Shiel, who tenanted Bowden Moor. Both had long leases, negotiated years before Alexander's arrival as factor, under the lairdship of David Ramsay Karr.

A lengthy series of negotiations and legal proceedings ensued, in which Alexander was assisted by Charles Erskine, Seton Karr's Melrose solicitor. Alexander demonstrated considerable persistence, patience and diplomatic flair. Best refused to pay the amounts he owed, and was finally evicted in 1802.[4] Alexander eventually extracted payments from one of Best's business partners.[5] The troublesome John Shiel was still in place in 1802, also through the grace of a business partner. However, Alexander had, by and large, got the better of him, and his tenancy of Bowden Moor was settled with satisfaction for all in May 1807, with Shiel replaced by a new lessee.[6]

The predicament for Alexander over Shiel's arrears and tenancy was compounded by poor relations between Shiel and his neighbour, Thomas Milne, a feu tenant of the Duke of Roxburghe at Lindean, adjoining Kippilaw. The comings and goings of unsavoury visitors at Bowden Moor, described by Alexander as 'Tinkers and Vagabonds', bothered Milne so much that he demanded a March Dyke (a boundary generally in the form of a ditch) be built between his land and that rented by Shiel.[7]

Alexander, always enthusiastic to create advantage out of adversity, agreed to this request and was spurred on to initiate the construction of a new boundary for the whole Kippilaw estate.[8] Unfortunately, his efforts failed to satisfy the tetchy Milne who decided, by the middle of 1802, that a full boundary adjustment was required between Kippilaw and Lindean, despite Alexander's careful survey indicating the contrary. The matter escalated and came before the Sheriff at Jedburgh for arbitration. Old Milne's anger eventually got the better of him as he 'died of Apoplexy [stroke] at his son's in Newark on Tuesday morning' 5 May 1807.[9]

This was by no means the end of his family's complaints regarding the boundary, as his son, Nicol Milne, carried on the argument.[10] Alexander again applied diplomatic skills to resolve the dispute. He assembled a cohort of witnesses, including John Murray, the tenant of Faughhill and Clarilaw, and cleverly inserted his friend Andrew Blaikie of Holydean as Milne's representative. Alexander's patience, gentle persuasion, along with his surveying and cartographical skills, eventually won out. He constructed a substantial March Dyke on the line of the stones fixed by him between Bowden Moor and Lindean, the cost shared by both parties to the satisfaction of John Seton Karr.[11]

The Excambion Between Bowden Mill and Holydean

In 1802 Alexander came up with a scheme to adjust the boundary between Bowden Mill and the Duke of Roxburghe's lands of Holydean, involving an *excambion*, or exchange of land. Andrew Blaikie, the feu tenant of Holydean, supported Alexander's suggestion. The proposal was for Seton Karr to give up Bowden Mill to the Duke, along with its thirlage (the right to mill grain), in exchange for part of the east side of Clarilaw, a corner cut off by a public road next to the section of Kippilaw called Restonrig Farm.

Blaikie wrote to His Grace's steward, James Haldane, arguing the case.[12] The advantages for the Duke, he said, were threefold. First, he would gain control of the water from Bowden Burn running through the Mill land, which tended to flood Holydean on an annual basis, as the water was held up for use by the Mill. Blaikie offered to clean out the drains and redirect the flow of the Burn at his own expense. Second, the removal of the Mill dam at Bowden Mill and 'making another sluice across Bowden burn, below the Kelso Bridge...would give His Grace's Miller the whole

Command of the water from Luckenhaugh, which he never had before.' The Duke's miller, William Swantson, would thus be able to grind grain year-round, instead of just when water was flowing through the Burn. Thirdly, the thirlage from the mill could be added to that of His Grace's miller.[13]

Despite the logic of Blaikie's arguments, and the agreement of the Duke, it took another three years to settle the matter. After the eviction of the miller Thomas Best, the arrival and departure of more tenants at Mill and Mill farm, the legal wheels began turning, with the excamb to be re-considered in 1805.[14]

Alexander again pressed the advantages with Seton Karr.[15] However, as it was not activated by February 1805, another tenant was found for the Bowden Mill land. Alexander negotiated a tight deal, involving the repair of buildings in exchange for a sixteen-year lease to Andrew Maither at a favourable rent, who proved to be good long-term tenant.[16] The matter of the excamb, which had been delayed so long by the 4th Duke's legal representative, was never settled as the Duke died in 1805, and his estates were sequestered until 1812.[17]

Bowden Mill is the first example found of Alexander's association with milling and the mechanics of mill design and construction, although he might have had exposure in Kelso, which was a milling centre. This foreshadows one of his son's mill-building in New South Wales. Further, the foregoing examples provide evidence of Alexander's growing ability as a land manager, surveyor and, unlike his interactions with the Kippilaw domestic staff, an effective negotiator.

The Rights of the Heirs of David Ramsay Karr

Another legacy from the previous lairdships of the Ramsay Karr family was not so easily or amicably settled. In 1801, John Seton Karr was in dispute with the other heirs of David Ramsay Karr regarding their rights over the lease income from Bowden Moor. This was but one of many issues that remained unresolved from the time of Andrew Ramsay Karr, who by his death in 1799 might have thought himself well rid of it. The matters were in the hands of the Ramsay Karrs' solicitor, Francis Napier WS, and Seton Karr's colleagues, Charles Erskine in Melrose and John Spottiswoode of Sackville Street, London.[18]

74

The precise nature of the dispute over Bowden Moor is not clear from the *Seton Karr of Kippilaw Papers*; it appears that Seton Karr had inherited a one fifth share, whereas there were four other Ramsays, each retaining a one fifth share. Seton Karr disputed these terms of the will, and commenced arbitration proceedings, with Spottiswoode preparing the submission and Decree Arbitral on his behalf.[19] A freak storm in early February 1801, described by Alexander as 'a perfect hurricane', destroyed most of the buildings on Bowden Moor, as well as damaging other infrastructure on the estate. Alexander prepared plans for the repair of these buildings which 'all needed to be [re]built from the foundations up as most were cracked and partly blown down by the recent tempestuous wind'.

Seton Karr was now faced, not only with a dispute over his ownership of Bowden Moor, but the expense of repairing the buildings on it.[20] He expressed his frustration in a letter to Spottiswoode, in which he described the other parties as 'irreconcilable & unreasonable' and without 'any Sentiment of Justice towards me, or any of my Mother's children.' He accused their solicitor of inaction, 'for Mr Napier means only to write, not to act; and if he gets his Way I shall be infeft in Melrose Abbey with my Ancestors before I am infeft in Kippilaw' (Infeftment is a Scottish legal term for investment with or possession of inheritable property).[21] He refused to agree to the conditions of settlement laid down by the Ramsays.[22]

Before leaving for Scotland for his summer holiday of 1801, Seton Karr consulted the Duke of Roxburghe's legal representative John Campbell, the future eminent Scottish lawyer, politician and man of letters, then studying at Lincoln's Inn.[23] Campbell, on behalf of the Duke, supported Seton Karr's case, but his opinion on the rents payable for the land further muddied the waters. The feu contract for the lease went back to 1647, which was supposed to restrict the inheritance of the land to a single successor.[24] However, several other parts of Kippilaw were held, together with Bowden Moor, under a single lease at a fixed rent. So, it was impossible to determine what proportion of the rent could be allocated to Bowden Moor without a full property assessment of the rental value of each piece of land. Here, Alexander's skills came to the fore.

Campbell wrote to Alexander requesting details of the rents obtainable from all the lands adjoining Kippilaw purchased by the late David Ramsay Karr.[25] Alexander duly consulted Seton Karr, being unaware of which properties were involved, and whether he should comply with Campbell's request.[26] In the meantime, he had completed the renovation of all the buildings on Bowden Moor, using the Kippilaw staff John Bichet and John Spiden. He received a further urgent request from Campbell for estimates of the rents on Bowden Moor, and so submitted his estimates without the laird's advice, thinking it would help his case. Unfortunately, Seton Karr had already written to Campbell stating his own estimates of the rental, which were different from Alexander's.[27] Consequently, the matter remained unresolved, in this case due to the laird's lack of effective communication and trust in his factor.

Alexander's depth of understanding of the legal complexities of these matters of the law of inheritance says something about his knowledge of land tenure and of his considerable intellect. Despite the application of several legal minds and Alexander's practical skills, John Seton Karr was, indeed, *infeft in his grave* before the matter was finally settled. But this was not to be Melrose Abbey, 'with his ancestors', but rather the cemetery of St James, Westminster, after he died at Golden Square, London.[28]

Chapter 6

War and Politics in the 'Land of Cakes' (1805)

I have been twice marked as a leader of the pikemen but have luckily got off – I would willingly take a musket or a Broad sword but a pike I hate…

Alexander Kinghorne, January 1806

Bonaparte Stirs Invasion Fears

Napoleon Bonaparte rose to prominence under the First French Republic and took power in 1799 as First Consul. In 1804, he crowned himself Emperor of France. Britain had faced his military strength when he launched an invasion of Egypt in 1798. The Royal Navy's response resulted in the defeat of the French by Rear Admiral Horatio Nelson at the Battle of the Nile on 1 August.

Britain was technically at war with France continuously between 1793 and 1815, known at the time as The Great War, with a brief interlude under the Treaty of Amiens from March 1802 to May 1803, as the French Revolutionary Wars transitioned to the Napoleonic Wars. She remained largely protected during this period by her naval supremacy.[1]

When hostilities resumed after the British occupied Malta in 1803, their objectives also transitioned, from restoring the French monarchy to stopping Bonaparte; as George Chalmers wrote to Seton Karr in October that year, nailing his Tory colours to the mast in a thinly veiled jibe at the latter's Whig associates…

> You see, we invade in place of being invaded. The French, however, persevere in their absurd project: and, we act upon the truest principles, when we prepare to make that project ineffectual…The volunteers are to be immediately called out; in order I presume, to show the best disciplined of them <u>real</u> <u>service</u>…We begin to think that Bonaparte will take Britain in his anger, and will come over. We seem now pretty well prepared for him. You are also preparing. I have seen Lord Minto's speech, at your meeting. I think he goes straight forward, though his

77

politics be crooked. There ought to be only one kind of politics at present.[2]

The renewed hostilities were viewed with trepidation in the Borders of Scotland, where the threat of invasion by Napoleon, through Scotland or from Catholic Ireland, caused some panic and the widespread muster of local militias to repel the threat.

On 17 January 1804, Alexander reported to Seton Karr that many were volunteering for the militia…

I have been twice marked as a leader of the pikemen but have luckily got off – I would willingly take a musket or a Broad sword but a pike I hate – In case of an invasion I have offered to serve as a Guide which I think I could well do as I know almost all the Roads & Fords in this and the two adjoining Counties – However I hope my service in that line will never be needed. Cap[t] Mein has shamefully neglected his Corps of Volunteers. He is still in London & I understand finds some difficulty in passing his acco[ts].[3]

These statements by Alexander were tongue-in-cheek. He was not a coward but, as his comments in subsequent letters suggest, he felt the preparations for invasion in Scotland were disorganised and pandered to the love of military pomp and circumstance, not to mention providing an excuse for carousing and jollity, for certain members of the aristocracy.

After Nelson's victory at the battle of Trafalgar in 1805, the Scottish Lowlands were placed firmly on a war footing, anticipating the imminent arrival of Napoleon's forces. J. G. Lockheart described the enthusiastic preparations for resisting the invasion…

Edinburgh was converted into a camp: independently of a large garrison of regular troops, near 10,000 fencibles and volunteers were almost constantly under arms. The lawyer wore his uniform under his gown; the shopkeeper measured out his wares in scarlet; in short, the citizens of all classes made more use of several months of the military than of any other dress; and the new commander-in-chief [the Earl of Moira] consulted equally his own gratification and theirs, by devising a succession of manoeuvres, which presented a vivid image of the art of war, conducted on a large and scientific scale.[4]

That same year, Alexander related another incident, also detailed by Walter Scott's biographer, about a false alarm that stirred Scotland from the Tweed to the Highlands. Scott was returning to the Borders from a visit to William Wordsworth in The Lake District. While overnighting with his wife at Gilsland, east of Carlisle, Scott received the news that a French force was about to invade Scotland...

> ...the alarm...spread far and wide; and a mighty gathering of volunteers, horse and foot, from the Lothians and the Border country, took place in consequence at Dalkeith. He was not slow to obey the summons. He had luckily chosen to accompany on horseback the carriage in which Mrs. Scott travelled. His good steed carried him to the spot of rendezvous, full a hundred miles from Gilsland, within twenty-four hours; and on reaching it, though no doubt to his disappointment the alarm had already blown over, he was delighted with the general enthusiasm that had thus been put to the test – and, above all, by the rapidity with which the yeomen of Ettrick forest had poured down from their glens, under the guidance of his good friend and neighbor Mr. Pringle of Torwoodlee...and after some sham battling, and a few evenings of high jollity, had crowned the needless muster of the beacon-fires, he immediately turned his horse again towards the south, and rejoined Mrs. Scott at Carlisle.[5]

Alexander's reaction to the excitement was one of amusement at the origin of the false alarm. Fire beacons had been erected along the coast, with others stationed at strategic points inland towards Edinburgh, as a signal for the militias to muster at a moment's notice. On this occasion, 2 February according to Scott, the watchman at Hume Castle saw what he thought was a beacon but turned out to be an 'accidental fire in the county of Northumberland'. The alert sentinel lit his beacon fire and the signal 'was immediately repeated through all the valleys on the English Border'. The alarm spread rapidly through the Border counties and the militias were rapidly armed and transported into their coastal command posts. There was a general panic as farmers and town people alike searched desperately for arms, and some remarkable distances were covered by those travelling to their rendezvous, as in the case of Scott's hundred-mile ride.

Sir Walter Scott commented in *The Antiquary*: 'The account of the ready patriotism displayed by the country on this occasion, warmed the hearts of Scottishmen in every corner of the world'. Alexander, on the other hand, merely saw it as 'an amusing folly'.[6] The irony of the situation was that Napoleon had, indeed, formulated plans for an invasion of

Britain by the 200,000-strong *Armée de l'Angleterre* from 1803, but called off the plans in 1805, around the time of the Scottish false alarm.[7]

There was a political storm surrounding the second term of Prime Minister William Pitt, and his decision to join the third coalition against Napoleon. In the wake of the Trafalgar victory, the coalition was defeated at the Battles of Ulm and Austerlitz. Alexander commented 'We have no news here but all cast down with the unfortunate accounts from the Continent – Mr Pitt surely has much to answer for at this time.'[8] Alexander's Conservatism was not blind as to consequences. However, he might have rued his comments, as he penned his letter only five days before Pitt's sudden death, which would have saddened him.

Alexander was intensely interested in public affairs. He kept up through the Kelso papers and those from London that Seton Karr sent him on a regular basis.

> I wrote you last Sunday, and on Tuesday I was favoured with No[2] of Cobbets political Register, for which I return you thanks, it is a great Treat to me – [9]

> I thank you most kindly for Cobbett I have received three of his numbers they are a very great feast to me and my wife.[10]

The *Political Register* was a weekly newspaper founded by William Cobbett in 1802. Originally Tory in outlook it gradually became radically Whig and is seen as a precursor of *Hansard*.[11] Betty's reading should be noted. Too often women's interests are hidden behind the written records. This gives an indication of the conversations at Kippilaw Mains. Betty's character would influence her children, and be an example to her daughters, who would become forthright in their own ways.

Alexander was an avid reader of the *Political Register* which, along with Seton Karr's comments on its contents, was formative of his political views. Alexander secretly felt some sympathy for the 'social conscience edge' of Cobbett's original Toryism. As a subscriber to the *Edinburgh Review* – which promoted Whig politics and romantic poetry – he did not confine his reading to the Tory press. The political influences of his mentors were an uneasy conflict: Seton Karr's aristocratic Whig politics, and Walter Scott's romantic Toryism. The Whigs had by this stage been so long out of government that softer views had grown in the Tory party, a kind of 'broad church', which was nevertheless not really Scott's cup of tea. Alexander seems to have absorbed these influences and settled somewhere in the middle.

Gossip and Dry Humour

Alexander would, on occasion, report to his employer local views on whatever was making headlines in London. In April 1805, he took an interest in the controversy that had arisen around Henry Dundas, 1st Viscount Melville, then First Lord of the Admiralty, described by Noel Mostert as 'a hard, ruthless, greedy Scott'. There was suspicion as to the financial management of the Admiralty, of which Dundas had been treasurer between 1782 and 1800, and a commission of inquiry was appointed to investigate in 1802. The commission reported in 1805, resulting in the impeachment of Dundas in 1806 for the misappropriation of public money. Though it ended in an acquittal, and nothing more than formal negligence laid against him, he never again held office.[12]

Alexander wrote that 'we have nothing talked of here at present but about the conduct of Lord Melville and Mr Trotter, [which] is a disgrace to the 'Land of Cakes'.'[13] Melville's was the last impeachment trial ever held in the House of Lords. Another reason for his retreat could have been the death of Prime Minister Pitt in 1806. An earldom was offered to Melville in 1809 but declined. Mr Trotter was Melville's financial agent and implicated in his dealings.[14]

The 'Land of Cakes', referred to by Alexander, was Scotland. Robert Burns used this expression to describe it in the opening line of his poem *On the late Captain Grose's Peregrinations tho' Scotland*: '…Hear, Land o' Cakes and brither Scots…'.[15] However, Robert Fergusson had previously used the expression in *The King's Birthday in Edinburgh*:

> …Oh, soldiers! for you ain dear sakes
> For Scotland's, alias, Land o' Cakes[16]

Both poems resonate the Scots' fondness for oatcakes, once a part of the staple diet, and still popular today. Alexander was, again, 'speaking' tongue-in-cheek as he parodied the local outrage to the alleged fraud by a member of the aristocracy, but with a tinge of Whig sentiment. Perhaps it was a dig at his employer, who was about to make the annual pilgrimage to Scotland:

81

All our living creatures are thriving, and my wife joins me in every good wish to yourself & Mrs Karr, hoping you will <u>all</u> have a prosperous journey to the 'Land of Cakes'[17]

Seton Karr's reply to these letters no longer exists, but in later correspondence, Alexander provided a more conservative view on the matter, bemoaning the lack of 'news here but are all happy that our Country man Lord Melville has been honourably acquitted.'[18] Had he been reprimanded for his previous flippancy?

Alexander was a bit of a gossip and had a rather dry sense of humour, reporting all sorts of goings on amongst the local aristocracy to Seton Karr. In mid–1805 he wrote that 'Co[l] Hunter has got a son by the Gardiner's daughter Past week – this is three – Two Girls & a boy.'[19] Lieutenant Colonel Richard Edgar Hunter, first Dragoon Guards, was the well-known and popular Laird of Linthill, the same who had admired Seton Karr's mare, the Countess. Hunter's illegitimate children were of no avail to him. He died unmarried and 'without any settlement – Riddell succeeds to the Linthill Estate without opposition – A Mr Edgar a clergyman claims the Berwickshire Estate which must be determined by the Court of Session.'[20] Alexander described the circumstances of Colonel Hunter's death as 'a melancholy story'...

> Co[l] Hunter our worthy neighbor came to the Heritor Meeting at Bowden on Thursday last to vote for our new schoolmaster and dine with the presbytery, he went away about half past 9 o'clock at night in company with our neighbor Mr Cochram and the Rev[d] Mr John Campbell but rode away from them at the Dam=head and having pushed his Horse against some sticks at the end of Mr Brockies Hynd's houses he was thrown off and killed on the spot – They searched for him the whole night but it was not till 6 o'clock on friday morning that he was found frozen quite stiff – The funeral is tomorrow...[21]

Alexander was to undertake private surveying work for Hunter's eventual successor, William Riddell, in 1820.[22]

* * *

Alexander's jibing of his employer indicates a level of intimacy in their correspondence that masked a developing rift. However, this rift was neither political nor a diminution of their personal relationship. Alexander professed to be a Tory, no doubt, for reasons of his aspirations to the gentry. However, he clearly harboured Whig sympathies, and expressed them here to Seton Karr, knowing it would not cause any adverse opinion of himself – many of the laird's clients and political associates were Whigs, as he was himself. But the time was fast approaching when Seton Karr would no longer be able to afford his witty but spendthrift factor.

Chapter 7

The End of the Beginning at Kippilaw (1805)[1]

I am very sorry you should think so little of the Return which Kippilaw makes

Alexander Kinghorne, January 1805

John Seton Karr's dissatisfaction with the returns he was getting from his considerable financial investment in his country estate began to emerge in early 1805. Alexander received a stern letter from his employer, as suggested by this response…

> I am very sorry you should think so little of the Return which Kippilaw makes – 'Tis true that the money laid out on Improvements have not yet paid, nor <u>can</u> Improvements of Land pay any person so soon, but they look as well, and promise to pay as much as any in the neighbourhood… The Buildings no doubt are junk money, but comfort cannot be had without some expence – The <u>Marle Moss</u> has certainly been a <u>continual Drain for Cash</u>, and has preyed much on my Spirits as well as yours; but this too is in a fair way of being done, as the Miners are advancing as well as can be expected, and I have no doubt of its paying you handsomely at the long run tho' not instantly –[2]

This is an unusually honest assessment of the situation without Alexander's usual hyperbole. However, Seton Karr was probably at the limit of his available funds for farm improvements and, as most of these had been planned and implemented by Alexander, his own limit on the long rein he had given him to manage them in his absence. But he was not consistent in his objections. The next expenditure to be lavished on the estate, the renovation and extension of the mansion house, although planned and supervised by Alexander, would certainly be at the laird's behest.

Seton Karr also maintained his concern that Alexander was unable to get on with the servants at the mansion house and was too lenient in dealing with the other farm labour...

> My Lenity to the servants has been studied to promote your interest – Harsh measures will never do good in this country – This is proven to a proverb amongst your neighbours – Good servants are ill to be found, and when they are found they ought to be treated gently, at the same time no misconduct ought on any account to be passed over without reproof, <u>and this I promise</u> it shall be my endeavour in whatever line I am placed always to do -

Alexander was not only lenient but also somewhat remote in his treatment of the farm workers, delegating considerable responsibility to the overseer John Bichet. There was a mass exit of the annually hired labour in 1805, which reflected badly on Alexander. He reported that 'they had resolved to a Man to leave your service at Whitsunday first, and they were all provided with Masters some time ago – This put an end to the conversation with my only saying, that I thought it was a duty they owed to their Master, to have at least informed <u>me</u> they were going before they went to seek any other place.'[3]

It seems the departure of the hynds on this occasion was not entirely due to poor management. Earlier in the year Bichet informed Alexander that 'Minto was to go which saved me the trouble of saying <u>he was to go</u> so <u>he</u> is out of the scrape.' Minto, who had been on the verge of being dismissed, decided to jump rather than being pushed. Another of the hynds, Goodfallow, whose wife was bondaged to the estate, stirred up the remaining servants. Mr Brodie, the new tenant at Clarilaw, told Alexander 'that it was no sooner known that he had got Clarilaw than <u>Goodfallow</u> had a messenger at him to see if he would engage <u>him</u> with <u>Old Jamie</u>, and <u>young Tom Henderson</u>.' Brodie 'behaved so well in the business' that he would not speak to any of these men until he had discussed it with Alexander, who told him 'he might do as he liked as I was determined none of them should remain longer here than Whitsunday.' Brodie ended up employing '<u>Jamie</u> & <u>Tom Henderson</u>' but Goodfallow ended up out in the cold.

By the time of the mass resignation, Alexander had already hired 'a very decent man & woman …William Hume, he has been 7 years at Holydean with Mr Blaikie – He is a Middle aged man, and has no young children, only one Daughter at home who is to work at any sort of job necessary on the farm.'[4] Alexander then launched into a general criticism of government policy on British agriculture. Here he was 'voicing' conservative views to Seton Karr, perhaps as a means of excusing his loss of so many staff, but also reflecting his fears that the amendment of the Corn Laws would further lower the returns to the estate, as it would open grain markets to foreign competition thereby lowering prices. His fears were, well founded.[5]

It took Alexander more than a month of intensive work to replace the farm labour at Kippilaw. He attended the hiring fairs at Kelso, Selkirk and Jedburgh, ending up with 'Thomas Nisbet from Langlee near Galashiels, & the other named William Fowler from Craig=Douglas in the parish of Yarrow – I only want a plowman.'[6] Thus, he satisfactorily resolved his problem of hired staff which, to his credit, seems to have been a typical contemporary issue: the hynds consorted with each other across the district to their own advantage, a foretaste of trade union bargaining.[7]

Much of Alexander's apparent leniency with staff was a consequence of his kindness to those in poor health or other difficulty:

> – the Hedger's son at the new Hedges in North park & Hay field weeding and cleaning – His father is a decent man & has been with Mr Blaikie there 7 years, he was quite well when I hired him, but had a fever in the beginning of May of which he is not yet quite recovered – I would not accept of him at Whit[y] but on condition that his son was to work along with him till Martinmas without any wages, as he himself could not be expected to be so able for work for sometime – he is getting stout again and I hope will soon be fit for work –[8]

He tried to give the impression that he was a tough master when required. He dismissed the groom, Hogg, who 'has not got a place nor will he get one in Roxburghshire – I shall take care that Toms daughter and her Brat shall march off at the term…His conduct to his Horses and his laziness are the reasons of my parting with him.'[9]

Alexander's management foibles were reflected in another incident with one of the hynds, Thomas Scott, hired in 1811. Initially, he painted a positive picture of Scott to Seton Karr: 'a stout young man, married, and only one child, he shapes very well as yet.'[10] However, he failed to keep a close enough eye on him. The neighbours already knew him as an inveterate poacher, but it took Alexander eight months before noticing Scott had been 'poaching in the night'. The practice had been carrying on for the previous year, he claimed, unknown to him, 'as none of the neighbours would inform against him…' The young hynd had been taking so much of Kippilaw's game that there was a noticeable scarcity during the Seton Karr's summer visit that year.[11] This was by no means the first time Alexander had misjudged a person's character.

Alexander's letters indicate that he had a free rein with hiring, firing, management and discipline of farm staff. However, in the absence of the laird's side of the correspondence it is not possible to be certain about this. A poor perception of Alexander's staff supervision might have been characteristic of Seton Karr's style, as a strict disciplinarian, or it might reflect Alexander's incompetence. He seemed able to retain the confidence and trust of many people at the same or at a higher social status than himself – for example George Chalmers and Lord Buchan, his neighbours John Murray, William Scott, and Andrew Blaikie. However, his relationship with those below him suggests kind support of good workers but failure to deal capably with the lazy and dishonest, or those with whom he was at odds, such as Molly Wilson.[12]

Were these permanent flaws in Alexander's character, which would re-emerge later in his life, or were they the consequence of youth and inexperience? He was 41 years old by the time he left Seton-Karr's employment. Twelve years later, he would be given a much more testing task as Superintendent of the Emu Plains government farm in New South Wales, with a deputy, overseers, staff and a workforce of convicts! How would he stand up to these responsibilities?

Chapter 8

Kinghorne Family Matters (1805–1812)

Alexander's Step-family

Alexander Kinghorne was the only child from the marriage of James Kinghorn and Margaret Eddington. Margaret died in 1775, a tragedy for both James and his young son, and the years which followed would have been marked by grief and difficulty for them both. After a period of three years, James Kinghorn remarried, Ann Smith of Kelso, on 29 November 1778:

> Andrew Smith & Alison Aimers both of this Parish – and James Kinghorn and Ann Smith also both of this Parish, are to be proclaimed on the 29 Nov[r] 1778. Witness David Glasgow & Andrew Kinghorn.[1]

Andrew Smith was a tailor in Kelso, and a trade colleague of James Kinghorn.[2] After their marriage, Andrew and Alison were to remain in Kelso, having three children. As for Ann Smith, it was a double wedding, and this suggests she was Andrew's sister.

The upshot of this for Alexander was that he gained a mother. Or, rather, a step-mother. There is little to suggest his reaction to this. He would have had to adjust from being the little centre of the household, to having a rival for his father's attentions, to being big brother, as the family grew. James and Ann would have seven children who survived infancy, quite filling what was probably not a large house. Alexander's step-family did play a part in his life, but it was not highly significant in the grand schemes of things. It is therefore opportune to summarise their lives at this point. (Details of their lives are in Appendix 3, Table 2.)

James and Ann's first child was a daughter, Isabella, born 17 September 1779, in Kelso, a little under ten months after the nuptials.[3] No further record of Isabella has been found in the surviving parish records.

Next was a brother, Andrew, born in Kelso a little over twelve months after Isabella on 20 September 1780.[4] Like Alexander, Andrew was not inclined to join his father's tailoring business. At the age of twenty-one, he set sail for Jamaica, as Alexander mentioned in a letter to John Seton Karr:

> My Brother sailed for Jamaica in March last but the painting can be got done by a young man who has begun business in that way in Melrose.[5]

Alexander had been lining up his brother to do the house painting at Kippilaw, but Andrew decided instead to seek his fortune in the colonies. It did not end well for him, though, as Alexander afterwards recorded in the Kinghorne Family Bible: 'Andrew...died at Jamaica June 1808.'[6]

Next was a sister, Margaret, baptized 11 December 1781 at Kelso, a good thirteen months after Andrew.[7] She married an innkeeper, John Scott, had three children, and died in Heiton, Roxburghshire in 1851.[8]

Next was a brother, James, baptized in Kelso 19 January 1784.[9] After Andrew left for Jamaica in 1801, Alexander and his father, then aged 55 years, had high hopes that James, then 17, would take over the family tailoring business in Kelso. In 1805, as James' involvement in the business grew, Alexander asked John Seton Karr if he would find him a placement with a London tailor to improve the then 21-year-old's skills. Alexander's gratitude for Seton Karr's assistance is shown in their correspondence...

> I thank you kindly for your attention in arranging a position for my Brother and informing me of his arrival – I hope he will behave himself in London with sobriety & industry – I thought his going there for a little time might brush him up a little in order to succeed my father in his business who is now an old man –[10]

One might suspect that 'sobriety & industry' were not hallmarks of James' character. He found London more to his taste and did not return to take up tailoring in Kelso. He married Jane Smith at St George Hanover Square in May 1808, and died in London in June 1821, leaving descendants including Mark Kinghorn a famous comic actor.[11]

The next child was John, baptized in Kelso on 10 February 1787.[12] John was to stay closer to his father, and the clothing trade, but again not with an aptitude for tailoring. He married a Greenlaw lass, Elizabeth Hunter, the bans proclaimed in May and June 1815.[13] John became a Woollen Hand Loom Weaver, a skilled trade at its best, making fine fabrics. In 1841, he and Elizabeth were living in a house in Roxburgh Street, Kelso, possibly James Kinghorn's old house. They had a family of at least four children. John most likely died before the 1851 census, and Elizabeth died in Kelso in September 1870. Their eldest son, James, was retired, and living in another house in Kelso in 1891.

The youngest brother, William, was baptized at Kelso on 13 August 1788.[14] It is unclear how he passed his early years, but it seems that by 1806 he had, with the assistance of Seton Karr, found employment as one of the gamekeepers at Fleurs, the Kelso estate of the Duke of Roxburghe. As part of this he had an interaction with Alexander in the matter of one of Seton Karr's favourite hounds:

> P:S: The Old Gamekeeper at Fleurs sent up one of my brothers last Wednesday desiring me to send down the young pointer LOT that he might train him for you to be ready for the Shooting Season – I accordingly sent him & wrote him to take particular care of him. [15]

William also died prematurely, at Kelso, 29 April 1813, just two months after his mother, Ann.[16]

His father died first, the sad events recorded in the Kinghorne Family Bible: 'James Kinghorne my father, died at Kelso, on Friday the 25th day of October 1811, Aged 65 years and 7 months.' And then: 'Ann Smith my stepmother died at Kelso on Thursday the 25th day of February 1813.'[17]

There were two further sisters: Anne was baptized in Kelso 24 May 1790.[18] She is next found at Stichill and Hume, where on 11 April 1817 she was married to Alexander Deans.[19] It is likely that after the deaths of her parents, Anne went to live with, or at least visit for an extended period, the family of her uncle, James' brother, Alexander Kinghorn and his wife Margaret Smith, who had long before taken up residence in Stichill and Hume. After their marriage, Anne and Alexander Deans moved to Cambusnethan in Lanarkshire, where they had five children. Anne died in 1869 in Braehead, Lanarkshire (Appendix 3, Table 2).

The last child, Janet Kinghorn (sometimes 'Jean'), was baptized in Kelso on 15 August 1792.[20] She also seems to have had a fortunate life. On 12 June 1818 she married John Lillie in Kelso.[21] Lillie was, by 1841, a road contractor, and they lived prosperously in Roxburgh Street Kelso, with six children aged from 20 to 10, probably not far from her brother, John Kinghorn, and his family. Afterwards, John and Janet Lillie and her family became farmers at Queenscairn, Stichill, where in 1861 they were still living, in their 70's, prosperously it seems. In 1871 they were living with their son in Lowick, Northumberland. John died later that year.

There appears to have been some correspondence between the family remaining in Scotland, and those in Australia, during the nineteenth century. A studio photograph of James, son of Alexander's brother John, is among the family papers, and on the back has the handwriting of Alexander's daughter, Isabella.[22] Otherwise, it seems, silence.

As remarked earlier, Alexander's step-family did play a part in his life, and this was probably more than has bubbled to the surface of the surviving documents. Nevertheless, they were not highly significant in the grand scheme of his endeavours. It was more an occasional interaction, using his connections to help them, but without major involvement himself.

Childhood Mortality

Meanwhile, Alexander and Betty Kinghorne's sixth child, named Alexander, was born on Friday 4 May 1804. Sadly, his older brother, John Karr did not survive childhood. He became ill in November the following year, as Alexander reported to his employer.[23] 'Little Karr' died at Kippilaw Mains on Saturday 7 December 1805 aged just five years and five months. To make matters worse, a month later, Betty's sister Helen Brockie caught a 'cold in the middle of January & died of a Galloping Consumption in five weeks ill.' Helen, who was unmarried and lived at Blainslee, was just twenty-one years old.[24]

The following year, on Monday 19 May 1806, Betty gave birth to another son, Thomas Kinghorne.[25] Therefore, by the middle of 1806, Alexander and Betty had six surviving children living with them at Kippilaw Mains, which had sleeping accommodation of just two bedrooms and a small nursery. The two-storey farmhouse was becoming crowded.

Young Thomas became ill during April 1807. Initially, the family thought it was just teething: 'Our youngest Boy has been very ill with a Teething Fever these 10 days which has alarmed us very much', wrote Alexander.[26] It was soon clear that his recovery was in doubt, as he was 'every hour worse and I dare say will not be in existence when you receive this Letter – I have not had off my clothes these four nights.'[27] Thomas died on Saturday 2 May 1807, aged eleven and a half months.[28]

Childhood mortality was a fact of life in early 19th century Scotland, when on average twenty to twenty-five percent of children died,[29] but this does not lessen the impact of the loss of a child on parents and siblings. It is a measure of the Kinghornes' devotion and care that they were able to raise eight of their ten children to healthy adulthood.

The circumstances of birth of their last three children were to be even more difficult than for the preceding seven.

Betty's Long Illness

Alexander and Betty were very shaken at the loss of a second son through childhood illness. Betty was weakened by the shock and physical exertion of caring for him, and she became ill herself soon afterwards. 'My wife is ill with a Quinsy in her Throat which has reduced her very much – she gets no rest Night nor day', wrote Alexander.[30]

This 'quinsy' was the beginning of a long, undulant illness, which waxed and waned for many years. In modern medical parlance, 'quinsy' is a peritonsillar abscess that starts as an inflammation of the tonsils and is accompanied by a sore throat. It usually affects one tonsil, in particular, but can develop into two pus-filled abscesses, one on each tonsil. This makes swallowing difficult, is very painful and often accompanied by fever and prostration.[31] At times Betty would be confined to bed for long periods, and at others she was able to do limited activities and look after her household and garden, but she never fully recovered her health.

The diagnosis given by Alexander cannot be taken as accurate and the medical advice available at the time was far from useful. Therefore, it is possible Betty had chronic tonsillitis, or something resembling glandular fever, but her doctors generally differed in their diagnoses, some thinking it was tuberculosis and others just a 'nervous' condition. 'Dr Spence is afraid she may fall into a consumption', wrote Alexander in June 1807. Spence then proposed a treatment that, over the years, Betty was to repeat on several occasions, a visit 'to Berwick Spittal' for the unusual activity of 'sea bathing'! She made this pilgrimage in the summers of 1807, 1808 and 1809.[32] As part of the 'treatment', Dr Spence ordered her also to take 'port wine…and…London porter which he said was the only Malt liquor she should drink'.

Despite perceived beneficial effects of the 'sea bathing' and, no doubt, regular doses of the medicinal liquors, Betty continued to suffer from her complaint, sometimes seeming to recover a little but suffering from a constant sore throat. [33]

Surprisingly, despite her medical condition, Betty was still able to conceive. On Saturday 19 of March 1808, she gave birth to her eighth child Elizabeth Margaret.[34] Betty's health continued up and down throughout 1809: 'She gets no rest Night and Day which distresses me very much, what it is to end in God only knows.'[35] Even Molly Wilson at the Mansion House expressed her concern for Betty's condition in a letter to Mrs Seton Karr:

> I do not no what tou thin of Mrs Kinghorn for she is verey bad and canot ceap out of hir bed and the pin in hir throt is severe that she throes hir self that I am afred she hurt hirself.[36]

In June 1809 Betty was again well advanced in pregnancy and feeling the benefits of the warm summer months. The gardens at the Kippilaw Mansion House were in full summer bloom with all the Laburnums, scarlet flowering thorns and Hawthorn in full blossom, 'the prettiest thing I ever saw' Alexander wrote.[37] But Betty varied between being much worse, with Alexander having to care for her night and day, and sometimes rather better, with never a mention in Alexander's correspondence that she was about to give birth. In fact, the happy arrival of John Ker Kinghorne on Tuesday 11 July 1809 seemed to come as a complete surprise to him. His only comment to Seton Karr was that his wife 'continued in the same lingering way'![38]

Betty continued in this 'lingering way' throughout 1810, sometimes able to get up and sometimes confined to bed. Whatever the nature of her complaint, she was able to conceive again in May 1810.[39] In January 1811, 'Clarkson… applied a blister to her Throat but it seems only to torment her and has done no good.'[40] Two local practitioners, Drs Clarkson and Douglas, had agreed 'that her complaint [was] purely Nervous and that there is no danger.'[41] But Alexander became so concerned with this unhelpful diagnosis that he sought an opinion from the doctor at Duns in Berwickshire, about twenty-eight miles north-east from Kippilaw. 'He has hopes of her Recovery, and has given her a Bottle of Drops and a Powder – she has begun to take the Drops this morning – He says they will do her no harm if they do not relieve.'[42] In the midst of her illness, Betty gave birth to their last child, Isabella, on Monday 18 February 1811.[43]

Within a month of Isabella's birth, Alexander was searching even further afield for medical assistance and dietary remedies for Betty. He consulted 'several of the most eminent physicians in Edin^h respecting my wife's case they all agree that her complaints are Nervous and order her nourishing Diet and air as the only treatment'.[44] In March and April 1811 she vacillated between weakness and slight recovery and, to make matters worse 'little Kerr and Helen are likewise up in a Fever – The Mains is quite like an Hospital.'[45] As the Kinghorne children recovered, Molly Wilson's daughter Mary became ill,[46] probably from tuberculosis, and within a month was in a very bad way.

> Molly's daughter is very fast going, nothing can be done for her, her disease is a rapid decline – Her only complaint is a great load at her breast, pain in her side, and a great spitting – Molly's daughter is fast going.[47]

Alexander did not record Mary's death, but she passed away in September 1811.[48]

In April 1812, Alexander obtained a position in the Royal Navy for his 15-year-old son William, through the patronage of Thomas Williamson Ramsay of Maxton. The Napoleonic wars were raging and had, by this time, spread to the North Sea, involving both Norway and Denmark.[49] In her debilitated state, Betty was terrified of losing yet another child and, it seems, a favourite one at that. Nevertheless, Alexander was determined to make the most of his connections by getting his second son into the Navy. On 9 April 1812, he wrote to Seton Karr that he was leaving 'with William tomorrow for Leith. I am afraid of the consequences of his mother parting with him, she is so very poorly'.[50] His concerns were justified, as he found Betty 'worse than he had yet seen' on his return to Kippilaw on 18 April.[51]

Betty remained confined to bed until Alexander was able to prevail upon her to try 'sea bathing' again. To this end she went to Leith, where he visited her at the end of August 1812, after which he took her to stay with her uncle, Thomas Brockie at Southfield near Port Seaton, a resort on the Firth of Forth east of Edinburgh. Here she would be able to continue regular exposure to the sea, until the weather cooled with the advancing autumn.[52]

Family Responsibilities

Betty never recovered from her debilitating chronic illness, although she was to live with it for another seven years.[53] It is hard to imagine the anguish, burden and disruption this caused to their lives. Alexander spent many hours personally caring for his wife, assisted by his eldest daughter Helen, then a stable and mature teenager. Alexander also had the assistance of a nurse while at Kippilaw, as there were five children under ten years old to be raised.

William had gone to sea and was to carve out his own maritime career in Australia. From early in 1811, Alexander's eldest son James, then seventeen years old, was fully participating in the farming operations at Kippilaw, assisting with land preparation, sowing and harvesting of crops.[54] However, James was also anxious to get a position of his own, as was Alexander to help him find one. James was 'tired of staying at home and does not like surveying,' wrote Alexander in March 1812, 'I am quite put about to think what to do with him.'[55] While James continued to take on responsibilities at Kippilaw during the Kinghornes' last year there, it was to be another two years before he would find a position of his own.[56]

At the age of forty-two, Alexander was facing the responsibility of providing for his children over many years to come. For the present, his plans were to remain at Kippilaw, supplementing his income where he could with outside commissions. But the time was approaching when his romantic ambitions would develop a grander plan for their future.

Chapter 9

The Renovation of the Mansion House at Kippilaw (1807–1811)

We are in great confusion and bustle as you may well imagine, but every thing gets on better than I could have expected...

Alexander Kinghorne, June 1808

From early 1807, John Seton Karr initiated major additions to the Kippilaw mansion house. Alexander had already completed several handsome new structures on the Kippilaw estate, all of which reflected his growing skill in the Georgian architectural style: the front gates and lodge on the Clarilaw–Bowden Road (1800), the tree-lined drive from these gates to the mansion house (1800), the magnificent coach house (1800), and the Kippilaw Mains farmhouse (1803). Perhaps his most attractive building was the regency villa at the nearby Gledswood estate, completed in 1805 for William Sibbald of Gledswood.[1] John Seton Karr was aware of these achievements and, despite reservations about Alexander's profligacy in matters of estate expenditure, entrusted him with both the architectural design and project management for what would become his largest and most impressive achievement to date.

The Seton Karrs arrived at Kippilaw in August 1807 for their annual country holiday. This time they stayed for four months, much longer than usual, a time of intense planning for the renovation, with Alexander taking on board all the laird's ideas, and proposing many of his own.

By December, Alexander had drawn up a 'Letter of Agreement' between Adam and James Hood, builders of Dalkeith, and 'John Seton Karr Esq respecting the Additions to be built to the Mansion House of Kippilaw.' He also prepared detailed specifications and plans, confirming that he was to be both the architect and manager of the project. The builders agreed to...

execute the <u>Whole work</u> furnishing every material and every kind

96

of service, in a substantial, Neat & workmanlike Manner for One Thousand, four Hundred and fifty six pounds seven shillings and two pence ster^g (£1456"7"2), The whole work to be conducted under the inspection of Alexander Kinghorne your Factor, who is to <u>have power</u> to reject or set aside any part of the Materials or Work he may find <u>not conform</u> to the above mentioned plans and specifications which are this day doqueted [warranted] and signed by us with reference hereto.[2]

The wording of the agreement, counter-signed by Seton Karr, clearly devolved control of the project to Alexander.

Accordingly, a long and arduous four years ensued for Alexander, as he struggled to make perfect every detail of the Seton Karr's new and imposing mansion. The house as it is today (2022) is not quite the same as that designed and built by Alexander in the early 19th century, as further external changes were made in 1886. However, Alexander's re-design was substantial and transformed the appearance of the house from a medieval Peel Tower with added 16th and 18th century two-storey rooms, into an imposing Georgian mansion of three floors.

Alexander appended a large neoclassical block on the north-east side of the old Peel Tower, changing it from a square to an L-shape, incorporating the simple embellishments of the Georgian style, such as symmetrical square windows and decorated cornices. The late 19th century renovations added further to the north side of the house, making the Georgian frontage asymmetrical, while other extensions were formed west and north of the original nucleus (Figures 13 & 14). Today, the only external trace of the original Peel Tower is on the south-east face of the main block.[3]

In essence, Alexander's design increased the two-storey 'old house' to three stories, by raising the height by nine feet. An additional three-storey wing, the 'new house', was integrated with the old at the point of the original central staircase. The new house comprised a ground, or 'principal floor' as Alexander called it, with hallway, kitchen and scullery, library, servant's hall, butler's pantry, and cellars that included the servants' accommodation. The second, or 'big room floor', contained a dining room, drawing room and two bedrooms; while the third, or 'bed room floor', housed six bedrooms, three with large walk-in closets and one with an adjacent 'water closet', an innovation for the times, that remains intact and in working order today. The staircase of the old Peel Tower was renewed *in situ* and another, concealed staircase installed beside it, so that servants could attend the upper rooms without disturbing the Seton Karrs or their house guests. All these features can be seen in Alexander's original sketch plans for the house. The project also involved landscaping the environs and garden of the mansion.

Construcion was undertaken in two stages: the first, spanning mid–1808 to mid–1809, was the building of the 'new house'; the second stage, renovating the 'old house', commenced in May 1809, all managed in meticulous detail by Alexander. By April 1811, when Alexander gave account to John Seton Karr, the project's costs had well exceeded the early estimates, some £1,830 – a very substantial over-run of £374 (twenty-five percent compared with the original contract price). This had been compounded by a long and acrimonious dispute with Hood the builder, fanned to an extent by Seton Karr's dissatisfaction with the quality of the latter's work, but left to Alexander to negotiate, resolve, and find work-arounds with other contractors.[4] Yet the house remained unfinished on the inside, and it would take until April 1812 for the interior fittings, painting, household linen, upholstery, wallpaper and other internal furnishings to be completed, in time as always for the Seton Karr summer visit.

Alexander had provided his master with a splendid country mansion, the Georgian symmetry of which survives in the structure as can be seen today, despite the confusing additions since. The pitfall was its enormous cost at a time when Seton Karr was entering a period of financial stress. Embarrassed for funds, but never dishonest regarding his obligations, he struggled to make timely payments particularly for the final stages of the build.[5]

Beyond that, Alexander had bitten off a very substantial piece of work, which distracted from his management of the agriculture of the estate and added burdens of time and anxieties. Seton Karr, while not overly interested in the agricultural enterprise, nevertheless was interested in the overall profitability of the estate, seeing as its purpose the support of his status and lifestyle. The cost of the renovation exceeded the returns from agriculture and rentals for the best part of a decade. This, compounded by him being straitened on other fronts, put further financial pressure on him, and on Alexander's position.

A lasting benefit to Alexander was that he had continued to increase his skills and achievements, with a series of projects as architect, structural engineer, building project manager and landscaper, of which the Kippilaw mansion was the largest so far. He had come from being a schoolteacher, a tailor's son who didn't want to be a tailor, and by 1812 was on his way to becoming a civil engineer.

Chapter 10

Alexander Kinghorne: Private Surveyor (1800–1812)

Theodolite – The small one mentioned by Mr Rennie will exactly answer my purpose

Alexander Kinghorne, March 1801

Notwithstanding the pressures of his work as factor at Kippilaw, Alexander continued regular private surveying work. Some commissions originated from recommendations by John Seton Karr to his clients and friends, while others came through Sir Walter Scott or Brockie connections.[1] The assignments were usually local to Roxburghshire but sometimes farther afield. Alexander scrupulously sought Seton Karr's permission before accepting each task. These requests were always reciprocated with encouragement. Whether this was out of generosity or a sense of mentoring on Seton Karr's part, or perhaps as a way of encouraging Alexander to pursue a bigger and better career, rather than remaining as Kippilaw's factor, will never be known. Certainly by 1805, Seton Karr gave the impression that he was trying to find ways for Alexander to spend other people's money, rather than his.

Early examples of Alexander's commissions included two weeks in March 1800 'on private commission, measuring land at Jedburgh' for an unnamed client,[2] eight days in 1802 'measuring the Job of Mr Scott of Harden's which I got last year when you was here'.[3] These were surveying and cartographic assignments, involving the measurement of an estate or piece of land followed by the production of a plan: showing its size, boundaries, topography and main features. Until 1801, Alexander might have used a compass, perambulator (measuring wheel), chains, rules and triangulation to determine angles and distances. To determine levels in the landscape, he would have employed either a 'plain' table and alidade, or a borrowed theodolite, having 'a good deal of practice in surveying with Theodolites of different kinds'.[4]

100

Early in his tenure at Kippilaw, Alexander asked Seton Karr to purchase a Theodolite for him in London – giving instructions that 'it should be firmly Jointed & accurately divided with two good Telescopes & Compass & if it shakes or is loose in any respect it is a sure sign of the inaccuracy of the workmanship – It should likewise be well polished and Burnished to prevent its tarnishing.' The best he ever saw was 'made by Mr Geo. Adams Fleetstreet – It cost eighteen guineas…I am sorry you should have had so much trouble with it.'[5]

Alexander was aiming for a high-quality theodolite in this case, as indicated by his request for one made by George Adams, and the price. Adams Senior (1709–1773) and his two sons were prominent instrument makers in London for over eighty years. All three, in turn, held the post of Mathematical Instrument Maker to the King, and wrote and published books on scientific subjects, especially scientific devices.[6] The theodolite in question had telescopic sights, with vertical arch affixed to a long axis and rack-work (geared) movement.[7]

The theodolite, the latest tool of trade of the surveyors of the time, was duly given to Alexander, possibly as a gift or perhaps in lieu of wages.[8] As secretary of the Crinan Canal Commission, Seton Karr was acquainted with the highly respected Scottish engineer John Rennie, whom he consulted regarding the theodolite. By the early 1800s, Rennie had already established his mechanical and civil engineering business in Holland Street, Blackfriars, and was in the process of supervising the construction of the Kennet and Avon Canal and the Rochdale Canal, in southern and northern England, respectively.[9]

> Theodolite – The small one mentioned by Mr Rennie will exactly answer my purpose – I have had a good deal of practice in surveying with Theodolites of different kinds & I know perfectly how to manage that Instrument – If it could be got ready before the end of April it would serve me very much, as after the Corn is up I can do little for sometime in the surveying way – [10]

In a few years, Rennie would become an important contact for Alexander through his involvement with the survey of the Berwick and Kelso railway.[11] The theodolite proved to be a very fine instrument, which Alexander was to use for many important commissions.

One of Alexander's extra-curricular assignments, which did not come through the connections of John Seton Karr, was to survey and recommend both land and building renovations at the small estate of Gledswood (or Gladswood). William Sibbald of Gledswood, a Leith merchant, had purchased the estate, which still dominates the beautiful view ('Scott's View') from the north side of the Tweed above Dryburgh Abbey (Figure 15). In undertaking this work Alexander sought his employer's permission and reported that his father-in-law, William Brockie, possibly the source of the assignment, would be assisting him in the task.[12] Seton Karr gave his approval, and Alexander set about conducting the survey and recommending 'improvements' in March 1803.

Alexander was also responsible for the construction of the mansion house at Gledswood, now the home of the Earl of Portarlington. It was to be his first major architectural project outside Kippilaw, and has been described as a 'classical country villa…having features in common with the early C19 Regency-style Leadervale House which has a curved Ionic-columned portico, and bows on the side elevations…but with a semicircular Doric portico' (Figure 16). An older Gledswood House, first built as a Peel Tower in the late 16th century by John Robson of Gledswood, was left intact and is now used as a barn. According to Cruft et al., in *The Buildings of Scotland*, the Gledswood House, dated by the modern (1994) architectural restorer Thom Pollock (of Pollock Hammond Partnership) as circa 1805, was both designed and built by Alexander Kinghorne.[13]

Sir Walter Scott described Gledswood house as a 'very handsome villa' when Sibbald put it on the market in 1815. Scott thought the estate 'in all probability, owing to the circumstances of the time, may be had very reasonably. I have a very selfish view in giving you this hint, for Gledswood is only five or six miles from my cottage.'[14] It was also a key element of Scott's favourite viewing spot in the Scottish Borders (Figure 15).

Alexander, or his eldest daughter, Elizabeth Margaret, was later to name her first home at Narellan, in New South Wales, Gledswood, where she lived with her husband James Chisholm Jnr. This choice of name for their first residence indicates that the Kinghorne family held the memory of this house, and perhaps its central place in 'Scott's View', strongly in their hearts.

County Appointments

Alexander had an official position as County Fiscal and Road Surveyor for Roxburghshire from 1800 to 1805. As part of that role, he was responsible for standards of measurement in the county. Much later, in 1821, he prepared an official compendium of weights and measures for the burgh of Selkirk at the behest of the multi-talented James Veitch (1771–1838) of Inchbonny (near Jedburgh), the notable physicist, mathematician, astronomer, inventor, writer and university principal…

> [James Veitch] being appointed by the Justices 'keeper' of the COUNTY STANDARDS, is authorized by them to Stamp & Regulate all WEIGHTS and MEASURES brought to him for that purpose, provided they are conformable to the ACT of Parliament.[15]

Veitch played a key role in the introduction of Imperial measurements to the Borders and consulted Alexander as a recognized expert in rural measurement systems. He would have been known to Alexander, either through Sir Walter Scott or because of Veitch's invention of the Scottish swing plough, for which he won an award from the Highland Society.[16] Alexander's document, indicating the various rates of conversion from local (county) to both Scots and Imperial standards, has been unfortunately lost from the old county records office at Hawick.[17]

By 1805 Alexander's 'official' surveying duties had become too taxing and he resigned from them, supposedly to concentrate on his work at Kippilaw, taking on only occasional private surveying contracts:

> I have resigned my office of Fiscal & Road Surveyor – The Justices required this year so much attendance with new Roads, Old ones repairing, setting the Assize of Bread, looking after weights & measures etc. etc. that I found I might give up every thing else if I was to attend them – I parted with them on the best of terms & much against their will but I could not do otherwise as our work at home must not be neglected -[18]

The following year, however, he was seeking appointment to another county position of Baillie, again with the encouragement of his employer, 'returning you my most Grateful Thanks for the Trouble you have taken respecting my Commission of Bailliary'.[19] The Baillie had been a heritable office in Scotland, originally responsible for the properties of a Burgh, but by Alexander's time more involved in executing the decisions of local

Courts. After 1748, it was described as a 'Commission of Bailliary'.[20] This shows Alexander's early interest in judicial roles, which he would have seen it as a step-up to becoming a magistrate, a role he later achieved in New South Wales. In terms of his ideas of social positioning, magistrates were drawn from the local gentry in both Scotland and England, and would be an important outward sign of status. This assignment, granted by the Duke of Roxburghe on the recommendation of the Sheriff, was either refused to Alexander or his commission was revoked on the death of the 4th Duke in 1805.[21]

The Melgrund Estate

The next important commission for Alexander was the Melgrund Estate. The owner was Lord Minto [Gilbert Elliot-Murray-Kynynmound (1751–1814), 1st Earl of Minto]. Minto's early education was, to say the least, unusual: at the age of twelve, he and his brother were bundled off to Paris to study under the Scottish philosopher David Hume. There they befriended the French revolutionary Honoré comte de Mirabeau, who encouraged Minto's radical streak,[22] expressed back in Scotland by his becoming a Whig, like John Seton Karr. The two wrote frequently, and had probably become friends in Edinburgh, where both were educated. Their correspondence was informal, Lord Minto signing his letters to Seton Karr as 'Gilbert Elliot', suggesting closeness.[23]

Lord Minto was an important and powerful contact for Alexander. Although he was a Whig member of parliament and friend of Edmund Burke, he became a member of the Privy Council under the Conservatives and Governor-General of India between 1806 and 1813. His early connections with Australia included the district of Minto being named after him in 1809, and his negotiation of the release of Matthew Flinders from imprisonment in Mauritius in 1810. As Baron (and later Earl) Minto of Roxburghshire and Viscount Melgrund of Forfarshire, he was in a position, not only to know Alexander through Seton Karr, but also to put local work his way and open doors to appointments throughout the British Empire. He might have been an early source of Alexander's ambition to emigrate to the colonies, but his death in 1814 precluded any direct patronage.

In 1806, before Minto departed for India, he approached Alexander, through his factor in Forfarshire, to undertake a complete survey of his estates in that county. While he lived in Roxburghshire, his Melgrund Estate, known as the lands of Netherton and Muirside, was in Angus in the north east of Scotland, some 133 miles from Kippilaw.[24] Ongoing arrangements were left in Lady Minto's hands who, as Alexander wrote to Seton Karr, 'pays all my expenses there and back again in the stage coach so that I have no need of a Riding horse, however I thank you kindly for offering me the countess'.[25] If Seton Karr were the source of this enquiry, his acquiescence to Alexander's usual request for permission would have been a mere formality. His offer to Alexander of the use of his mare, the Countess, suggests a favourable disposition towards the project. However, Kinghorne's helpful friend Sir Walter Scott, who was related to Minto through the Scotts of Buccleuch and well acquainted with their family, might have been the person behind the scenes who initially arranged this assignment. [26]

This was one of Alexander's earliest private commissions for which his cartography is still extant. The resulting plans could be best described as 'early work'. His opinion of the estate, which he conveyed privately to Seton Karr, was less than favourable…

> I arrived home on Friday from Forfarshire…I had fine weather and never lost one days work all the time – The Estate of Melgund is really a fine place but completely lost for want of improvement – most of the good land being covered with Furze [gorse] and Broom –[27]

The plan, hand-drawn by Alexander, is primitive compared with his later, published work. It comprises a coloured scale drawing of the two properties, which are adjacent to each other but not connected: Netherton was bounded by the River South Esk in the north and separated from Muirside in the south by the main Forfar to Brechin road (Figure 17).[28] The plan shows the main geographical features of the estate, such as arable fields, meadows, heath and moorland, burns and other water-courses, together with its main buildings, and a written description of the areas, comprising some 622 acres in total. He signed the document 'attested by Alex^r Kinghorne Surveyor.'[29]

Alexander included some historical ruins on his plan, reflecting his interest in antiquities, noted earlier in connection with George Chalmers' *Caledonia*. A close examination of the drawing reveals the structures, marked as small red rectangles, but only the Mill on Netherton is named. The U-shaped structure to the west of Netherton Mill is Melgund Castle. At the time of Alexander's survey this was an extensive ruin that had been built in the second half of the 16th century in imitation of a 15th century keep. The castle was in an L-plan, consisting of a keep and stair tower, with an adjoining 16th century hall. A range of domestic buildings ran east-west across Muirside, terminating in a round tower with shot-holes, depicted in the north-east of Alexander's Muirside plan (Figure 17).[30]

The features of these early plans by Alexander are significant, as they reflect the level of detail he continued to use in all his cartographical work into the future. His farm plans, such as that of the Emu Plains Convict Establishment, drawn to a similar scale for the New South Wales Governor some 20 years later, also included topographical and water features, acreages of crop and pasture lands, boundaries and structures marked as labelled rectangles.[31] However, Alexander's finest works were to be his large-scale cartographical maps of the counties of Roxburgh and Selkirk.[32]

Work for the Duke of Roxburghe

William Bellenden Ker succeeded as 4th Duke if Roxburghe, after the death of the 3rd Duke, John Ker, in 1804. The 4th Duke appointed John Seton Karr as his commissioner and auditor. In 1804, being elderly, he also executed a trust deed in favour of Seton Karr, so that he could act as trustee in the disposition and management of the Roxburghe estates after the Duke's death. In congratulating Seton Karr on these appointments, Alexander requested 'if you think fit to employ me in any way in which I can be of use to His Grace I shall be very happy to serve you to the utmost of my power'.[33] Seton Karr had initially arranged several days surveying a march dyke at Ormiston for the Duke's factor, James Haldane, in January 1805.

Soon after completing his work for Lord Minto, Seton Karr duly directed Alexander to conduct another survey of a farm, Crookedshaws, for the Roxburghe estate. It was located south-east of Kelso, equidistant from Yetholm, Morebattle and Mowhaugh.

> I have been at CrookedShaws since Thursday seenight and only returned yesterday – I have finished the survey of these lands but have not yet got

done with the calculations – its extent is nearly 500 acres – but I will write you pointing as to this and my opinion of its value on Friday first –[34]

Alexander submitted a very favourable report on the farm on 9 May 1806. This provided a plan, measurements of infield, arable and hill pastures, and detailed estimates of their rental and sale value.

Taking the above Rental at 25 years brings its whole value (as Lands presently sell in that neighbourhood) to Ten thousand six hundred & fifty pounds ~~ I have given Mr Haldane the particular measurement as above but my opinion of its Annual and Total value only in Round numbers – Crookedshaws is a very neat little Farm, and will certainly meet with several purchasers as it is situated in a very pleasant Country and amongst people of Capital –[35]

Crookedshaws is still (as viewed by the author in 2014) the viable commercial farm, incorporating hill and arable country, as described by Alexander in 1806. It is very picturesque, with its highest point forming the summit of one of the Cheviot Hills. It lies on the course of St Cuthbert's Way and rises to an altitude of one thousand feet, three miles west of the English border. This old farm has drawn the interest of RCAHMS because it retains traces of contour cultivation, the old run-rig system, spread over the moderately steep slopes of Crookedshaws Hill.[36] It seems the 6th Duke of Roxburghe subsequently purchased the life-rents of Crookedshaws, and it remained as part of his estates for many years.[37]

* * *

These commissions proved a springboard for Alexander, who undertook other surveying contracts for members of the aristocracy, including on the Marquess of Lothian's Mount Tiviot estate:[38]

[March 1808] I was duly favoured with your Letter of the 29th past and would have wrote you sooner but I was from home on Monday, Tuesday, and Wednesday last at Tiviotside measuring for one of the Marquis' tenants –[39]

As was the case with Crookedshaws and Mount Tiviot, he often provided a combined land management service to his clients: this involved both a detailed survey, sometimes with a cartographic plan, and recommendations for 'improvement' of the estates from a farming perspective.

In 1810 he was engaged to survey the estate of Wester Eccles in Berwickshire by Mr James Kyd WS from Cupar, who was in the process of purchasing it from Nicholas Brown for £48,000. A plan of the estate had been drawn up in 1807 by William Blackadder, a well-known local surveyor.[40] Based on the available information, Kyd paid a deposit of £18,000 for the estate in 1809 and a further payment in 1810, but when the next payment fell due on Whitsunday 1811, he failed to pay and raised objections to the size of the land. He maintained that he had a right to 646 acres Scots, 'whereas, according to a measurement made for him … by a skilful surveyor, Mr Kinghorn, the lands extended at most to 604 acres, 3 roods and 16 falls, or to 582 acres only, if the ground occupied with fences, roads, plantations, and houses were deducted.' On this basis, he claimed an abatement of the price. Brown brought an action against him in the Court of Sessions [41] and Kyd lost his appeal in 1813.[42] It is uncertain whether Alexander was paid for his trouble.

The Maxton Estate

In 1811, Alexander undertook a detailed survey for Thomas Williamson Ramsay of the Maxton Estate which he had recently purchased.[43] This led to a further commission for the renovation of Maxton Kirk. Like so many others in the Borders, the kirk was dedicated to St Cuthbert, and is reputed to have been a place of continuous worship since *circa* 1100. The church had a plain oblong shape with a thatched roof in 1790, when the thatch was replaced with slate. Alexander remodelled the building in 1812, the date of the pair of windows now with 19th century glazing 'on each side of a centrally placed oculus, and the bird-cage bellsote with ogee-profile dome on the w. gable' (Figure 19). The interior of the church, with its 'plastered coomb ceilings' and fine painted furnishings are also dated to Alexander's renovation.[44]

Alexander completed his work on the Maxton Estate, and the renovation of the church building in 1812, and there is little doubt he was paid for his work through the arrangement of a commission in the Royal Navy for his son, William, by the grateful Thomas Williamson Ramsay.[45]

Employment by Sir Walter Scott

Largely remembered for his literary works, Walter Scott was also educated in the law, and practised as a WS in Edinburgh. Between 1808 and 1815 he was Sheriff-Depute of the Court in Selkirk. Here he employed Alexander to undertake surveys on commission in connection with his legal judgements.

The first, in 1808, concerned a disputed boundary between the lands of J. E. Johnstone of Lewinshope and John Boyd of Broadmeadows, over the building of a march dyke (boundary) between their farms. Johnstone, against Boyd, disputed the line of the march so, to assist in his understanding of the issues, Scott decided to visit the site and 'perambulate the Marches in presence of the parties'. After the visit, Scott wrote that he disapproved 'the intended line of March Dyke…as rendering necessary a very large and unusual excambion of property.' This could be avoided by keeping the boundary nearer to the original March of the farm …' He appointed 'parties to attend with Mr. Kinghorn the surveyor on next at the place called the ferkings' where he would 'lay down the line of March at the sight of all parties.' Scott, 'having again visited the March in dispute in presence of the parties and Mr. Kinghorn, Sworn Measurer', made the decision that the march dyke should be built upon his recommended line.[46] Subsequently, Alexander was granted a commission by Scott 'to fix any farther marks which may be necessary for the more accurate ascertainment.'[47]

In August 1810, in a dispute over the measurements of a building in the case of William Douglas and Andrew Hope, masons in Selkirk, against William Evans, 'taylor in Selkirk', Scott again called upon Alexander's services to survey the building in question. His measurements in the case were declared to differ 'very little from that of Mr. Watson' (the original surveyor of the building) and Scott found 'the defender liable in expenses, and allow[ed] an account thereof to be given in.'

In another argument over the size of a farm in March 1815, in which the lease payments were disputed, both Kinghorne and Watson were employed by the court to re-measure the boundaries of the farm 'that the real extent thereof may be ascertained reserving consideration upon which party the expense shall ultimately fall…' Alexander had apparently measured this farm in 1802, having an area of 233, rather than the 250 acres that appeared in the lease, and Scott upheld his judgement in the court decision.[48]

These relatively simple matters of measurements and recommendations for the Sheriff-Depute, would have been based on Scott's prior knowledge of Alexander's abilities. No evidence has been found of the pair working together before 1808, but their association since school days suggests that Scott was well aware of Alexander's abilities. While these were the only cases involving Alexander recorded by John Chisholm is his book of 1918 – *Sir Walter Scott as Judge, His Decisions in the Sheriff Court of Selkirk* – Scott must have utilised the skills of his former school friend on many occasions over the years and would certainly have recommended him for other survey work. Yet his notable influence on Alexander would be firstly, like a generation of Scots, the development of a love for the romance of the families and antiquities of his native land and secondly, his encouragement of Alexander to realise his dreams of advancement through emigration to the colonies.

The Roxburghe Succession Dispute

William Bellenden Ker, 4th Duke of Roxburghe, died in October 1805 at the age of 77 with no surviving issue. According to her husband's wishes, the Dowager Duchess sequestered the whole lands of the Dukedom, apart from those that were left to her as part of her marriage contract, anticipating the forthcoming dispute.[49] The 4th Duke had issued two deeds to tailzie (cut off the legal course of succession),[50] in favour of John Bellenden Ker, his first cousin's son.[51] John Seton Karr, who was staying at Fleurs Castle when the Duke died, had been ordered to act on these deeds. Accordingly, he immediately implemented the infeftment (inheritance) of John Bellenden Ker.

Sir James Northcliffe Innes and Brigadier-General Walter Ker made immediate claims to the estate, but the Sheriff initially refused them. Thereafter, a legal battle ensued for the succession of the title, encompassing seven years of constant litigation. After appeals to the Scottish Court of Sessions and the House of Lords, the 4th Duke's power to execute the deeds of tailzie was eventually overturned in the House of Lords, and James Innes Ker became the 5th Duke of Roxburghe in 1812.[52]

Duke William had appointed Archibald Swinton, WS, 'as principal factor and receiver of the rents of his estate, with power to name sub-factors under him', at an annual salary of £500 per annum.[53] Swinton appointed James Haldane as Sub-Factor of the estate of Wester-Grange at Sprouston (lands given to the Dowager Duchess as part of her marriage contract) and paid him a fee of £300 per annum. These arrangements also became, as late as 1825, the subject of another dispute between the 5th Duke James Innes Ker, and Swinton, which was also taken, on appeal, to the House of Lords.[54]

From 1806, when John Seton Karr was representing the 4th Duke's nominated heir, John Bellenden Ker, in his unsuccessful campaign to retain succession to the Dukedom, Alexander was, unsurprisingly, a strong supporter of his case in the local community:

> I rejoice that you have good hopes of the issue of the Roxburgh cause in favour of our friend Mr Bellenden Ker.[55] We have no news here but much talk about the Roxburghe question – Co[l] Hunter was in Edin[h] last week and informs me that Mr Bellenden Ker is certain to succeed, which may God grant – The Ancrum farms are much run after and will fetch a great advance of rent – I suppose the sale of Crooked-shaws is given up –[56]

Throughout his tenure as factor at Kippilaw, Alexander was to maintain his intense interest and wild optimism, even after the case was finally lost in the House of Lords on 11 May 1812. He was full of disbelief after receiving 'notice about an hour ago that the court of session have given a decision against Mr Bellenden Ker and in favour of the General – I hope this is not the case.'[57] He was 'very upset at Mr Bellenden Ker's ill success in the Court of Session I hope he will still succeed in the House of Peers where he will be without prejudice.'[58] Alexander's encouragement continued throughout 1808 with 'great anxiety respecting the issue of the Roxburghe question – God grant Mr Belenden Ker every success',[59] and 'I wish Mr B: Ker success, it is reported here that he will have a great majority respecting the feus'.[60]

Alexander fell out with many of the local populace because of his loyalty to John Seton Karr over this issue, including his close friends Andrew Blaikie and Rev'd William Balfour, who were supporters of James Innes. He was genuinely devastated at the House of Lords final decision, decrying 'the foolish people of Bowden with Maxpoffle, Balfour, & Blaikie, at their head making Bonfires and an illumination on Sir James Innes's succession to the Roxbro' estates – They got all drunk on the occasion, I thought it prudent to keep all our people at home, and did not countenance them myself'.[61]

This episode in Alexander Kinghorne's life highlights one of the pillars of his character, that of loyalty. It also calls into question his flexibility in handling a situation which was essentially political. His persistent support for the cause of John Bellenden Ker shows he was prepared to take a position opposite to those held by many of his closest connections, his friends and neighbours in the district. This was his personal view of the justice of the case, the wishes of the 4th Duke for whom he had worked briefly, but with whom, in Alexander's scheme of things, he had a personal connection. However, his stance was primarily the expression of his loyalty and support for Seton Karr, the affection and high regard he held for the man who had given him so many opportunities in his life.

The consequence was that this ended his closeness with Andrew Blaikie, who for many years had been his mentor and friend. Alexander accused him of being 'a great sycophant' in supporting the cause of the pretender to the Dukedom,[62] and after this Blaikie does not figure in Alexander's affairs. It is difficult to tell from this distance what passed between the two, and how absolute the rift. One would have hoped that a friendship of depth would have survived a difference of opinion, even on a matter of significance in local society. But then, not too many years had passed in Scotland since people had fought and died over such things or suffered exile and ruin.

As a lawyer, Seton Karr knew well the shame and disaster of a debtor's prison. Unlike Duke William's factor, Archibald Swinton, he escaped the ignominy of further litigation, by dying three years after the disaster, in 1815. Nevertheless, he had staked everything on his personal loyalty to the 4th Duke, to whom he was not related, and on his confidence in the case. Now, he was sharing the financial burden of the decision. Not only had he acted for the estate *pro bono*, but as a co-applicant he was liable for his share of the costs. The loss was to impact him severely, both financially and personally.

For Alexander, the ramifications were multiple. Firstly, a perfect storm: his work as a private surveyor, alongside the succession matter, lay across

112

the period of renovation of the mansion house. They added to the stresses his workload made upon him, and the complexities of negotiations with the builders, while Seton Karr was increasingly less able to finance the renovation to his own high standards. Alexander's principal task as factor was the viability of the Kippilaw Estate as an agricultural enterprise, but his attentions were spread everywhere. Secondly: it strained or ended friendships with people who had been important to him, a significant matter to Alexander, who placed such store in his connections both for his present and future advancement. Amidst all of this, the patronage of the Duke of Roxburghe had been shaping as a key asset, but Alexander was left stranded in the losing camp. Thirdly, and in consequence: the House of Lords' decision would have a serious downside for his future at Kippilaw. His job and the wellbeing of his family were on the line.

Chapter 11

The Beginning of the End at Kippilaw
(1806–1812)

I have spent much more Money than I could afford and there is an absolute Ne-
cessity for stopping which I cannot explain in writing which grieves me much...
John Seton Karr, April 1812

As the expenses of the Kippilaw Estate increased, and its income decreased, John Seton Karr became more anxious about Alexander's ability to control the staff and his ineffectiveness as a financial manager. He was praiseworthy of his initiatives and innovations directed at improvement but concerned that this was not paralleled by a sound financial plan and consequent income. Considerable allowance needs to be made for the prevailing economic conditions during the early 19th century. The winters from 1798 to 1801 were excessively cold, as described above, the crop yields low, and livestock prices stagnant.

These economic conditions persisted until the middle of the Napoleonic wars in 1808, which gradually increased the demand for beef. Then from 1808 onwards the winters returned evil, with reports of heavy snows and late thaws. Seton Karr's letter above came on the tail of severe snowfalls in March and April of 1812, which halted work on the estate – a year with half a Spring. This did not improve much until after 1816, the 'Year without a Summer' when the eruption of Mount Tambora in the East Indies cast the whole of Europe into darkness, storms and famine.[1] Alexander's last years at Kippilaw, and indeed John Seton Karr's last on earth, should be seen against this backdrop of adversity.

One result of the poor circumstances was a steady decline in the total returns from the rented parks, from £225–10 in 1805 to £106–10 by 1811 (Table 3), a fall of 53%.

Table 3. Kippilaw Park Rents for the years 1805 to 1811.[2]

Name of Park	1805 £	1806 £	1807 £	1808 £	1809 £	1811 £
Hothams	36	35	31	34	27-10	Not let
Lodge Park	33	30	30-10	33-15	23	Not let
Restonrig West Park	34-10-"	Not let	Not let	Not let	Not let	Not let
Ansons	27-15	21	22-10	24-15	Not let	Not let
Hawke's	25-10	21-5	Not let	Not let	Not let	Not let
Saunders	27-15	24-5	26	26-10	Not let	Not let
Edwards	23	Not let	Not let	Not let	Not let	Not let
New limed Park	18	25-5	In crop	Not let	Not let	Not let
Lady Park	Not let	27-15	29	31-15	28	25
North Park (Keppels)	In Hay	39-10	35-5	Not let	23-5	Not let
Restonrig East Park	Bar[y] & Oats	Not let	27-10	Not let	21	Not let
Park East from Lodge	Not let	Not let	Not let	28	Not let	Not let
East or West Whinny Park	Not let	Not let	Not let	26	Not let	14
Park next Maxpopple	Not let	Not let	Not let	Not let	26	21
Dam Head Park	Not let	Not let	Not let	Not let	42	25-10
North Mains	Not let	Not let	Not let	Not let	Not let	21
Total Rent each year	£225-10	£224	£202-10	£204-15	£190-15	£106-10
Average per Park[3]	£28	£28	£29	£29	£27	£21

Every year, Alexander had to justify the Park Rents to Seton Karr, who always hoped they would cover most of the expense of running the estate. They never did. Moreover, the rents were generally in line with, or better than those received by comparable lands in the district, as Alexander explained his logic for trying to rent them earlier than most…

You think the parks bro^t a low Rent, but I can assure you if they had been to let now they would not have fetched half as much as they are looking worse than in December – Marchment & Old Melrose parks are considerably lower, & Minto parks which were rouped the other day though in a sheltered situation could hardly be got off at any rent –[4]

It is notable that Alexander managed to keep the average rents above £20, even in the hardest year of 1811 (Table 2). Moreover, the names of those renting the parks reflect the effort he made to 'recruit' tenants from prominent local families, of an 'appropriate social class'. These included William Scott of Maxpoffle, Robert Turnbull of Bewliehill, John Rutherford of Sandy Stones, Mr Simson of Headshaw near Selkirk, Mr Hills of Harestains near Jedburgh, Mr John Park of Selkirk (brother to the famous explorer Mungo Park), Mr Thorburn of Sunderland Hall near Selkirk, and William Laidlaw of Philiphaugh (maternal uncle of the poet James Hogg). These were not ordinary yeomen, rather well-connected and reliable locals; some were gentry and members of the aristocracy, others literary and romantic connections of Walter Scott.[5] Alexander even recruited further tenantry from his wife's family! These included his brothers-in-law, George and John Brockie, who tenanted Kippilaw Parks for three years each, and his wife's uncle, Thomas Brockie from Prieston, with whom Alexander was a business partner.[6]

The early 1800s were also characterised by gradual tax increases as Britain built up her naval and military resources in response to the French threat. Alexander reluctantly explained the situation in 1806 as follows:

> Expenses continue to increase:
> Your Taxes payable on 5th April stand as follows viz
> Property Tax 1804 £13-1-11
> Assessed Taxes £16-13-4
> Land Tax £8-13-0
> Sum £38-8-11

And as there is another years property Tax payable at the same time, it will not be in my power to answer all these demands, so I am obliged, very much against my will, to request a remittance of about 50 or £60 pounds in your next – I declare I can make the money go no further than I have done and am ashamed to have so many demands on you –[7]

Alexander clearly felt deeply embarrassed by his inability to meet the expenses of the estate from its income, but Seton Karr seemed either unsympathetic, or oblivious to the prevailing agricultural circumstances. During 1806, his concerns about Alexander's inefficiency intensified, with a series of written instructions, demanding that jobs should be completed with more haste and less expense, and that more precise details be given of daily work and expenses. Despite the onslaught and the atrocious winter weather, Alexander's replies remained calm and polite...

> I am glad nothing escapes you tho' at so great a distance, neither do they escape me, nor never did, but it is not so easy a matter as you imagine to get over these small Jobs executed – I only wish you were one whole season in the Country when you would see whether it is to be imputed to my negligence in giving orders according to your instructions, or whether I write you <u>the Truth</u> or not – I assure you of...doing every thing in my power to promote your interest, is no easy matter for me to support – but as I have repeatedly promised since you left Scotland that these Jobs <u>shall be done</u> you may rest assured <u>that they will</u>.[8]

Alexander was, properly, concerned with the overall management of the seasonal agricultural operations at Kippilaw and gave them as much priority as he could over Seton Karr's garden and cosmetic requirements. He prepared his employer for a bad result with the park rents for 1806, indicating that it would 'not to be a good year for letting Grass as Cattle bring so poor prices & very few in proportion were reared in the Country last season.' He expected, based on the result at Old Melrose, that the rents would decline by one third compared with 1805. However, despite his reservations, the roup of parks for that year went well in the prevailing circumstances, yielding much the same income from eight Parks as the previous year (Table 2).

The visual condition of the Parks at the time of the roup was critical to the price bid. Alexander prudently managed the improvement of these Parks, year-by-year, so that those recently re-sown with grass, or which had been heavily cropped the previous season, would not be let for a low rent but retained for use by the estate for a year. His decisions were vindicated, because even in years such as 1806, when the overall rents were down, the rents for the newly improved Parks (in this case 'New Limed Park', 'Lady Park', and 'North Park'; Table 2) made up the deficiency. Alexander wrote that the rents obtained 'plainly testify what benefit you are to expect from the improvements of your Estate with your own Marle, which will now cost you a very trifling expence, & will soon pay you all the money already laid out.'[9]

By early 1807, Alexander was looking for alternative employment to supplement his income. He heard that the factor to James Maitland, 8th Earl of Lauderdale, had been killed by a fall from his horse, the Thirlestane Estate where Alexander's father-in-law, William Brockie was a tenant. Brockie suggested that His Lordship would need a replacement factor, and Alexander threw his hat in the ring, with the aid of Seton Karr.[10] However, he was unsuccessful. It seems likely that Alexander's father-in-law might have acted as Lord Lauderdale's unofficial factor for several years, as he began to manage building projects at Thirlstane.[11]

Despite depressed grain and livestock prices, Alexander, through his connections, continued to maintain good prices for the annual roup of parks into 1807, increasing the average rent per Park from £28 to £29 (see Table 2). As he pointed out to Seton Karr, 'Ours are the only parks in this neighbourhood that have maintained last years rents or rather advanced from 29/- sh to 30/6 pr acre – Camieston, Whiting, and Old Melrose, are each fallen a full third from last year'.[12]

The 1808 roup maintained the average at £29 per Park (Table 2). In 1809, however, the district rentals were not looking good, and Alexander prepared Seton Karr for the worst by pointing out the fall in rents at 'Fleurs – Mr Baillies – Whitfield – Torwoodlee, -- and Lauder are down a third – Haining had not one offerer, Kelso News Paper is almost filled with Grass Parks, one half of which will not be let, as far the 3 years past Farmers have almost given up breeding stock.'[13] At Kippilaw that year, only seven Parks were rented at 'a very small company and a dull Roup, but the Rents on the whole are far above any expectation.'[14] Despite the heavily depressed livestock economy, Alexander had managed to maintain an average Park rent of £27 (Table 2).

In 1809, some of the expenses beyond Alexander's control were the brewer's bill (£13-9)[15] property tax (£46–5) and assessed and land tax (£31-18-2).[16] By 1811 the property tax had fallen to £37-17-1 and the land tax £8-8-9,[17] but this was to be one of the worst years for the roup of Parks. The depressed rents were partly due to the continuing lack of interest in grazing livestock, but also it 'turned out a very tempestuous day and very few people appeared' so Alexander was reduced to letting only three Parks; another two were subsequently let by private arrangement with neighbours.[18] The following year, 1812, saw a considerable improvement in the Park rents, as Alexander's program of pasture improvement began to take effect and the Napoleonic wars reached their climax. While the data on these rents has not been found, the average rent, based on per acreage price, returned close to £30 per Park.[19]

Despite Alexander's careful management of the Parks, expenses from the Kippilaw Estate rose substantially from 1809 onwards. These came mainly from the prodigality of both the excavation of the Marle Moss and the renovation of the mansion house. With the external building works nearing completion in January 1809, things came to a head over the control of expenditure, with Seton Karr demanding 'no new works this year'.[20] Alexander did well to keep his letters calm, with only a hint of the prickliness he felt at having to balance expense on the farm with the wanton extravagance at the mansion house, including preferential allocation of precious conserved fodder to the dairy cows and the pigs which, at this time of year, were only feeding a skeleton staff of servants.[21]

Dissatisfaction from Seton Karr over the expense of the renovation of the mansion house continued, alongside his wish to get every detail perfect[22] Complaints continued about the cost of the farm operations. Alexander rightly pointed out that it was not 'farming' but 'improvements' that contributed the most expense:

> If you would attentively look over all your Expenses since you succeeded to Kippilaw, you will find but a very small part of Expenditure on what can really be called Farming – Draining the Moss to be sure was a heavy expense, but I shall maintain that this is the best laid out money that could have been done on the Estate…These at this moment are paying Double what they ever did before – But all the produce of the farm is quite sunk and can never be seen whilst so many other works are going on and if you would look over the money expended on Buildings, Fencing, Planting and Clearing Alone, you will find your Farming & Breeding costs you a very small sum indeed – and it is impossible that Horses, Cows, Dogs & Poultry can be maintained without raising either Corn and Straw for their support or purchasing it at a far greater expense – These observations I have been forced to make, very much against my will, but your complaints are now so frequent and heavy that my life is quite unhappy under them, particularly as I am conscious

of no mismanagement, but on the contrary have exerted myself to the utmost in Improving and Beautifying your Estate and that at the smallest expense.[23]

Here was the crux of the disagreement between Alexander and his employer. It was the beginning of the parting of the ways and the main reason the Kinghornes eventually left Kippilaw. There was truth on both sides of the argument, but clearly Kippilaw under Alexander Kinghorne was a major financial drain on Seton Karr. It was a place where Alexander lived out his dreams of being the up-to-date agricultural scientist and landed gent, advised by the leading lights and ideas of the day.

The Seton Karrs, on the other hand, expected the mansion house to be the envy of all and sundry, and afford them a lavish lifestyle when they were in residence: bacon prepared, beef and butter on the table, plenty of milk, beer and porter, horses in peak condition for riding and the drawing of the carriage, Argyll cattle arranged in a picturesque manner on the pasture, garden blooming around the mansion pile – every detail meticulous, and costly, and cumulatively beyond their means. Indeed, as much a mirror of the estates and parks of the aristocracy as the resources of a Scottish lawyer would allow.

Amidst this increasing impasse, Alexander and Seton Karr maintained their friendship, the latter encouraging and arranging for Alexander to develop his outside commissions, already established as a surveyor, into the area of civil engineering. This was an important new direction for Alexander, one that he approached with characteristic enthusiasm, and was to carry into the rest of his life. It was, with their mutual agreement, additional to his continuing duties as factor, but this only compounded the pressures outlined in this chapter.

Chapter 12

On the Railway Tracks (1809–1813)

Mr Kinghorne has now made a fair beginning upon the real Survey at Berwick,
and if the Weather proved favourable, will, I have no doubt, make speedy progress
Thomas Telford, September 1809

Thomas Telford FRS, FRSE (1757–1834) and John Rennie FRS, FRSE (1761–1821) were, arguably, the foremost British civil engineers of the Georgian era. Telford came from an impoverished background at Eskdale in the western Borders. After establishing his reputation as an architect, then canal, road and bridge builder in Shropshire, he designed and implemented the early 19th century communications systems of southern Scotland that became harbours, roads, bridges and canal systems, such as the famous Caledonian Canal.

It was in the latter capacity, that he was in close contact with John Seton Karr in 1803. This was an old family connection, as Karr's uncle, the former laird David Ramsay Karr, had been one of Telford's early mentors while he was architect of the new buildings at Portsmouth docklands in 1784. Moreover, Telford and Seton Karr were in company as members of the Scottish intelligentsia in London, where both lived on-and-off between 1782 and 1790, and their correspondence suggests an ongoing personal friendship. Seton Karr, in his capacity as Secretary of the Crinan Canal Company, used Telford as a witness in the Company's 1804 funding petition to the House of Commons Select Committee on the Caledonian and Crinan Canals. Telford resided at the Salopian Coffee House in Charing Cross from 1800, not half a mile from Golden Square, and at that time would have attended various government committees with Seton Karr.[1]

In 1809, a committee under Sir James Stewart Denham of Coltness commissioned Telford to report on the possibility of building a railway from Glasgow in the west of Scotland to Berwick-upon-Tweed in the east, some one hundred and twenty-five miles, to provide a new communication route across the country. The planned route ran through the Monkland coalfield, Carluke, Peebles, Melrose and central Berwickshire, to Tweedmouth. Many years before the advent of steam trains, this line was to be constructed with iron rails to support carriages pulled by horses.[2] The rationale for such wagon-ways was, quite simply, the coal that fuelled the burgeoning iron-based economy of the industrial revolution.

At this time Scotland was limited by its lack of transport routes: there were few navigable rivers and canals, but plentiful open sea routes from Leith to London, Newcastle and east coast Scottish ports, and from Glasgow to Lancashire or Ireland. For the most part, inland transport of heavy goods depended on roads, which were poorly constructed and largely unfit for wheeled vehicles, necessitating the use of packhorses or horse-drawn sledges. Iron 'rail-roads', once constructed, required less maintenance and deteriorated at a much slower rate than turnpike roads, even those constructed using the new methods of Telford and McAdam.[3] The initial approach for transporting coal was by water, with most early collieries located close to the sea, particularly the Firth of Forth. The canal projects, so important in early inland coal transport in the English Midlands, did not result in the development of new collieries in Scotland. Even the Caledonian Canal had only limited carriage of coal and it yielded no new mines along its length.[4]

So, the possibility remained to use wagon-ways to link the coal pits with the nearest navigable waterway. Some thirty-one of these horse-drawn arrangements were constructed in Scotland between 1772 and 1824, ranging in length from 1½ to five miles. In the same period, nineteen wagon-ways, from one to one hundred and twenty-five miles long, were planned but not constructed! The wagon-ways became 'railways', when they moved from the province of the coal owners to that of subscribed public companies established under acts of parliament. The Glasgow to Berwick Railway Company was to be the longest and most ambitious of these public projects.[5]

The Glasgow to Berwick Railway

John Seton Karr recommended Alexander Kinghorne, by letter, to Thomas Telford to conduct the survey of the line for the Glasgow to Berwick Railway. Telford replied on 29 August 1809 from Melrose that he was 'only making a general inspection of the proposed Line which has been proposed for the Rail Road – I have to attend a meeting at Edinburgh before I am authorized to begin a Survey, but from what I have now seen of the Country, I am inclined to think it will take place'. He continued in his typical busy style…

> From the strong recommendation you have given, I am very much disposed to employ your friend, but as it is a work of importance and nicety [not for public knowledge], you will be aware of propriety of my proceeding with caution – I shall be glad to see and converse with the person you have mentioned. –
>
> As Kippilaw I find is considerably out of the way and as I am much pressed for time, I cannot, this journey, pay my respects to you, which I regret, if the Survey is proceeded with, I shall avail myself of your invitation, but as I mean to be this evening at Kelso, perhaps your friend will think it worth while to meet me there, or if he is from home, or otherwise engaged, he may be disposed to take a ride to Edinburgh, where I shall be, on Saturday and Sunday next –
>
> If the Survey is agreed on, I shall proceed instantly –[6]

Telford's hands-off approach to this commission was in accord with his usual *modus operandi*, which were to utilise the best available local expertise but retain full control of, and acclaim for, the project. As with many of the schemes and projects that made Telford famous, his biographer Julian Glover highlighted 'something of a gap between the role he allowed others to believe he had played and the probable reality of what happened'. This letter confirms the busyness of the man, who was always on the move and had several projects on the go simultaneously. It also confirms his trust in Seton Karr's opinion, as Telford only chose people of 'quality' to work with him. He would be relying on Alexander's survey to accurately reflect the veracity of his conclusions.[7]

This was nevertheless a major opportunity for Alexander to associate himself with one of the most ambitious projects ever proposed in Scotland. Like Thomas Telford before him, Alexander was then transitioning from surveying to architecture and, with this project, had the opportunity to be involved in engineering. He duly met Telford 'on the banks of the Tweed below Melrose' on Monday 13 September 'when after settling on a proper situation for a Bridge we went to Melrose that evening, and ran a Level forward to Kelso on Tuesday'. Telford was impressed with his short time with Alexander and wrote again to Seton Karr from Edinburgh on 22 September:

> I have been so pushed as to time that I have not hitherto been able to get as far as Kippilaw, but hope to be enabled to pay my respects to you about the beginning of Nov[r] when I make a final inspection of Railway Line – Mr Kinghorne has now made a fair beginning upon the real Survey at Berwick, and if the Weather proved favourable, will, I have no doubt, make speedy progress –[8]

Telford's mention of a 'fair beginning' and his assessment that Alexander would 'make speedy progress' was an unusual encomium from a man who rarely praised others. It says something of his high opinion of Alexander, and his trust was not misplaced.

Alexander left Telford to travel to Berwick via Edinburgh, arriving on 21 September. Here he began his survey 'from the Quays' and headed in as direct a line as the terrain north of the Tweed River would allow in the direction of Kelso. He remained based in Berwick until 28 September when he moved his quarters to the village of Paxton, some five miles west of Berwick.[9] His survey took him north of the Tweed, reaching Ednam in Roxburghshire on 21 October. Here he received further instructions from Telford 'to call on Douglas Ainslie Esqr at Cairnbank by Duns,[10] one of the Committee for the Rail Road, and report [his] progress in Berwickshire'. Alexander was in easier country now and his 'line of road' rapidly reached Newton Don, near Kelso and then Mertoun near Melrose.[11]

Next, Alexander moved west from Mertoun to 'make the necessary surveys through Peeblesshire.' While undertaking this part of the survey, he arrived in the home town of a young man (unnamed) who was later an editor of *Chambers' Edinburgh Journal*. This man later wrote...

> Mr Kinghorne erected his theodolite in the street, and explained its uses to my brother and myself, to our infinite pleasure, and with the effect of awakening in our minds a reverence for the instruments of exact science, and indelibly impressing upon us a pleasing recollection of the kind demonstrator himself.[12]

Alexander's enthusiasm for describing the precise science of the theodolite to the young men, so that their minds were awakened to 'a reverence for the instruments of exact science', reflected his own philosophy and enthusiasm for the subject. Based on Alexander's survey work, Telford produced a detailed report on 'the proposed cast-iron railway' line, which he published on 12 March 1810. As was his way, the report fails to mention Alexander Kinghorne. The line was to follow the Tweed River from Peebles, crossing it in several places, including Peebles, Melrose and Dryburgh, then proceed north of the Tweed, and south across Leet Water (near Duns) to Berwick. After consideration of the best mode and manner of construction, and the route to be taken, Telford provided a full costing of £365,700 and nine pence. He followed this with an estimate of the business that would be contracted by the railway and the revenue to be earned, £55,559 per annum, mainly from the carriage of Lanarkshire coal and lime eastward and Borders grain westward, giving a return on capital of twelve percent; a projected rate of return that turned out to be wildly optimistic.[13] Telford concluded that he had stated the facts from all points of view 'which are necessary for a thorough understanding of its nature. It is one of the most important which has ever come under my consideration; and I have no doubt but when the public have been enabled to judge of its merits, the means will soon be provided to carry it into effect.'[14]

The second half of the report included an 'opinion' written by another civil engineer, the English-born William Jessop (1745–1814). Jessop is remembered as a mentor to both Telford and Rennie. However, his earliest encounter with Telford had been less than amicable when, in 1792, the ambitious younger man usurped Jessop's position as chief engineer on the Ellesmere Canal project in Shropshire.[15] Jessop had considerable experience with iron carriageways, having completed the Surry Iron Railway from Wandsworth to Croydon and on to Mestham in 1803. Despite past differences, the amiable old gentleman, with a few minor suggested improvements, was highly supportive of Telford's scheme, indicating that the subscribers 'will have no reason to be dissatisfied with any other part of it; and that it is a plan which, when carried into execution, will be highly beneficial to the public'.[16]

Telford published a full survey plan of the line from Glasgow to Berwick in 1810, in this case duly acknowledging Alexander Kinghorne as the surveyor.[17] Subscription papers were produced and lodged, among others, with Charles Erskine in Melrose and Alexander Kinghorne at

Kippilaw.[18] Unfortunately, the project disappeared without trace, and Alexander's hopes of this gaining him status as an engineer would be dashed. Once out of the hands of the coal barons, horse-drawn wagonways were never able to carry the tonnage that would deliver the economic rates of return prospected by Telford. It would not be until the age of the steam locomotive that this would be a possibility, after Telford had died and long after Alexander Kinghorne had left Scotland.

The Berwick and Kelso Railway

In 1809 the Scottish Civil Engineer John Rennie (1761–1821), another designer of bridges, canals and docks, began to work on a similar railway project that encompassed part of the original route of the Glasgow to Berwick railway.[19] In this case, the initiative for the railway came from coal consumers, rather than producers. Rennie and Telford were not always on good terms and were clearly in open competition for this railway project.[20] Rennie modified Telford's original concept for the Glasgow to Berwick railway to a shorter twenty-two-mile section from Berwick that terminated in Roxburghshire.[21] As the man on the ground, Alexander found himself in the middle of an argument:

> We have had another meeting about the Rail road – Telford is paid off and Mr Rennie employed – I was desired to meet him at Kelso on Thursday last, Harden was there, as also Sir John [Scott of Ancrum], Sir George Douglas, Walker of Wooden and Dr Douglas. I think Rennie a sensible man, he seems to hold Telford very cheap indeed – I think we will now get the two contending parties brought to a reconciliation – Harden seems determined to oppose Rutherford in carrying forward the line to Ancrum bridge –[22]

Rennie produced a full report in November 1809, pre-dating the publication of Telford's analysis of the longer railway, and a pen-and-ink plan of the new route in 1810.[23] In this report Rennie suggested that the countryside and topography along his proposed path, different from Telford's, appeared 'favourable for an Iron Rail-way, yet the expense of crossing … rivers and brooks will be found considerable.' The main economic advantage of the project, according to Rennie, as for Telford, was for the transport of coal and lime but in this case, it was to be imported by sea to Berwick and then by rail to local districts.[24]

It is unclear whether Rennie conducted a new survey of the area independently, or whether he used the earlier 1809 survey of Alexander Kinghorne. Both Rennie's and Telford's plans are extant.[25] Rennie makes no mention of Alexander, who had worked so hard on Telford's plan.[26] Nevertheless, in 1811, Alexander remained hopeful of employment for himself and his eldest son, James, on the project. He tried to contact Rennie, through Seton Karr, several times between January and June 1811:[27]

> I am glad you have met with Col Lockhart – I have heard nothing from Mr Rennie yet.[28] As the work on the Railway will soon commence and as it will be necessary that some person should lay out the line with accuracy to the Workmen, and occasionally survey them as they proceed, I would propose myself as a person qualified for such an undertaking, and now that James is of age and I am training him to that line of business it would be a fine introduction for him – Mr Rennie has every thing in his power provided he has no other person in view for it –[29]

Seton Karr duly approached Rennie on Alexander's behalf, but there is no record of any response:

> I do not know how to express my thanks for your kindness in accommodating me to Mr Rennie – I am extremely anxious to get James employed now that he is able, my young family are all my comfort at present –[30]

In May 1811, based on Rennie's 1810 report, an act of parliament was passed, giving permission to build the horse-drawn railway from Spittal, near Berwick-upon-Tweed to Kelso.[31] It is notable that this was the first parliamentary authorization for *passenger* transport by rail in Britain.[32] As Rennie began to investigate the details of the route, the Railway Company gave Alexander some involvement, mainly at the urging of the local aristocracy, such as Sir Walter Scott of Raeburn and his son William Scott, and Hugh Scott of Harden,[33] who were important subscribers of the Company…

> The Berwick and Kelso Railway is expected now to go on. I was employed about a month ago in improving their line, and fixing on a situation for a Bridge atop the Tweed near Twisel Castle – Mr Rennie may now be of some use to me if he has no other person in view, I know Mr Scott of Harden will support my interest, as he would not leave Scotland till

I surveyed the proposed line, and gave him my report to lay before Mr Rennie, indeed he attended me whilst making the survey.—[34]

It is clear from the above that Alexander was, by May 1811, conducting some work on the route, whether Rennie was aware of it or not. He was excited about the prospect of being retained long-term, as he might have seen this as the next stage of his career after leaving Kippilaw. However, he was not the only surveyor involved, as Rennie's trusted assistant, James Hollinsworth, is recorded as surveying part of the route at this time.[35]

When Alexander finally left his employment at Kippilaw in 1813, he still retained a strong expectation that he would be able to gain employment on the railway once construction started. But Alexander was Telford's man, a serious competitor of Rennie, so it was unlikely that Rennie would favour Telford's choice above his own man, Hollinsworth. Alexander continued to hold out hope and again sought Seton Karr's support to lobby Rennie on his behalf; fortunately, he had another surveying job lined up with the Duke of Buccleuch. As it turned out, the latter was to be more fruitful than the former, which never eventuated.

The Berwick and Kelso Railway Company struggled on, without being put into action for want of funds. However, Rennie's work on the line was not wasted, as he used his design concept for the line to implement the famous Stockton and Darlington Railway in 1821. Remarkably, the legislation for England's first railway to use steam locomotives was based on the unexecuted Kelso and Berwick Act of 1811.[36]

Ever the optimist, Alexander kept his hopes up. Several local lairds remained strong supporters of the railway project, including Lieutenant-Colonel William Elliot Lockhart of Borthwickbrae, MP for Selkirkshire from 1806 to 1830, James Pringle of Torwoodlee, Sheriff of Selkirkshire, and William Scott of Maxpoffle, old Raeburn's heir.[37] Lockhart had been a supporter of Alexander in his bid to obtain employment on the line, and had visited him at Kippilaw at Seton Karr's behest.[38] Despite their continuous efforts, and the retention of Rennie and William Jessop's son, Josias Jessop, as consultant engineers, it proved extremely difficult to raise the capital needed to commence construction.

Proposals for horse-drawn railways linking to inland waterways were never going to provide the financial and logistical benefits hoped for them. By 1824, after Alexander had left Scotland, the whole project had been revised based on the new steam-powered technology. Jessop advised the employment of 'the Newcastle system' developed by Robert Stephenson.[39] The survey conducted by Alexander Kinghorne for Telford in 1809 remained, much modified as the basis of Jessop's steam railway plans, but this proposal also failed to materialise. The York, Newcastle and Berwick Railway eventually opened a similar line in 1849. From 1865, it was also possible to travel from Berwick, via Reston to St Boswells, using the Duns Branch and the Berwickshire Railway, until the route was closed to passengers in 1951 and finally abandoned in 1965 because of the Beeching Report.[40] Somewhere at the core of this improvement to industry in the Borders were glimmers from the imaginations of Thomas Telford and Alexander Kinghorne.

Alexander Kinghorne, Engineer

From 1813 onwards, Alexander Kinghorne described himself as an 'Engineer' or 'Civil Engineer'.[41] He would do this over the coming decade, and his patrons would perpetuate this in recommending him for a position in New South Wales. So, the question arises as to the basis on which he was able to call himself an Engineer.

The Institution of Civil Engineers in London was not formed until five years later, in 1818, with Telford as its first president. It once held two original plans associated with the Berwick and Glasgow Railway: these were entitled 'A plan of continuation of the line of the Berwick and Glasgow railway surveyed by A Kinghorne for T Telford' and 'Plan of part of the proposed rail road from Berwick and Glasgow surveyed under the direction of Thomas Telford by Alex[r] Kinghorne'. These documents were sadly destroyed in 1906, but their description survives. This confirms that Alexander surveyed and drew up the plans under Telford's direction. It was unusual that Telford allowed Alexander Kinghorne's name to appear on these documents; for Telford, this was high praise. But this did not confer on Alexander recognition other than as a surveyor.[42]

It was as a surveyor that Alexander's name appeared, on government or private commissions, so that his career has been recently described in the 'Dictionary of land surveyors and local mapmakers of Great Britain and Ireland 1530–1830' (1997), as 'a railway and estate surveyor with links to Angus, Berwickshire, Lanarkshire, Midlothian and Roxburghshire'.[43]

Prior to 1840, there was no tertiary training in civil engineering and prior to establishment of the Institution in 1818 no body to provide accreditation. The trades which were employed in large engineering projects often had such structures, but the design and management of projects did not. Generally, persons who called themselves engineers trained through tutelage, were recognized by an established engineer or potential clients, or took over their family's business.[44]

It was different with Alexander's related role as architect, where design and construction management had been included traditionally in the trade of masons and builders since medieval times. Once again, Alexander had not received accreditation through apprenticeship to one of those trades, but had by-passed them, undertaking this work as part of his employment as John Seton Karr's factor.

So, what in Alexander's 'experience' qualified him in engineering? He had undertaken work for Telford, which involved responsibilities for the design and selection of routes, within parameters given him by Telford, and subject to the latter's agreement. This was not just ordinary surveying, the description and mapping of topography. Similarly, Alexander's role with his surveys of estates was often not just descriptive but identifying potential for improvements. Alongside these were the larger works he had undertaken at Kippilaw: the architecture and construction management on the buildings, gardens and topography of the estate; the hydraulic engineering in the draining of the Marle Moss, celebrated in verse.

It was based on these that Alexander would hang up his shingle as an Engineer at a time (in 1813) when there was still no professional accreditation. His work in this profession would be gained through reputation, patronage and chalking up successes. The railway projects were a mixed blessing, because while they showed certain skills, and recognition to an extent from Telford, neither of the projects got to construction.

Chapter 13

The Kinghornes Leave Kippilaw
(1812–1813)

*...your place is now in pretty good order, and when I am gone and the place begin-
ning to pay very possibly somebody else will get the merit and praise...*

Alexander Kinghorne, March 1813

For several years the writing had been on the wall for Alexander's
employment at Kippilaw. That it went on for so long was a mark of the
esteem and friendship between himself and John Seton Karr. Fortunately,
it seems their eventual parting also was amicable. Over the years Seton
Karr had put various commissions and contacts Alexander's way, so he
had been established with a reputation as a local surveyor and engineer.
The Seton Karr family were left with a magnificent new Georgian manor
house and a productive estate; approaching double the useable acreage
after bog drainage and a long-term supply of marle-based fertiliser that
increased production per acre. The next manager of Kippilaw, William
Foggo, inherited Alexander's improvements, and required little ingenuity
to benefit from the increased productivity that began to be manifest from
1811 onwards.

The Seton Karrs' visit to Kippilaw in August-December 1811
was a happy one, and they were able to enjoy the luxury of the newly
renovated mansion house. Despite the ongoing difficulties with expenses,
relationships seemed to be good after the family left for Stockton, and
those with Molly and the house staff much improved compared with the
previous years:

> Every thing here goes on as well as you could wish and I shall take
> care that the greatest economy is observed in every department on
> the Estate...– The men are plowing in the Easter fallow park next
> Camieston – John attending the Cattle, and Cessford occasionally lead[g]
> Turnips and in the Garden. – The sheep are all sheared and doing well.
> Every other living Creature thriving. – The swine are in the Court all

the day and go regularly down to their Houses and sleep all night –
Molly thought this the best plan and I approved.[1]

However, John Seton Karr was by now financially embarrassed over the
burgeoning expenses from the house renovation and taxes, unbalanced by
the meagre income from the estate. In 1812 he was hit with the extreme
financial burden from his involvement in the failed succession of his
candidate for the Dukedom of Roxburghe.[2] In the same year, property tax
increased to £33-3-9, assessed taxes to £40-6-4, and Seton Karr was liable
to a hefty share (£12-19-4) of the stipend for the Bowden kirk minister,
Rev'd William Balfour; not to mention 'Molly, the Hynds, Insurance,
Shearers, Graham etc etc.' As Alexander pointed out 'the Cattle can never
pay all.'[3]

Despite it all, Seton Karr maintained a great affection for Alexander
and his family, as indicated by the following rare letter from 1812. The
letter also sets out his need for expenditure to be curbed:

Golden Square, Monday 20th April 1812

Dear Alexander,

Since I wrote you on the 11th I have your Letter of 9th instant and I
observe the weather is good and you are busy sowing which I hope
is now well over if not finished – I shall be anxious till you write how
many Parks are let & the Rents. I am sorry to be under the necessity
of stopping the fitting up the Two Rooms in The Old House, such of
the Finishings as are already prepared and Wood provided for that
Purpose must be deposited in the Rooms to serve hereafter when they
are finished – I am also to desire you not to proceed with Building My
Pillars and putting up The Gates behind The House nor to do any New
Work whatever but you will take care to fence out the Cattle from The
Lawn by the wooden Path and Bard being sound and high – I suppose
you have already spread the Earth on The Rock and planted The Lawn
and then you must stop and in general not to lay out one Shilling which
can be avoided and saved and to practise the strictest Accuracy in your
Management only keep all in Repair as for things have occurred here
lately which are the Cause of this Sudden Revolution, I have spent much
more Money than I could afford and there is an absolute Necessity for
stopping which I cannot explain in writing which grieves me much. You
must put the best Face on it you can – Let me know if you have bread
and what quantity of Ale & Beer. I hope Will is now on board and that
He likes the ship – Mrs Karr has been very ill lately. I am quite uneasy

about Her and trust in God she will soon get better. She joins Me in best Wishes to yourself Wife and family – Believe me

Yours sincerely

J. Seton Karr [4]

John Seton Karr had 'spent much more money than [he] could afford' but his urging for restraint was, at this stage too late, as the damage to his finances was already done. Alexander was drawing his time at Kippilaw to a close. A substantial proportion of the estate was about to be leased and the next generation of tenants was to reap the benefits of his 'improvements'.

William Foggo Replaces Alexander Kinghorne

John Seton Karr's financial circumstances had become so difficult by 1812 that he considered advertising part of the Kippilaw estate for lease, including the entire Kippilaw Mains farm. He informed Alexander about his thinking. Alexander was already resigned to the fact that his time at Kippilaw was ending. Rather than arguing his case, he responded, typically, with a dispassionate analysis of the likely outcome. He had 'considered what you mention about letting the Estate, and I cannot but approve your plan, provided you can get a respectable tenant.' There followed a detailed analysis of the likely rents obtainable for the Mansion house, the remaining lands and the '800 Cart loads of Moss & Marle' which could be obtained annually, all totalling £452. As well as providing these estimates, Alexander raised the issue of leaving Kippilaw, as this must have been intimated in his employer's previous correspondence:

> I shall say nothing to any person about it till I see or hear from you on the subject, but I presume you mean me in the interim to be looking out for some place to go to as we cannot remain here after the place is let.[5]

The departure of the Kinghornes would be the obvious implication of the proposed changes, as Kippilaw Mains was to be leased as a whole, including the farm buildings and the Mains house. In August 1812, Alexander 'wrote [to Seton Karr] enclosing a Copy of the Conditions of the Lease of Kippilaw Mains,' in order that a time could be arranged for a prospective 'young Gentleman's meeting with me to look at the farm.'[6] Alexander, loyal to the end, continued to look after his employer's interests.

133

Yet the die was cast. With the Mains leased, the estate would be much smaller, requiring only a working baillie to steward it, commanding a lower wage than Alexander. His letters from June 1812 onwards give the impression that he and his family were setting things in train for their departure, while still maintaining those important little luxuries that would be expected by the Seton Karrs when they next arrived at Kippilaw:

> The Brewing was finished before the hot weather set in, and I think the Ale and Beer will be good. James has done the best in his power but I shall not say the article will please every person about the place. Molly has the Key of the Cellar and I hope will take care of the Beer till you arrive. – The New Hynds, Robert Oliver, and Thomas Watson, are doing very well as yet, and I hope will continue to give satisfaction.[7]

Alexander's financial situation was compromised at this time by an unexpected shortfall in revenue and increased expenses. These included the costs associated with his son William's entry to the Royal Navy, although his position had been procured by Thomas Williamson Ramsay.[8] The revenue shortfall also came from a continuing debt owed to him by Sir Alexander Lockhart of Carnwarth, for surveying work on his estates:

> He [William Kinghorne] has cost me nearly a Hundred Pounds for outfit and all this will be lost, which with his mothers very melancholy situation, and what I must lose by Sir Alexander Lockhart who owes me £200, and for which I was obliged last week to rank amongst his creditors, and when we are to receive even the Interest none can tell, as all his Estates are conveyed in Trust – to a Mr Claud Russell accountant in Edinburgh. – These things press very heavy on me and I am far from being well otherways ... Lockhart leaves me tomorrow for Carnwarth – I have just received £100 to account but £50 of that goes to pay for Clothes & other necessaries he has got since he came.[9]

Lockhart was the MP for Berwick-upon-Tweed. Early in 1811 he became 'for some time in a very dangerous state of health' and did not contest Berwick in 1812. He died on 22 June 1816, aged 40, from injuries received in a carriage accident. By then he was considerably in debt, to the tune of £4,000, which was only slowly discharged by his executors. Alexander had been most fortunate to receive £100 on account in 1812, indicating either Lockhart's respect or affection for him.[10]

The relationship between laird and factor was maintained at a cordial and respectful level but, by July, Alexander's letters reflected some tension between them, and confirmed the approaching end of his time at Kippilaw...

> You are <u>heartily welcome</u> to my Horse when you want him, and I only thought it proper to mention his <u>Fault</u>. As to his standing in your stable that has certainly been the case but on your arrival and on examination you will find that he has never bit your <u>corn</u> or <u>straw</u> without a <u>full greater</u> quantity being brought from Maxton with Mr Ramsay's own Horses & Carts, neither has he been <u>shoed</u> at your expense, and if you think proper I am willing to pay for the Grass he has got – I am sorry you should have taken amiss any thing I wrote in my last, I declare I am not conscious of having said any thing to offend you, nor did I mean it in the least degree.[11]

Between August and December 1812, Alexander Kinghorne ceased to be the factor of Kippilaw. The Kinghornes remained in the Mains farmhouse until Whitsunday 1813, but William Foggo took over as manager of the estate. The Baillie family of Mellerstain had previously employed Foggo as their estate manager, suggesting that Alexander might have had a hand in his recruitment.[12] There was an arranged handover period of six months, during which Alexander had a supervisory role with Foggo, whom he praised cautiously, as he 'seems very attentive as yet, but I can form no opinion of his abilities as a Farmer from the short specimen of his operations.'[13]

On taking up his duties, Foggo had some difficulty with a particular servant, the gardener Mr Cessford, who had also been troublesome for Alexander. Foggo wrote of this to Seton Karr:

> Cessford was in garden on Wednesday at thrashing & turnips on Thursday holling and Furze [gorse] on Friday and today is carting home turnips. He was saying to me yesterday that you had agreed with Mr Kinghorne not to dig any more Furze just now than what was spoke for, and that Mr K. was to find people to dig up the reminder in Spring. This I know nothing off but in my opinion the sooner they are taken up the better as the ground stirred up by digging them out has a better chance of getting green the earlier they are taken out. – You left no orders to Mr Cessford to do what I order him, as he understands that he has three days of the week to cart Turnips, and the other three at his own disposal.[14]

135

This was the first of many difficulties for William Foggo in his relationship with the domestic servants at Kippilaw, but this was no longer a concern for Alexander. It does, however, suggest that the latter's ongoing disputes with them might not have been entirely due to his mismanagement.

In March 1813, Alexander began clearing up the final accounts of the estate and selling livestock, as arrangements were made for the lease of the Mains farm.[15] On 19 March he 'took a House, Garden, Stable, Byre & Cows Grass from Raeburn at Lessudden' in preparation for moving permanently from Kippilaw. This rented house and small farm, named Crossflat, was located between St Boswells and Maxton.[16]

On 21 March 1813, as a final offer of explanation, Alexander wrote a long letter to Seton Karr regarding his past difficulties at Kippilaw:

Kippilaw Mains, Sunday 21st March 1813

John Seton Karr Esqre

29 Golden Square, London

Dear Sir,

I wrote you on Friday last, and by the same post I received your Letter of the 15th instant = I assure you the intercourse between Mr Foggo and me is the most friendly, and when he consults me on any matter I always give him my best advice for the advantage of all your concerns here – and tho' during the time of my having the management of your Estate the Outlays have been great and the returns very scanty, yet it was always my wish to be as frugal as possible – and now when I am about to leave you, I declare it shall give me the greatest pleasure to hear of your prosperity, and I only wish it was in my power to put you on any plan to get back from Kippilaw the money you have expended on it in my time. – I still flatter myself that by persevering in the Improvement of the soil you will ultimately be paid. – you know I had many things to struggle with having found every thing in ruins – your place is now in pretty good order, and when I am gone and the place beginning to pay very possibly somebody else will get the merit and praise of what has been done by me and so little thought of not by you but by others who in your presence have sometimes thrown it in my teeth – but this I don't mind and I impute the whole to the same source which perhaps interrupts the intercourse between Mr Foggo and my family – he seems a sober decent man and I shall do him all the good in my power whilst I am near him. – I shall get him the seed Barley & Grass seeds in proper time – and I shall do the best in my power to get the parks let to advantage, but I really am much afraid it will be impossible, as stock is scarce and dear and farmers turning all their attention to corn. – It affords me much satisfaction that Foggo is in the spot when the Parks are offered this year as he will be a witness of my diligence and will report to you whether it is my fault or not. – We have the finest weather ever I saw, and every thing going well on and all the living creatures thriving. --- I remain, Dear Sir,

Your most obed^t hum^le Servant

Alex^r Kinghorne[17]

His next letter to Seton Karr on 1 May 1813, is even more revealing of the issues that had finally convinced him to leave the laird's employ. It opens with an apology for the low rents obtained for the 'Parks', occasioned by the excellent season resulting in a glut of pasture available in the district. He also explains that the number of livestock on the estate had always been inadequate to consume the feed available, which had been reserved, against his recommendations, to feed the house milking cows. This came as a direct criticism, in no uncertain terms, of the staff at the mansion house and, indirectly, of their being favoured unfairly by the Seton's Karrs:

> This idea I have always combated since I knew Kippilaw, and this was one among many of the reasons of my being so unpopular with these Harpies. – Such things as this, with many others of the like kind will be now practiced on you, but they ought to be curbed in time.[18]

This on-going bone of contention had, according to Alexander, significantly decreased his ability to optimise the profitability of the estate. Such angry words, describing the domestic staff as 'Harpies', reflect not only his frustration with his situation but also his inability to resolve the dispute – perhaps he felt emboldened by Foggo's confirmation of the problem! Sent one week later, Seton Karr's last letter to Alexander was typically business-like, seeming a little too formal given the circumstances and the content of Alexander's previous letter:

Golden Square, 7th May 1813

Dear Alexander,

I have this day received your letter of 1st inst and enclose my Note for £100 payable at Messrs Drummonds 25 days after Date to pay the assessed Taxes & Property Tax amounting per your Letter of 21st past to £77"7"10, after which there will remain £22"12"2 to be applied to other uses – These Taxes you will not fail to pay at Melrose on Saturday the 22nd inst. – I observe what you say about the Parks and Foggo writes that he ment[d] to you that he might spare the Park East of the Damhead one but I do not know how it can now be disposed on – if you can let it good & well but if not might not Cattle be taken in to Grass for the Season – My Rental is lower now than ever – I am sorry your wife is no better but I hope she will get better as the Season is favourable – I shall be glad to know when you propose to move as Whitsunday fast approaches – you and Foggo will of course make out compleat Inventories of the Live & Dead Stock – These must contain Carts, Ploughs, Harrows & every thing moveable in & about the Farm --- House & Offices and specify all the Fixtures – you know very well how they should be made out & I depend on your Accuracy & Attention – One Copy must be signed by & left with him & another signed by him & given to you to prevent Disputes hereafter – I cannot be more particular unless I was on the Spot, which is impossible …As I shall be anxious for your Answer write me soon – I enclose a Letter for Foggo and with best wishes to ye all particularly for your Wifes Recovery I am Dear Alexander

Yours sincerely

J. Seton Karr[19]

On 29 May 1813, William Foggo wrote to Seton Karr, informing him of the departure of the Kinghorne family.[20] As far as the authors can ascertain, they never returned to Kippilaw. Despite the ire of their final correspondence, Alexander and Seton Karr remained on very good terms until the latter's death in 1815, just four years after the completion of the mansion house renovations.

So ended a long relationship, of more than fifteen years, that provided Alexander with many opportunities to make important connections and continue to operate in the private sphere.

Chapter 14

The Cultivation of Patronage
(1804–1824)

...a celebrated Civil engineer in North Britain...
Cleaveland Gazette & Commercial Register, August 1818

It can be seen from the preceding history, that Alexander Kinghorne became well connected with prominent people throughout his young life in the Scottish Borders. To rise in his profession, and to throw off the shackles of his trade origins, he recognised early that he needed patronage. He sought it, used it and made his way by it. A summary of all the connections made throughout his life is provided in Appendix 1. The list includes the great and the good as well as the lowly and seemingly unimportant. Even so, they represent a cross-section of rural, landed and aristocratic society, some of whom would aid him in his emigration to New South Wales, and a few provided fellowship in his old age after returning to Scotland.

Alexander had the good fortune to be at school, if briefly, with Sir Walter Scott. By 1815, with the publication of *The Lay of the Last Minstrel* (1805), *Marmion* (1808), *The Lady of the Lake* (1810), *Waverley* (1814) and *Guy Mannering* (1815), Scott had become a well-recognised and respected poet, author and magistrate. Alexander also had significant connections to important men of science, such as Thomas Telford and John Rennie, and with the peerage, including primarily the 11th Earl of Buchan, but also Sir Hugh Scott of Harden, Lord Minto, Sir Walter and his son William Scott of Raeburn, the 4th Duke of Buccleuch and the 3rd and 4th Dukes of Roxburghe. The latter connection was lost when the 4th Duke died unexpectedly and John Seton Karr's client, the likely successor to the dukedom John Bellenden-Karr, failed to regain the estate. Nevertheless, by 1815, through the kindness and support of Lord Buchan, Sir Walter Scott and, before his death, John Seton Karr, Alexander had a formidable array of potential patrons to help promote his career as a private surveyor and civil engineer. But there were still further connections already made, and some to be made.[1]

In 1804, 'Alexander Kinghorne of Kippilaw', together with one hundred and seventy others, notably the 'Countess of Buchan', 'Rev. William Balfour of Bowden', 'James Haig of Bemersyde', 'Sir Henry Hay Macdougall' and the bard Walter Scott himself, had subscribed to one of James Ballantyne's early publications, *Poems on Various Occasions*, by James Pace.[2] The abovementioned subscribers were persons with whom Alexander had, or would soon have, a privileged association. He cultivated the patronage of the Earl of Buchan who had come to know his family well.[3] Balfour was the Kinghornes' minister in the Bowden Parish, who had recently baptized five of their children. Haig was the laird at Bemersyde where Betty Kinghorne's father, William Brockie, and brother, Alexander Brockie, were feu tenants. It would be reasonable to say that the main sources of Alexander's patronage were, in order of contribution but not restricted to, Sir Walter Scott, John Seton Karr and Lord Buchan. Of these, Seton Karr had been by far the most active in promoting Alexander's interests, and the family's departure from Kippilaw would lessen the ease of that influence, casting him somewhat adrift from a major source of commissions. Other important connections would need to be found.

Sir Henry Hay Macdougall

Among these useful connections was Sir Henry Hay Macdougall (1752–1825) 4th Baronet of Mackerston, a distant cousin to Sir Walter Scott through his uncle, Walter Scott of Raeburn.[4] In 1819, Macdougall's eldest daughter married Sir Thomas Brisbane.[5] Scott's comments about this new relationship give an insight into the importance of the Macdougall connection for Alexander:

> We had a visit from a very fine fellow indeed at Abbotsford, Sir Thomas Brisbane, who long commanded a brigade in the peninsula. He is very scientific, but bores no one with it, being at the same time a well informed man on all subjects, and particularly alert in his own profession, and willing to talk about what he has seen. Sir Harry Hay Macdougall, whose eldest daughter he is to marry, brought him to Abbotsford on a sort of wedding visit, as we are cousins according to the old fashion of country kin; Beardie,[6] of whom Sir Harry has a beautiful

140

picture, being a son of an Isabel Macdougal, who was, I fancy, grand-aunt to Sir Harry.[7]

The patronage of Sir Henry Hay Macdougall, through his connection by marriage to Sir Thomas Brisbane, would be valuable in Alexander's transition, and that of his two eldest sons, from Scotland to New South Wales a few years later, by which time Brisbane had been appointed that colony's Governor.[8] Moreover, the next of Alexander's patrons, Lord Buchan of Dryburgh Abbey, was also a mentor of Sir Thomas Brisbane.

The Earl of Buchan

David Steuart Erskine (1742–1829) was born in Edinburgh, the second son of Henry David Erskine, 10th Earl of Buchan, and Agnes Steuart (Figure 18). He became the 11th Earl, Lord Cardross, in 1767, an ancient mormaerdom of the family of Comyn, descending from the earliest divisions of the Scottish Kingdom.[9] His chief claim to fame was as founder of the Society of Antiquaries of Scotland in 1780. Buchan's biographer, Ronald Cant, comments:

> There can be little doubt that the long and complex history of the Buchan earldom and its association with so many of the most famous families in Scotland exercised a powerful influence on the mind of the young Lord Cardross. In 1781, when it seemed possible that he might have to bear most of the expense involved in securing a home for the newly founded Society of Antiquaries, he professed himself prepared for the 'sacrifice of my domestic convenience to the honour of my country and the promotion of useful learning' adding: 'To aspire after Fame founded on the performance of noble and disinterested actions is no less than habitual to the family from which I have the honour to derive my descent.'[10]

Buchan's insatiable curiosity and independence of thought and action had been developed through an extensive education. At first this was home-based under the influence of the Edinburgh intelligentsia, including the mathematician Colin MacLaurin, the artist Alan Ramsay and the philosopher David Hume. He later attended the Universities of St Andrews, Edinburgh and Glasgow. At the latter he studied under Adam Smith among many notables. He was called to the Scottish bar in 1768 but exhibited the persona of a dangerous radical in his early years. After

Benjamin Franklin's visits to Scotland in 1759 and 1771, Buchan became his friend and later that of George Washington, discussing with Franklin Britain's 'foolish oppressive conduct towards the colonies' on Franklin's visits to London. He became well known amongst American intellectuals, particularly in the northern United States. This alienated him from the British Government after the American Revolutionary War. Buchan mellowed during the Napoleonic wars, however, and by 1818 had been accepted back into the fold of British aristocracy as a competent, if rather eccentric, political commentator and scientist.

Buchan was indeed a well-rounded, if rather eccentric, polymath and 'remained a devout Christian throughout his life'. On accession to the Earldom of Buchan he became a successful 'agricultural improver' of the family estates, introducing new methods of production, better breeds of livestock, 'enclosure' and tree-planting, combined with the gradual replacement of estate buildings. Buchan was, among all these talents, an antiquarian.[11]

The Dryburgh connection

Like many monasteries in Britain after the Reformation, Dryburgh Abbey was still in ruins at the beginning of the 18th century. Nevertheless, the peaceful, ivy-covered remains attracted the attention of Lord Buchan. He purchased Dryburgh House and the Abbey in 1786 and set about creating a charming, tranquil landscape, in which the ancient Abbey figured prominently.[12] It is notable that there are not many graves within the precincts of the Abbey; among a few others are those of Buchan himself,[13] the Haigs of Bemersyde[14] and the relatives of Sir Walter Scott, including the bard himself.[15] Surprisingly, amidst these notables, are the memorials of the tenantry of the Bemersyde Estate, including a number of the Brockie family.

Lord Buchan and the Kinghornes

It was in this setting, the burial ground at Dryburgh Abbey, that the connection with the Kinghornes developed. Through his feu tenancy at Bemersyde, Betty Kinghorne's father, William Brockie, and his family, had the right to burial in the Abbey.[16]

By 1788, Buchan had enlarged and remodelled the Dryburgh Mansion

House adjoining the Abbey ruins in an appropriately romantic style and had withdrawn from public life to a forty-year residence as a country gentleman. Here, he liked to entertain distinguished visitors, old friends and neighbours 'in the manner of a cultural patrician land-owner.'[17] Mention has already been made of Buchan's role as an encourager of Alexander's interests in the antiquities of the Scottish Borders. Alexander might have been influenced by his *Discourse*, presented at the foundation meeting of the Antiquarian Society of Scotland in 1780, which outlined the development of antiquarianism in Scotland from the earliest times.[18]

Given Buchan's education, political views, interest in agricultural science and the antiquities of Scotland, and his connection to the tenants of Bemersyde, including the Brockies, it is not surprising that Alexander was attracted to him as a like-minded mentor.

Alexander might have met Lord Buchan early, while a student at Kelso Grammar School. Sir Walter Scott recorded that Buchan had examined him (Scott) there in 1782, awarding him a prize for proficiency in translation of Latin verse.[19] Alexander might have been examined also, and if so, it would have been hard for him to forget the eccentric peer. Years later, in 1823, Buchan would write of Alexander, that he had 'been known to me from the first dawn of his merit, and in a <u>certain respect</u> classes with those individuals who in the course of my long life have attracted my notice before their powers of genius were known in Society.'[20] There is no help in this for fixing a date, but one would think they met early, perhaps in connection with the Bowden Statistical Account in the early 1790's. Who made the connection has not been discovered; it might have been through Alexander's father-in-law William Brockie, or Andrew Blaikie or Walter Scott, or it might have been Seton Karr, if a few years later. All of them were acquainted.[21]

Alexander's crusade of 'improvement' at Kippilaw could be said to have mirrored, on a small scale, Buchan's efforts to restore the fortunes of his family estates; although John Seton Karr perceived Alexander's innovations as a pecuniary drain rather than profitable. Like Andrew Blaikie, Buchan used his experience to guide and advise Alexander on crop and pasture rotations, the appropriate use of tree-plantings, and on livestock improvement. It has already been noted that Alexander obtained animals and plants directly from Lord Buchan, so he no doubt also received his wisdom, if not his close friendship.[22]

This friendship was such that Buchan helped the Kinghorne family as a whole and became one of their most important patrons. Buchan's biographer described his friendships as characterised by 'intense emotional attachment'.[23] This was likely the nature of his relationship with Alexander Kinghorne, who described him as 'my friend and patron [who had] granted me and my family a burial place [at Dryburgh Abbey] next to that of my schoolfellow the celebrated author of Waverley'.[24] It was in 1791 that Buchan had made over the ancient burial place of the Haliburtons at Dryburgh Abbey to Sir Walter Scott's father and uncles, as heirs of this family through their mother. However, his promise of a burial place to Alexander Kinghorne, though fully within his purview, might have been a passing whim of old age eccentricity. Unfortunately, the exaggerations and absurdities of conduct that were well-documented in Buchan's old age, and his ebullience of temperament, 'inclined [him] to advance proposals in … abundance and with…little concern for the difficulties involved.'[25] Nevertheless, there is no doubt of Buchan's affection for the Kinghornes, confirmed by his close interest in their personal welfare. In a little note to the family in 1823, for example, he wrote 'complements to Miss Kinghorne [referring to Isabella], wishing her joy [and] hopes to hear of her tooth-ache being gone or of her tooth being drawn.'[26]

The close connection with Lord Buchan became particularly useful, a year later, when Alexander accepted his patronage in support of his emigration, with his family, to New South Wales. With the passing of John Seton Karr, Lord Buchan and Sir Walter Scott were probably Alexander's most enthusiastic supporters. The eccentric Buchan was also a friend of Scott, who was not beyond pointing out the Earl's foibles. At the declaration of the Collector of Cess (a tax) in April 1820, for example, Scott described a comic pair of old men holding court over the occasion:

> Lord Buchan and Old Raeburn…the two most absurd figures I ever beheld stuck themselves like two Roman Senators into the two great curule chairs which are usually occupied by the Lords of Justiciary and thus sublimely seated sate winking like a brace of barn-door owls not understanding a single word of the procedure.[27]

Scott's son-in-law and biographer, Lockhart, described Buchan as 'the silliest and vainest of busy-bodies' and Scott recorded in his Journal when

Buchan died in April 1828 that he was 'a person whose immense vanity, bordering on insanity, obscured, or rather eclipsed, very considerable talents. His imagination was so fertile, that he seemed really to believe the extraordinary fictions which he delighted in telling...'[28] It is perhaps fortunate that Lord Buchan was not the only highly-placed patron that Alexander cultivated. Yet, he was exactly the right one to pave the way for Alexander's family to emigrate to New South Wales, where Buchan's friend and protégé, Sir Thomas Brisbane, had become Governor in 1821.[29]

The Erie Canal

His connection with Buchan led to Alexander's involvement in a review of the Erie Canal proposal in the United States. Thomas Jefferson thought it was madness, but the 6th Governor of New York was not a man to be trifled with: DeWitt Clinton was very well-connected. His father had been the longest serving Governor of that State. Clinton had been a United States Senator, a candidate for the American Presidency and the Mayor of New York City for some twelve years. As Mayor, he had joined the Erie Canal Commission, making it the project of his life. He became its driving force when elected Governor of New York in 1817, despite vehement opposition from Tammany Hall.[30]

Clinton's grand plan was to link the Atlantic Ocean, via the Hudson River, with the largest of the North American great lakes, Lake Erie, with a navigable waterway, similar to those engineering marvels that had been such an integral component of the industrial revolution in Britain and France.[31] This would establish a much-needed transport link for freight and passengers, and open up the industrial potential of the mid-western states. As the *Charleston Times* described it:

> History presents no parallel to so stupendous and magnificent an undertaking. What were the Roman roads, what are all the internal improvements of the whole continent of Europe, for the last century, contrasted with this sublime spectacle exhibited by a single state in the new world?[32]

It was the year 1818. There was spirited opposition to 'Dewitt's Ditch', as its opponents called the canal, but Clinton had managed to persuade the New York legislature to fund his grand project. He was now gathering as much political and scientific support as possible to persuade the state of

Ohio to build the canal linking the Ohio River with the lake at Cleveland, and so provide a free waterway all the way through the city of Cleveland and on to Charleston in what is now West Virginia.[33]

Clinton started to call in many favours, and he made the best use of his connections throughout the world. A letter that had just arrived on his desk in Albany was a key component of that strategy. It came under the auspices of a supporter of the American independence movement, Lord Buchan of Dryburgh. Clinton had asked Buchan to seek the opinion of the best engineering mind in Scotland on the prospectus for the route, costs and returns from the Erie and Ohio Canal, and the aristocrat had passed the task to the man he considered most qualified to produce an informed and independent critique.

The letter Clinton read at his desk on that day in 1818 was not from James Watt, Robert Stevenson, John Rennie or even Thomas Telford. Surprisingly, it came from a little-known Scottish civil engineer…

St. Boswell's Green,
12th April, 1818
Honoured Sir,

Sometime ago the right honourable the Earl of Buchan, most obligingly put into my hands, the plan, profiles, reports and estimates of the proposed inland Navigation from Lake Erie to the Hudson river, and from thence to Lake Champlain, requesting my observations on them. I have attentively and with much pleasure examined the whole, and from the particular and minute description of every part of the line, I have every reason for believing that the surveys have been made with due attention, and that the choice of ground had been well considered. In regard to the estimates of the expense and the calculation of the probable amount of the products which may be conveyed on the canals and from which must arise the remuneration to the state, I am incompetent to judge – but from the very luminous and distinct reports of the canal commissioners, of 15th February, and of the joint committee of the Legislature of New York, dated 19th March, 1817, I cannot think these gentlemen at all too sanguine in their expectations on this part of the subject.[34]

This extract is all that remains of the letter from Alexander Kinghorne to Governor DeWitt Clinton. The editor of the *Cleaveland Gazette and Commercial Register* described Alexander as 'a celebrated Civil engineer in North Britain' and that the letter highlighted 'the Opinion which is entertained on that subject by a competent judge in Europe'. The little-known Scottish engineer was learning the value of publicity.

In a few years' time, immigrants arriving in New York City were heading west via the Hudson River, Erie Canal and Great Lakes, and vast tonnages of grain were returning on the same route from the breadbasket of the American mid-west, feeding the industrial revolution in Europe. As the grain traversed the waterway that had been so strongly approved by the 'visionary Scottish Engineer',[35] Alexander was planning his own much longer journey to the colony of New South Wales.

Chapter 15

The Kinghornes at St Boswells (1813–1824)

...after a long and painful illness of not less than twelve years, which she bore with Christian fortitude...amongst these splendid ruins my beloved spouse was interred on Monday the 23rd of August 1819...

Alexander Kinghorne, February 1833

Alexander's work for Thomas Williamson Ramsay, surveying the Maxton Estate and renovating the Maxton Kirk, had been completed in 1812.[1] This was timely, as it made him familiar with the district around that estate at a time when he was looking for a new home. In early 1813 he was able to locate and arrange the lease, from Sir Walter Scott of Raeburn, of a 'House, Garden, Stable, Byre & Cows Grass' nearby.[2] At the end of May, Alexander and his family left Kippilaw Mains and moved to Crossflat Farm. This small holding was situated next to the main road between St Boswells (then known as Lessudden) and Maxton. It was eventually incorporated into the Maxton Estate and is today (2022) its main farmhouse, known as St Boswellsbank. The Kinghornes were to remain at Crossflat, with their address 'care of the post office at St Boswells Green', until they left Scotland in 1824.[3]

Three Plans

While living at Crossflat Farm in 1813, Alexander produced three cartographic plans, two of which were for new lines of road between Selkirk and St Boswells Green.[4] He also constructed a large plan of the farm of Faughill (or Faugh-hill), one of the properties adjoining Kippilaw. This was undertaken on behalf of James Innes Ker, the newly infeffed 5th Duke of Roxburghe, who owned the land. It would have been commissioned by the Duke or his factor James Haldane. It shows that Alexander's support for the losing side in the succession dispute had not excluded him, although there would be few commissions from that source of patronage. Alexander's plan is still held privately by the current Duke (Figure 21).[5]

Faughill Farm at Bowden is today eight hundred and fifty acres, carrying three hundred sheep and one hundred cattle. Its main crops are oilseed rape (or canola), potatoes, wheat, barley and turnips. Apart from the oilseed rape, the stock and cropping rotations are little changed from those adopted for 'improvement' of estates in Alexander's time. Faughill now has six tractors, whereas it relied on fifteen draught horses in the early 18th century under the tenancy of John Murray.[6] The land is hilly and three quarters of it used for the grazing of sheep and cattle, one quarter for crops and the lower parts incorporate Lady Moss (a loch) and various streams and old quarries.[7]

Alexander's 1813 plan shows a slightly smaller acreage compared with the modern farm, as it excluded the forty-eight-acre 'Old Lady Park' belonging then to Holydean. Otherwise, the boundaries remain much the same today, with the farm adjoining Holydean and Kippilaw in the south, Bowden Moor, Faldonside and Whitelaw in the north, with the Eildon Hills to the east. The land in 1813 was divided into twenty-one enclosed fields. Their individual acreage is not shown on the extant plan but were probably provided in a separate table, according to Alexander's usual method; some fields are hand-coloured light blue, mauve or yellow, possibly as an indication of their use, but this also is not detailed on the plan. The farm surrounds the village of Bowden and its Common.

Typical of Alexander's and other contemporary plans, miniature sketches of prominent antiquities and buildings are included, some of the latter only represented by rectangular shapes in this case. These include Bowden kirk and village (every building is outlined), Faughill farm, Bowden Mill, Old Holydean Castle, and various barns and farm buildings. The plan incorporates details of all roads, watercourses, lakes, tree lines and reserves, boundary marches and their construction (hedges or dykes).

These features, incorporated in his plan of Faughill, are instructive of Alexander's developing cartographical style. This was first seen in the plan of Netherton and Muirside (1806) but would reach a pinnacle with his plan of the Linthill Estate (1820; this Chapter) and culminate in his fine maps of the counties of Roxburgh and Selkirk (1822, 1824; this Chapter).

The Passing of John Seton Karr

Alexander had already entered a period marked by the deaths of those closest to him. He had lost his brother Andrew in 1808 in Jamaica, his father James in 1811, his stepmother Ann and youngest brother William in 1813, all closer to home in Kelso. More were to come.

John Seton Karr died on 27 April 1815. He was buried at St James Anglican Church, Piccadilly, with Lady Seton Karr, his wife, who had died just three months earlier.[8] While it was nearly two years since Alexander had been at Kippilaw, he must have been shaken by the death of his employer, who had been his friend, mentor, and so influential in his life. The laird died without issue, so his nephew, Andrew Seton (eldest son of his brother Daniel), succeeded him at Kippilaw, and received the surname of Seton Karr by grant of the King.[9] Andrew Seton had been absent from Scotland for almost twenty-four years; he served in the Bengal Civil Service from 1791 to 1811 and became Resident of Haripal and at Maldah. Alexander would have been unknown to Andrew Seton Karr and, along with his wife Alicia, he probably wished to make his own mark on the Kippilaw Estate that had been so much improved by his uncle and former factor.[10]

There was no possibility, nor would Alexander have wished, to regain his position at Kippilaw after the death of John Seton Karr. On leaving the estate, he had obtained commissions for survey work, which one suspects kept the wolf from the door, but only just, while he planned his family's future. His principal concerns at this stage were the careers of his eldest son, James, who from the previous year had been working as an estate manager in Pembrokeshire, and the next son William. At the time of Seton Karr's death, William was still enlisted in the Royal Navy, at war in the North Sea. However, after the Battle of Waterloo (15 June 1815), and having participated in the repatriation of the army, he was paid off in August. By May 1818, it is known that he was active as a merchant Captain in the North Sea, but for a period of the interim would have been at St Boswells, and another subject for Alexander's concern.[11]

Betty Kinghorne's Death and Burial at Dryburgh Abbey

From 1811, after complications associated with her on-going throat Quinsy, Alexander wrote that his wife was confined to her bed for 8 years

150

and finally died on 20 August 1819 'after a long and painful illness of not less than twelve years, which she bore with Christian fortitude', aged '50 years and 8 months'.[12] He also reported her burial near her father and mother at Dryburgh Abbey, just across the River Tweed from St Boswells: 'amongst these splendid ruins my beloved spouse was interred on Monday the 23rd of August 1819...'[13] The authors have located the memorial gravestone of Betty's father William, among other close Brockie relatives, but there was no marked grave for Betty extant at Dryburgh Abbey in 2016.[14]

The prospect of Betty's death would have filled Alexander with dread and hung over much of the first half of that period at St Boswells. Her death was devastating, even for a person of characteristic optimism. His words in the family Bible expressed only a part of the immense loss both for himself and his family group, as they clung onto the threads of their former life.

The years that followed led Alexander to re-assess his life completely. His long desire to improve the status of his family had led to achievements and some accolades, but they were living precariously on his commissions, and did not own the floorboards underneath their beds. What was the path that would lead them to true social advancement, when they would be as equals among the society of the gentry, to which they had already achieved some degree of admission?

Alexander Kinghorne's Coat of Arms

> 'What! Is it possible? Not know the figures of Heraldry! Of what could your father be thinking?'[15]
>
> Sir Walter Scott, *Rob Roy*

This sentiment expressed in the novel *Rob Roy* was undoubtedly Sir Walter Scott's own. He placed it in the mouth of Di Vernon who, with indignant surprise, asked Frank Osbaldistone of what his father could have been thinking, that he had been permitted to grow up without any knowledge of heraldry. Sir Walter Scott believed in the value of heraldry as an important element of education. He led the way to that revival of a popular sympathy with every expression of medieval antiquity. It was a visible statement of one's ancestry, holding in its emblems one's principal claims to nobility. Scott himself had recently been awarded a coat of arms with the inscription 'Scott of Abbotsford'.[16]

Therefore, it is not surprising that by 1820, Scott's protégé Alexander Kinghorne commissioned a coat of arms from the Edinburgh heraldic house of Alexander Deuchar, of which the surviving copy is a printed colour plate, pasted into the Kinghorne Family Bible (Figure 20). The original Family Bible is located in the Nowra Museum.

The plate records that the arms were 'Extracted from a MS Collection of Arms V. in the Heraldic Library of Alex Deuchar, Seal Engraver to His Majesty George IV'. Alexander Deuchar (1777–1844) was a fabricator of arms, a romantic reviver of Templar heraldry in Scotland, and a member of a family initially Jacobite, who became Hanoverian turncoats. The only suggestion of the royal patronage, claimed by the inscription, was that the company, which Deuchar inherited from his father and uncle (David and Alexander Deuchar, respectively), had made a seal for the Prince of Wales (later George IV), in 1784 during one of that personage's Lowlands rampages. There is no evidence that Alexander Deuchar held letters patent of royal appointment.[17]

The arms nevertheless reveal something of Alexander Kinghorne's idea of himself, as well as how Deuchar operated. An inscription on the bottom left of the plate reads 'Ducs of Este' and the helm and crest (with 'lion rampant') are the same as for the coat of arms of Francesco I d'Este, a 17th century Duke of Modena and Reggio in Italy. His connection with Scotland was that he was the grandfather of Mary d'Este of Modena, the second wife of King James II, the last Stuart King of England and Scotland, and the mother of the Old Pretender, James Francis Edward Stuart. The d'Este helm and crest were part of one of the base templates, which would have had a blank central field, onto which Deuchar would introduce heraldic devices more particular to his client, using the contents of his Heraldic Library to aid the process of invention.[18] The d'Este helm and crest might have been popular in Scotland among Jacobites, and probably for Deuchar was a tongue-in-cheek gesture to the then royal house, who loved to dress up in tartans when in Scotland. But for Alexander, if he realised, it must have been horrific. He had no Jacobite sympathies, and all his esteemed connections were Hanoverians.

The motto selected, 'fortis in arduis' (strong in adversity) was appropriate to Alexander himself, albeit from amongst Deuchar's treasury, perhaps not realising it was the motto of the Middleton Clan of

Scotland, to whom Alexander was not related. It reflects his then outlook: fortitude, stoicism and indeed valour, in the face of opposition and cruel circumstance. By 1820 he had lost his mother, his father, his wife, two of his children, his permanent employment, and was now working freelance, facing attendant difficulties with the flow of monies for living expenses. He was, nevertheless, at the age of fifty, launching into the next phase of his life with whatever energy and assurance he could muster. This idea of himself as persevering against a world which was set against him would recur into the future.[19]

It is less likely Alexander selected other elements of the crest, rather they were put together by Deuchar, based merely on Alexander's surname and that of his mother. The 'castle triple towered' was part of the crest of the Burgh of Kinghorn in Fife. The 'savage heads couped' were part of the crest of the noble family of Edington, to whom Alexander was not related, although it was his mother's surname. Every element of an armorial crest is full of symbolism, but there is little to suggest Deuchar did other than select them in this fashion from his library of templates.

Alexander Kinghorne admitted his coat of arms was fabricated, writing in the Bible: 'The Smaller are the arms of the Burgh of Kinghorn...the old are the arms of Edington mother of A.K.'[20] Such fabrications were common among nouveau-riche families in Britain and Europe, seeking to underpin a newly acquired social status with beautifully presented but fanciful family trees, complete with coats of arms. There was little concept that 'nobility' could be achieved through trade, as was sometimes expressed on the Continent, for example in the mercantile centres of Lyon and Marseille in southern France. A 'scientific' approach to genealogy had not developed yet, although there was a tradition of works on the peerage, for example Debrett's *New Peerage*, first published 1769. Still now, in modern times, one can buy pre-printed coats of arms for many surnames for a few pounds, no questions asked. However, for a coat of arms to be authentic in the United Kingdom, it must be granted under letters patent by the College of Arms, a royal corporation. Alexander, or his family, had not been granted a right under letters patent, whether by birth or for services to the Crown. His coat of arms was a piece of fiction.

Along with the coat of arms in the Kinghorne Family Bible is a journal article about the origins of the Kinghorn family name, claiming it originated with the 'Horne x Child of Havelock' (or 'King-Horne of Havelock') in Anglo-Saxon literature.[21] The article is dated June-September 1826 (that is, six years after). Alexander was by then in New South Wales, facing another crisis in his identity in his relationship with Governor Darling and the politics of the Colony. Significantly, it is pasted in the Bible as a flap over the coat of arms.

The inference from these elements is that Alexander had little idea of his family background, his family's origins in Fife, and was unlikely to have been able to trace much further back than his tailor grandfather. Had he been able to, he would have recorded what he knew in the Family Bible, instead of clutching at straws.

He nevertheless held a romantic desire to have been descended from nobility and saw the arms as a reinstatement of his family's ancient status. There was this belief that his ancestors must have been noble but had fallen upon hard times – a common theme in the romantic literature of the day, including that of Sir Walter Scott. In this context, the Anglo-Saxon legends of the 'King-Horne of Havelock' had a place, or notions of descent from the nobility of old Fife, or King Robert the Bruce (above Noble ancestors).

Alexander might have believed that Deuchar had the necessary means, through his Heraldic Library, to open for him his lineage through the Kinghorne and Edington names. If so, he would have been disappointed.

The Plan of the Estate of Linthill

William Riddell inherited the Estate of Linthill after the death of his first cousin, Lieutenant-Colonel Richard Edgar Hunter in 1807.[22] Riddell moved there with his family in 1812 to occupy the beautiful 18th century Linthill House, built by descendants of the Rev'd William Hunter (1657–1736), the minister of Lilliesleaf and laird of Union Hall.[23] The estate was located due south of Kippilaw and Clarilaw, situated east and roughly equidistant from the villages of Midlem and Lilliesleaf, and west from Cavers Carre. Clarilaw Burn bordered the Mansion House in the north and the Water of Ale in the south.

Walter Riddell Carre, in his book *Border Memories*, described how Linthill came into being, when the Hunters of Union Hall purchased the neighbouring estate of Midlem Mill…

We come now to Elliots of Midlem Mill, from whom the noble family of Minto are descended…as their estate of Union Hall was only separated from Midlem Mill by the river Ale, they took down their old mansion, which stood near to the present garden of Linthill, built a bridge and enlarged the house of Midlem Mill, which in the days of the Elliots had, I have understood, a thatched roof, calling the united properties Linthill, and there the Hunters resided, till the death of the last member of the family, the well known and justly popular Colonel Edgar Hunter, who was killed by a fall from his horse at Clarilaw Burn in 1807. Having died intestate, he was succeeded by his cousin and heir, William Riddell, whose father had married a sister of the Colonel's father … But that gentleman soon sold it, being a good deal embarrassed, when the late Mr Currie bought and entailed it …[24]

The precise nature of William Riddell's 'embarrassment' is not known but would have been financial. Walter Riddell Carre stated in 1874 that Riddell 'sold [Linthill] to Mr Currie, the father of the present William Currie, Esq. of Linthill.'[25] In 1820, some two years before the sale, Alexander produced a detailed survey and plan of the entire estate, including surrounding geographical and antiquarian features. It is likely that William Riddell commissioned the survey in preparation for the sale, choosing Alexander as his former neighbour and a respected local surveyor.

Alexander's map of Linthill survives in its original hand-drawn form in private hands, but the authors viewed a full-scale copy at Thomas Thomson House in Edinburgh. Figure 22 presents a scaled-down photographic copy of the original.[26] It is a beautifully drawn, large plan of the estate and surrounding districts (two pages each measuring 506 x 760 mm), among Alexander's finest work for a private estate (cf. Figures 17 & 22). It shows details of the village, kirk, glebe and moss of Lilliesleaf in the middle left, Craggs Steading, Midlem Mill and Portous Croft. The course of the Water of Ale, and the locations of chapel steading, a ruined peel tower, and the Linthill gardens and offices are drawn in some detail. The miniature drawings of buildings and antiquities are more detailed than in his previous work.

Alexander's survey measured a total area, excluding Lilliesleaf Moss, of 757 acres and 33 perches, comprising the Mansion House with a staggering 116 acres of landscaped lawns, 28 acres of woods, and five farms: Lilliesleaf, Chapel, Toft Barn, Crays and Childknow (see details in Figure 22). The neighbouring estates were also included to some extent, including parts of Clarilaw and Cavers Carre. The plan incorporated an insert, showing William Fairdairn's 1788 plan of Curling Farm at Midlem Mill, then part of the estate. Linthill estate is now smaller (some 130 acres) than it was in 1820 and was recently sold (2013), after subdivision into several lots.[27]

It is notable that Alexander attested the frontispiece accompanying the Linthill plan as 'Alex' Kinghorne, Engineer and Surveyor [top right hand corner]…St. Boswell's Green, 1 May 1820 [top left hand corner]' (not shown in Figure 22). This indicates that by 1820 he considered himself to be principally an engineer, having progressed from the titles of surveyor and architect.[28] The Linthill plan exhibits a quality not found in much of Alexander's earlier work and would have impressed nearby landowners.

The Plans of Roxburghshire and Selkirkshire

By the early 1820s, Alexander was assisted in his survey work by his eldest son. Both James and William Kinghorne had been trained in surveying by their father, but only James followed him into the profession of estate management as his apprentice at Kippilaw.[29]

In 1814 James had obtained a position in his own right, engaged as Land Steward by John Dunn Esquire of Tenby, the lessee of the Crickmarran estate in Pembrokeshire. Most likely, the position had been arranged for him through John Seton Karr, who knew the owner of the estate Sir John Owen Bart., MP for Pembrokeshire. James, aged 19 years and 8 months, departed Leith by ship for Wales on 8 April 1814. There he remained in Dunn's employ for five years. After his return home in June 1819, James collaborated with his father on new surveying commissions. In this period, Alexander was describing his own profession as Engineer or Civil Engineer, and that of his son as Land Surveyor.[30]

The survey of Roxburghshire was a significant undertaking and, while first published in 1822, commenced much earlier. Alexander mentioned it as a private project in 1813 to John Seton Karr, and expected the Duke of Buccleuch to be his patron for both the Roxburgh and Selkirk Surveys,[31] but there is no indication Alexander received funds from the Duke of Buccleuch, let alone from the Duke of Roxburghe, whose demesnes he mapped. Lord Napier was involved in the plan of Selkirkshire, but the financial side is unclear.

However, Alexander did find a publisher. The map of Roxburghshire finally appeared in 1822, published by John Thomson and Company of Edinburgh. The plan had been redrawn to prepare a plate for printing, but had all the characteristics of Alexander's earlier work, as described for the Plan of Linthill.[32] The names attesting this plan were Alexander Kinghorne, Engineer & Surveyor, James Kinghorne, Land Surveyor, George Cranston, Road Surveyor, and John Clark, Land Surveyor (Frontisepiece). Alexander's original drawing has not survived.[33]

It seems William was involved as well. On 28 May 1821, the year before Thomson's publication, Alexander wrote to Sir Herbert Taylor, military secretary to the Duke of York, enclosing 'two plans' of James and William's 'own delineation and survey, that His Royal Highness may judge for Himself of their talents.'[34] These might not have been the final maps of Roxburghshire and Selkirkshire. James was named on the published versions of both, but William on neither.

The map of Roxburghshire covered the whole county but was eventually published in two parts, Northern and Southern, presumably to fit into the standard paper sizes for atlases of the day, while retaining the levels of detail in the original hand-drawn plan (Frontispiece). The map is divided into individual parishes with coloured boundaries. Elevated land is shown in relief, but without the contours seen in modern survey maps. All major and minor watercourses are included with their relative sizes indicated figuratively. Each parish is detailed to the level of individual villages and estates.

The Bowden Parish plan, for example, shows the size and location of the main towns (Bowden and Midlem), together with the buildings and mills, but not the boundaries, of the estates. Prominent antiquities, such as the tower at Holydean, and the mansion houses, are clearly drawn in place but, of course, out of scale and perspective.

Beautifully engraved views of the Abbeys of Jedburgh and Melrose are included as inset pictures on the published map; these would not be Alexander's work but are unattested additions by the engraver. The engraving of the map, by N.R. Hewitt of London, retains the fine details of land relief, as well as parish boundaries, rivers, roads, woods, parks and settlements (Frontispiece).[35]

The quality of the plan of Roxburghshire, and its favourable reception in Scotland, soon led to further work, notably the plan of Selkirkshire (Figure 23), for the Right Honourable William John Napier, 9th Lord Napier (1786–1834). Napier is notable as the first Administrator in Canton, and for recommending the British settlement at Hong Kong. The commission of the plan of Selkirkshire was made in the year of Napier's election as a Scottish representative to the House of Lords. It was most likely a memorial to his father who had been, until his death in 1823, Lord Lieutenant of Selkirkshire. The initial connection for Alexander might have been Colonel William Elliot Lockhart. Lockhart, a friend of both Sir Walter Scott and John Seton Karr, was MP for the county of Selkirk, and had earlier mentored Alexander in his bid to work on the Berwick to Kelso railway.[36]

In this case, John Thomson claimed that the map he published in 1824 was based on 'the original survey of the county in 1784–5 by John Ainslie'. He wrote that 'after various additions and corrections by William Johnson, it met with the approbation of Lord Napier, who called in the assistance of the most skilful assistants in the country to make it accurate.'[37] The plan is inscribed 'Attested by The Right Hon[ble] Lord Napier', and lists those responsible for its production as John Corse Scott Esquire of Sinton, Thomas Mitchell, Road Surveyor, Alexander Kinghorne, Civil Engineer and James Kinghorne, Land Surveyor.[38]

Among these, Thomas Mitchell described as 'Road Surveyor' was the same Lieutenant-Colonel Sir Thomas Livingstone Mitchell, who became Surveyor General of New South Wales in 1827, one of Australia's most celebrated early explorers and map-makers. The Kinghornes would meet and collaborate with him on the opposite side of the earth.

Alexander's involvement in the plans of Roxburghshire and Selkirkshire was significant in the history of the mapping of Scotland. These were the first comprehensive plans of the two counties since General Roy's military surveys of 1754–5.[39] Initially published individually, they were included in Thomson's Atlas of Scotland of 1832. There were other mapmakers at work in the two counties but, according to Thomson, none had matched the accuracy and finesse of his cartographers.[40]

These plans, and Alexander's 1802 survey for George Chalmers, were the forerunners of the Ordnance Survey maps of the counties, produced from the mid-nineteenth century.[41]

PART II

NEW SOUTH WALES

Chapter 16

A New Life in the Colonies (1819–1824)

I was often with the renowned Sir Walter while he was writing his novels and never was further than 9 miles from his residence till I embarked, by his advice, to try my fortunes in New South Wales in April 1824. [1]

Alexander Kinghorne, February 1833

Around 1819, shortly after the death of Betty Brockie, Alexander Kinghorne made the decision to move his entire family from the depressed Scottish Borders to seek a new life in the Colony of New South Wales. This would not have been possible in Betty's lifetime, as her illness kept them to St Boswells. People grieve in different ways. In the Kinghornes' case, as remarked previously, they did not own the floorboards under their beds, and so would not have had that attachment to their home. Alexander's financial circumstances were deteriorating also, doubtless exacerbated by needing to be close to Betty during her illness, but also due to the loss of his most active job-finder, John Seton Karr, and a decline in economic circumstances in Scotland, all affecting his commissions.

David MacMillan, in his book *Scotland and Australia 1788–1850*, wrote that between 1820 and 1830 there were 'ample evidence of the effects of high rents and of the fall in prices in the Lowlands, and of the decline of the tacksmen in the Highlands, of commercial distress in the cities and depression in the small country towns'.[2] Not content to weather out the post-war economic recession at home, many Scottish merchants and professionals were adventurous enough to undertake the hazardous voyage to the colonies during this period, even though some took considerable wealth with them.

Alexander Kinghorne had not been in full employment since losing his position at Kippilaw in 1812. Sufficient income came from the commissions he received, but not to a level suited to his aspirations. If he were to achieve these, he needed to chart another course.

Sir Walter Scott encouraged him to consider emigration, as can be seen in the hand-written note, quoted above, from his edition of *The Monastery*. The opportunities available in New South Wales were threefold: first, to earn a respectable salary as a senior colonial employee, a position gained through the influence of his highly placed connections; second, to be granted the land he needed to acquire his longed-for social status as a 'gentleman'; and third, with land he could use his agricultural skills to build a fortune.

The Eldest Sons of Alexander Kinghorne Leave Scotland

The first phase of the plan was for his eldest sons, James and William, to go out and report on the family's prospects there. James, after returning to Scotland from Pembrokeshire, was again working with his father as a surveyor. William, retired from the Royal Navy, would have been anxious to return to the sea but was unable to do so in European waters, because his involvement in the infamous Bodø incident made him persona non grata in the Baltic trade, as described in the authors' previous book.[3] Therefore, encouraged by Scott, Alexander sought endorsement and support for his emigration plans. He launched a campaign of letter writing, seeking the necessary permission for assisted emigration for James and William, with guarantee of employment on arrival.

Alexander first garnered letters of support from his existing patrons, either directly or through Sir Walter Scott: these were Scott himself and Lord Buchan, and Scott's cousin Sir Henry Hay MacDougall. He then ensured that other highly placed connections, the Earl of Minto, Colonel Elliot Lockhart and George Chalmers, were agreeable to provide favourable references. Then, a letter to Sir Herbert Taylor, Military Secretary to His Royal Highness The Duke of York:

St Boswells, Roxburgshire
28th May 1821.

Major General Sir Herbert Taylor K.C.B.
Military Secretary to
His Royal Highness the Duke of York, etc. etc. etc.

Sir

In taking up my pen to do myself the honour of addressing you I must plead a Father's interest in the welfare of his two sons:– and I know when that motive is explained to His Royal Highness, from what one would say of the warmth of his heart He will hold me blameless in taking so great a liberty.

Sir, I am by profession a Civil Engineer & Land Surveyor. I educated my two sons in their youth to the same profession. My eldest (James) aged 26 has for several years conducted the improvements of a considerable farm in the highly cultivated Vale of the Tweed where I reside. My second son (William) aged 24 has been educated to the Nautical Profession:– he served 3 years & a half as Midshipman in the Nightingale Sloop of War, and since the peace has had the command of a Merchant Vessel. – He is a complete navigator & has a competent knowledge of Marine Surveying, planning, etc.

I am at present fitting them out as free Settlers in New South Wales and they sail for that province on the first of July. I do not wish them to go to that distant region without making it known to His Royal Highness that they are both equal to make Military Surveys of the Country; and as I know they will do credit to the instructions they have received. I do myself the honour of enclosing two plans of their own delineation and survey that His Royal Highness may judge for Himself of their talents.

I have the recommendation of Sir Henry Hay Mackdougal Bart father of Lady Brisbane, to his son-in-law Sir Thomas – of Sir Walter Scott Bart, and the Earl of Buchan, in their behalf:– and I would most anxiously solicit His Royal Highness Patronage and recommendation to the Governor and Commander in Chief of New South Wales and Van Diemen's Land, which will be the means of my young men being employed by Land or Sea usefully to His Majesty's Government in that very interesting Colony – and as His Royal Highness may wish to have a reference to some persons to whom I am known, I beg leave to mention the Earl of Minto; Colonel Elliot Lockhart M.P. and George Chalmers Esq F.R.S. Chief Clerk to the Board of Trade Whitehall London; who is in possession of certificates to the Colonial Secretary of State which I hope will be satisfactory to His Royal Highness.

I again beg leave to apologise for so great a liberty as I have taken:– and I have the honour to be with great respect

Sir
Your most Obedient
and
Very devoted humble Servant
Alexd^r Kinghorne[4]

The Duke of York was to be the final and most exalted connection Alexander sought to cultivate: Frederick Duke of York was Commander in Chief of the armed forces and heir presumptive to the throne, as his brother, George IV, was without an heir.[5] To obtain the patronage of the Duke of York would have been a major coup. Consequently, Alexander's manner of address was particularly obsequious – 'Your most obedient and very devoted humble servant' was more than the usual formula 'Your most humble and obedient servant.'

Alexander's approach was through Sir Herbert Taylor, who later became Master Surveyor and Surveyor-General of the Ordnance from 1828.[6] As the Duke's Military Secretary, Taylor would be familiar with his current survey work. By sending him maps of Roxburghshire and Selkirkshire, presumably the hand-drawn originals that he, James and possibly William had made, he provided strong evidence of their worth in a context that Taylor would understand. Alexander clearly had confidence in the quality of the cartography and knew it would have an impact. He emphasized the colony as the 'means of young men being employed by land or sea usefully to His Majesty's Government' and presented his sons' qualifications in their best light, suggesting their utility for such tasks as 'military surveys of the country'.

Alexander also marshalled the full complement of his patrons, aforementioned, to back up his argument to the Duke. How could His Royal Highness fail to be impressed by this retinue of prestigious connections and not support Kinghorne's request for patronage?

The answer to this question is unknown. There is no evidence that James and William carried the Duke's recommendation to New South Wales, and their father received no more than a courteous acknowledgement, as was the case when he wrote again, two years later. On that occasion, Alexander thanked His Royal Highness for his assistance and sent him the gift of another map, possibly the published version of the map of Roxburghshire. Sir Herbert Taylor replied, thanking Alexander for his 'attention in sending him a map of the County of Roxburgh'.[7] Nevertheless, as the result of Alexander's efforts, his sons did carry weighty recommendations.

In August 1821 James and William set out for New South Wales on board the *Castle Forbes*. The letters they carried were sufficiently influential that, when they reached Hobart Town in early February 1822, William was immediately offered, and accepted, a position as a ship's Master in the Colonial Marine service of Lieutenant Governor William Sorrell. William remained in the maritime service of Van Diemen's Land for more than 18 years before settling on dry land in New South Wales around 1836.[8]

James Kinghorne was equally fortunate. He was 27 years old when he arrived in Hobart with his brother but, unlike William, continued to Sydney in the *Castle Forbes*, arriving on 26 April.[9] Here, under the patronage of Governor Brisbane, he secured employment as Assistant Superintendent at the government prison farm at Emu Plains, commencing his duties on 1 June 1822.[10] The appointment was, again, based on his impressive letters of introduction and on his qualifications and experience as an estate steward in Wales. However, in the case of James Kinghorne, there was the additional recommendation from Sir Thomas Brisbane's father-in-law to provide him with a senior government appointment.

Their reports back to Alexander would have been favourable. They had received largesse and seen the opportunities openly available.

Further Letters of Introduction

The next phase of Alexander's plan was thus activated, to emigrate with the rest of the family. Sir Thomas Brisbane had replied in the warmest terms to Lord Buchan's letter carried by James and William, no doubt confirming their reports.[11] Alexander continued to seek Lord Buchan's support for his own emigration plans, and received the following response from Dryburgh Abbey on 28 December 1822 (Figure 24):

> Your letter to me of the 21st current of which I send you a copy for preservation afforded me great satisfaction, and I will cheerfully join in recommending your petitions to the Colonial Secretary of State along with your other friends in this country who are particularly acquainted with your character & abilities, which have been known and esteemed by me for many years, and which I am confident are truly deserving of countenance and support.[12]

Buchan further replied to Governor Brisbane's on 5 February 1823, clearly setting the scene for the emigration of the remainder of the Kinghorne family:

My dear Sir Thomas

Your letter of the thirtieth of August from the chief seat of your government gave me great satisfaction, and I entertain no doubt that with the uniform aid of your prudent administration, on the principles you have done me the honour to communicate, the Colony of Australia will continue to prosper.

Alexander Kinghorne the worthy father of your young settlers has been known to me from the first dawn of his merit, and in a <u>certain respect</u> classes with those individuals who in the course of my long life have attracted my notice before their powers of genius were known in Society.

I take therefore the liberty of recommending Mr Kinghorne and his promising family to the continuance of your favour, and entertaining no doubt that they will prove really useful to your government. I have mentioned them favourably to Mr George Chalmers of the Board of Trade and to all those of my particular acquaintance who may probably have it in their power materially to support Mr Kinghorne in obtaining assistance to his settlement under your government and I am confident that his abilities are such as if encouraged would materially promote the prosperity of your Australian Country.

With my affectionate respects to Lady Brisbane
I remain dear friend
Yours truly
Buchan[13]

Lord Buchan became the main instigator of Alexander's campaign, working behind the scenes and compiling a 'Journal of Transactions relating to New South Wales' – containing letters of recommendation from himself, Scott, and Chalmers – which he forwarded to Lord Bathurst.[14] Buchan's recommendations and those of Scott have not survived, but were effective. On 29 July, Elizabeth Kinghorne received this hastily written note from Buchan's secretary (Figure 25):

Dryburgh Abbey
July 29th 1823

Miss Kinghorne

I am happy to inform you that My Lord has desired me to say that Sir Walter Scott called this day to inform His Lordship that Lord Bathurst had ordered a Grant of a Thousand Acres of Land for your Father in Australia.

I am Madam
Your Most Obt Sert
Ebenezer Faichney[15]

Soon afterwards Alexander, who had been away surveying during July, received a copy of the letter from Downing Street, addressed to Sir Thomas Brisbane from Lord Bathurst, indicating that the bearer, Alexander Kinghorne, had been 'given permission…to proceed as a Free Settler to the Settlement of New South Wales – and I am to desire, that you will make to him, upon his arrival, a Grant of Land, in proportion to the means which he may possess of bringing the same into cultivation.'[16]

His desire to become a landed gentleman was to be fulfilled. But to what extent was yet to unfold.

The Prisoner of Hope: Alexander Kinghorne and Family Leave Scotland

Turn you to the strong hold, ye prisoners of hope:
even to day do I declare that I will render double unto thee.
Zechariah 9:12 (King James Version)

Preparations were well in hand by the beginning of 1824 for Alexander Kinghorne and his family to leave Scotland and follow James and William to New South Wales. His other children had little choice unless they were to go against his wishes. One of his sons refused him. Andrew Seton had married Helen Aimers, the daughter of Robert Aimers, a Galashiels miller,[17] and was establishing himself in the wool manufactories of that town. Try as Alexander might, he could not persuade him.

As the date of departure approached, he wrote to Andrew Seton, showing both the pressures and anguish he was feeling:

[March 1824]…every Mortal on Earth. – Even <u>Mrs Ramsay</u> and <u>those about her</u>, who have in their pockets, and have wrested from me <u>Hundreds</u> five times fold to which they never were entitled, I <u>forgive</u>, and only hope <u>she</u> and <u>they</u> may never experience the hardships and distress which at this moment they have made me and my poor family suffer. I declare to you most solemnly that they force us to <u>Exile</u> with only <u>Twenty</u> <u>three</u> <u>shillings</u> between us <u>all</u> and <u>stern</u> <u>Poverty</u> ! ! ! But I will not distress you further as we must join in prayer to almighty God for <u>His</u> Blessing to aid our humble efforts here, for it is <u>His Blessing</u> alone which 'maketh rich and addeth no sorrow'[18]

You have all the blessings of an affectionate Father whose <u>Tears</u> drop…

167

[illegible] of you all hoping, still trusting that on this ... [illegible] will yet see an embracing aged parent, and yet there is nothing I can add more, my feelings...[illegible] and such that I can scarcely express what I am writing. All your Brothers and Sisters are well and join in kind love...[illegible].

My dear Andrew,
from your loving and affectionate Father
Alex' Kinghorne
P.S. I shall write you from every place on our voyage when I have every opportunity.
A.K.[19]

Alexander's 'Tears' were real, because parts of this letter are rendered illegible by the 'drop[s]' which have left their mark, dissolving the ink where they struck the paper. The letter expresses pity for his family having been brought to suffering and 'stern Poverty'. Here is the realisation that his whole life in Scotland had come to very little, a few shillings, his family certainly, the contents of their cases, his precious letters of introduction ... He had been forced into 'Exile', the word capitalised and underlined, his thoughts upon the exiles of Israel in the Bible, in Egypt, in Babylon. He commits himself and his family to 'almighty God', placing them under 'His Blessing'. He quotes Proverbs 10:22, 'The blessing of the Lord, it maketh rich, and he addeth no sorrow with it.'[20] They were now facing uncertainties, not only in New South Wales, but the voyage out often enough ended in shipwreck, disease or other calamity. Only God could protect them and, 'render double' to them, as Zechariah put it, quoted at the head of this Chapter.

The reference to Elizabeth Ramsay is a sad reflection on the wife of his patron and friend Thomas Williamson Ramsay, his landlord at St Boswells,[21] 'and those about her', who have in their pockets, and have wrested from me Hundreds five times fold to which they never were entitled.' The circumstances of this dispute, otherwise unknown, had left him in severe distress. Even his last stronghold, his family home, had been turned against him, leaving them 'with only Twenty three shillings between us all and stern Poverty!!!'

From Leith to Hobart

Alexander, with five of his eight surviving children – Alexander Jnr, John Ker, Helen (Nellie), Elizabeth and Isabella – departed Leith aboard the Australian Company's migrant ship *Portland* on 1 April 1824.[22] The *Portland* was carrying 87 passengers (73 in steerage and 17 in cabins, according to Alexander). The Kinghorne family shared two cabins. The captain, William Snell, was an experienced former Royal Navy Lieutenant, who had served at Trafalgar while still a midshipman, and left the Royal Navy in 1821 to join the merchant service.[23]

Among the passengers were several families similarly making the voyage as emigrants, planning to leave the ship at Hobart or Sydney as free settlers. The Kinghornes would have got to know many of them. Alexander might have introduced the Pitcairn family to his son William on arrival in Hobart, as the youngest son, Robert, became William Kinghorne's agent and solicitor.[24]

Five days out from Leith, Alexander penned a few lines to Andrew Seton from the deck of the *Portland* while she lay at anchor in the Orkneys. His words give some indication of the difficulties associated with a sea voyage in the early 19th century, as well as the advantages of travelling on a well-provisioned migrant ship. His main concerns were for his family, including the future technological improvement of Andrew's practice as a millwright. Nevertheless, his romantic notions still came through in the description of their situation. He wrote encouragingly of the conditions on board the *Portland*, reporting it well-provisioned with 'beef and plum pudding four times, and pork and peas three times per week.' At this early stage of the voyage they had 'never tasted anything <u>salt</u>. The pilot brings plenty of eggs at 4d per dozen and fine fat fowls at 8d each'.

After leaving Ham Sound in the Orkneys and crossing the Pentland Firth, the *Portland* headed into the Atlantic Ocean, making for the Island of Madeira. Alexander carried a letter of introduction to the family of a friend in Madeira:

> On parting with Mr James of Stow, he generously put into my hands 20 sovereigns new from the Bank of England and a package and letters of introduction to his son-in-law and daughter at Madeira – This, you will no doubt say, is a providential relief to us <u>Poor Exiles</u>. We must now trust the Almighty for a prosperous passage and happiness hereafter.

169

His letter went on to encourage his son in an upcoming trip to Glasgow, describing arranged visits to mechanised factories, possibly as a form of study tour to learn the latest wool milling technology. He had 'left word with Ja^s Airth at the Foundry, who will pay every attention to you when you call on your way to Glasgow. Mr Anderson also promised to show you every part of his work, and also the Card Wire Manufactory. I hope you will glean all you can in the Steam Engine way and other improvements at Glasgow...'[25]

Alexander held strong aspirations that Andrew would follow the rest of the family to New South Wales and join his brother, Alexander Jnr, in developing a millwrighting business: 'on your coming to the Colony, I shall take care that an establishment of the most respectable sort is set going for you and Alexander.' He expressed his confidence that he had secured his 'interest with the Governor and Attorney General... [which] must lead to something handsome for me, and all the family.' The final words for his son were loving, with the hope that the family would soon be reunited: 'Adieu, dear Seton – May God prosper and bless you. Your brothers and sisters join in best wishes till we have the pleasure of meeting you.'[26]

Leaving Madeira, the *Portland* headed south-west towards Brazil, stopping in for supplies at Rio de Janeiro. Alexander wrote again to Andrew Seton from that port. The letter not being extant, but is known of from a short note from Lord Buchan:

Dryburgh Abbey, Nov 9th 1824

Lord Buchan with kind compliments to Mr A.S. Kinghorne returns his worthy Father's letter from Rio de Janero with which Lord B. is greatly pleased & hopes his young friend Andrew will carefully preserve it & all his Fathers letters, which will become hereafter very interesting.

Buchan[27]

The *Portland* left Rio on 10 July, setting a south-easterly course for Cape Town. It seems that the remainder of the five-month winter voyage to New Holland was largely uneventful, although they might have experienced further storms and bad weather, particularly rounding the Cape of Good Hope or in the Roaring Forties as they traversed the Southern Ocean in winter. Migrant ships often touched at Cape Town, or at Port-of-France roughly half-way across the Indian Ocean, but there is no report of the *Portland* doing so, and the speed of their transit suggests they kept to the southern route.[28]

The *Portland* arrived in Hobart Town on 10 September 1824.[29] The passengers expressing their thanks, and doubtless relief, in an open letter to Captain Snell, published in the *Hobart Town Gazette*:

> With regard to the provisions we cordially agree in stating that they were, both in quantity and quality, entirely to our satisfaction; and as to the conduct observed towards us by the officers of the ship, and of yourself in particular, we as cordially assent in testifying, that to have been always directed towards our comfort, and altogether characterized as that of Gentlemen. With our sincere wishes for your prosperity, and of the Company whose ship you command.[30]

Alexander, despite the brevity of his stop-over in Van Diemen's Land, was presented with a significant opportunity to progress his reputation as a civil engineer in the colonial context.

The Kinghorne Family Transit through Hobart[31]

Upon arrival, the family were reunited with William. Then, likely with William accompanying, Alexander along with his younger sons and charming daughters, called promptly at Government House with his letters of introduction. On 23 September Lieutenant Governor George Arthur commissioned Alexander to undertake a survey for the township of Brighton, and the prospects for relocating the capital there:[32]

> Alex. Kinghorne, Esq.
> Civil Engineer
>
> SIR. – As I deem it of great importance to have the township of Brighton very particularly surveyed, for the purpose, of ascertaining its local advantages, for the establishment of a large town, I desire to avail myself of your services on this occasion. It is important, that you should minutely examine the ground marked out for the township, and fully report thereon; you will then see whether there is an abundant supply of fuel; whether water, with moderate labour and expense, can be brought into the township, from the river which runs at its foot, or from any adjacent springs; whether lime-stone, stone for building, or clay for making bricks, can be easily procured…[etc. etc.] [33]

171

The commission seems remarkable for a migrant who had only just arrived in Hobart, en route to Sydney.

On 24 September 1824, Alexander, 'accompanied by my son [possibly Alexander Jnr], and furnished with four government servants being as pioneers, proceeded to the spot where I continued till yesterday, in perambulating, examining, and taking accurate levels of the surrounding country for several miles...' Seven days after the date of the Lieutenant Governor's order, Alexander duly completed his survey and, on 30 September, submitted a detailed report recommending 'Brighton Plains' as highly suitable for the construction of a township so that 'the seat of Government [could] be removed from Hobart Town ...'[34]

The move of the seat of government never eventuated. However impressed Lieutenant Governor Arthur had been by Alexander's connections and qualifications as a 'Civil Engineer', the survey was a ploy, a political gambit to set in the teeth of the more troublesome elements in Hobart. To make the capital in Brighton, a rural backwater some 19 miles north of Hobart, would have been folly. It would have been a kind of Swiftian Brobdingnag, a kingdom in the sky, in which Arthur was little interested, because if he was to exercise power he needed to be at the centre of things in Hobart. Nevertheless, Alexander swallowed it. His report addressed the suitability of the countryside, planned the layout for the township, but not the impossibility of the location for Government. Arthur persisted with it for a while, later turning his attention in similar vein to New Norfolk, but neither were going to happen.

Alexander thought he was off to a good start, ensuring that his commission from the Lieutenant Governor, together with an extensive report, were published in the New South Wales Gazette.[35] But his support for the project would come back to haunt him at a time he little needed it.[36]

On 3 October 1824, the Kinghorne family re-boarded the *Portland*, and set sail for Sydney, just three weeks after their arrival in Hobart.[37]

Figure 1. Line Engraving of the town of Kelso, 1834, by J.M.W. Turner RA, engraved by R. Wallis; from Scott's Poetical Works. [Tate Britain, T05137; licensed to author]

Figure 2. Sir Walter Scott, 1821. Detail of engraving by John Horsburgh (1791–1869) after Thomas Lawrence (1769–1830). [Kruizenga Art Museum, 2012.2.7; licensed to author]

Figure 3. Smailholm Tower. [Author's photograph, 2018]

Figure 4. Silver serving spoon, part of a set presented to Alexander Kinghorne and Betty Brockie on their marriage, 1793; silversmith hallmark: David Marshall, Edinburgh, 1789.
[Author's collection]

Figure 5. Brockie family graves in grounds of Dryburgh Abbey. [Author's photograph, 2014]

Figure 6. Old Bowden Schoolhouse. [Author's photograph, 2014]

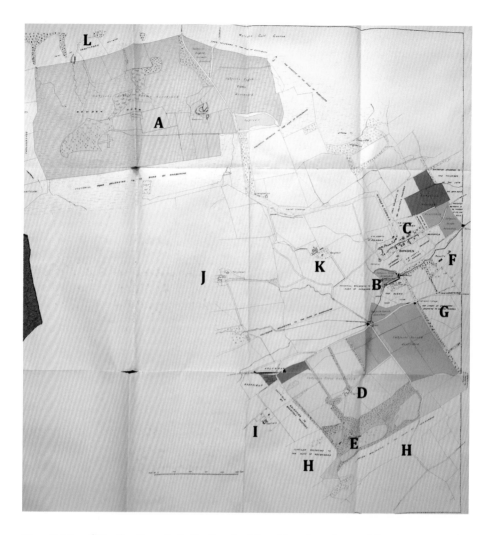

Figure 7. Map of Kippilaw Estate including Bowden Moor. The coloured areas of the map represent the extent of the Estate in 1907. The letters on the map indicate the approximate positions of (A) Bowden Moor, (B) Bowden Mill, (C) Bowden village, (D) Kippilaw Mains, (E) the Kippilaw Mansion, and the neighbouring Estates of (F) Maxpoffle, (G) Camieston, (H) Clarilaw, (I) Eastfield, (J) Holydean, (K) Faughhill and (L) part of Abbotsford. [Seton Karr of Kippilaw Papers, NRAS2970]

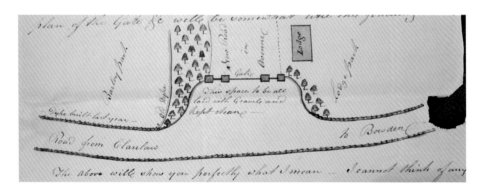

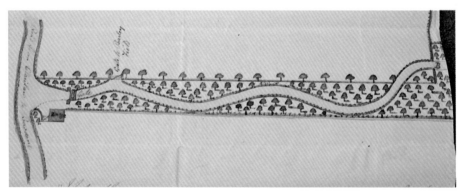

Figure 8. Alexander Kinghorne's sketches for the new gate and avenue at Kippilaw, 1800. [Seton Karr of Kippilaw Papers, NRAS2970]

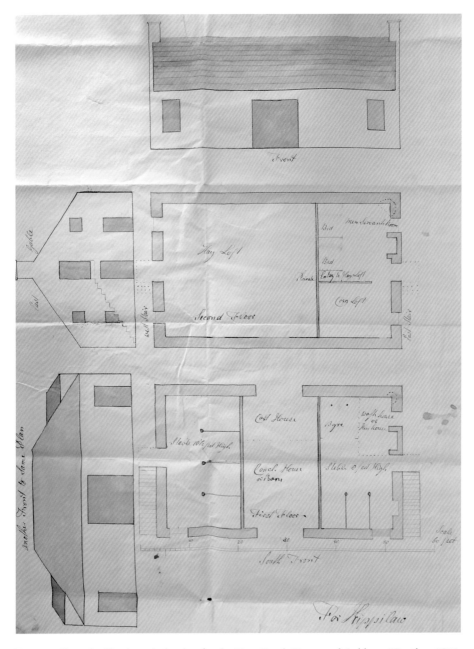

Figure 9. Alexander Kinghorne's sketches for the New Coach House and Stables at Kippilaw, 1800.
[Seton Karr of Kippilaw Papers, NRAS2970]

Figure 10. Coach House and Stables at Kippilaw. [Author's photograph, 2014]

Figure 11. Kippilaw Mains farmhouse, completed 1803. [Author's photograph, 2014]

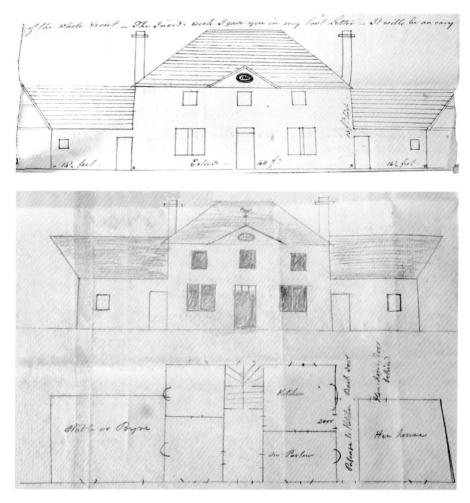

Figure 12. Alexander Kinghorne's rough plans for the renovation of the farmhouse at Kippilaw Mains.
[Seton Karr of Kippilaw Papers, NRAS2970]

Figure 13. Sketch plan for the Georgian frontage of Kippilaw Mansion House by Alexander Kinghorne, 1807. [Seton Karr of Kippilaw Papers, NRAS2970]

Figure 14. Georgian frontage of Kippilaw Mansion House. [Author's photograph, 2014]

Figure 15. Scott's View. [Author's photograph, 2016]

Figure 16. Gledswood House, Berwickshire. [RCAHMS, SC 1382685, ©Crown Copyright: HES]

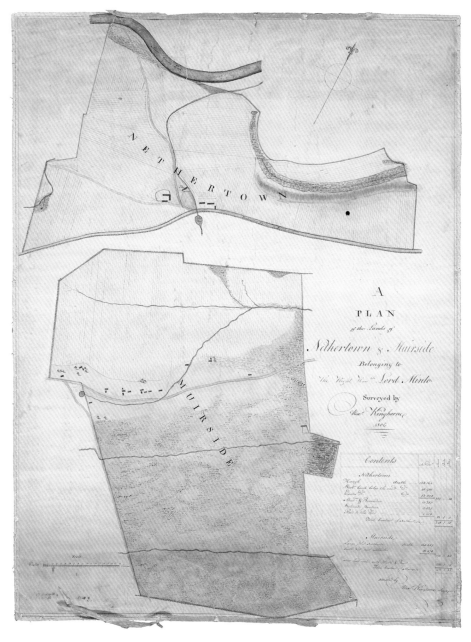

Figure 17. Plan of Netherton and Muirside (Melgrund Estate) by Alexander Kinghorne, 1806. [NRAS RHP 03634-00001]

Left: Figure 18. David Steuart Erskine, 11th Earl of Buchan, by John Finlayson (after Sir Joshua Reynolds, 1764) mezzotint published 1765. [National Portrait Gallery, London D893; licensed to author]

Below: Figure 19. Maxton Kirk. [Author's photograph, 2016]

Figure 20. Alexander Kinghorne's coat of arms, from Kinghorne Family Bible, Nowra Museum.
[Author's photograph, 2022]

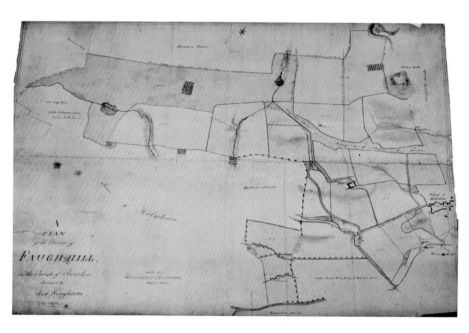

Figure 21. Plan of the farm of Faugh-hill, 1813, by Alexander Kinghorne. [Courtesy of the Duke of Roxburghe]

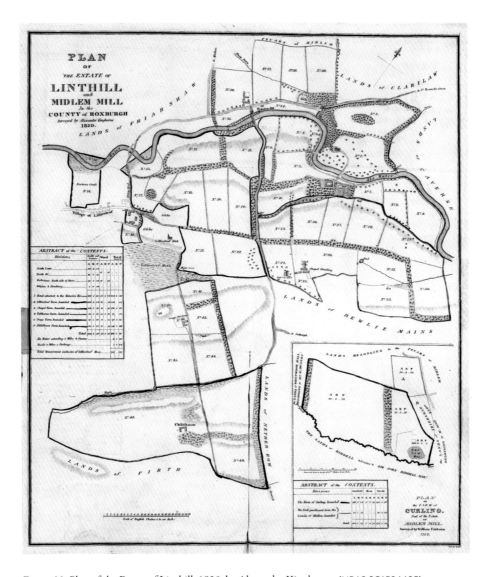

Figure 22. Plan of the Estate of Linthill, 1820, by Alexander Kinghorne. [NRAS SC1524405]

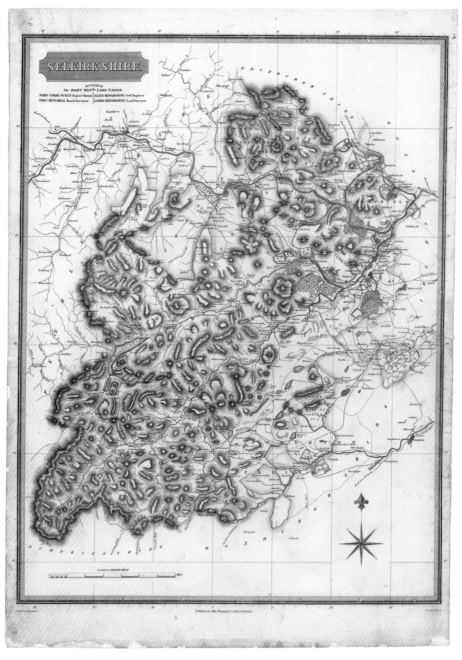

Figure 23. Plan of Selkirkshire; attested by Rt. Hon. Lord Napier, Thomas Mitchell, road surveyor, Alexander Kinghorne, civil engineer and James Kinghorne, land surveyor, Edinburgh: engraved by William Johnstone; Edinburgh: John Thomson & Co., 1824. [Author's collection]

To Mr Alexander Kinghorne, at St Boswells Farm

Dear Sir,

Your letter to me of the 21st current of which I send you
a copy for preservation afforded me great satisfaction,
and I will with chearfuley join in recommending your
petition to the Colonial Secretary of State along with
your other friends in this country who are particularly
acquainted with your character & abilities, which have
been known and esteemed by me for many years, and which
I am confident are truly deserving of countenance and
support. Buchan

Dryburgh Abbey December 28th 1822.

Dryburgh Abbey
July 29th 1823

Miss Kinghorn

I am happy to inform you
that My Lord has desired me to say
that Sir Walter Scott called this day
to inform his Lordship that
Lord Bathurst had ordered a
Grant of a Thousand acres
of Land for your Father. in
Austrailia.
I am Madam
your most Obt Ser
Ebenezer Faichney

have you had any letter from
your father

Above: Figure 24. Lord Buchan to Alexander Kinghorne, 28 December 1822. [Author's collection]

Left: Figure 25. Ebenezer Faichney, on behalf of Lord Buchan, to Elizabeth Kinghorne, 29 July 1823. [Author's collection]

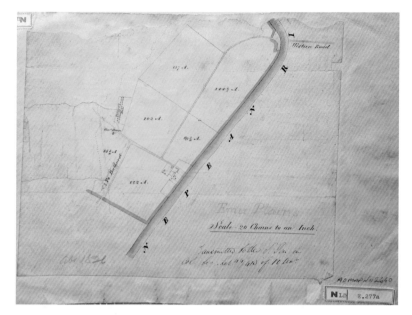

Figure 26. Map of Emu Plains Convict Farm by Alexander Kinghorne, 1826. [NSW State Archives, map 2660, Crown Plan E-277A]

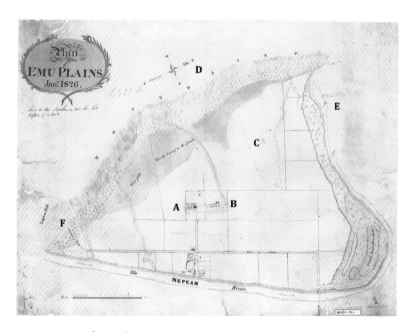

Figure 27. Map of Emu Plains Convict Farm by Alexander Kinghorne, 1826. The letters on the map indicate the approximate positions of (A) 'Government House', (B) convict huts, (C) Sydney-Bathurst Road, (D) Sydney-Bathurst Road zig-zag, (E) Alexander Kinghorne Jnr's Mill, (F) Old Bathurst Road. [NSW State Archives, map 2661, Crown Plan E-277B]

Figure 28. View of the Colonial Secretary's Residence, Sydney, by Conrad Martens, 1839. [State Library of NSW ML1618]

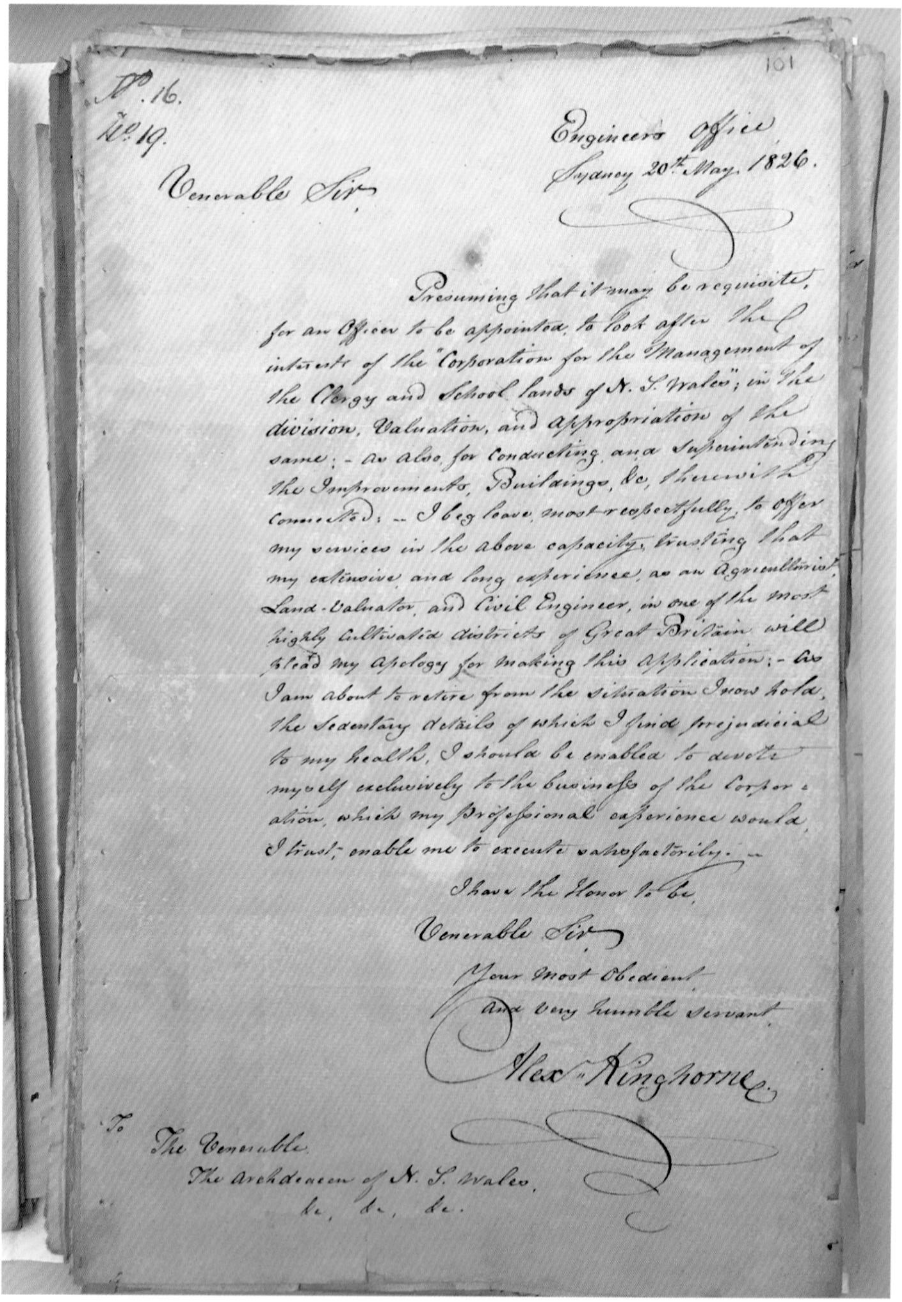

No. 16.
No. 19.

Engineers Office
Sydney 20th May 1826.

Venerable Sir,

Presuming that it may be requisite, for an Officer to be appointed, to look after the interests of the "Corporation for the Management of the Clergy and School Lands of N. S. Wales"; in the division, Valuation, and appropriation of the same; - as also for conducting and superintending the Improvements, Buildings, &c, therewith connected; – I beg leave most respectfully to offer my services in the above capacity, trusting that my extensive and long experience, as an Agriculturist, Land-Valuator, and Civil Engineer, in one of the most highly cultivated districts of Great Britain will plead my apology for making this application; - as I am about to retire from the situation I now hold, the sedentary details of which I find prejudicial to my health, I should be enabled to devote myself exclusively to the business of the Corporation, which my Professional experience would, I trust, enable me to execute satisfactorily. –

I have the Honor to be,
Venerable Sir,
Your most Obedient,
and very humble servant,
Alexr. Kinghorne

To
The Venerable
The Archdeacon of N. S. Wales,
&c, &c, &c.

Figure 29. Letter from Alexander Kinghorne to Archdeacon Thomas Hobbes Scott, 20 May 1826.
[NSW State Archives, 4/346, 101. 11]

Figure 30. Bonnyrigg House, Male Orphan School. [Author's photograph, 2015]

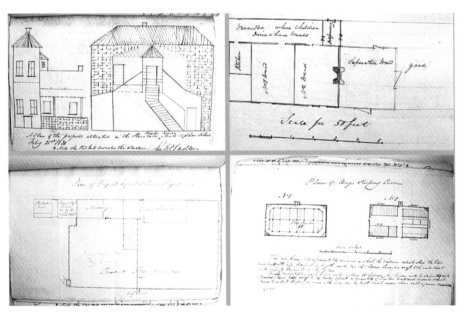

Figure 31. Copies of Plans for Male Orphan School buildings, Bonnyrigg, 1831, by Lieutenant Richard Sadlier. [Thorp, Bonnyrigg House, Plans 1 & 2: 148-9]

Figure 32. Drummond House, Terminus Street, Liverpool, ca 1960. [Op den Brouw, Glen, Town's First Fleet Power Couple, Liverpool City Champion, 1 April 2019]

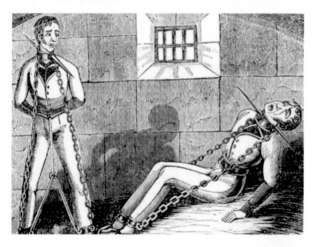

Figure 33. Cartoon of neck collar and irons worn by Privates Sudds and Thompson, 1826. [Hall, Refutation of Lieutenant-General Darling]

Figure 34. Large Cavern in the Wellington Valley. Engraving showing James Kinghorne and Thomas Mitchell in Cathedral Cavern, Wellington Caves, 1830. [Oldroyd, In the Footsteps of Thomas Livingstone Mitchell, 357]

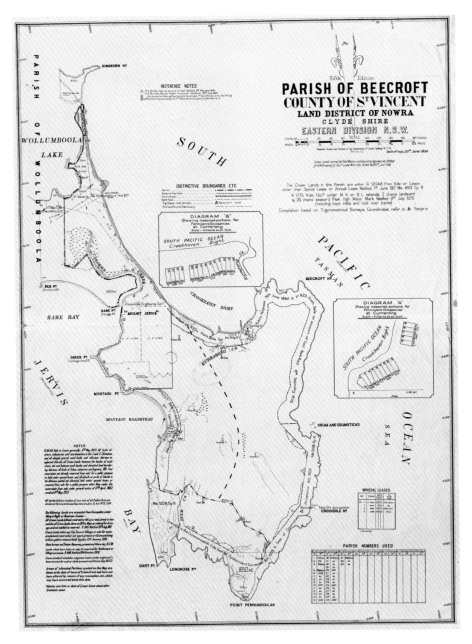

Figure 35. Map of the Parish of Beecroft, County of St Vincent, 1936. The boundary of Portion 1, Alexander Kinghorne's property Mount Jervis, is outlined in red. [State Library of NSW]

Figure 36. Montagu Point, adjacent to Mount Jervis, Jervis Bay, NSW. [Author's photograph, 2013]

Figure 37. View across Wollondilly River to Kippilaw, Goulburn, NSW. [Author's photograph, 2017]

Chapter 17

Superintendent, Emu Plains Convict Farm (1824–1825)

...a picture of comfort, regularity and discipline...
Sydney Gazette, Thursday 15 December 1825

The *Portland* came to anchor in Sydney on the balmy spring morning of Saturday 16 October, after a thirteen-day passage from Hobart Town. She remained docked at the King's wharf throughout the following two weeks while her 'valuable and extensive' cargo was unloaded.[1] James Kinghorne might have come to meet his family, whom he had not seen for more than three years. He had moved on from Emu Plains to Bathurst earlier in 1824, a journey of three to four days by horse from Sydney.[2] But he must have been anxious to greet his siblings – if not his father – to see how his brothers and sisters had grown in the intervening period and get the family settled.

The Kinghornes found temporary lodgings in Sydney, while Alexander made it his business to present himself and his letters of introduction to the Governor, Sir Thomas Brisbane. The Governor was expecting some of these letters: from his friend and Whig mentor Lord Buchan and the vice-regal father-in-law, Sir Henry Hay Mackdougall.[3] He would have been impressed by the letter from Sir Walter Scott, who two years earlier had become a baronet and entertained King George IV in Edinburgh. Scott was in the process of transforming the relationship of the monarchy with Scotland, and in so doing was one of the most influential men in Scotland, if not Britain; declared by the King '...The man in Scotland I most wish to see!'[4]

However, Alexander's letters were a mere formality, as his earlier groundwork ensured his recommendation to Brisbane by Earl Bathurst. His future was already in train. The position of Superintendent at the Emu Plains convict establishment had been allocated to him, the government notice of his appointment pre-dating his arrival in Sydney by five weeks.[5] James Kinghorne, previously Assistant Superintendent at Emu Plains in 1822, would have given the family full details of its location, function and history.

Alexander was entering what was perhaps the happiest period of his life, in which all his experience up to that point would bear fruit.

Over a century has passed since the artist Elioth Gruner visited Emu Plains and painted some of the most memorable evocations of rural life in the Sydney Basin, including *Morning Light* (1916) and *Spring Frost* (1919), both winners of the Wynne Prize. [6] Gruner's was an idyllic Australian landscape touched by the light of a sun which, a century before him, would have overwhelmed the senses of Alexander Kinghorne, used to the Scottish Borders and the vagaries of 'the weather'. It was also in Alexander's time an 'open' landscape, different in appearance to the Borders, little 'improved', but uncrowded by boundaries and pompous landowners. The scene today has changed considerably, with urbanisation across the high ground, seeking to avoid, not always successfully, the flood prone areas along the Nepean River, beautiful until it spills out and destroys people's homes and livelihoods. In Gruner's day urbanisation had scarce begun, and in Alexander's not at all. People who visited there in the 1970's might remember driving beyond the urban areas into open grasslands, on the old road that led to the mountains, which in turn held the memory of what the Europeans called 'The Emu Plains', roamed by distinctive Australian birds, and the aboriginal people whose ownership of this land stretched back tens of thousands of years.

This was the demesne over which Alexander would have oversight as Superintendent, but what would confront him in 1824 was a different scene again, because it was a hub of government-run industry. The convict-worked farm of two thousand acres had been in operation since 8 September 1819 when it was established by Governor Macquarie to cater for excesses of convicts arriving in the colony: those who could not be allocated to government construction, work gangs or free settlers.[7] The location of Emu Plains was strategic: west of the Nepean River, away from major settlements but close enough to the watercourse to benefit from its rich alluvial soil; and at the foot of Lapstone Hill, the beginning of the road across the Blue Mountains to the western counties of Westmoreland and

Roxburgh, and the plains beyond. Convicts, often sent directly to Emu Plains for training before re-assignment, arrived there on their way to and from more remote locations, such as the government establishments at Bathurst and Wellington Valley. Others remained at Emu Plains, as overseers, storekeepers, blacksmiths, butchers or clerks.

It was good land. Comparable terrain further north along the Hawkesbury River had been farmed since 1797 and found to be the best in the Colony to that point. By the time of Alexander's arrival the land at Emu Plains had been cleared and was increasing in production.

The Convict Farm was a major piece of government infrastructure, a staging point for the convicts, settlers, goods and stock travelling between Sydney, through Parramatta, across the closely located Nepean Ferry to Emu Plains and then on across the mountains to the west, or vice versa. The management of this facility would be a significant increase in responsibility compared with anything Alexander had experienced in the past.

Meeting James Chisholm Snr

Not long after his arrival in Sydney Town, Alexander Kinghorne made an accidental but most important acquaintance. As he walked along George Street he was 'accosted by an elderly Scotchman', James Chisholm Snr, who politely asked him the time of day. As they exchanged pleasantries it became clear that Chisholm and Kinghorne had something in common. Having established their Scottish heritage, they at once became 'favourably impressed' with each other; 'and after a little conversation on the street, Mr Kinghorne was invited by the other to partake of his hospitality'. The day must have passed pleasantly enough, but on returning home, Alexander was 'much concerned' at having been the guest of a person quite unknown to him. He 'feared he might have compromised his character by accepting hospitality from a convict'! Having made inquiries about James Chisholm, he was much relieved to find his newly acquired friend had never undergone a conviction and was 'in every way a respectable individual'.[8]

Despite his initial reservations, Alexander probably recognized the advantages of associating himself with such a prominent and influential citizen of the colony as James Chisholm. The two men became firm friends and played no small part in ensuring that their children had ample opportunities to meet.[9] The irony of Alexander's concerns is that James Chisholm had been regimental tailor to the New South Wales Corps until 1810. As Alexander himself was descended from a family of tailors, the two men shared the same origins.[10]

In the years ahead, Chisholm's townhouse in George Street, Sydney, would become a second home for Alexander, as he travelled between Emu Plains, Liverpool and Sydney on business.[11] Their friendship would be an important source of personal contacts for Alexander as he navigated the complexities of the colonial administration. More importantly, James Chisholm was a like-minded confidant for Alexander, not only sharing his cultural origins but, at a deeper level, his Presbyterian Christian faith.

Superintendent of the Emu Plains Convict Farm

Alexander and his family spent Christmas 1824 in Sydney. They travelled through Liverpool and arrived at the Emu Plains establishment on the afternoon of 29 December. James Kinghorne had been Assistant Superintendent under Peter Murdoch after his arrival in the colony and might have accompanied the family that day on his way back to Bathurst. However, the group who arrived and remained for the next year comprised Alexander and his sons Alexander Jnr (20) and John Ker (15), and daughters Isabella (13), Elizabeth (18) and Helen (then 27 years old).

The accommodation that awaited them was comfortable, particularly for a family of six. The building of 'Government House', as the Superintendent's house was called, had been commenced in 1820, on a site chosen by Governor Macquarie: a 'fine situation and commanding an extensive view of nearly the whole of the plains.'[12] By 1822 it had become a two-storey brick residence, comprising a total of eleven rooms, with special accommodation for the Governor when he visited. On the ground floor were two sitting rooms, two 'sleeping rooms', two servant's rooms and a pantry. As was usual for the times, the kitchen was detached at the rear, to avoid the risk of fire spreading to the main residence from the cooking fire. It had an associated storeroom and office. There were a further four rooms in the upper storey.[13]

The French naval explorer, Hyacinthe Yves Philippe Potentien, Baron de Bougainville (1781–1846), visited the Emu Plains establishment in

August 1825. He described the Superintendent's abode as 'the attractive residence of Mr Kinghorne' and 'a fine house surrounded by an attractive fence and gardens.' This must have been a comfortable and welcome sight to the three Kinghorne daughters when they arrived from the relative squalor of Sydney.[14]

Most of the other infrastructure at the Emu Plains farm had been established by the first Superintendent, Richard Fitzgerald, from 1819. This included a commissariat store, near the river for convenient movement of stock and provisions, a sturdy cabin, stables and stockyards, and log huts with bark walls, each holding eight to ten people. By 1825, these huts provided accommodation for nearly five hundred convicts. They were located on a hill about half a mile from the river, lining a single street, some with their own gardens, along with a bakery, tobacco factory and barracks for six soldiers.[15] About half a mile north from these huts was a smaller cabin, labelled 'accommodation for invalids & idiots'. Later, other separate houses allowed for the accommodation of the storekeeper and principal overseer. The military detachment of twenty-one soldiers had their own barracks and guardhouse, and there was a small gaol and a hospital. There was also a kitchen garden, granary and store, and two barns with lofts for storage of produce. Several crops were under production, including tobacco, wheat, maize, potatoes, turnips, peas and beans.[16]

Alexander Kinghorne's arrival heralded a distinct change in culture at Emu Plains. The previous Superintendent, Peter Murdoch, operated in a climate of fear, where the emphasis was on convict punishment, rather than reform, which suited his style of management.[17] He had been joined by James Kinghorne as Assistant Superintendent on 1 June 1822. James was the only other freeman on staff who might have been influenced by Murdoch's style. Unlike his father, James was described by his superior as 'a rigid disciplinarian', based on his successful control of the convicts sent there to break their 'improper connections'. He had direct supervision of the principal overseer, Joseph Peters, with whom he had an excellent relationship.

Peters, from Birmingham, had been convicted at Warwick Assizes on 25 July 1818 and sentenced to seven years transportation. He arrived in Sydney on the *Granada* in 1819 when he was about 21 years of age, although his convict records provide various estimates of his birth date between 1798 and 1802, suggesting he probably did not know his age. He had been a skilled artisan, described as a 'Tortoise Shell Worker' and proved a very adept manager of workmen and agriculture. He was appointed to Emu Plains in 1820, soon after his arrival, as he claimed to have worked out his sentence by 1825. In that year, supported by Alexander, he submitted a memorial to the Governor, requesting his freedom, which was granted on 28 July 1825. Peters was later to work for James and John Ker Kinghorne as overseer at their father's properties, Cardross and Maxton, near Goulburn.[18]

James Kinghorne resigned as Assistant Superintendent in January 1824 to manage Thomas Icely's newly acquired Saltram Estate at Bathurst.[19] Lorraine Stacker, in her book, *Chained to the Soil on the Plains of Emu*, suggests the relationship between Murdoch and James Kinghorne, who shared accommodation at the Superintendent's residence, 'appeared amiable and loyal'. But James 'was…not totally satisfied with his position, choosing to move on and further his managerial and administrative experience'.[20] Whatever his motives, James was to become the main developer of the family's pastoral estates after his father returned to Scotland in 1840.[21]

Commission of Enquiry into Prostitution at Emu Plains

A number of women convicts were assigned to Emu Plains while James Kinghorne was Assistant Superintendent. This was to relieve pressure on the Female Factory at Parramatta, which had become 'extremely crowded' with the many new female convicts arriving in the colony. The first consignment of 25 women arrived at Emu Plains in May 1822, with instructions from Governor Brisbane that they were to undertake light duties and be kept separate from the male convicts.[22] The administration was criticised for sending female convicts to Emu Plains, but Brisbane had a high opinion of Peter Murdoch and believed he could keep things under control. The Governor believed that the women would be properly and appropriately cared for, and his personal and regular inspections of the establishment gave him no reason to believe otherwise.[23]

While Brisbane's purpose was founded upon a desire to employ the women productively, the aspiration forbidding contact between the male and female convicts was wishful thinking. In May 1823, Rev'd Henry

Fulton, the minister at Castlereagh, informed the Colonial Secretary of 4 convicts at Emu Plains, all overseers in charge of the women, who wished to marry.[24] While marriage among convicts was encouraged, any sexual relations outside the sanctity of wedlock was regarded as prostitution on the part of the women.[25]

In 1824, a damaging letter was published in the London newspapers, reporting the immoral and improper use of convict women at Emu Plains, and implying that prostitution was rampant. It added 'that, in consequence of the promiscuous intercourse and prostitution existing among the females at Emu Plains, many of the men there had become diseased with the Venereal'. Under growing criticism, Brisbane was forced to establish a commission of inquiry in 1825, not long before the end of his governorship, to which James Kinghorne was recalled from Bathurst as a witness.[26]

The commission members – Lieutenant Governor William Stewart, John Stephen, Solicitor General and Rev'd William Cowper, Senior Assistant Chaplain – were to determine the veracity of the report 'which had been widely circulated and which was very injurious to the character of the government...in regard to sending women to Emu Plains for impure purposes...'[27] They interviewed 11 witnesses, including Dr West, the surgeon attending Emu Plains, Dr Henry Gratton Douglass, the Medical Superintendent of the Female Factory at Parramatta, and from Emu Plains, Peter Murdoch, James Kinghorne and the Principal Overseer Joseph Peters.

James Kinghorne gave evidence that the women were separately housed, about a mile distant from the male huts, that the men and women at Emu Plains had been worked separately and that the Governor's orders 'not to permit any illicit intercourse' between them had been strictly adhered to. He provided minute details, later confirmed by Joseph Peters, on how this was achieved using random musters, nightly observations and activities strictly timed by the ringing of a bell! He reported that he 'never received or ever heard of any orders to permit any intercourse between the men and women; on the contrary, [he] had strict orders to prevent it.'[28]

Despite James' assurances to the contrary, Murdoch revealed under questioning that 'absentees from the women's huts occurred occasionally.' He actually expressed his surprise that, with so many male and female convicts present, they 'had shewn so little desire to counteract my Orders, and meet together for illicit intercourse.' Joseph Peters further stated that 'almost all the women, who did visit the men contrary to orders, were afterwards married to the men whom they respectively visited'; Peters' own wife, Mary Robinson, was punished for this offence, with him, and was sent back to the Female Factory pregnant! [29]

Interestingly, James Kinghorne revealed under questioning that, at the time of his departure from Emu Plains, 'there was only one woman remaining there unmarried of the original number'.[30] It is difficult to imagine how these marriages came about without some meeting between the male and female inmates, even though some of the husbands were overseers!

The commission's report noted that, out of 32 females sent to Emu Plains, 24 had been married to 'Constables, Overseers and other Persons, with whom they now live[d] in comfort…[having] formed an intimacy [with them] at Emu Plains'.[31] Governor Brisbane reported to Lord Bathurst that the 'whole charge of women being improperly sent' to Emu Plains was 'a cool, deliberate and most outrageous misstatement of the facts…'[32] Despite the findings of innocence, the evidence showed that some of the men and women at Emu Plains had 'formed an intimacy' – in fact they had been 'found in bed' together – and had become betrothed and married.[33] This was not prostitution. Rather, it was an expected and natural consequence of their presence at the same establishment, regardless of Brisbane's protestations to Earl Bathurst that his policy of separation was effective. An almost Shakespearean Comedy. Ah, Cupid, and his swift arrows!

Comfort, Regularity and Discipline

The first and second Superintendents at Emu Plains, Richard Fitzgerald and Peter Murdoch had, over five years, established an effective agricultural establishment that was economically productive and assisted the government with its administration of convicts. Both Superintendents had worked well with their government administrations, under Macquarie and Brisbane, respectively. Brisbane reported to Earl Bathurst that, despite shortages elsewhere, the establishment 'yields a surplus, which has been gradually increasing and will no doubt, in a few more years, afford a considerable public revenue'.[34] The following five years would highlight the contrasting styles of both the Brisbane and Darling administrations, and of the next two Superintendents, Alexander and James Kinghorne.

Alexander was to remain just twelve months as Superintendent. Nevertheless, Emu Plains flourished under his administration and exhibited 'a picture of comfort, regularity and discipline'. For his part, Brisbane was impressed with Alexander's management of the farm, and particularly its inmates, for it turned an 'idle disorderly vagabond...[into] a regular industrious servant'.[35]

With the arrival of Alexander's daughters and sons, the Superintendent's household presented a picture of wholesome family life not seen before at the establishment. This was reflected in Alexander's style, which Lorraine Stacker has described as a fundamental change of focus: away from discipline and brutality, towards 'compassion and loyalty not only towards the farm but also to the convicts in their charge'. In accord with government policy, convicts were under 'correction' at Emu Plains, but they were also being retrained with the skills they would most need for the rest of their lives.[36]

Hyacinthe de Bougainville, at the time of his visit to Emu Plains on 8 August 1825, noted that 'the convicts appeared to be as happy as their condition would permit and well-disciplined'. His notebook and published account are revealing of Alexander's management style:

> ...the [200] convicts lined up in front of the door [of Alexander's house] and a clerk read prayers aloud for quarter of an hour. The convicts listened bare-headed and with the most decorous attitude; they were quite well-dressed, seemed to be in good health but I did not see a single face that was remotely distinguished...[their] good health...said a lot for their treatment here and the salubrious climate...The settlement of Emu Plains seemed to me well-organised in every respect and is managed by a very enterprising and knowledgeable man. The convicts appeared to be as happy as their condition would permit and well-disciplined...Unaccustomed to agricultural work and far from strong, they had failed to find employment on the settlers' properties. The results of the experiment have confirmed that they could still be put to good use, and the large property at Emu Plains, developed over such a short period of time by inexperienced workers under the supervision of talented managers, will serve as a model for any similar establishment.[37]

The convicts were required to attend regular church parades and services, reflecting both government policy and the importance which Alexander placed on their spiritual salvation. Their dress and good health were the consequence of Alexander's care for the physical man as well as the reform of his character. Bougainville's glowing report, certainly reflecting Governor Brisbane and Alexander's words, nevertheless provides an independent picture of 'comfort, regularity and discipline' that characterised the year of Alexander's superintendence.

A Good Deed by the Governor's Noble Guest

One of the convicts Bougainville met that day is worthy of further comment. Among those lined up for prayers outside Alexander's house was 'a 25-year-old Frenchman named Théodore Constantini' (or Costantini).[38] The convict record reveals the Parisian-born Constantini was tried and found guilty at the Old Bailey of 'larceny in a dwelling house' and sentenced to life at the Old Bailey on 23 October 1822, although his sentence was commuted to seven years transportation. Constantini ended up at Emu Plains in 1825, presumably after some misdemeanour at Bathurst where he had been assigned to T.H. Hawkins.[39]

Alexander was interested in and had encouraged his artistic talent.[40] On introduction, Constantini explained to Bougainville that he had been 'deported from London because of his excessive passion for a local woman', an unlikely story given the official record, but one that appealed to the romantic French aristocrat. He asked Bougainville 'to intercede on his behalf with the governor'. Bougainville wrote in his notebook that the prisoner's 'good behaviour since his arrival here convinced me to pledge my support for him...He is a fine young man with a pleasant face and was deported for rape, having made excessively amorous advances to the wife of a greengrocer'. On speaking to the Governor six days later, 'Brisbane promised to gather information about him'. Constantini was pardoned just ten days later and embarked for England on 30 August aboard the *Mariner*.[41] His good fortune was short-lived. By 1827, the hapless Frenchman was in trouble again, this time for theft, and was transported again for seven years to Van Diemen's Land, ending up at Macquarie Harbour in January 1828.[42]

Despite his felonious habits, Constantini made positive contributions to Tasmania's colonial history through his artwork: his pen-and-ink and watercolour landscapes of the settlements at Macquarie Harbour and, later (1831–33), Port Arthur.[43] Famed later for his portraits, he was, in a small way, influenced by his associations with the Kinghorne family: first, through the recognition of his talents by Alexander, who assisted him obtain his pardon through the auspices of Baron de Bougainville; and secondly, through his association with Alexander's son, William Kinghorne, a captain in the Colonial Marine of Van Diemen's Land. William likely transported him from Hobart to Macquarie Harbour on the *Prince Leopold* in January 1828, and certainly did so to Port Arthur, either on the same vessel or, after April 1831, the *Isabella*.[44] In Port Arthur, Constantini was mentored by William Kinghorne's friend, the Commissariat Officer Thomas Lempriere, also a French speaker and an accomplished artist. While guilty of further misdemeanours at Port Arthur, Constantini later settled in mainland Tasmania where he remained an artist of naïve watercolour portraits and landscapes.[45]

Management and General Operations at Emu Plains

Alexander Kinghorne inherited several existing senior staff with his appointment at Emu Plains. Among the 200 employees was John Stewart, Assistant Superintendent, Joseph Peters, who remained as principal overseer, James Scott the storekeeper, and Christopher Dodding, the experienced overseer of the tobacco gangs.[46] This staff was a significant responsibility for a man with an equivocal track record in the management of farm workers in Scotland. However, at Emu Plains his style was clearly suited to the personnel structure. He did not directly supervise most of the workforce, as this responsibility fell largely to John Stewart through his various overseers. So, Alexander's leadership was more directed at setting the tone and character of the establishment, liaison with the government administration and relaying the orders he regularly received through the Colonial Secretary.

Emu Plains became, under Alexander, an important intermediate station between Sydney and the western establishments at Bathurst and Wellington Valley.[47] With this expanded role came the responsibility for transiting stock and supplies to the gangs working on land clearing and the upgrading of roads. Alexander, as Superintendent, had to supply

James Scott with the correct number of men, convicts and employees, who required daily rations. Scott, as a commissariat officer, was somewhat independent of Alexander. He worked with the commissariats at Sydney, Parramatta and Windsor, his responsibilities having to tie in with requirements elsewhere, including to the west: a major logistical exercise.

The farm had its own livestock, mainly horned cattle, and of course crops for its ration requirements (see Figure 26), but also supplied meat, grain and other produce to convict gangs, their military escorts and into the other commissariat stores. Each month, Alexander sent returns of the establishment to the Colonial Secretary, detailing staff, convicts and stock. Rations supplied to convict gangs and other establishments were also included, and the returns had to be counter-signed and verified by the Assistant Superintendent.[48]

Alexander Kinghorne Junior's Flour Mill

The production of flour was of paramount importance for the convict population and staff at Emu Plains. Among other rations, each convict received ten pounds of flour per week, which had to be obtained by the storekeeper from the commissariat's sources.

On 24 March 1825, Governor Brisbane informed Under Secretary Horton that a 'compact bed of Millstone' had been discovered at Cox's River, about fifty miles west of Emu Plains.[49] Two of these granite stones were to be tried out for grinding flour at Emu Plains. Hyacinthe de Bougainville wrote that the stones had been discovered by Alexander Kinghorne Snr, while prospecting for mineral samples, which was his hobby.[50] Alternatively, Lorraine Stacker suggests that the discovery had been made by Alexander Kinghorne Jnr, who had trained as a millwright, along with his brother Andrew Seton, in Galashiels.[51]

There is no evidence that the young Alexander was constructing a mill at Emu Plains at this time, as tenders were still being called for 'persons desirous of undertaking to grind and dress wheat and maize' for that establishment at the end of the year.[52] However, he *was* practising his trade at a very close geographical site, having constructed a new flour mill for William Bowman at Castlereagh. This mill, right across the river from the Emu Plains tobacco field and a few miles downstream from the ford at 'Bird's Eye Corner', was known as Jackson's Mill after Alexander

184

Jnr sold the mill to Jackson.[53] The mill remained in operation until the 1860s.[54] It is depicted on the map of Emu Plains, produced by Alexander Kinghorne Snr in 1826, located across the river at Castlereagh, marked 'New Grinding Mill, Alex^r Kinghorne Junr' (see Figure 27).[55] Alexander Jnr was to build further flour mills in New South Wales, including at the family properties of Cardross, near Goulburn, Raineville and St Boswells, on the Fish River near Bathurst, and also at Holwood, Blayney.[56]

The Emu Theatre

Alexander Kinghorne's superintendence of Emu Plains was marked by social change and stability, influenced by his refined tastes and his willingness to encourage the reform of its convict inhabitants.

Early in his tenure, he was approached by a group of unknown convicts, who suggested the construction of a theatre and the performance of plays; Alexander approved the idea and allowed them to build a rough bark auditorium. It had a ramshackle appearance, prompting Hyacinthe de Bougainville to comment: 'the theatre of Bobèche [alias Mardelard, a contemporary French clown and wit] would seem like the Paris Opera' in comparison. He also noted that the theatre had 'caused quite a stir in the colony…Much ado about nothing'.[57] The Sydney press, however, hailed the project as providing convicts with 'a congenial relief from the rigours of compulsory servitude [and] an agreeable mode of beguiling their leisure hours, which might otherwise hang very heavy on their hands'.

The first performances, held on 16 May 1825, were *Barissa or the Hermit Robber*, *The Farce of the Mock Doctor: or The Dumb Lady Cured*, and the favourite *Bombasters Furioso*.[58] *The Australian* newspaper complained, tongue-in-cheek, that the 'Emu Theatre' had created 'a greater variety of pleasure and entertainment in the Bush than in Sydney…[leaving] us of the town far behind in the powers of invention, and in the art of pleasing'.[59] Similarly, 'A Lover of Rational Pleasures', writing to the Editor of the *Sydney Gazette*, pointed out that it was 'rather mortifying…to the lovers of drama, in this metropolis, where is to be found the concentration of our colonial respectability and gaity, that in this species of fashionable entertainment, the amateurs of Emu Plains have taken the lead of them'.[60] While the Emu Plains productions were probably quite amateurish, the chosen plays were mainly popular contemporary farces, by the likes of

Fielding and Garrick, which had completed successful runs in the London west end theatres.

Further performances were held in July of the mock-heroic farces *Bombasters Furioso* and *The Lying Valet*.[61] Local dignitaries honoured the performers by their presence. They included Alexander himself, along with two of his daughters and Alexander Jnr, the Blaxlands, George Cox and his wife, Henry Cox, Mr and Mrs McHenry, and the neighbours over the river in Castlereagh, Sir John Jamison and his son. Jamison pompously showered benefactions on the performers, donating a ten-pound note to the company. Further visitors from Sydney began to attend the regular performances, paying a 'dump' entry price.[62]

After Baron de Bougainville first visited Emu Plains, he received a personal invitation, written by Alexander on 'a fine poster' in French, 'asking [him] to name a day for a gala performance in the theatre'. Bougainville asked one of his companions to reply in English, 'which he [could] write correctly', indicating that his company would attend the following Saturday 13 August. That Saturday evening Bougainville and his colleagues, who for the past five days had been exploring the lower Blue Mountains and Hawkesbury regions, returned to Emu Plains, and dined with the Kinghornes. After dinner, at 6.30 pm, they took their seats in the theatre, 'alone in one box in the front row of the stalls', apart from five soldiers and two ladies.[63]

In his notebook, Bougainville wrote that the 'prologue in verse was recited by a small man with a ghastly face', whom he thought was the director of the company. They watched performances of *The Lying Valet*, *The Village Doctor* (based on *Médecin malgré lui* by Molière)[64] and *Bombasters Furioso*. The former play starred two convicts, dressed as women, who 'made us laugh until we cried' and the Molière play incorporated an English dance accompanied by a tune played 'at a frenetic pace and with great gusto on a violin which formed the entire orchestra'. Bougainville described the last play as 'a gibberish farce that was completely baffling'.

Despite his bewilderment, Bougainville apparently enjoyed the performance and, characteristically, the company of Alexander's daughters at 9 pm after the performance, whom he described as 'very pretty'.[65] The French mariner's wandering eye fell on many attractive young ladies of the right social class, including Sir John Blaxland's three 'pretty daughters'. He continued an ongoing infatuation, if not passionate love affair, with Harriot, Blaxland's eldest daughter, who was married to the Calcutta merchant Alexander Ritchie.[66] Fortunately for Helen and Isabella Kinghorne, Harriot Ritchie, being at the peak of Sydney's social stratum, was even more attractive to the romantic Frenchman than they were. Bougainville departed Sydney with his two ships on 24 September 1825, lamenting his fleeting affair with his Sydney paramour.[67]

Thespian activities did not outlast Alexander's term as Superintendent. Governor Darling put a stop to the 'Emu Theatre' in 1826. This was not an isolated dislike of theatricals. In 1828, he refused the application of Barnett Levey to open a theatre at the rear of his property in George Street, believing that such an entertainment operated by a man of the 'lowest class' would attract an audience of undesirable elements that would be a detriment to public order.[68] As for the Emu Theatre, Darling had no interest in offering any form of leniency or positive reformation to convicts, favouring appropriate punishment and discipline as the only means of rehabilitation.[69]

The Land Board of Van Diemen's Land and the Demise of New Brighton

The plans Alexander had developed for the removal of the capital of Van Diemen's Land from Hobart to New Brighton had remained in his mind as a key claim to his advancement in the Colony. The prospect of being involved in the development of a new city seemed a considerable enhancement of his fame as a civil engineer – the sort of fame enjoyed by Telford and Rennie. Accordingly, William had been placed on watch for any senior government opportunities that might be of interest to his father or brothers.

On 2 June 1825 an article appeared in the *Sydney Gazette* reprinted from the *Hobart Town Gazette*, stating the removal of government had been 'postponed', and referring to 'A long report, written by a Mr. KINGHORNE, to the Lieutenant Governor, strongly recommending this removal was produced; in which it was stated, that water in abundance for 20,000 persons could be obtained at Brighton at all seasons; that there was plenty of fuel as well as all the necessary building materials, and that it possessed all the requisites for a great and splendid Town.' The article went on to describe Arthur's ambivalence towards the project, still playing off one faction against another. [70]

Stung into action by the prospect of his project being shelved, Alexander wrote to Governor Brisbane on 12 June 1825, requesting consideration 'as a candidate', having been informed by William of a vacancy on the Valuation Board of Van Diemen's Land. He reminded His Excellency of his 'education and long experience, as an Agriculturalist and Land Valuer, in one of the most improved districts of Great Britain:– and that [his] extensive practice, as a Civil Engineer, and Surveyor, enable[d] [him] to know and appreciate the local advantages and disadvantages attending lands in every situation'. He further reminded the Governor of the original letters of introduction presented on the arrival of the Kinghorne family in Sydney, and of his work on the survey of New Brighton for Lieutenant-Governor Arthur, whom he felt sure would concur with his appointment 'provided your excellency would be pleased to nominate me as a commissioner'.[71] Such a posting would have been a step down the ladder from Emu Plains, and indicates his view of New Brighton as his flagship project.

However, Governor Brisbane was not pleased at the prospect of losing his Superintendent at Emu Plains. Moreover, the decision had been made, although not yet officially, to abandon any move of the capital from Hobart to Brighton, as suggested in both the *Sydney* and *Hobart Town Gazettes* on 16 June.

> Colonel Arthur, therefore, in order to obey the instructions with which he was invested, as soon as practicable, commissioned Mr. Kinghorne, Civil Engineer, to examine, survey, and report upon the capabilities or incapabilities of Brighton, as the site of a town, and of the future capital of the sister Colony…From September till April the Civil Engineer's Report lay dormant-His Honor hereby evincing, although his instructions were positive (the reasonableness of which he could not doubt when taken in an enlarged political view), that tardiness and deliberation which the present interests of the Hobart Town residents most unquestionably demanded.[72]

The *Sydney Gazette* reprinted the original letter from Colonel Arthur, commissioning Alexander to survey New Brighton, as well as his report of 20 September 1824. In a thinly veiled attempt at obfuscation, the newspaper revealed that the decision against moving the capital had been made by Brisbane, and not Arthur. They further suggested that the idea for the move to Brighton originated with the 'Honourable the late Commissioner of Enquiry' [Thomas Bigge], and that the policy would have been transmitted as an order to Brisbane from Earl Bathurst. While Commissioner Bigge's recommendation to establish Van Diemen's Land as a separate colony was later implemented, this particular hypercritical detail, the removal of the seat of government to 'an inland spot, where, from its more central position, it would unavoidably tend to facilitate the views of the Executive Authorities, and ensure that greatness to which these Colonists already aspire', was neither favoured nor supported by Governor Brisbane.[73]

The demise of the government move to Brighton, and later New Norfolk, was fully disclosed in an article which appeared in the *Colonial Times* a year later:

> For months, the removal to Brighton was fixed, we may say decreed by the laws of the Medes and Persians, Surveyors, Assistant Surveyors, Engineers, Brickmakers, and Workmen out of number, were sent to Brighton. Plans for Government-houses, Churches, Courthouse, Gaol, Factories, &c. &c. were submitted and decided upon, and land bought for Wharfs, to the extent of near £1000. When all on a sudden, the line of operations are changed and New Norfolk became the scene of action, and by the touch of the Magician's wand, the Capital is removed from Brighton to New Norfolk, the fine Aqueducts, Reservoirs, and Squares of Mr Kinghorne, all vanish.[74]

Alexander's flagship project had turned into mockery of him, the 'Government-houses, Churches, Courthouse, Gaol, Factories…the fine Aqueducts, Reservoirs, and Squares of Mr Kinghorne, all vanish.'

The Map of Emu Plains

Two plans of the Emu Plains Establishment, drawn up by Alexander Kinghorne and dated January 1826, are held in the State Archives of New South Wales (Figures 26 and 27). They were based on surveys and earlier drafts undertaken in 1825, while Alexander was Superintendent. The maps are of historical importance, not only for their record of the buildings and agricultural activities at Emu Plains, but as a snapshot of the nearby topography, features and roadworks associated with the crossing of the Blue Mountains.

189

Plan E227A (Figure 26) is a detail (20 chains to the inch) showing the layout and areas (in acres) of paddocks, and the locations of structures adjacent to the Nepean River between Emu Ferry and the intersection of the main Western Road. The intersections of Western and Bathurst Roads are clearly shown, together with the locations of 'Government House', the prisoners' huts and, to the east, the commissariat stores adjacent to the river.[75]

Plan E227B (Figure 27) is a larger-scale map of the entire establishment, showing the full extent of the Sydney-Bathurst Road, Lapstone Hill, the buildings and other infrastructure on the farm, the various paddock divisions (without acreage), and including a detailed survey and drawing of the course of the Nepean River and its associated sand and gravel banks.

The map was annotated in pencil to indicate further features. These include the produce grown in each paddock, the line of the new Bathurst Road under construction, and the location of the grinding mill constructed by Alexander Kinghorne Jnr (later Jackson's Mill) on the northern side of the river. Lorraine Stacker believes these pencil additions were made by James Kinghorne in November 1827, when he was Superintendent.[76] An addendum to both maps in red, not in the hand of Alexander Kinghorne, indicates that they were 'transmitted to the Surveyor General and Colonial Secretary 44/413 of 10 Decr'. James Kinghorne reported, in his correspondence with the Colonial Secretary, that a plan of the farm, drawn up by his father, was still in his father's possession, suggesting that this annotated date is likely December 1827.[77] Lorraine Stacker has pointed out the importance of the annotated plan in providing the earliest confirmation of the various crops, structures and roads on the farm.

Plan E227B shows the position of the Old Bathurst Road, which conforms well with its location in present day Emu Plains (2022). It reveals the road passing through the farm and immediately ascending Lapstone Hill. The ascent of the Lapstone monocline, close to the crossing of the Nepean River at Emu Plains, had been a challenge to all road builders, but especially to the surveyors and convict gangs seeking to make a viable dray road to Bathurst over the mountains. Cox and Evans chose the southerly route in 1814, which attained the level ridge at Blaxland near the site of the future Pilgrim Inn. This part of Cox's Road had always been hard to maintain in trafficable order.[78] In 1826, when traffic over the mountains was increasing, a radically different route was created, starting and ending at the same places, but lying much farther to the north and pursuing straighter line, as can be seen on Alexander's map.

This new road, now called the Old Bathurst Road, was constructed in 1826 by convict labour under the direction of William Dumaresq, as inspector of roads and bridges.[79] In April 1826, *The Australian* reported that he had marked out another line for the crossing of the mountains, specifically mentioning Mount York and Mount Blaxland, but Dumaresq likely also laid out the new ascent of Lapstone Hill at this time. The new road was completed by the end of 1826. It is clearly marked as the new 'zig zag' on Alexander's map of Emu Plains (Figure 27). Despite its steepness and a series of very sharp bends, supported by high retaining walls, it was a significant improvement over the previous route.

* * *

In all, Alexander's time at Emu Plains appears to have been happy, a stark contrast with the darkness and impasse of his departure from Scotland. He had arrived in a new country, with his family all but intact. His letters of introduction from carefully cultivated patrons had quickly raised him to some prominence in colonial society, without the constraints of the class system in Scotland. They assured him of an excellent position, with authority over many. He and his family were comfortably accommodated in 'Government House' which, after all, was what they called the Governor's big house in Sydney. He had a comfortable relationship with Sir Thomas Brisbane, the highest person of the land, entertained foreign nobility in his own accommodations, such as Hyacinthe de Bougainville, and made important connections and friends in colonial society, James Chisholm Snr not the least. His children settled to their respective new roles: his sons either had good positions, or every prospect. He had undertaken a significant commission planning a city in Van Diemen's Land, which would assure him lasting fame. (This did not start unravelling until the following year.)

His first land grant was in the pipeline, promised by the colonial authorities, and with every expectation of delivery. The granting of this would immediately confer a status Alexander longed for, that of a landed gentleman. The ambitions and hopes of his life had every prospect of a brilliant resolution.

Lorraine Stacker has described Alexander Kinghorne at Emu Plains as 'a kindly, proud man who was respected by his peers as well as the convicts with whom he dealt. He was neither a harsh disciplinarian nor a brutal man and showed considerable compassion and understanding for the convicts and their circumstances'.[80] It is a worthy thing that he should be remembered thus after only a year's tenure. The character of his regime would be continued by his son, James, and both influenced many convicts to emerge from their sentences and make their lives and families in New South Wales. Of all, this might be Alexander's finest achievement.

During the year that Alexander was Superintendent, he managed the productivity and growth of the convict farm to the highest satisfaction of the Governor. Despite the instructions received by Brisbane from Earl Bathurst to close all government farms in the County of Cumberland, he was determined to defend the two jewels in his government farming crown: Grose Farm and Emu Plains. Brisbane understood the value of the latter as a producer of grain and produce for the supply of the colony, and as a buffer against hard times and the price-controlling activities of some private farmers. Moreover, as he wrote to Bathurst, Emu Plains was 'the best School of Reform in the colony' where 'many an idle, disorderly vagabond…[had been transformed into] a regular industrious servant'. Along with taking up surplus convicts in the system, it had a 'far better and more permanent effect than all the scourgings or lessons of morality in the world could produce'. Under Alexander Kinghorne's light and even-handed management, Emu Plains never waned in Brisbane's esteem as one of the most valuable assets within the colonial service.[81]

Unfortunately, the colonial government's high opinion of Alexander's ability was to be short-lived, as the liberal and delegatory style of Sir Thomas Brisbane was soon to be replaced by the austere and conservative administration of a new Governor, Lieutenant-General Ralph Darling.

Chapter 18

The Colonial Civil Engineer (1825–1828)

I have selected an experienced and scientific person as Civil Engineer.
Lieut. General Ralph Darling, February 1826

On 7 December 1825, six days after the end of Sir Thomas Brisbane's term as Governor, Major John Ovens died.[1] Ovens was a veteran of the Peninsular War, where he had served under then Brigadier-General Brisbane as his aide-de-camp. He came to New South Wales in 1821 with the newly appointed Governor, who made him colonial Civil Engineer. Part of his responsibility in this role was the allocation and supervision of convict gangs. He also acted on occasion as the Governor's private secretary and was ordered to undertake two exploratory expeditions, with Mark Currie to the Monaro and with John Oxley to Twofold Bay.[2] He was indeed a confidante of Sir Thomas Brisbane.

On the departure of Governor Brisbane, Lieutenant-Governor William Stewart became the administrator of the colony for the interim of eighteen days until the arrival of the new Governor, Lieutenant-General Ralph Darling. Stewart had already had dealings with Alexander Kinghorne out at Emu Plains over the local operation of the postal service,[3] and was familiar with his qualifications and background, or Alexander had made sure that he was.

In the closing days of Brisbane's administration, Stewart fulfilled some earlier promises to Alexander: formalising his land grant of two thousand acres in the county of Argyll and appointing him Justice of the Peace.[4] Four days before Darling arrived, the *Sydney Gazette* provided a favourable report on the 'most flourishing condition' of 'the Establishment at Emu Plains, under the Superintendence of Mr. Kinghorne…[it] exhibits a picture of comfort, regularity, and discipline, which reflect the highest credit upon [his] zeal and ability.' The source of this report was described as 'a high official quarter'.[5] It might have been William Stewart, or it might have been Alexander himself, according to his former practice of ensuring the publication of his achievements.[6]

During his earlier tenure as Lieutenant-Governor, Stewart had been interested in the proper regulation of the postal service and the formation of a mounted police force. Now, as acting Governor, he was able to make some decisions on these issues.[7] Notably, he created 'Stewart's Mounted Police', fixed the postal rates and recommended to the oncoming Governor that Alexander Kinghorne should be appointed postmaster at Emu Plains.[8]

Darling arrived to take up the reins of government on 19 December 1826. He had married Eliza Dumaresq while acting Governor of Mauritius and brought his wife and brothers-in-law, Henry, Edward and William, with him to Australia. Henry Dumaresq had been Darling's private secretary in Mauritius and continued as such in New South Wales, arriving in Sydney earlier than the Darlings, in October 1825, to make arrangements for their occupation of Government House.[9] Edward accompanied the Darlings to Australia but remained in Van Diemen's Land. Captain William Dumaresq, who came on to Sydney with the Darlings, was an experienced military engineer, having served in the Peninsular War and in Canada where he was engaged in the construction of the Ottawa Canal.[10]

Darling made himself familiar with the operations of the Brisbane administration well before his arrival. He was unhappy about the levels of responsibility Brisbane had given to 'Chief Engineer Ovens': the arrangements for superintendence of convicts were 'totally unorganised' and 'without any particular System or principle'. Under Brisbane, the Superintendent of Convicts had been subordinated to the Civil Engineer who, as the principal employer of prisoners, had a substantial say in convict management, raising potential conflicts of interest.[11]

Ovens, in addition to his general duties, had controlled the extensive public works programme and directed the labour and allocation of prisoners; described by Darling as being 'given at the caprice of the Civil Engineer to whomsoever and in such numbers as he pleased'.[12] Consequently, the new Governor reduced the engineer's powers over government convicts, by allocating this responsibility to a newly created land board; but Darling retained the right to reject its decisions and, where necessary, distribute convicts on his own initiative.[13] He further

194

restricted the Civil Engineer's activities by creating an inspector of roads and bridges. This new position had responsibility for road parties and clearing gangs. With three inland roads under construction, this was an important office that required an increase in staff.[14]

Under Darling, the Civil Engineer was to retain overall control of public works and, specifically, 'the erection and repair of the Public Buildings and the preparation of plans and estimates for these undertakings'. His yard made 'carts, harnesses, ploughs, etc', and he also handled the 'lighting and drainage of the towns'. These 'innumerable' and 'vexatious' duties were made 'more harassing and unsatisfactory' by the convicts' aversion to 'habits of industry'.[15] Nevertheless, the newly allocated duties of the Civil Engineer were seen by Darling as being more manageable than under Brisbane's administration.

It is with these rearrangements of responsibility in mind that Darling instituted a series of staff moves, which were soon to elevate and then curtail Alexander Kinghorne's public service career.

A Very Short-term Appointment

O quam cito transit gloria mundi[16]

Thomas à Kempis, *De imitatione Christi*, 1418

Soon after his arrival, Governor Darling filled the void created by the death of John Ovens by appointing William Dumaresq as acting Civil Engineer.[17] Then, on 6 January, Darling announced the appointment of Alexander Kinghorne to the newly created land board and as Civil Engineer, with William Dumeresq becoming Inspector of Roads and Bridges, effective 10 January.[18] Alexander's experience with the management and distribution of prisoners sent to Emu Plains was undoubtedly seen as a primary qualification for the former position and he had made his case as a qualified engineer on a number of occasions, including in his petitions for land grants.[19] The other members of the land board were William Stewart, Lieutenant-Governor, and William Lithgow, the Colonial Auditor. 'I have selected', Darling wrote, 'an experienced and scientific person as Civil Engineer.'[20] Darling's personal 'selection' of Alexander is unlikely, as events would soon prove. He might have been recommended by William Stewart, with whom Alexander had cosied himself and who was favourably disposed towards him.

On the same date, 10 January 1826, James Kinghorne replaced his father as Superintendent at the Emu Plains convict farm. Alexander's joint salary for his two appointments was £350, and James' salary was £250.[21] James was to remain at Emu Plains until September 1829.

With these 'promotions', the fortunes of the Kinghorne family in New South Wales appeared to have reached a zenith. On 4 February Alexander was one of only thirty-one invitees to a farewell dinner for the retiring Colonial Secretary, Frederick Goulburn, at the Sydney Hotel. The dinner was organised and chaired by William Stewart. Among the other guests was Thomas Icely, James Kinghorne's erstwhile employer at Bathurst. It was an exclusive evening, attended by invitation only, reflecting the heights of society to which Alexander had soared under Governor Brisbane's administration.[22]

However, his rise was to be short-lived. Alexander's signature, along with the other members, appeared on only three pieces of land board correspondence after his appointment.[23] Already in early February, Darling commented on his appointment that 'his duties are extensive, and I fear will be burthensome, as they are not confined to the town of Sydney alone, but to the charge of all Public Buildings and the other points, specified in the general arrangement, throughout the Colony...'[24] The first set-back came within the month, when Alexander was relieved of his position on the land board, together with its £100 salary. He 'ceased to act as such 17th February 1826 as consequence of [his duties as] Civil Engineer...being of so extensive a nature as to occupy his whole Time and Attention'; he was replaced by John Thomas Campbell.[25]

It can be concluded from this hand-written addendum to the Returns of the Colony, that Alexander was not coping with the 'extensive, and... burthensome' responsibilities of both positions and, as a consequence, was failing to adequately meet Darling's expectations with respect to convict allocations and superintendence. A further interpretation is that Kinghorne, like Ovens, Forbes and others, was associated in Darling's perception with the liberal Whig policies of the former Brisbane administration.[26] The new Governor was bent on gathering around him like-minded Tories, such as Alexander MacLeay and his Dumeresq brothers-in-law, whom he could trust to support and carry out his conservative policies.[27] None of Darling's new appointments, including Alexander, was confirmed by the British government, leading to accusations of nepotism by Francis Forbes and, later, the editors of *The Australian* and *Monitor* newspapers.[28] The reader will recall that Alexander Kinghorne had received some of his political formation back in Scotland from William Cobbett,[29] upon whom Edward Smith Hall modelled the radical Whiggism of the *Monitor* newspaper. Like Cobbett, he had a strong social conscience, and was described by Brian Fletcher as 'a man of principle and integrity, …unshakeable in his convictions which he pursued with…complete disregard for the consequences…'.[30] The irony was that Alexander was otherwise conservative in outlook, although his approach to convict management at Emu Plains might have confused the matter, along with his friendship with James Chisholm, who was a reformist, associated with the Governor's enemies, and Darling might have joined the political dots.

On the same day that Campbell replaced Kinghorne on the land board, Darling wrote to the chairman of the Quarter Sessions in response to complaints from the grand jury about the poor state of the infrastructure in the town. Their 'Presentment' listed such items as their want of a meeting place for the court – provided in May by renovation of the police office,[31] the poor state of the gaol and prison hulk, and the lack of a proper water supply for Sydney. In his letter, published in the *Sydney Gazette*, Darling requested the chairman of the Quarter Sessions and the foreman of the grand jury to meet with the Civil Engineer, so that 'the most appropriate remedies' for 'the subjects of the Presentment' could 'be proposed'.[32]

On the same page of the newspaper, the Lieutenant Governor and William Lithgow were named as apparently running the land board single handedly. It seemed the board was meeting 'almost daily for the purpose of expediting the public business that crowds in upon this new Department', with the two gentlemen able 'scarcely to sleep, so indefatigable and laboriously are they employed in their several and important duties'.[33]

Again, in the same issue of the *Sydney Gazette*, under government order No. 11 of 21 February, the Colonial Secretary outlined the requirement for the Civil Engineer to prepare a weekly statement minutely detailing 'all work carried out under his Direction, and the purpose for which it was intended'.[34] There is no record of such a statement ever being prepared. Darling's micromanagement was very different from the laissez-faire approach of the previous administration. The storm clouds were gathering around Alexander's role as Civil Engineer, as he was becoming overwhelmed by the workload and pen-pushing. Gone were the liberal days of Governor Brisbane, who ruled by delegation. Alexander, that 'man of science', was stuck in an office, with an arduous desk job that was keeping him from fulfilling his stated responsibilities, disrupting his family, and was not at all to his liking.[35]

A Want of Competency

The second set-back came less than three months after the first. On 3 May 1826, Darling wrote to Earl Bathurst expressing his disapproval of Alexander, the 'Civil Engineer', in no uncertain terms:

> The repair of the public buildings and other Works is impeded from the want of a competent Civil Engineer. Captain Dumaresq of the Staff Corps is the only person here at all qualified for that appointment, and I at first placed him in it. But the Charge of the Roads and Bridges, which is of great importance to this country, requiring much personal activity and skill, appearing to me a more legitimate employment for that Officer and his company, I appointed him Inspector of Roads and Bridges. I am, however, apprehensive that I shall be under the necessity of reinstating him as Civil Engineer … The want of an efficient Person at the head of the Civil Engineer's Department is a very serious embarrassment at the moment. The Buildings originally appear to have been so imperfectly erected that they are in constant need of repair, and the quantity of work to be performed, necessary to their preservation and other indispensable objects, is in fact beyond the means of the Government.
>
> It has been my intention for some time past to transmit to your Lordship a detailed statement of the Public Buildings and the Works carrying on; but I have not been able to procure the necessary information from the Civil Engineer. It shall however be forwarded as soon as I can obtain it.[36]

Alexander's problems with personnel management and poor focus, which retarded his effectiveness as factor at Kippilaw, had seemingly returned. But Darling's criticisms went beyond that: Alexander was accused of withholding information regarding the state of public buildings 'and the Works carrying on'. Darling offered the excuse that 'the Buildings originally appear to have been so imperfectly erected … and the quantity of work to be performed … is in fact beyond the means of the Government.' Nonetheless, he believed that Alexander, 'though a man of science, [did] not possess the necessary activity or skill in management'.[37]

Within a few days of Darling's letter to Bathurst of 3 May 1826, Alexander was summarily sacked from his position as Civil Engineer, without the approval of Earl Bathurst. On 24 May 1826 the *Sydney Gazette* confirmed the 'changes about to take place in the Engineer Department':

> Mr. KINGHORNE, the respected Chief Engineer, has resigned that arduous post, and is about to return to his former situation at Emu-plains, as most accordant with his health. Captain DUMARESQ, the Inspector of Roads and Bridges, it is said, will become the CHIEF ENGINEER, and henceforward reside in the capital.[38]

The government order replacing Kinghorne with Dumeresq, published on 31 May, was more direct, that 'Mr Kinghorne, who has assisted in carrying on the Duties, [was] required for another Service'. This short, brutal announcement was placed in stark contrast to the preceding few words in the same newspaper report, announcing the resignation of Assistant Justice John Stephen: 'His Excellency begs to express his Acknowledgement for the services rendered by Mr Stephen…and for the zeal, which he has manifested, on all Occasions, in the performance of the important Duties which have been confided to him.'[39]

A complicating factor in Alexander's original appointment, was that Earl Bathurst had already appointed John Busby to the post of Civil Engineer, notice of which had not reached Darling until late February 1826, after Darling had already appointed Alexander. At the time, Darling invented a neat solution by giving Busby another title:

> THE Governor is pleased to notify, that the Employment of Mr. John Busby, as Mineral Surveyor and Civil Engineer, is not affected by the recent Appointment of Mr. Kinghorne as Civil Engineer, their Duties being totally distinct; and that it is His Excellency's Intention, immediately to avail himself of Mr. Busby's Services, in the important Objects for which he was originally sent to this Country, by His Majesty's Government.[40]

Nevertheless, when Alexander was dismissed, it was Dumaresq who was favoured, not Busby. It was five months before Earl Bathurst received Darling's message of 3 May, outlining the problems he was having with Alexander. Bathurst wrote back that he should 'carry on this Branch of the Public Service without the necessity of making an additional appointment...'. An ambiguous instruction, but more likely referring to Busby, who was Bathurst's appointee, than to Kinghorne. However, there were months of sea lag in correspondence, which could be compounded by obfuscations, which allowed Darling all the flexibility he desired. Bathurst's message, written 19 October 1826, was immediately dispatched on the ship *Guilford*, but it was a further ten months before Darling acknowledged receipt on 7 August 1827; far too late for Bathurst's order to have any effect.[41]

Darling's zeal for reforming the colony's administrative structure was under strict instructions from the secretary of state for colonies,[42] but his response here was nepotism. Alexander's replacement, Dumaresq, was Darling's brother-in-law. Anticipating this charge, Darling covered his bases with Robert Hay, the conservative first permanent under-secretary at the colonial office, by 'endeavouring to impress upon [him] the importance of sending out, with as little delay as possible, a *Competent Engineer...,*' recommending that Major Buchanan be recalled from Mauritius.[43]

At the time of Alexander's dismissal, William Dumaresq was already Inspector of Roads and Bridges, a job he enjoyed. Despite asserting that he had neither experience nor time to be Civil Engineer, he was ordered to fill that office as well, and did double duty for the next three years until London sent out another soldier to relieve him.[44] Darling's plan to surround himself with his family and trusted friends in the key administrative positions was all but complete; but he was leaving himself wide open to accusations of partiality, of which William Charles Wentworth, and others, were to take full advantage in their future vendetta against the Governor.

The Achievements of the Civil Engineer

In the short 108 days that Alexander occupied the position of Civil Engineer, there were few, if any, achievements recorded against his name in the official colonial archives. Moreover, he is not mentioned in any of the published histories of this period, with the notable exception of Lorraine Stacker's history of the Emu Plains government establishment.[45] However, while not completed by Alexander, he was responsible for proposing, designing and supervising several government building projects. Most of these were finished under the supervision of William Dumeresq, to whom they are generally credited. A complete listing of these is beyond this history, as Alexander's level of direct involvement is difficult to ascertain, but they included repairs to the Old Sydney Gaol and Carter's Barracks on Pitt Street, construction of new offices at the Commissariat Stores, completion of the Watch House in Erskine Street, plumbing the Parramatta Barracks, repairs to the Female Orphan School at Parramatta, construction of a drainage system for Sydney streets, repairs to Hyde Park Barracks, supervising the planning for St Thomas' Anglican Church Port Macquarie, Moreton Bay Gaol, and the expansion of the residence of the Colonial Secretary on Macquarie Place.[46] Two of these, for which the records allocate design directly to Alexander, are detailed below.

The Colonial Secretary's House

On his arrival in Sydney, the new Colonial Secretary Alexander MacLeay found his residence most inconvenient. His daughter, Fanny, described the house, built in 1810, as 'the worst & ugliest in Sydney', its rooms 'holes…unfit for a cat to sleep in they are so small and close'.[47] Alexander proposed a substantial remodelling to accommodate the needs of the MacLeays and their six daughters, adding to the structure…

> …four…Rooms by raising each Wing 6 feet higher; these Rooms will average 12ft by 15ft and 9ft 6 in Height. The front of the House is at present exposed to the direct influence of the Sun in Mid-day, which in the height of summer, makes the Rooms very oppressive and unhealthy. To obviate this it is proposed to have a neat Verandah fixed, which besides the utility will improve the appearance of the house.[48]

More modest renovations were completed under the supervision of William Dumeresq in December 1827.[49] The finished product is beautifully illustrated in Conrad Martens painting of 1839 (Figure 28).

Gas Lighting for Sydney

A further substantial engineering plan, which did not reach the light of day until ten years after it was first proposed, was Alexander's design for gas lighting the city of Sydney. The Australian Gas Light Company (AGL) was formed in 1837 to supply town gas for the first public lighting of streetlamps. In that year it received a royal charter to start construction, and the first lamps were lit on 24 May 1841. The roots of the company, however, lie in one of the tasks undertaken by Alexander as Civil Engineer. He was commissioned by the Colonial Secretary to prepare a report and estimate, on the cost and returns of lighting Sydney with gas, that included a plan for the layout of gas lamps along the main city streets. [50] According to a 1937 article in *The Sydney Morning Herald*, there was considerable public opposition to the government's proposal for gas lighting in 1826 because

> ...not only was the town very small and the difficulties very great, but also many of the settlers were convinced that the proposed innovation would interfere with the Creator's intention that the world should be dark after sunset. Some of them feared, too, that illuminated streets would embolden thieves and conduce to all manner of depravity, drunkenness, and chest complaints.[51]

No further action appears to have been taken in the 1820s, as Sydney residents continued to rely on candles and oil lamps. However, the proposal was revived in 1836, when Rev'd Ralph Mansfield founded AGL with the support of Governor George Gipps. [52]

While Alexander's gas light plan is not extant, it is mentioned in the first prospectus for AGL, which appeared in the Sydney newspapers in September 1836. This detailed the costs and potential profit from a system of lamps to be laid out initially only in George Street and its branches. The Directors had obtained 'from the Office of the Honorable the COLONIAL SECRETARY a copy of a Report and Estimate, on the cost and returns of lighting Sydney with Gas, prepared so far back as the year 1826, by ALEXANDER KINGHORNE, Esq, J.P., then Colonial Civil Engineer, by direction of the Government.' The AGL Board had used this document in the formulation of their plans and had compared its financial estimates with their own, finding that it agreed with their plans 'in general facts', and that 'their calculations of profit [were]...below the rate officially computed [by Alexander] more than ten years ago.'[53]

In response to objections made by a shareholder regarding the calculations of income and expenditure published in the prospectus, the secretary of AGL, under the pseudonym 'Another Shareholder', responded in a letter to *The Australian*. The calculations, he wrote, 'were made under the supervision of one of the most experienced Gas engineers in the colony, whose estimates have in part been verified by Invoices received by the Directors from London and Scotland' and they 'compared [favourably] with those drawn up by the Colonial Engineer in the year 1826, for the use of the Government'.[54] The worthy Directors of AGL thereby endorsed in their prospectus the work undertaken by Alexander on the design for Sydney's gas lighting, but also confirmed his tendency for overestimating business economy.

* * *

For Alexander, *the dismissal* was a major blow. This was his first position at a high government level, a position which bore the title at least of his profession as a civil engineer. The Governor, the highest person in the land, had called him incompetent, a slur which was doubtless echoed by his peers, Darling's cronies at the heads of government departments. The abruptness of the newspaper announcement left no doubt he had been sacked, after just six months. He had been dealt with arbitrarily by a high-handed autocrat, and the likeness of this to the attitudes engendered by the class system in Britain would not have escaped him. Suddenly the sun, which had seemed so bright at the end of 1825, was covered by a pall. His flagship project at New Brighton, which he had hoped would bring him lasting fame, had by then unravelled, and later in 1826 the final disastrous article in the *Colonial Times* would label him little more than a dreamer.[55]

Chapter 19

The Clergy and School Lands Corporation
(1826–1827)

I have likewise added sundry other conveniences which will be found <u>absolutely necessary</u> for…an establishment of such Magnitude.

Alexander Kinghorne, August 1826

As colonial Civil Engineer, Alexander had responsibility for the maintenance of government buildings including, at that time, the Female and Male Orphan Schools, located at Parramatta and Liverpool, respectively. These institutions operated combined programmes of welfare and training for underprivileged children. They have been described by Vernon Goodin as the earliest examples of government welfare in the British Empire.[1]

The Female Orphan School was originally located in William Kent's former residence in Sydney, which had been purchased for the purpose in 1800 by Governor King at the urging of Rev'd Samuel Marsden.[2] A new building at Paramatta was commenced by Governor Macquarie in 1813 and the orphans moved there in 1818. It was in a state of disrepair after only eight years of occupation when Alexander, as Civil Engineer, assumed responsibility for its maintenance. A 'perpendicular fracture' had appeared in the face of the building and there was a 'want of sufficiently good wholesome water', among many other problems.[3] During February 1826, Alexander supervised a survey and major alterations to the building, dealing either with the works superintendent at the Parramatta engineering office, William Aird, or sometimes directly with the contractor.[4]

The Male Orphan School also was located, from January 1819, at William Kent's former residence, after it had been vacated by the female orphans.[5] Its purpose was to house, and basically educate, destitute boys aged between seven and ten. The school was relocated in 1823 to the orphan schools grant at Cabramatta, deeded by Governor King in 1803 as 12,300 acres. The school was first sited on the 'Old Farm' section of this grant, where the orphans were housed in temporary timber buildings.[6]

Through his supervision of the repair work at the Female Orphan School, Alexander encountered Rev'd Robert Cartwright, the Master of the Male Orphan School.[7] Cartwright was of the evangelical persuasion, and, over the next three years, he and Alexander became close colleagues and friends.[8] As one of the nine senior chaplains of the colony, and incumbent at St Luke's Liverpool, Cartwright was a trustee of the Clergy and School Lands Corporation (CSLC).

A draft charter of incorporation for the management of the church and school estates had been sent from Earl Bathurst to Governor Brisbane on 30 June 1825. The charter created CSLC trustees, such as Cartwright, who would manage certain lands to provide for the maintenance of the Church of England clergy and the education of children. The corporation was inaugurated when the trustees met for the first time on 27 April 1826 and a committee was formed to draft by-laws, regulations and rules for proceedings. Legislation was prepared to enable the orphan school lands to be vested in the CSLC and the corporation became responsible for their management. The new committee was chaired by Archdeacon Thomas Scott and had as members Saxe Bannister (the Attorney General), Hon. Robert Campbell (as a member of the Legislative Council), James Holland (the Solicitor General), and Rev'ds Samuel Marsden and Charles Cowper (clerk).[9] Hon. John Macarthur also attended some committee meetings from 21 June 1826.[10]

From his role as Civil Engineer, and his contact with Cartwright, Alexander knew that the Male Orphan School was about to be relocated to the 'New Farm' site at Bull's Hill on the Cabramatta orphan schools grant (present day Bonnyrigg Heights), about four miles north-west of Liverpool. Here, replacing existing log huts, a new master's residence, dormitories, schoolhouse and outbuildings were to be erected.[11]

The plan for these improvements, together with a separation in the operations and accounts of the Male Orphan School from the Orphan School Farm, had been instituted in 1825 by Governor Brisbane. In August of that year, the surveyor and engineer John Busby, then in the process of planning a new water supply for Sydney, visited the orphan school lands.

He confirmed that the current site, at Bull's Hill, had the best water supply, sourced from rainwater tanks and a spring-fed pond. Busby had a close interest in the school, as his 24-year-old son, James, had overseen the surrounding Orphan School Farm ('Agricultural Establishment') since October 1824.[12] James had arrived in New South Wales with his parents, John and Sarah, in the same year. A trained viticulturalist, he was to take charge of the farm, and teach animal husbandry and viticulture to its inmates.

On 15 May 1826, Cartwright wrote to Archdeacon Scott and placed before him the unsatisfactory nature of the buildings at Bull's Hill. They were too small; there was overcrowding; and the distance between them caused problems when it rained and in winter. At that time the orphans in residence numbered 121, ranging in age from five to more than twelve. Ninety-eight of these attended the school and twenty-three of the older boys had been apprenticed as farm workers to James Busby.[13]

The Male Orphan School

At this point, the transition of Alexander Kinghorne from colonial Civil Engineer to 'another service' requires further consideration.[14] Alexander was dismissed as Civil Engineer on or about 20 May 1826.[15] On the same day, while clearing his desk at the engineer's office in Sydney, he wrote to Archdeacon Scott, suggesting the creation of a new position within the CSLC – for himself!! He presumed 'that it may be requisite, for an Officer to be appointed to look after the interests of the Corporation… in the division, valuation and appropriation of the same:– as also for conducting and superintending the Improvements, Buildings, etc., therewith connected'. He presented his qualifications, in those familiar old terms of 'long experience, as an Agriculturalist, Land Valuer and Civil Engineer, in one of the most highly cultivated districts of Great Britain', pointing out that he was 'about to retire from the situation I now hold, the sedentary details of which I find prejudicial to my health' (Figure 29).[16] These were similar to the words published in the *Gazette* on 24 May announcing Alexander's 'resignation' as Civil Engineer.[17]

While this was Alexander's face-saver for an unwanted sacking, it was opportune that he had extensive background with Rev'd Cartwright in the Male Orphan School.[18] The Colonial Secretary, Alexander Macleay, who had extensive dealings with Alexander regarding the renovation of his house, might have seen a convenient escape route for the unhappy and unwanted Civil Engineer.

At its 9 June meeting, having received his letter, the CSLC Committee resolved to invite Alexander to meet them. At the same meeting they approved the draft legislative bill, to be sent to Governor Darling, enacting their role.[19] The Act effectively implemented the recommendations of Commissioner Bigge, to transfer the responsibility for the orphan schools from the government to the CSLC.[20]

On receiving the committee of trustee's invitation from its clerk, Charles Cowper, Alexander duly rode his horse from Emu Plains to attend its next scheduled meeting on Wednesday 21 June, at which 'the subjects on which he was to be employed were stated to him'. He was asked to deliver a proposal for his new position by the following meeting. In the meantime, he was to visit the site of the new Male Orphan School and prepare recommendations on the location and construction of the buildings.[21] The final details of his contract were not finalised until September, and these were employment half-time for one year, at the significant salary of £250, with additional payments for any extra time worked.[22] It is hardly a coincidence, that the agreed salary is the same as he had received as colonial Civil Engineer.

The day after his interview, Alexander duly rode to Liverpool and arranged a meeting at Bull's Hill with Cartwright and Charles Throsby, then a member of the legislative council.[23] He likely took the opportunity to find lodgings for his anticipated frequent visits to Liverpool. On Friday, he 'perambulated the ground' at the Male Orphan School estate with Cartwright and Throsby, agreeing on a site for the buildings 'three quarters of a mile from Cabramatta Creek' and only a little over a mile from Liverpool church. He spent another day meeting the CSLC Committee there and surveying the chosen site, so that he could prepare 'a rough sketch of the proposed Buildings'. This he sent to Cowper for consideration by the committee.[24] Cowper, on behalf of the committee, instructed him to proceed with a plan and specifications, and in early July Alexander started sourcing local building materials.[25]

Alexander attended the CSLC committee meeting on 5 July 1826 with proposals for erection of the new schoolhouse at Bull's Hill. He received orders to start clearing the land and to procure 'Stone, Lime, Bricks and sawn Timber'.[26] After further meetings with members of the committee on sight, work proceeded apace. Alexander continued measuring and drawing up detailed plans as workmen were employed in felling and burning trees and shrubs to clear the site. On Tuesday 18 July he rode to Sydney and delivered the plans to Charles Cowper. He attended the committee meeting the following day and received 'instructions to procure Tenders and Materials' for the construction of the master's house and six dormitories. The minutes of the CSLC committee indicate that the dormitories, capable of housing 180 boys, were to comprise the 'left wing' of a two-wing school building; the right wing presumably to house classrooms.[27]

A thorough archaeological investigation of the Bull's Hill site, conducted in 1982 by Wendy Thorpe, confirms the orphan school originally comprised log huts, fencing, a bridge over the Cabramatta Creek, the master's house (now called Bonnyrigg House), dining room, probationary school, infant school room, privies, staff bedroom and kitchen, watch house, hospital, stable and yard, coach house, office, tailor's shop, lower school room, school room, bakehouse, nursery, storekeepers house, clothing store, dormitory, kitchen and wash house. Of these, the stone bridge, master's house, dining room and dormitory were designed by Alexander.[28] Bonyrigg House is intact, and Thorpe identified archaeological remains of the dormitory block, water supply, parts of the school wing, and some other structures such and paths and fences.[29]

James Busby was authorised to assist Alexander in matters of access to the school buildings through the surrounding agricultural lands.[30] In less than a year's time Busby would be dismissed due to a dispute with the CSLC.[31] Initially, he was vitally involved with Alexander in the process of construction and, particularly, the clearing of land for the livestock and cultural components of the agricultural establishment to be associated with the school. He was responsible also for ensuring access to regular supplies for the school, including flour, salted meat, and other consumables.[32]

Some of the building work was undertaken by older orphan boys who became 'apprenticed' to the various trades involved. Alexander was ably assisted by boys considered to be 'the most troublesome and expensive,

although' Cartwright reported, 'to their credit and that of their overseer…
they are now doing as well as boys under such circumstances can be
expected to do.'[33] Alexander had a flair for engaging the boys in their
work and in teaching them useful skills.

Alexander's detailed cost estimates and tender recommendations of 28
July were duly accepted at the CSLC committee meeting on 3 August, which
he again attended in person, travelling from Liverpool.[34] The following
days were occupied at the orphan school supervising the 'apprentices',
employing labourers, purchasing building supplies and fixings. Access to
the site was via a carriageway and bridge to be built over the Cabramatta
Creek.[35] There was always close consultation with Cartwright about the
building works, the grounds in the immediate vicinity of the school, and
the construction of a 'garden'. This turned out to be a wise collaboration,
as Alexander was not employed for the full term of the project.

Other Church and School Projects

The Male Orphan School was a significant commitment of Alexander's
time but, in the course of his employment by the CSLC, there were plans
to establish and maintain church schools and parish churches in other
areas around Sydney. During 1826, the committee was planning new
schools at Bringelly, Prospect, Castlereagh and the Kissing Point portion
of the Field of Mars. Alexander had a limited supervisory role in some
of these projects but, despite suggestions of wider involvement in the
literature, his direct contribution can only be confirmed for two of them.[36]

In September, Alexander was asked to make recommendations for
repairs to St Luke's Church Liverpool. He met Cartwright at the church
on Saturday 23 September 1826 and submitted his recommendations to
the CSLC committee, which were approved on 27 September.[37] During
October, in association with Rev'd Fulton, Alexander also supervised the
selection of a site for a new schoolhouse at Evan, on the Nepean River at
Castlereagh. Four acres of land were purchased for this purpose from a 'Mr
Appledore', and Alexander spent considerable time seeking tradesmen to
tender for its construction. On 31 October, he eventually employed a 'Mr
Goff from Clarendon' for the purpose. The schoolhouse was completed
after Alexander left the employment of the CSLC.[38]

Bonnyrigg House

Alexander's 'Journal' records an extensive programme of land clearing and the commencement of excavations for building foundations for the masters' residence at the Male Orphan School. However, the entries for 1827 leave a clear impression that, apart from these initial works and the building of a road and bridge over the Cabramatta Creek, little was done apart from the preparation of plans, the calling of tenders, and the purchase of locks, glass, and other building sundries.

When rumours of the termination of the project first began to circulate, as early as October 1826, Alexander continued to advance the work. Thousands of bricks were made on site, timber was prepared for the bridge and carts were carrying bricks, lime and sand. By the end of the year one building, the schoolhouse wing, was completed.[39] On 1 January 1827, Alexander was given a minute from the general court of CSLC suspending all works at the orphan school. He was paid and released from his duties on 17 January 1827.[40] Nevertheless, within the next year, the semi-completed buildings on Bull's Hill were finished. In Alexander's absence, the work was progressed by Cartwright using the convict carpenter (Benjamin Wilson) and other trades Alexander had employed and based on the plans he had prepared.[41] The accounts clearly show that activity on site did not stop, and details of the work, which continued until 1829, are also given in the archaeology report of Wendy Thorpe.[42]

Neither the 'Journal' nor the CSLC committee minutes give reasons for Alexander's termination, or details of any planned abandonment of the project. Both documents leave the impression that the committee could not agree on the programme, having underestimated the costs and tried to get Alexander to do it on the cheap. In August 1826, for example, the workmen refused to accept Alexander's order from the committee 'to purchase window glass, locks, hinges and the requisite tools, also a cart and dray', as the prices the CSLC had fixed were too low and unrealistic.[43] Wendy Thorpe suggests that Alexander might have been the victim of a change of management, who rejected the work programme whether on economic or political grounds.[44] However, she also commented on Alexander's activities towards the end of 1826, as follows:

210

With regards to the alterations in the plan it does begin to appear that, in being given such a free hand, Kinghorne was letting the project get out of proportion by creating additions and the like.[45]

The idea that Alexander was, once again, displaying his old profligacy, is supported by his letter to Charles Cowper on 28 August 1826:

You will herewith receive the plan of the proposed New Orphan Institution, which I have altered and enlarged according to the Instructions of the Archdeacon communicated to me in your letter of the 17th and Note of the 18th instant. I have likewise added sundry other conveniences which will be found <u>absolutely necessary</u> for containing the stores Etc, Etc, connected with an establishment of such Magnitude.[46]

These words could have come directly from one of Alexander's letters to John Seton Karr, some 16 years earlier, during the renovation of the mansion house at Kippilaw in Scotland. The formerly spendthrift factor was still a perfectionist! Had Alexander's desire to make 'every thing perfect' got the better of him again?[47]

His architectural legacy remains in the completed Bonnyrigg House, as his plans were eventually implemented in the final construction (Figure 30).[48] His original elevations for the house are not extant, but copies from 1831 remain, which are shown in Thorpe's archaeology report (Figure 31).[49] Bonnyrigg House has been described by the Heritage Council of New South Wales as a unique example of early colonial Georgian architecture, and 'the only surviving example of the Civil Engineer Alexander Kinghorne's work'.[50]

A surviving family record provides another possible explanation for Alexander's departure from the Male Orphan School. Writing to her brother in Scotland, about a year later, Helen Kinghorne commented…

I think I mentioned in my last letter the Church had been prevented from taking possession of their land owing to some error in the Charter, and that consequently, my father's services were not required in the situation to which he had been appointed. Since then he has not held any public situation.[51]

Whether or not Helen's interpretation of the trigger for her father's dismissal is correct, shortly afterwards the CSLC sold 8,309 acres of the orphan estate at Cabramatta. The reason for these sales is not on the record, but the costs of running the orphan school farm were getting out

211

of hand and eventually led to the dismissal of James Busby.[52] The funds raised from the land sale, more than £8,000, would have gone some way to offsetting the costs of construction of the school, which had so limited earlier progress.

Interestingly, 3,321 acres of the orphan school estate were sold to Alexander's friend, James Chisholm Snr, through Chisholm's business partner, the auctioneer John Paul.[53] At this time, Chisholm was well on the way to becoming one of the largest landholders in the County of Cumberland and beyond. With this undeniable impetus, Alexander, too, was beginning to accumulate agricultural land to secure the future of his family. His first grant, promised by Governor Brisbane in 1825, was in the County of Argyle, in a location soon to become the centre of landholdings for both the Kinghorne and Chisholm families.

The Kinghornes Move to Liverpool

During 1826, while colonial Civil Engineer, and afterwards as engineer to the CSLC, Alexander and his family remained domiciled at the Superintendent's residence, 'Government House', at Emu Plains. Whether officially sanctioned, or not, this arrangement persisted after James Kinghorne became Superintendent.[54] Alexander would travel to Liverpool to supervise works at the Male Orphan School and to Sydney for meetings of the committee. He rode his own horse and covered many miles between Emu Plains, Parramatta, Sydney, Liverpool and elsewhere in the performance of his duties, accompanied only by a manservant.[55] He had temporary lodgings at Liverpool, but when in Sydney he stayed with James Chisholm Snr in George Street.[56] It is likely that he stayed there also in early 1826, during his tenure as Civil Engineer.

In a letter to the CSLC committee, dated 6 September 1826, in which Alexander outlined the conditions of his superintendence of the Male Orphan School works, he requested the provision 'of a residence near the proposed new Buildings, with rations for a man servant, and rations for two horses', along with separate rations for his family. This request was deferred by the CSLC, but it confirms that his family continued to reside at Emu Plains.[57] On 16 November 1826, however, Alexander asked the Committee to grant him an advance on his salary of £150, as he had 'a considerable sum to pay…for stock which I have been purchasing for my farm...' This request was approved.[58]

The 'farm' in question was known locally at Liverpool as 'Drummond Farm'. The authors' book, *The Merchant of Sydney*, describes how this property became available for rent:

> James [Chisholm]...acted as executor for John Drummond, a mariner who had been Beach Master at Norfolk Island in 1796–1812 and then lived at Liverpool with his wife Ann on a small pension...When Drummond's grave was robbed not long after his burial, seemingly only to steal the shroud in which he was clothed, James stumped up a reward for the arrest of 'the Offender in the above named vile Depredation'. [59]

In handling the estate, James Chisholm was generous, as Drummond's wife was unable to pay for his services. John Drummond died on 1 July 1827 and his wife Ann followed him in September 1828. At the time of her husband's death, she would have been in her early sixties and in need of an income.[60] James Chisholm, aware of Alexander's need for accommodation at Liverpool, and his desire for a farm, made the necessary arrangements.[61]

First, though, Chisholm advertised Drummond farm and residence 'for let by private contract over three or five years' in the *Sydney Gazette*, starting one month after Drummond's death, as was required of him as executor: the advertisements appeared weekly between 1 and 31 August 1827. The farm comprised one hundred acres, and included 'a commodious built house, containing seven rooms, a kitchen dairy, a large granary, and other requisite out-houses; there [was] also an excellent vegetable garden, together with an extensive orchard well stocked with a variety of choice bearing fruit trees'.[62]

It is not certain when Alexander began renting Drummond Farm, but his letter to Cowper of 6 September 1826 suggests he already had tenancy of the farming land. The first firm evidence of Alexander's lease appeared in March 1828, when Ann Drummond placed the following advertisement in the *Sydney Gazette*:

CAUTION

FOR THE TWO-FARMS BELONGING TO the late Mr. John Drummond, of Liverpool, the one let to Mr. Kinghorn, of Liverpool, and the other let to Mr. William Tuck of Bringelly persons are requested not to pay any rent to any one except to the widow of the late Mr. Drummond, as she is the Executrix of the Estate, and entitled to receive

213

the rents. She hopes the above caution will be sufficient without any further notice. ANN DRUMMOND. Parramatta, February 24, 1828.[63]

However, evidence from two Sydney newspapers indicates that the family relocated to Drummond Farm in August 1827, after James Chisholm found lodgings for Ann Drummond at Parramatta.[64]

The parliamentary records of the Sudds-Thompson affair (Chapter 20) confirm that Alexander Kinghorne Jnr was present at Emu Plains, at least until June 1827.[65] Moreover, the entire Kinghorne family, excepting James, accompanied by three adult convicts and a nine-year-old child servant, were domiciled at Drummond Farm according to the 1828 census.[66] In October 1828, Helen Kinghorne, in a letter to Andrew Seton back in Galashiels, also mentioned the family's domicile in Liverpool:

> My father, my two sisters and myself are at present residing at Liverpool, where I think I mentioned in a former letter, he has purchased a small cottage and rents a small farm until he gets a house erected on his own land for which he is preparing.[67]

The small cottage Helen mentions might have been elsewhere in the town of Liverpool, or Drummond House itself on what is now Terminus Street, Liverpool. This old house survived until the 1960s, when it was destroyed by fire (Figure 32).[68] Alexander was later to build his own home on the town block he was granted at the corner of Macquarie and Elizabeth Streets. He would remain living principally in Liverpool for the next fourteen years.[69]

Death of the Mentors

After the death of John Seton Karr in 1815, Alexander Kinghorne's surviving mentors, Lord Buchan and Sir Walter Scott, had been active supporters, and in the case of Buchan organiser, of his migration and that of his family to New South Wales. They were both physically well and active when the family left Scotland in 1824. However, Buchan's biographer, Ronald Cant, suggests that by the 1820s he was 'growing undeniably eccentric, a tendency that became more pronounced after the deaths of his brother Henry in 1817 and of his wife in 1819'.[70]

Buchan had known Walter Scott since examining him as a schoolboy in 1783 and awarding him a prize for proficiency in translation of Latin verse.[71] On one occasion, when Scott became ill in Edinburgh, the old Earl tried to force his way into the sickroom, as he said, 'to embrace him before he died' and to assure him that he would personally supervise all the funeral arrangements and pronounce an appropriate oration. As it happened, Scott outlived Buchan, if only by three years.[72]

Late in 1829, when Alexander Kinghorne had been in the colony of New South Wales for five years, he read the news of the death of his friend and mentor Lord Buchan…

> The Earl of Buchan died at his seat at Dryburgh Abbey on the 19th April, in the 88th year of his age. His Lordship was uncle to the present Lord Erskine.[73]

Buchan's passing would have struck him deeply, as he retained fond recollections of the eccentric aristocrat's persistent kindness and support.

Sir Walter Scott, having attended Buchan's funeral at Dryburgh on 20 April 1828, entered in his diary the oft-quoted observation: 'Lord Buchan is dead, a person whose immense vanity, bordering upon insanity, obscured, or rather eclipsed, very considerable talents'.[74] This comment was perhaps harsh, and only applied to the very end of Buchan's life. Alexander would have harboured no such view of the man who had, more than any other, encouraged and supported him in the twenty-four years between his appointment as factor at Kippilaw and his departure from Scotland. Cant comments that if 'Buchan had done no more than found the Society of Antiquaries of Scotland it would still entitle him to the gratitude of his countrymen, but this achievement can be seen as part of a general and truly commendable concern to preserve and enhance every aspect of the historic identity of his native land.' This certainly applied to his mentoring of Alexander Kinghorne, whom he both valued and encouraged in his agricultural, antiquarian, surveying, engineer and, finally, colonial pursuits.

After the Kinghornes left the Borders, Sir Walter Scott had suffered financial ruin through the collapse of the Ballentyne printing business, in which he was the major shareholder. Determined to write his way out of debt, Scott produced six novels between 1826 and 1832 and many other works including histories of Scotland and Napoleon Bonaparte. Scott's approaching demise, eight years after the Kinghornes sailed from Leith, was widely heralded. He first fell ill, probably from a stroke, in October

1831. Updates on his condition appeared, almost weekly, in the colonial press, as they arrived on ships from Leith and London, some five months after the event. [75]

Scott attempted to cure his illness with a Mediterranean voyage, but on his journey home he had a final stroke. He was transported back to Abbotsford where he died on 21 September 1832. The following reports appeared in the colonial newspapers, reprinted from Scotland:–

> Sir Walter Scott arrived at Leith on Monday. We cannot conceive more affecting circumstances than those under which our illustrious countryman returns amongst us— he comes indeed to lay his bones at rest for ever in that land which gave him birth, and over whose history and literature his genius has shed a fadeless splendour, and secured for himself a deathless name.[76]

> All hope of a recovery is abandoned. He continues in a very feeble state of body, and is now unable to recognise his attendants.[77]

> London, Saturday evening, 7.30 pm, 22 September 1832. DEATH OF SIR WALTER SCOTT. This distinguished person breathed his last at twenty-five minutes past one o'clock yesterday (Friday). He expired softly and easily, but had suffered a great deal for several weeks before. Scotland may well mourn the loss of the man who has spread the glory of her literature far and wide: but the event will awaken a feeling of grief in every part of the globe to which civilization extends.[78]

Scott was laid to rest in Dryburgh Abbey on Wednesday 26 September. The melancholy procession left from Abbotsford around one o'clock in the afternoon, the hearse drawn by Scott's faithful horses to Dryburgh. According to a popular story, the horses stopped at Scott's View, on the summit of the hill at Bemersyde, as was their custom, to allow their master to pause and observe the vista of remarkable richness which he so loved.[79]

Five months later, Alexander Kinghorne was deeply moved by the news of Scott's death. He recorded his personal feelings as a footnote, on pages 20–28 of his own copy of Scott's novel, *The Monastery*.

> 'De Haga', the ancient family of Haig of Bemersyde (in Berwickshire), lineally descended in the Male line from the race of the Picts. Their ancient Tower or Fortalice is situated on an eminence overhanging the Tweed, and from it the 'Monastery' of St Mary's can be distinctly seen; as likewise the beautiful ruins of the Abbey of 'Dryburgh' as faithfully represented by the Engraving on the title page of next volume. Here

the Noble proprietor, the Earl of Buchan, my friend & patron, granted me and my family a burial place, near to that of my schoolfellow, the celebrated author of Waverley, Etc., Etc., and amongst these splendid ruins my beloved spouse was interred on Monday 23rd Augt 1819; Lady Scott in 182–; – And here, all that was Mortal of the renowned Sir Walter was deposited on the 27th Sep^{tr} 1832. He died at 'Abbotsford' on Friday the 21st of that month in his 62nd year. –

His Name is Immortal

An Account of A. Kinghorne
Liverpool, N. S. Wales
28th Feb^{ry} 1833
An account of Sir Walter Scott's funeral is annexed, from the Edinburgh Courant. A.K.[80]

On reading the newspaper reports of Sir Walter's funeral, Alexander's mind might well have drifted to Scott's View, with its soft light illuminating the Eildon Hills as they cast their shadows over his beloved vale of Tweed. His ambitions in the colony were now only for his family, while his personal hopes were gradually shifting back to his homeland, the burial place of his wife and heroes, and the son he had left behind.

Alexander's annotations in *The Monastery* date from around 1833. In them he recalled some of the real people and locations on which characters and places in the book were based, as well as the circumstances of his discussions with Sir Walter about them. He also highlighted a passage in the book bewailing the showy verbosity of Sir Piercie Shafton:

But alas! where is the man of modest merit, and real talent, who has not suffered from being outshone in conversation, and outstripped in the race of life, by men of less reserve, and of qualities more showy, though less substantial ? and well constituted must the mind be, that can yield up the prize without envy to competitors more unworthy than himself.[81]

While most of Alexander's annotations were written in ink, this passage was bracketed in pencil, which could have been done any time after he obtained that edition, published in 1822. These words surely reflect his feelings about his own circumstances, whether in Scotland or New South Wales.

Chapter 20

The Death of Private Sudds and its Consequences (1826–1835)

I saw him lie down in them at full length, and am almost sure that I saw him turn while lying on the floor with the irons on him.

James Kinghorne, May 1827

The Sudds–Thompson Case

Joseph Sudds, from Devizes in Wiltshire, was 22 years old when he enlisted as a private in the 57th (West Middlesex) Regiment of Foot at Chatham. It was 16 March 1825.[1] On 10 April, along with thirty-six others under the command of Lieutenant Henry Shadforth, he departed Chatham as a convict guard on the *Minstrell*, arriving in New South Wales on 22 August.[2]

After a year in the Colony, Private Sudds wanted to be free of army life. He claimed to have a wife and child back in England,[3] and faced the prospect of many years of colonial service without home leave.[4] His discontent must have been acute, as Sudds resorted to desperate measures to escape further military service. In November 1826, Sudds and an accomplice Patrick Thompson were indicted for stealing twelve yards of calico, the property of Michael Naphthali.[5] The two soldiers deliberately planned this theft so as to be convicted and discharged from the army; despite Governor Darling's warning that any troops who tried such an exit ploy 'would be held up as examples of just abhorrence to their comrades'.[6]

On 8 November, according with their plan, Sudds and Thompson were arrested and sentenced to seven years transportation by magistrate Francis Rossi at the Sydney court of Quarter Sessions.[7] Three days later, Sudds became unwell and was admitted to the Sydney Gaol Hospital but was later discharged.[8]

On 22 November 1826 at Wynyard Barracks, Sudds and Thompson were

218

paraded before their regiment in special chains designed by Governor Darling, and manufactured under supervision of Captain William Dumaresq, by then in full bloom as the Colony's Civil Engineer. These were no ordinary shackles: each set weighed about 14 lbs and comprised an iron neck collar with two protruding spikes linked by chains to ankle irons (Figure 33).[9] The Governor's order commuted their sentence to hard labour. They were to work in chains for the duration of their prison term and then return to the army. The regiment then watched as the soldiers were stripped naked, dressed in convict clothes, and made to stand as their irons were riveted around their necks and ankles. The Rogues March was played by the regimental band and they were marched back to gaol.[10]

Twenty-four hours later, Sudds complained again of feeling ill and was readmitted to the Gaol Hospital, where his irons were later removed.[11] On 25 November *The Australian* newspaper, backed the 'unusual severity' of the soldiers' sentences but noted that the manacles prevented them from 'laying their heads down to rest' and made it difficult for them to breathe.[12]

Then, on 27 November, Private Sudds died.

The editorial tenor of *The Australian* then changed radically, and it caused an uproar in the streets of Sydney. Robert Wardell, the paper's editor, criticised the Governor's treatment of Sudds and Thompson and carried the dramatic news of Sudds' death, which was added to the newspaper 'when the ink was hardly dry'. He accused Darling of unlawfully commuting their sentences, having exercised 'greater power in New South Wales than the King of England has in England' and of cruelly exacerbating Sudds' illness by the application of heavy irons and draconian treatment.[13]

Governor Darling responded to *The Australian's* criticism, unofficially, through an anonymous letter from 'A Subscriber'.[14] He also answered, officially, by instructing Alexander Macleay to write to the newspaper outlining the Government's side of the affair.[15] In this letter, Macleay gave the weight of the irons as 13 lbs 12 oz and denied they would prevent their wearer from stretching out and sleeping. Irons of this weight were made available for press scrutiny.

However, the furore continued in the press and among reform-minded citizenry, and over the coming weeks elicited a concerted attack on Darling and his government. Critical to the argument was the weight of the irons, and whether their design had ended Sudds' life. Darling responded by ordering an Executive Council inquiry in December 1826, which considered what happened, not the legality of the Governor's actions.[16] The Governor's version that the irons 'were...intended to produce an effect on those, who were to witness the Ceremony, and not to subject the Prisoner to any extraordinary punishment' – was endorsed.

Curiously, Patrick Thompson was considered irrelevant to the controversy he and Sudds had aroused, and it was not until April 1827, that he was called to give evidence to a second inquiry by the Executive Council. He told them that, on Monday 27 November 1826, he was taken 'to the lumbar yard' at Sydney Gaol...

> to get my irons removed,[17] and Sudds's [irons] put on...collar and all... At the end of eight days I became unable to work...I remained in gaol till Friday morning, when Mr McHenry ordered the irons to be taken off by the orders of the Governor...On our arrival at the camp in Emu Plains, another pair of irons were put on me, being the usual irons of the gang...[18]

This was later confirmed by the evidence of William Dumeresq, James Kinghorne and George Plumley, who were examined by a third Executive Council inquiry in 1829: the order had been communicated through Dumeresq, to James Kinghorne, and by him to Plumley, the overseer to whom Thompson had been assigned.[19]

In *The Australian*, Wardell did carry some further news of Thompson's adventures, claiming he was worked in his chains, and sent by cart to the convict establishment at Emu Plains, where James Kinghorne was now Superintendent.[20] Thompson then said he became too exhausted to work and was sick. He was subsequently taken to Penrith goal. There he appeared as a minor celebrity when the paper claimed all Windsor had turned out to see him.[21]

The Kinghornes are Embroiled

The arrival of Sudds' irons and chains at Emu Plains, by then worn by Patrick Thompson, was the point at which the Kinghorne family became deeply involved in the Sudds-Thompson case. James Kinghorne had been Superintendent at the Emu Plains convict farm since February 1826 and became responsible for these irons in the way described above by

Thompson.[22] James' family, including his father, brothers and sisters were still living at the Superintendent's house, where the chains remained in storage. James' brother Alexander Kinghorne Jnr, then 23 years old, was at Emu Plains in May/June 1827, when a military contingent from Bathurst visited and asked to examine Sudds' irons and chains.

Meanwhile, the outspoken reformer and barrister William Charles Wentworth, formerly Wardell's business partner at *The Australian* newspaper, was taking a strong political interest in the case. On 15 December 1826 Wentworth, ignoring the colonial office instruction that all correspondence should be forwarded through the Governor, wrote directly to Earl Bathurst urging Darling's impeachment. He had been too busy to prepare a proper report and asked Bathurst to hold off deciding on Darling's behaviour until he sent a complete statement, through the Governor, 'by the next conveyance'. It was a promise he did not keep until March 1829.[23]

In the meantime, Wentworth was busy organising a public meeting for Anniversary Day, Friday 26 January 1827, at which he took the lead with his lively reformist oratory.[24] A petition to the King was supported by the meeting, requesting constitutional reforms, and studded with criticisms of Governor Darling, which would not have been there but for the death of Sudds.[25] Darling forwarded the petition to Bathurst, after adding several of his own enclosures which countered the petitioners arguments.[26] Despite all this preliminary sabre-rattling, it took three years before Wentworth and Wardell felt 'armed [with sufficient] proof' to 'invite [His Excellency] to trial'.[27]

In early 1829, a new player entered the public vendetta against Governor Darling. In a letter to Wentworth on 3 January, the commander of the Royal Veterans of the 57th Regiment, Captain Robert Robison, wrote he had tried on Sudds' chains at Emu Plains, which weighed '40 lbs or upwards'.[28] The implication was that the irons earlier made available for public scrutiny were not those which had been used on Sudds, and ended up at Emu Plains with Thompson.

Robison was another aggrieved victim of Darling's autocratic government, having been recently placed under arrest and court marshalled for sedition.[29] He had arrived in the colony in September 1826, in time for his Royal Veterans to witness the degradation of Sudds and Thompson. Robison would not let his perceived injustice at the hands of Darling rest. His complaint was raised in the House of Commons by petition in 1833,[30] and he was to be the main witness at a parliamentary select committee of inquiry into Darling's administration in 1835.

In March 1829, Wentworth finally produced his 25,000-word indictment of Darling. This contained little substance, apart from blaming Sudds' death on the Governor's iron collar, but the letter caused the Colonial Office in London to seek an opinion from the Solicitor General.[31] The matter was reopened in the third inquiry by the Executive Council at Sydney in May 1829.

James Kinghorne was interviewed by the Executive Council on 7 May. He confirmed that Patrick Thompson had been sent to a road gang near Emu Plains wearing irons for about seven days. James had received orders from the Governor, via Captain Dumeresq, to remove the irons from Thompson, in consequence of his good conduct: 'They were brought to me and kept in the government house in which I reside…for twelve months, perhaps longer'. He stated that Mr Ranken, Mr Lawson, Lieutenant Vachell, Captain Robison and Lieutenant Christie, en route from the Bathurst district, had asked to see the irons in May or June 1827. Captain Robison tried them on and '[James] saw him lie down in them at full length, and [was] almost sure that he saw him turn while lying on the floor with the irons on him.' James was further able to 'recognize the same set of irons [presented at the inquiry] from several marks', stating they were the ones given to him as having been worn by Thompson and 'there were no other chains of the same description at Emu Plains.' These, he said, were the same ones tried on by Captain Robison. James 'did not ascertain [their] weight, but…judged it to be from twelve to fourteen pounds.' He further testified that – when Lieutenant Christie, who had been present when Robison tried on the irons and chains, observed that they must weigh sixty pounds – his brother (Alexander Jnr) 'who was standing by said "no such thing", and taking them up in his hand and stretching out his arm, added "Do you think I could hold out sixty pounds in this way?"'[32]

Alexander Kinghorne Jnr then appeared before the Executive Council on Thursday 14 May 1829.[33] He confirmed that both Captain Robison and Lieutenant Christie had been at Emu Plains to see the irons originally worn by Sudds. Alexander Jnr was also able to identify the irons presented to him by the Council as those that had been at Emu Plains and tried on by Robison: 'he knew them from a nail in one of the basils.' He was able to confirm all his brother's evidence regarding the weight of the irons, when examined by Christie and Robison 'in about the month of May 1827'.[34]

> I recollect Mr Christie saying they would weigh about sixty pounds. I took the irons in my hand, and stretching out my arm said, 'it was impossible I could hold out sixty pounds in that way.' Captain Robison and Mr. Christie said it was all habit. I might perhaps hold out a hundred weight.

Alexander Jnr then confirmed that Captain Robison had tried the irons on, had lain down on the floor and turned himself with them on.[35]

The evidence given independently by the Kinghorne brothers was vitally important, and damning for those opposing the Governor, because they confirmed that the irons fitted to Sudds (and later Thompson) were lighter than the weights sworn by Christie and Robison. The Kinghorne brothers were capable of accurately estimating the weight of the irons, without the aid of scales, throwing considerable doubt on the motives of Captain Robison, who, on cross-examination, blamed the poor candlelight for his gross over-estimation of their weight (60 lbs).[36]

Robison's evidence became even more elaborate and evasive when, in 1835, he was examined in London by the House of Commons Select Committee enquiring into the conduct of Governor Darling. He tried to discredit the evidence of the Kinghornes, suggesting that the irons he saw before the Executive Council were lighter than those at Emu Plains. He invented stories about further persons trying on the chains at Emu Plains, that James Kinghorne had ascertained the weight of them to be 60 lbs from one of the by-standers, and that Alexander Kinghorne Jnr (whose name he could not recall) had been unable to fully lift the irons with his arms outstretched.[37] His unreliable memory had been elaborated with the passage of time and in accordance with his enmity for Governor Darling.

These details were critical to the case that was finally placed before the House of Commons committee in London in 1835, which resulted in the exoneration of Lieutenant-General Ralph Darling.[38] The Kinghornes' evidence had the ring of truth amongst all the invective and diatribe, despite Edward Smith Hall's best efforts to discredit them, in the

Monitor newspaper.[39] It is surprising that their specific evidence has not been previously highlighted by historians.[40] James' and Alexander Jnr's testimonies were factual and honest, showing no sign of a political bias.

Alexander Kinghorne Snr, for his part, was not called to give evidence regarding the Sudds–Thompson case. He was present at Emu Plains in 1827, when Robison and the other military gentlemen examined Sudds' irons. His only contribution might have been to encourage his sons to tell the truth at the Executive Council Enquiry, and this evidence was conclusive at the select committee of inquiry into Darling's administration in 1835. It is uncertain what Alexander's personal views might have been as there is no comment from him documented. He did not write to the newspaper in 1830, after Edward Smith Hall used his name in his case against Darling and tried to discredit his sons' evidence in the *Monitor*. The irony remains, that the Kinghorne brothers' evidence contributed to saving the reputation of the Governor who deprived their father of his career, at a senior level, in the colonial administration of New South Wales.

Chapter 21

James Kinghorne at Emu Plains and Wellington Valley (1826–1832)

Imagination cannot fancy anything more beautifully picturesque than the scene which burst upon us.

John Oxley, August 1817

From his appointment as Superintendent of the Emu Plains establishment in January 1826, until his move to Wellington Valley in September 1829, James Kinghorne oversaw a period of heightened productivity, through the growing of wheat, maize and tobacco. The movement of large numbers of government stock was also an important aspect of the farms' activities but cropping gradually overtook livestock production under James' management. In July 1826 there were 392 bushels of wheat in the granary, 4,000 bushels of wheat in stacks, and 6,256 bushels of maize in the stores at the farm. James' achievement was to maintain the high farm productivity that had been established by his father, despite one of the worst droughts in the colony's history that lasted from 1827 to 1829. During this period, Emu Plains was responsible for supporting many of the other agricultural and penal settlements in New South Wales especially Rooty Hill, Bathurst, Wellington Valley, Moreton Bay and Norfolk Island.[1]

Alexander Kinghorne Snr continued to influence the operations of the farm well after he ceased to be Superintendent. He and his family remained domiciled at Emu Plains until August 1827, and he occasionally took over from James when he was absent. Alexander Jnr occupied himself by supporting his brother and involving himself in the mechanisation of agricultural operations. In June 1827 he constructed a threshing machine which, driven by horse or bullock power, was able to separate wheat from stalks.[2] When Alexander Jnr requested payment of £300 for his efforts, the Colonial Secretary asked William Dumeresq, as Colonial Engineer, to inspect the work.[3] The funds were eventually paid in 1828, after a delayed inspection. James Kinghorne utilised the threshing mill as best he could, but its output was limited by the availability of suitable horse or oxen power.[4]

The Emu Plains establishment remained a major staging point for government officials travelling over the mountains to Bathurst, including the Governor and Chief Justice Francis Forbes, who was a regular guest at 'Government House'.[5] The continued residence of Alexander and his family in the house made for convivial, if somewhat cosy evenings over dinner. Doubtless, Alexander would have made the most of these opportunities to curry favour with the guests of the establishment.

James' superintendence at Emu Plains was not without controversy and he, like his father, suffered the wrath of Governor Darling. An early reprimand came in June 1826 and resulted in the dismissal of James' most trusted overseer, Joseph Peters, who had been in continuous service at Emu Plains for six years, well after his original sentence had expired. Peters, suspecting that stock were being pilfered from the station, instituted an audit that indicated 130 pigs were 'unaccounted for' during the previous six months. He estimated that thirty of these pigs had been stolen and the remainder had perished from disease and the severity of the winter. Peters notified Alexander Kinghorne Snr of the suspected theft, who reported it to the Evan Bench of Magistrates. The unfortunate Peters found that counter-charges had already been laid against him as the thief![6]

Contrary to Alexander's intentions, the bench found Peters guilty, despite James' protestations of his innocence to the Colonial Secretary. Peters appeared to have lost the respect of the convicts in his charge, who associated his sympathies more with the Superintendent than with them. Darling insisted that his dismissal had to stand, presumably as a scapegoat, although he indicated Peters was probably innocent of the charges. He reprimanded James for failing to solve and check the situation before it placed Peters in such a vulnerable position. James was 'sorry that the Governor should think him negligent' but explained he could not oversee every department on the farm all the time. Even when he was absent from Emu Plains, his father was there in his place, so that he tried to '[see] everything with [his] own eyes and never depend upon reports'.[7]

James was further censured by the Colonial Secretary on several occasions during his four-year tenure as Superintendent. His official correspondence at times reflected frustration with constant policy changes and lack of consultation from the government. For example, on 30 December 1826 he received a stern letter from Alexander Macleay with a reprimand for not strictly adhering to government orders. A convict, Peter Davidson, had bypassed James and sent his memorial for an indulgence directly to the Colonial Secretary. James was admonished that he must observe the 'Orders' and 'keep the people under your orders fully informed of regulations'.[8] These transgressions were kept on James' record and eventually counted against him.

In September 1829, John Maxwell took over from James Kinghorne, who replaced Maxwell at the Wellington Valley government station, then considered the outer limits of the colonial frontier.[9] Maxwell had been Superintendent of Government Stock at both Bathurst and Wellington Valley. James' move to Wellington was effectively a demotion for him, and a promotion for Maxwell, whose primary responsibility became wider than Emu Plains, encompassing all government stock in the colony.

When James Kinghorne departed, the Emu Plains staff had reduced to a hundred men, less than half the number present at his appointment in 1826. The emphasis had changed from agricultural production to the control and movement of government stock. Alexander had by then moved the family base to Liverpool. So, as the Kinghorne era at Emu Plains ended, the future 'no longer would be a picture of comfort, regularity and discipline'.[10]

James stayed at Wellington Valley until the establishment was closed in January 1832. It was a pleasant but remote rural appointment. John Oxley had described it in these words when seeing it for the first time on 18 August 1817:

> Imagination cannot fancy anything more beautifully picturesque than the scene which burst upon us. The breadth of the valley to the base of the opposite gently-rising hills, was between three and four miles, studded with fine trees, upon a soil which, for richness, can nowhere be excelled. The westward rocky-range was covered to the summit with cypresses and acacia in full bloom. In the centre of this charming valley ran a strong and beautiful stream, its bright transparent waters dashing over a gravelly bottom intermingled with large stones, forming, at short intervals, considerable pools, in which the rays of the sun were reflected with a brilliancy equal to that of the most polished mirror.[11]

Oxley was so impressed he named it Glenfinlass: the glen of many windings. The Macquarie River at this point was wide, with a considerable area of alluvial soil along its banks, making it ideal for agricultural purposes. The convict settlement has been established there in 1822 under the command of Percy Simpson, followed by Lieutenants Brown and Christie, and John Maxwell, and finally James Kinghorne.

At its peak, Wellington Valley comprised a substantially fenced farm of 300 acres, divided into several paddocks where wheat, maize and tobacco were grown successfully. The convicts were housed in white-painted brick huts, 'where all was neatness and comfort' and James resided in 'a rustic cottage at the head of the valley, built on a gentle eminence'. The Macquarie River, close by, was wide and flooded regularly. There were plenty of fish in the river, including large Murray Cod. Gradually, large grazing estates were taken up in the vicinity.[12]

James Kinghorne developed an intimate knowledge of the surrounding areas through his good relationships with the local aboriginal people.[13] He undertook several forays of his own under their guidance, including extensive investigation of the nearby subterranean caves. His land explorations extended far to the west, where he became acquainted with the Macquarie marshes and the Bogan and Orana regions.[14] This experience would serve James well in the future, as he expanded his family's landholdings into western New South Wales. At Wellington, he was also to renew his acquaintance with his old colleague Thomas Mitchell, and assist him with his exploration, locally and beyond.[15] This first recorded interaction between the Kinghornes and the aboriginal people, whose land it was, seems to have been harmonious, and not officious or predatory.

After James left, the settlement was abandoned with the exception of 'half a dozen stockmen and soldiers, who remained to protect the building from the mischievous spoliation of the natives'. The London based Church Mission Society then moved into the settlement to create an aboriginal mission.[16]

Chapter 22

Court Service (1827–1840)

...are you one of Kinghorne's constables...for taking bushrangers...
Michael Finnegan, August 1830

In the forty years between the establishment of the colony of New South Wales and the arrival of Alexander Kinghorne, the criminal court system had changed from a military tribunal, without judge or jury, to something resembling that operating in Britain. The New South Wales Act of 1823 introduced the so-called 'Third Charter of Justice', proclaimed on 17 May 1824. The arrangements under the charter established the first Supreme Court, presided over by a Chief Justice, Francis Forbes.[1]

This court had jurisdiction to hear cases of treason, piracy and crime. All such offences were to be prosecuted in the name of the attorney general, and issues of fact were tried by the judge and a 'jury' of seven 'commissioned officers of His Majesty's sea or land forces'.[2]

Matters of civil law in the Supreme Court were different. They were tried by a judge, together with two assessors – these being magistrates specially appointed to this duty. In addition, the accused parties in civil cases had the privilege of choosing to be tried by a twelve-man 'jury of civil inhabitants', sometimes known as a 'common jury'.[3] Trial by jury remained confined to civil issues only until 1833, when the provision was extended to criminal cases by an Act of Council. In criminal cases after 1833, the accused could choose to be tried either by seven military officers, or by a jury of inhabitants. However, the application for cases to be heard before juries was still rare in Alexander's time. Most civil trials in the Supreme Court, for example, were before a judge and assessors (170 trials), with special and common juries less often (on average seventeen and six trials per year, respectively, between 1830 and 1834).[4]

Below the Supreme Court were the courts of Quarter Sessions and local courts (or Petty Sessions). The Quarter Sessions was an intermediate court with more powers than the local court or bench but not as over-riding as those of the Supreme Court. It could hear all crimes and misdemeanours not punishable by death. The Quarter Sessions court met three times a year at various locations throughout the colony, and was composed of two or more magistrates, presided over by an elected chairman who served the entire colony. The local courts, presided over by Justices of the Peace, had jurisdiction to deal with most minor civil and criminal matters.

Between 1825 and 1840, Alexander Kinghorne served at all three levels of the legal system of New South Wales, as a local magistrate in Liverpool, a grand juror, foreman and witness in the Sydney court of Quarter Sessions, and as an Assessor in the Supreme Court.

Justice of the Peace

Alexander's legal service commenced when he was appointed as a Justice of the Peace. In colonial New South Wales, the role of a JP was not as it is today, involving considerably more than administration of oaths and the certification of documents. There was, then, a judicial power, status and responsibility associated with the appointment. The announcement of appointment as a JP, published in the *Sydney Gazette*, usually opened with the declaration: 'George the Fourth, by the Grace of God, of the United Kingdom of Great Britain and Ireland, King, Defender of the Faith, and so forth' followed by a list of names, selected by the Governor, to be given the King's 'commission of peace'. A long 'Greeting' followed, witnessed by the Governor, which admonished the appointees to fulfil a series of articles, ordinances and statutes 'for the Preservation of the Peace, and for the quiet Rule and Government of our people'. JPs had authority over sheriffs, constables, gaolers and other government officers. Their legal powers included the sentencing of felons and rebels to fines, punishments and imprisonment, making enquiries about them and sitting in judgement over them, 'according to the Laws and Statutes of England'. They were, therefore, honorary magistrates, of which there were 119 in the colony in 1830.[5]

Until 1825, JPs were drawn exclusively from the colony's landowners, civil and military officers, but paid police or stipendiary magistrates were introduced from the mid-1820s, eventually eroding the powers and responsibilities of JPs. However, the general magisterial power was still in place when Alexander Kinghorne and his family moved to Liverpool in 1827.

Alexander was first appointed JP by Governor Brisbane on 12 November 1825.[6] The main qualification for this appointment, apart from his service as Superintendent of Emu Plains, was his recent grant of two thousand acres of land in the County of Argyle, near Goulburn.[7] He was reappointed JP in June 1827, a couple of months before he moved himself and his family to Liverpool.[8] There, he took an active role as a magistrate in the local court, being reappointed every two years until 1840.[9] Alexander sat on the bench, usually along with two other local magistrates, hearing relatively minor cases, sometimes directed to them from a higher court.[10] The Liverpool bench of magistrates operated from the courthouse and sometimes the police office, whence they both issued orders and dispensed justice.[11]

A Reliable Witness

Alexander was a regular witness in the courts, particularly giving character assessments for convicts who had been under his superintendence at Emu Plains. Some of these individuals reoffended over the years, so he was called to give evidence about the same person more than once between 1826 and 1840.

Perhaps the closest of these to Alexander's heart, was the Emu Plains convict overseer Joseph Peters. He was in trouble with the authorities on several occasions over the five years he served under Alexander and James Kinghorne, the latter when both assistant and principal superintendent. On Thursday 12 October 1826, for example, Peters appeared before the Windsor Quarter Sessions accused of attempting to 'suborn [induce] witnesses on a criminal prosecution', always a potential misdemeanour for an overseer of convicts. Peters' defence counsel was able to impeach the evidence of witnesses against him, and Alexander spoke passionately 'of the defendant's character, as a good overseer, active and industrious, and consequently opposed to the misconduct of the men sent to this establishment, and thereby very much disliked'. Rev'd Fulton spoke also in Peters' defence, having some experience of him appearing before him, as local magistrate, when Peters had been falsely accused in the past by disgruntled inmates of Emu Plains. The jury found Peters not guilty without retiring. [12] The hapless Peters was eventually dismissed from Emu Plains under the orders of Governor Darling,[13] wherefrom he continued long service of James Kinghorne as the overseer at Cardross, near Goulburn.[14]

Emu Plains was not always the situation of Alexander's acquaintance with accused felons, as in the case of Alexander Dick, a free settler and silversmith, whom the Kinghornes met on the *Portland* during their voyage to New South Wales in 1824. Dick and an accomplice, Thomas Jasper, appeared in the Sydney Supreme Court in May 1829 accused of receiving stolen goods, twelve silver dessert spoons, which Dick was said to have falsely hallmarked – a form of silver laundering – and restamped with his mark ('AD'), after they had been made 'smooth, filed, scraped, annealed, and pickled'. Alexander testified that 'during the voyage he had frequent opportunities of observing Dick's conduct, which, connected with his behaviour in this country, he had every reason to be satisfied with. He believed him to be an upright, industrious young man' – an assessment that proved wayward as the evidence of his silver forgery emerged. The judge in this case, Mr Justice Dowling, was well known to Alexander, who served under him as an assessor in the civil court.

The case of Dick and Jasper was widely reported in the Sydney newspapers, in considerable detail, as the spoons in question had been stolen in November or December 1826 from the Colonial Secretary, Alexander MacLeay's residence in Macquarie Place. The prisoners were prosecuted by the Attorney General and defended by Wentworth and Wardell. The defence argument rested on the spoons being passed to Dick as revenge for mistreatment of the main witness against him, his former convict servant, of whom Dick had instigated a lashing. Nevertheless, the case was clearly proved, and both men were found guilty.[15] Alexander was not alone in testifying to Dick's character. The merchant Samuel Terry, watchmaker James Robertson and engraver Samuel Clayton were among those who provided favourable endorsements, and forty leading citizens, including a reluctant Alexander MacLeay, signed a memorial to Governor Darling on behalf of Mrs Dick. On 1 February 1833 Governor Bourke pardoned Dick, stating that 'some favourable circumstances have been represented to me on his behalf'.[16] Notably, the pardon required a change of Governor.

Jury Service

From 1834, juries could be made up of four *special* jurors or twelve *common* jurors or 'civil inhabitants'. A special jury list was published each year in the *Sydney Gazette* from 1831.[17] Esquires, or 'persons of higher degree', JPs, merchants or bank directors were eligible to serve as special jurors, receiving a fee of 15s per day.[18] The system was imbued with notions of class and the importance of position within the community, and the idea that possession of valuable property somehow denoted the honesty and fairness of the possessor. This was a curious concept in a colony where property was amassed by all manner of both sanctioned and nefarious means. Nevertheless, the appointment of Alexander Kinghorne as a special juror, and later as a Supreme Court Assessor, confirmed that he had gained significant recognition in the colony.[19]

Alexander served as a special juror on the Supreme Court between 1830 and 1833, after which he was appointed an Assessor. In most cases, he was selected on juries under Sir James Dowling – a 'tactful, genial and kind man',[20] but on occasion Chief Justice Forbes, or John Stephen. Stephen, who often 'independently asserted himself with unmistakable energy', could be 'blunt to the point of rudeness' and was a thinly disguised enemy of Governor Darling.[21] Despite their varying characters, Alexander got on well with the Supreme Court judges, and was regular and prompt in his attendance, sometimes acting as jury foreman.[22] This might have contributed to his selection as an Assessor, although there is no specific evidence to that effect. Alexander sailed blithely and unerringly through all the intrigue of the early colonial legal system. He rarely occasioned public comment, with the exception of certain of his magisterial pronouncements that ended up in the press (see this chapter, The Liverpool Magistrate, and Something Strange).

Quarter Sessions Jury Service

As opposed to the Supreme Court, jury trials were used in courts of Quarter Sessions from October 1824, after Chief Justice Forbes had established them 'by judicial declaration'.[23] In these courts, both 'grand' and 'petty' juries were empanelled, from which both convicts and emancipists were excluded. Grand juries, composed of local inhabitants, were a uniquely colonial institution. Their purpose was to inform the court about breaches

233

of the peace, and other matters requiring its attention, based on local knowledge.[24]

Alexander first appeared in the Windsor Quarter Sessions on 2 January 1827, as a member of a grand jury under the foremanship of John Bingle Esquire. Other local dignitaries on the jury included his son James, George Bowman, William Faithful, Thomas Arndell and Richard Rouse.[25] The jury were presented with the cases of James Dunn, charged with stealing a piece of calico, John Blackmore for stealing a water cask, William Lahy for possession of stolen goods, Ann Rushtin for stealing a cloth jacket, John Trowell for stealing two tether ropes, Henry Ruth for stealing promissory notes, Edward Devine for 'pig-stealing' and a charge of larceny against Esther Croughwell. The grand jury considered each case individually, generally for fifteen to twenty minutes, giving findings of guilty or not guilty. The grand jurymen also made a field visit to examine conditions at the local gaol but had no 'presentment to make' about it. The prisoners found not guilty were then discharged and the session terminated. Such was the usual business of the Quarter Sessions court.[26] Mundane as these court sessions might have been, they provided Alexander with invaluable judicial experience for his appointment as a local magistrate.

The Liverpool Magistrate

Alexander became a local court magistrate after moving to Liverpool in 1827. The first record of him sitting on the bench appeared in the newspapers in 1829. He likely started serving earlier than this, as he was already on the list of Liverpool JPs, along with the other five magistrates (Charles Throsby, Thomas Moore, William Browne, Patrick Hill and Richard Brooks) from September 1827.[27]

The newspaper record indicates that the most regular magistrates sitting together on the Liverpool bench, from 1830, were Thomas Moore and Alexander Kinghorne, whereas the other gentlemen were often far too busy with their landed pursuits.[28] It was clearly a service that Alexander enjoyed, and he would have been well schooled in its workings by Thomas Moore: a prominent citizen of the colony who had been a magistrate since 1810 and was then the senior magistrate of New South Wales. Moore, another like-minded evangelical Christian, although Church of England, contributed generously to the establishment of other institutions, including the Sydney Scots Church and the Liverpool courthouse, where Presbyterian and Wesleyan services were held on Sundays. It is likely that Moore had a significant and beneficial influence on Alexander as a mentor.[29]

In one of Alexander's more curious cases, one Michael Finnigan – a reprobate who would not have been expected to be literate – wrote to the editor of the *Monitor* from Sydney Gaol. The letter complained that he had been wrongly imprisoned by Magistrates Kinghorne and Moore for assaulting Constable Donohoe at Liverpool on 24 August 1830.[30] Ten days later, three affidavits, sworn before the same magistrates by Constables Donohoe, Young and Perry, also appeared in the *Monitor*, each confirming the assault by Finnigan. He had been imbibing at the nearby Elephant and Castle on the evening of the incident. He first addressed Donohoe as 'Donnolly', then 'Connolly',[31] becoming abusive, and asking 'are you one of Kinghorne's constables…for taking bushrangers?' He then struck Donohoe and tore his shirt.[32] Despite the testimony of the constables, the *Monitor's* outspoken editor, Edward Smith Hall, added the following footnote:

> On perusing the above, we think Finnegan has a good action against the Justices, if he chose to indulge in gambling in the law, Ed.[33]

It should be noted that Hall, at this time, was also in Sydney Gaol, having been convicted of libel against Governor Darling three years earlier. He might have written the original letter, which Finnegan signed, after hearing the complaint directly from him. So, why did he publish such clearly false comments about the magistrates in the face of overwhelming evidence? One possibility is that the letters, comments and editorial statement were associated with Hall's campaign to discredit the evidence of Alexander's sons, James and Alexander Kinghorne Jnr, in support of Robert Robison against Governor Darling.[34] Public criticism of their father could be construed as another component of Hall's haranguing efforts against Darling, although it could have been just a general diatribe against the judiciary.

As if to place himself in Hall's favour, Alexander had been on the jury in another Supreme Court suit, a month earlier, which exonerated the outspoken newspaperman. The Crown was attempting to recover penalties Hall allegedly incurred for breaches of an Act of Council that seemed specifically designed for *him*: 'for preventing the mischiefs arising from the printing and publishing of newspapers, and other papers of a like nature, by persons not known and for regulating the printing and publication of such papers in other respects, and also for restraining the abuses arising from the publication of blasphemous and seditious libels'. On this occasion, the jury found for the defendant.[35]

Hall was released from prison on 6 November 1830, in honour of the accession of King William IV, but continued his campaigns against the Governor until Darling was relieved of command on 1 October 1831.[36]

Alexander might have held some sympathy for Hall, either because of even-handedness or his changing political stance. Hall's friend James Chisholm shared his reformist agenda and would have carried some influence with Alexander. Moreover, by December 1831, Darling had been replaced as Governor by the far more liberal Richard Bourke. In 1833, Alexander participated in the movement for the introduction of a legislative assembly.[37] Along with James Chisholm in Sydney, Alexander became a member of the General Petition Committee for Liverpool, as was his son, James Kinghorne, for Argyll.[38] By the 1830s Alexander was becoming aligned with the reformists in New South Wales.

* * *

Alexander's long service as a local magistrate was, perhaps, overshadowed by his appointments to more senior roles in the courts of Quarter Sessions and the Supreme Court. Nevertheless, his status as a magistrate gained him invitations to important civic and vice regal events. In January 1836, he was present with other Liverpool and Campbelltown magistrates to welcome the new Governor, Sir Richard Bourke, at the opening of the Lansdowne Bridge over the Prospect Creek at Liverpool. Alexander had been a signatory in the various petitions, encouraging the construction of the bridge. Along with the other dignitaries, he presented the Governor with a picture of the new bridge by Conrad Martens.[39] In May of the same year Alexander, along with other prominent merchants, landowners and judiciary, attended a 'Levee' at Government House in honour of the King's birthday.[40] In January 1837 he became a trustee of the Town Common of Liverpool.[41]

Without doubt, in terms of New South Wales Society, Alexander Kinghorne had arrived. However, his magisterial role was not all plain sailing.

Something Strange

In October 1837, Alexander had a run-in with a Wesleyan Minister. Rev'd Daniel Draper came from Parramatta to preach at Liverpool one Sunday afternoon. Despite twenty years of Wesleyan ministry at the Courthouse, Alexander sent a constable to prevent Draper entering the premises, where the services were usually held; a correspondent to *The Colonist* described Alexander's behaviour as 'Something Strange' and the affair as 'grotesque'.[42]

The circumstances were as follows. Rev'd James Allan, Presbyterian minister at Parramatta, intending to conduct occasional services at Liverpool, had written to the Liverpool Bench, informing them of his wish to do so. He requested 'the use of any edifice within their power'. The only place 'within the gift' of the magistrates was the courthouse, where the Wesleyan minister had held services, by his own account at 3 p.m. 'every Sunday'. As it happened, Rev'd Allan chose the same Sunday as the Wesleyan minister, at the same crucial hour, and so the courthouse became double-booked. The *Sydney Gazette* suggested 'the magistrates' were unaware that Rev'd Draper was preaching there on the same day, and that it was not until Sunday morning that the mistake was discovered, when a message was sent to Draper, apologising to him and requesting him to 'vacate the building' and make other arrangements.[43]

The *Sydney Gazette*, scrupulously avoiding the mention of any particular magistrate's name, reported that Draper 'was more desirous to be considered a martyr, than a man of sense', as he returned an angry message to 'the magistrates', who ordered the constable to turn both him and his flock out of the Courthouse. Rev'd Allan arrived, after the disturbance had subsided, oblivious of any problem, but held a short service as only nine or ten people turned up due to insufficient notice. Then Allan encountered Draper on his way home. He was confronted with 'a violent towering passion of abuse' that left him mystified. Allan eventually calmed the 'furious Wesleyan', explained what had happened and apologised.[44]

Unfortunately, this was not the end of the story. On October 10, Rev'd Daniel Draper, his ire not having subsided, penned a long letter to the Editor of the *Sydney Gazette* regretting that he had been misrepresented by them and setting the record straight. In this he implicated 'Mr Kinghorne and a lady' in barring him from the courthouse...

> Mr. Allan advanced to me, and offered, his hand, which I took. I observed to him that such a mode of proceeding was very improper, to which he replied that he had 'a document' which fully justified him in the steps he took. Mr. Kinghorne then said something, but I have forgotten what, and I immediately informed the people that I should preach at the school; to which place everyone followed me.[45]

The matter was still not at an end. Several letters to the editor of the *Sydney Gazette* ensued from Wesleyans, who had been ejected from the Courthouse, supporting at some length Rev'd Draper's claims. One of them described how it was Alexander Kinghorne who was the villain of the piece, in collusion with the presbyterian minister.[46]

There the matter rested, with no further correspondence, and there is no evidence of Alexander making any statement about it. Whatever the truth of the incident, he had been accused of denominational bias, and of falling short in both judgement and communication. Not good for a judicial official.

Supreme Court Assessor

Alexander was appointed Assessor in the Supreme Court of New South Wales in 1833. The Assessors were rostered in groups of three and, on the day of sitting, two were selected to sit with the judge.[47] Alexander first appeared with His Honour Mr Justice Dowling, along with fellow-Assessor John Campbell, on Wednesday 12 June 1833. This was a civil case between two brothers, Lyons v. Lyons, represented by Wardell and Wentworth, respectively, for recovery of funds owed.[48] This was typical of many litigations Alexander assessed on matters relating to the recovery of money, often by barristers to recover their fees, for breaches of agreements and for damages resulting from trespass. Up to six trials were heard at each sitting.[49]

In most cases, the sitting judge could make a direction to the Assessors, like the direction to a jury, before they made their decision on a matter.

For example, an unusual lawsuit before Justice Dowling in September 1834 concerned an action for damages by Mr Ducey against Mr Grant for the loan of a horse and cart by the defendant as lessee of the Government Punt at Bedlam Point, 'in consequence of the absence of the necessary precautions for preventing the horse from backing itself overboard'. His Honour regretted that some arrangement had not been made between the parties, instead of bringing it into court, 'as they were very poor persons, and must necessarily involve themselves in ruinous expenses'. Dowling 'felt bound to direct the Assessors to find for the plaintiff' but declared that the defendant was hard-done-by. He 'generously moved a subscription' on Grant's behalf, to which he immediately contributed two guineas. The Assessors, Alexander and John Edye Manning, subscribed their fee for the day, and some of the 'gentlemen of the law added their mite in behalf of the poor suitor'.[50]

Alexander continued as an Assessor in the Supreme Court until 1839, although he appeared less often after the end of sittings in 1835,[51] when he began to acquire more rural property on behalf of his sons. From 1836–40, he concentrated on the acquisition and management of his estates, perhaps as a consolidation of assets for his family, as he prepared for his return to Scotland. He was spending more time in Goulburn at his Cardross estate, and even acted as Police Magistrate in that town.

Chapter 23

The Vision Splendid: Property in New South Wales (1827–1840)

And the bush hath friends to meet him,
and their kindly voices greet him
In the murmur of the breezes and the river on its bars,
And he sees the vision splendid of the sunlit plains extended,
And at night the wond'rous glory of the everlasting stars.

Banjo Paterson, *Clancy of the overflow*

The heart of the Kinghorne colonial landholdings were in the County of Argyle on the Goulburn Plains, just six miles west of that town. This area of the New South Wales southern tablelands would have reminded Alexander of Tweedside, in the Scottish Borders: its long views, soft undulating topography, occasional higher hills and riverine alluvial soils (Figure 37). A detailed consideration of these lands was given in the authors' previous book, *The Master of Hell's Gates*.[1] A link to the full list of Kinghorne land grants and pastoral properties may be found at Appendix 7.[2] This history considers only the lands granted, purchased and disputed while Alexander was resident in New South Wales (1824–1840).

For the 'honor of Tweedside'

It is unlikely that Alexander Kinghorne visited his Argyle land before 1828, as the location was not chosen by him, but for him, by his future son-in-law, James Chisholm Jnr. Alexander's first grant had been recommended by Earl Bathurst in 1823, before he left Scotland, and promised by Governor Brisbane on 19 October 1824.[3] After a year in the colony, Alexander felt the need to remind the Governor that he had yet to receive any land…

> I beg leave to request, that Your Excellency will be pleased to cause a Reserve of Two Thousand acres of Land to be made out in my Name, which, in the event of my quitting the employ of Government, may be

240

converted into a Grant from the Crown.

I am emboldened to solicit this favour from the circumstances of my assistant superintendent holding a Grant of Land, and many other officers (who are under the same circumstances with respect to land as myself), receiving similar benefit and indulgence. [4]

An area of two thousand acres was requested, either based on Brisbane's original promise, or as a new claim based on his government service. Part of the supporting argument from Alexander was that his Assistant Superintendent at Emu Plains, John Stewart, had just been awarded a grant. Stewart, like Alexander, had arrived in the colony in 1824 and was appointed to Emu Plains on 16 February 1825. Stewart's land was promised in December 1824, reserved and granted on 23 May 1825 and, in response to a further memorial, increased from 100 to 1,000 acres on 10 November 1825. [5] Likewise, Alexander's son James, formerly Assistant Superintendent at Emu Plains, had already been promised a grant of 1,000 acres in the Cowpastures. [6]

Brisbane wrote on Alexander's letter that his request was 'confirmed if p[e]r regulations', necessitating a further formal memorial, explaining the 'means he possessed to bring the land into cultivation'. Alexander's ensuing memorial did not mention funds or assets, but concentrated on his ability, experience and education…

I beg leave most respectfully to thank Your Excellency for your kindness, in directing your Private Secretary, on 19th of October 1824, to communicate to me, 'That the Surveyor General would be instructed to make unto me a Grant of Land so soon as I should show, through some respectable channel, the Means I possessed for bringing the same into cultivation'. –

I have now been upwards of twelve Months in the Colony, and most of the time employed under Your Excellency's own eye, in directing and Superintending, the Various Works and Improvements on His Majesty's Grand Agricultural Establishment of 'Emu Plains'; – And I have more than once, had the honor of being complimented, on the spot, by Your Excellency, for the manner in which these Improvements have been conducted: – And, from the Certificates and other documents, which I have laid before Your Excellency, of the Means I possess, and of my character from earliest life. – I hope Your Excellency will have no hesitation in Ordering me a Grant of Two Thousand acres of Land: – which I pledge myself shall be so Managed and Cultivated, as to do

241

credit to myself, and add honor to the district of 'Tweedside' (where I was educated, and practiced as an Agriculturalist and Land Valuer, etc., on an extensive scale for 20 years), and from which all my Improvements in the Colony have been, and shall be copied. [7]

Alexander's agricultural practice 'in the Colony', with which he had ensured Brisbane was familiar, had been and would continue to be 'copied' from that conducted by him in 'the district of "Tweedside"'. This had been mainly the improvement of the lands of John Seton Karr of Kippilaw, with whom Brisbane had been acquainted through Lord Buchan, and which encompassed both infrastructure and agricultural developments. Alexander's practice would indeed improve his own lands in New South Wales, but the agents and beneficiaries of the improvement would ultimately be his children and their descendants, rather than himself.

Brisbane noted on this Memorial that he was 'satisfied as to the extent of means proposed by Mr Kinghorne & direct[ed] He may be placed in the same parity as other Principal Superintendents', thus maintaining his precedent of granting land for government service. The grant of two thousand acres was ordered on 4 November and Alexander was notified by letter on 18 November 1825.[8]

Up to this point, the process of obtaining his first land grant had been lengthy but relatively straightforward. However, even at this early stage, Alexander believed he had been hard-done-by, and that the intentions of Earl Bathurst and the promises of Sir Thomas Brisbane should be seen as separate.

Disputed Claims

By 1827, Alexander was laying claim to his entitlement to three portions of land on the Goulburn Plains. These claims were based on three premises.

The first was that his original letter from Lord Bathurst, received while he was still in Scotland, promised him one thousand acres. This was based on the copy of this recommendation he had received in 1823 from the Colonial Office and confirmed by Sir Walter Scott through Lord Buchan. Bathurst, however, made no mention of the area of land to be granted, writing in general terms of proceeding 'as a free settler' and 'mak[ing] to him, upon his arrival, a Grant of Land, in proportion to the means which he may possess of bringing the same into Cultivation.' Scott, on the other hand, specified that 'Lord Bathurst had ordered a Grant of a Thousand Acres of Land for your Father in Australia.'[9] Alexander would have felt anxious about this grant from the time he first arrived in New South Wales. Hence, his two letters abovementioned to the Governor in September and October 1825.'[10]

Secondly, Alexander believed that he had asked for two grants of two thousand acres and was entitled to a third. This notion originated from separate claims, reflected in the appearance of his name on two lists, both indicating a grant of two thousand acres, but with different dates of promise, 4 and 8 November for 'a grant' (no fees) and 'a reserve for purchase' (quit rent payable), respectively.[11] The desire for a second two thousand acres was, eventually, fulfilled, when James Kinghorne's thousand acre grant at the Cowpastures was converted to a two thousand-acre grant in the County of Argyle, in recognition of his government service at Emu Plains and Wellington Valley.[12] However, Alexander's other claim for a reserve of two thousand acres, became a third claim for one thousand acres, and remained a matter of dispute.[13]

The idea of three grants continued to be held firmly by the Kinghorne family, but the disagreement of the authorities became confused by regular changes to land grant regulations and legislation, as colonial settlement expanded. From the earliest time of occupation, however, the Kinghornes were running stock on a far larger area of the Goulburn Plains than Alexander's original grant. To legitimise this, from February 1830, Alexander held a 'Depasturing Licence' to run stock on an additional four thousand acres on the south and south-west of his original grant.[14]

Remarkably, these early lands of Alexander and James Kinghorne, including the disputed 1,000 acres, are now together again (2022) as a single holding. This property bears the original name given to it by Alexander Kinghorne – Cardross – in memory of his mentor, David Steuart Erskine, Lord Cardross and 11th Earl of Buchan.

Taking Possession

Alexander Kinghorne formally took possession of Cardross, and the adjoining land he intended to include with it, in 1828. He was still negotiating with the Colonial Secretary regarding his tenure in June 1827. This was around the same time the family left Emu Plains and moved to

Liverpool. Alexander MacLeay wrote to Alexander on the ninth of that month:

> With reference to my former letter of this date inquiring whether you wish to rent with a view to purchase two thousand acres of land therein alluded to and situated ... in the south side of the Wohoridilly...his Excellency the Governor has no objection to your occupying the same under the prescribed rent of 20/- per annum for every hundred acres until His Majesty's pleasure be made known on the subject as until the survey and valuation of the parish in which the land is situated shall be completed when it will be put up to sale...'[15]

When Alexander did the sums, he informed MacLeay that the quit rent on two thousand acres was too much for him to afford. Based on this, the Colonial Secretary wrote on 31 December to Surveyor-General Oxley as follows:

> ...respecting the claim advanced by Mr Kinghorn for two distinct portions of Ground of (2000) two thousand acres each I am now directed by His Excellency the Governor to apprise you Mr Kinghorne has been this day again informed in reply to a subsequent representation that it appears quite clear that he has a claim to only one (2000) two thousand acres in the whole as a reserve confirmed by grant on his quitting the employment of the Government and that this opinion is confirmed by the practice at the time ... Mr Kinghorne having stated that he is unable to rent at the established rent of 20/- per hundred acres per annum more than 1000 acres he has been required to notify to you the particular spot which he wishes to obtain in order that possession may be given in addition to the 2000 acres above mentioned upon the normal conditions.

The final sentence of this communication 'that possession may be given in addition to the 2000 acres above mentioned' confirms Alexander's belief that he was to obtain an additional one thousand acres, as a reserve for purchase, for which he presumably intended to pay the quit rent as specified. This land was duly surveyed, probably by Robert Hoddle, and marked thereafter on the official survey maps as belonging to Alexander Kinghorne, adjoining the Cardross grant on its eastern boundary.[16] Alexander named it Cardross Grange, which remained in the possession of the Kinghorne family for the next fifty-five years, until it was disputed by selectors, and eventually returned to the government as crown land.

In any event, the years 1825–1827 saw Alexander granted a substantial estate of agricultural land on the Goulburn Plains, greater in size than many in Scotland. He had become what he had always dreamed, on paper at least: a landed gentleman. The challenge remained to turn what was in fact excellent pastoral land, into full development, and productive of wealth.

Marriage of Elizabeth Kinghorne and James Chisholm Jnr

The initial meeting between Alexander Kinghorne and James Chisholm Snr in 1824 had flourished into friendship. They shared a reformed evangelical faith, were from similar origins in the lowlands of Scotland, had benefited from aristocratic patronage and were bent on 'improvement'. Whereas Chisholm was 'gruff but quietly spoken' and a little rough around the edges having missed the benefits of an education, Kinghorne had been to grammar school and could 'turn a phrase' with the best of them. Nevertheless, they had much in common and there would have been many meetings between them.[17]

Alexander resided with James Chisholm during his short employment as Colonial Civil Engineer, and during visits to Sydney from Emu Plains, during 1826 and 1827. There is little doubt that the Chisholm family would have been guests at 'Government House', Emu Plains, on several occasions. These meetings led to opportunities for their children to meet, for James Jnr and Elizabeth to form an attachment, and the necessary arrangements to be made in the fullness of time.

On 9 June 1829, James Chisholm Jnr married Elizabeth Margaret Kinghorne at Liverpool.[18] The parish record of the marriage 'certifies that James Chisholm of Minto, bachelor, aged 23, to Elizabeth Kinghorne of Liverpool, spinster, aged 21, were this day married after proclamation of the banns there several times according to the customs and institutions of the National Church of Scotland, by me, John Dunmore Lang, Presbyterian Chaplain, Liverpool New South Wales, 9 June 1829'. The witnesses were the respective fathers of the groom and bride, James Chisholm Snr and Alexander Kinghorne Snr.[19]

James and Elizabeth Chisholm, aided by Alexander and James Snr, started accumulating land along the Wollondilly River to the west of Cardross soon after their marriage. The first two blocks, totalling 1,265 acres, had been purchased by James Chisholm Snr from his auctioneer friends John and George Paul on 9 April 1829.[20] The second of 1,280 acres, initially promised to Rev'd Robert Cartwright in November 1822, and one of the first grants in the Goulburn district, was purchased by James Chisholm Snr on 23 August 1830.[21] The third was a marriage portion of 1,280 acres, granted by Governor Darling in 1831 to Elizabeth Chisholm.[22] Upon this land James Jnr and Elizabeth were to build a fine homestead, commencing in 1831 and completed in 1836.[23] A further six hundred acres was purchased from Mrs Bunker on 3 September 1833.[24] The estate so-formed adjoined further Chisholm land to the west, so that James Chisholm Jnr eventually owned much of the land on the south side of the Wollondilly River, stretching from the western boundary of Cardross, upstream to Thomas Woore's Pomeroy Station, a distance of about ten miles.[25]

Elizabeth Chisholm named the amalgamated property Kippilaw, after the Seton Karr estate in Scotland where she had been born and her father had been factor for thirteen years. One can only suspect that she had reserved the use of this name, with the agreement of her father, before he settled on the name for Cardross. Both were clearly named in 'honor to the district of "Tweedside"'.

Pastoral Expansion

Alexander Kinghorne chose the location of his first land grants on the recommendation of his future son-in-law. While James Jnr and Elizabeth were married in 1829, their courtship, and the consequent growing together of the families, might have been ongoing since 1824. After James Chisholm Jnr finished an apprenticeship in the Sydney commissariat stores in 1826, he moved to Minto to take care of his father's estates there, and to commence building the house that would eventually be named Gledswood.[26]

James Jnr, like his father James Chisholm Snr, had a pioneering streak in his character. He wanted better agricultural land and searched for it further afield than Gledswood, which was located in the poor sheep country of the County of Cumberland. According to his son, James Kinghorne Chisholm, he first visited the Goulburn Plains in 1826. This was part of the area then known as 'the new country', south of the Bargo

Brush. It was 'officially discovered' by Hamilton Hume, James Meehan and Charles Throsby in 1818, although there had been many earlier visits by white settlers.[27] When James Jnr explored it in 1826, he travelled alone on horseback, leading a packhorse loaded with supplies. According to Ransome Wyatt's *History of Goulburn*, James found one solitary shepherd's hut standing on the hill that today is the city of Goulburn. The pastoralist William Bradley, a future member of the Legislative Council and owner of Landsdowne, Goulburn, was already running more than ten thousand sheep on the plains by the late 1820s. In later years, James Jnr was fond of describing the appearance of the Plains west of Goulburn, when he first travelled through them, where he carefully selected a site for a future land grant that was to become his home. In the romantic language of the 1930s, Ransome Wyatt claimed that James Jnr 'being of true pioneering spirit,... carved from the wilderness a great holding which still stands today'.[28]

James Chisholm Jnr chose well when he selected the area for the family settlement in the County of Argyle. However, it was Alexander Kinghorne who first took advantage of it as the site for Cardross. This was located to the south of the Wollondilly River, in the Parish of Baw Baw, six miles west from the site of the town of Goulburn.

In August 1826, perhaps fortuitously, Governor Darling forced James Kinghorne to dismiss Joseph Peters, his principal convict overseer at Emu Plains, over the case of the missing pigs.[29] Unwilling to allow Darling's pedantic scapegoating to ruin the life of a good man, the Kinghornes took the opportunity to send Peters straight to the Goulburn Plains as overseer at Cardross. This might have been as early as 1827,[30] soon after his departure from Emu Plains; the record has him on-sight on census day 1828, as 'overseer for A. Kinghorne, Cardross, Goulburn Plains'. This capable and loyal retainer continued working for the Kinghorne family for most of his working life.[31] The census indicates that he was a tenant on a three-hundred-acre block named 'Oak Brush', presumably part of, or close to Cardross, where he had cleared and cultivated thirty acres. He lived there with his wife, Mary, and their now one-year-old daughter, also named Mary. Fifty of the two thousand acres of Cardross had been cleared, twenty-five acres cultivated, and it was carrying two horses, 203 horned cattle and 256 sheep, all suggesting that Peters and a team of convicts had been hard at work for at least six months.[32]

In the absence of James Kinghorne at Wellington Valley, the young and adventurous John Ker Kinghorne was sent to join Peters at Cardross in early 1828. He was nineteen years old. In October of that year, his older sister, Helen, reported his departure in a letter to brother Andrew Seton Kinghorne, back in Galashiels:

> Ker has now grown a stout fellow and has gone to take charge of the farming concern at Cardross which is the name my father gives to his grant of land. I am happy to inform you that he has been particularly fortunate in concerns there. He has now a good part of the land under cultivation, and likewise a good stock of sheep and cattle.[33]

In 1830, Alexander had been granted a four thousand-acre licence to 'depasture stock' in a location between Cardross and James Chisholm's adjoining property to the west.[34] Ker was on site in September 1830, when William Edward Riley passed 'the huts of Mr Kinghorne' on his way to 'a grant of Chisholm's where he has a herd of cattle in fine order...'.[35] These cattle were running either on the neighbouring land, that was to become Kippilaw, or on leased country at Captain Mark John Currie's grant, Gatton Park, eight miles further west on the Wollondilly river, which James Chisholm Jnr would later purchase.

Agricultural production at Cardross had advanced by February 1832, when Ker wrote to his father reporting the dispatch of ten bales of wool. The description of the clip suggests the sheep flock was still in the region of five hundred:

> You will receive by Will[m] Chadwick and William Graham (10) Ten Bales of wool, some dirty wheat and Bran, and 9½ lb starch the Bags that is marked with a X is lambs wool. There is some coarse Twead wanted for the men and a Brace and Bit which I think James forgot to mark down.
>
> I would have sent the Dray off a day or two sooner but it rained so heavy on the Wednesday after James left that I could not get the Lambs shorn. I hope the Bull[ks] got down right and that you have got a good price for them. I have seen two or three lots pass this and have heard that there is a great many on the road.
>
> Mr Futter has taken all his Flour away from this mill. He is to send 40 bushels more tomorrow. Mr McFarlane sent over 29 Bushels on Saturday.[36]

Cardross was turning off saleable bullocks, which in those days required two to three years to finish on pasture. Moreover, these were no ordinary bullocks, as the following short item from the *Sydney Herald* of 9 July 1832 suggests:

> Mr. Hyland has purchased a bullock of Mr. [JK] Kinghorne for £10; the animal, at present, is on its journey to Sydney, from beyond Goulburn's Plains, and is so fat that it can only travel six miles per diem. It is expected to turn out 1600 lbs.[37]

Allowing for journalistic hyperbole, these animals were likely of above average sale weight for their day.[38] A flour milling operation was also in full swing, grinding wheat from the district's farmers, as far afield as Mr Futter of Bungonia.[39]

Ker's brother James joined him at Cardross after leaving Wellington Valley in February 1832.[40] James would have enjoyed reuniting with Joseph Peters, his former overseer from Emu Plains. Peters continued to assist Ker to run the operation at Cardross, as James began to look further afield for suitable land. In 1833, 2,240 acres was granted to James, adjoining Cardross on the north side of the Wollondilly River. Alexander named this new grant Maxton, after the estate of Thomas Williamson Ramsay back in Scotland.[41] The Argyle property was completed, in 1837, with the purchase from Henry Howie of the Strathern block, at Baw Baw, for one thousand guineas.[42] The addition of this 960-acres on the Goulburn side of Cardross, took the Kinghornes' holdings in Argyle to 6,200 acres (Appendix 7).[43]

In 1835, Alexander applied for and was granted a further ten lots of land, totalling 10,010 acres on the Boorowa River, under the yearly leasehold system applying at that time.[44] This was a substantial addition to their livestock grazing capability. Again, James Chisholm Jnr was soon to lease a similar sized block adjacent to the Kinghorne land at Boorowa.

On 20 June 1836, John Ker wrote a long letter from Cardross to his brother Andrew Seton Kinghorne in Scotland, informing him of developments at Argyle. He revealed that his father, along with James and Alexander Jnr, had erected a wind-powered grinding mill at Cardross, which Ker now owned and operated. The mill was in full operation when David Waugh, a local settler, had his grain turned into flour there, in 1836. Waugh was a 'school fellow' of Ker, as he explained in his letter to his brother, and had been 'in the country' since 1834...[45]

> I have not got up to the farm yet. A law suit, for the tenant's expulsion, is going on at Sydney; but I have nothing to do with it, so I built a house

for myself at the station, and live there; I come down now and then ten miles, stop a day or two with the Kinghorns, and see the news. They have been very kind to me, and lent me what wheat I need, on paying it back out of my first crop. I have four men from government of my own, all good and civil fellows, two English and two Irish; but, as I do not need all till I get into the farm, Mr. Kinghorn has got the loan of two; it is a favour to him, as he is short of hands, and saves me their rations.[46]

Ker was also looking after his brother's 1,200 sheep at Cardross, these presumably belonging to James, who was living with Ker at Cardross. James had 'over 2000 acres joining my fathers [Maxton], running 3000 sheep and some horses [text missing]. [His] father ha[d] about 3000 sheep and 800 head of cattle...' together with 30 draught oxen. They were selling 'seventy bales of wool ... 800 fat sheep and 60 Bullocks' each year together with a significant number of stock retained for feeding a large staff of forty shepherd and herdsmen convicts and overseers. Ker was also running a dairy herd of a hundred cows. As for cropping, they 'had [produced] an excellent crop of wheat – [retaining] 500 Bushels to share after keeping [their] own rations. [Ker was] selling it at 10/- per Bushel. [They had] about 1000 acres enclosed and divided into fields for [their] milking cows, working oxen and horses'.[47]

So, in 1836, John Ker and James Kinghorne were managing a substantial, well-established enterprise on the Goulburn Plains, as well as a large pastoral station on the Boorowa River, 'about 200 miles from this in the west of the country'. This enterprise had taken eight to nine years to establish.

The Kinghorne's property at Boorowa, named Cucumgilliga, was eventually expanded to thirty thousand acres. A further two hundred thousand acres of pastoral country, was obtained by James and John Ker between 1839 and 1851. These properties were spaced widely apart in different environments, stretching from the upland Monaro to the Murrumbidgee River flats in the south, and the productive sheep country, along the Marthaguy Creek, in north-western New South Wales.[48]

In addition to the selection of his prime agricultural land south of Sydney, Alexander had a grand 'vision splendid' to acquire land in the County of Westmoreland, near Bathurst, and the County of St Vincent on the New South Wales coast, 130 miles south of Sydney. He planned to drove his produce – wool and surplus stock – from the Bathurst region,

250

via Argyle to St Vincent, where transport could be completed by sea to Sydney. Consequently, he proceeded to acquire land, by grant and purchase, on the Fish River south-west of Bathurst and at Jervis Bay.[49]

Bathurst

James Kinghorne had been superintendent of Thomas Icely's Saltram Estate at Bathurst Plains from 1824 until January 1826, when he replaced his father as Superintendent at Emu Plains. During this period, he was friendly with George Ranken of nearby Kelloshiel.[50]

In 1830, after constructing the grinding mills at Emu Plains and Cardross, young Alexander Kinghorne Jnr moved to Bathurst and continued his practice as a millwright. His initial employment, arranged by his brother James, was to construct a flour mill for George Ranken at Saltram, newly acquired from Thomas Iceley.[51]

James was then Superintendent at the Wellington Valley convict farm. Later the same year he accommodated George Ranken and Thomas Mitchell at Wellington and assisted them in the exploration of the nearby limestone caves.

A Subterranean Diprotodon

James would have remained in touch with Mitchell, his former colleague from Scotland, where they had worked together on the first topographical survey of Selkirkshire.[52] James and Ranken had already explored several Wellington Caves, so he was the obvious companion and guide for Mitchell, who wanted to explore the main cavern during his visit. A contemporary traveller from Bathurst to Wellington Valley described this cave in December 1831:

> A mile from the entrance of Wellington is the mouth of the subterranean vaults...having found it, you descend a few yards in a horizontal direction till you arrive at a kind of lobby, from which two passages, that afterwards meet, lead you to a great vaulted chamber, capable of holding four or five hundred people...On the far side of the vault stands a huge mass of petrifaction, throwing up innumerable spires and minerals, bearing the appearance of a Gothic altar, or the front of a large cathedral organ...The extent of the cavern is about four hundred feet; and, although several apertures appear in the sides of the passages, not a glimmer of light is discernible. Visitors provide themselves with

torches, made of oakum, tar, and grease, the flame from which destroys the damp and unhealthy exhalations which assail the sense on entering. The excessive ruggedness of the ground fatigued us greatly, but we were amply repaid by the sombre grandeur of the scene.[53]

On the occasion of the 1830 exploration,[54] the party lead by Mitchell and Kinghorne found many bones in the caves, including the fossilised remains of a Diprotodon, the largest of the extinct marsupial megafauna that ranged Australia during the Pleistocene epoch (Figure 34). James provided the boxes to carry the more than one thousand specimens, for the Rev'd John Dunmore Lang to take with him to the University of Edinburgh.[55]

On the return journey to Bathurst, Mitchell was 'detained' on 10 July 1830 'moving, unpacking and repacking the large specimen from Wellington'. He stopped overnight at George Ranken's property, where his fellow dinner guest was a local landowner Robert Lambert and his daughter Jane, whom Mitchell observed was 'very pretty'.[56]

Alexander Kinghorne Jnr – Marriage and Millwrighting

In 1831, Alexander Jnr was engaged by Rev'd Samuel Marsden, through the agency of George Ranken, to design a mill and mill-house to be built at Kerikeri in the New Zealand Bay of Islands. At this time, James Kinghorne also introduced him to the Lambert family, where he and Alexander Jnr were dinner guests. Nature took its course, and in the fullness of time, Alexander Jnr married Jane, the eldest daughter of Robert Lambert, on 20 December 1834.[57]

Soon afterwards, Alexander Jnr purchased a small block of 100 acres at Queen Charlotte's Ponds, near Bathurst, for £600, naming it Mount Edgcombe.[58] He built a water-powered flour mill on this land, which he operated for a short time before selling the property and milling operation for £800 in 1836.[59] Alexander Jnr and Jane Kinghorne had a son, Alexander [III],[60] born 30 October 1835. After the sale of Mount Edgecombe they moved, as tenants, to Raineville. This former estate of Thomas Raine was located about fourteen miles east from Bathurst in the Sidmouth Valley. Here, Alexander Jnr commenced building another water-powered flour mill on the Fish River at a location now called Kinghorne Falls. He and Jane lived at Raineville in a cottage of six rooms; they also had a good stone barn, stockyards and 120 acres of cultivation paddocks.[61]

Meanwhile, Alexander Snr started to put his plans into action to obtain land at Bathurst, with the intention that it would be managed by Alexander Jnr. On 13 October 1835, he was granted a reserve of 1,221 acres of crown land in the County of Westmoreland, directly adjoining Raineville on its eastern boundary. He named it St Boswells, after the location of his final home in the Scottish Borders. The following year he initiated negotiations to purchase the neighbouring 2,000-acre estate of Raineville, which was then under the administration of Thomas Inglis.[62]

Alexander Jnr built a second, larger water mill at St Boswells, where there was also a miller's cottage and two small cultivation paddocks. The production of flour was good business in the growing agricultural district near Bathurst and continued to be profitable until the recession of the early 1840s. Both properties were in excellent agricultural areas with good alluvial soils and were productive in the short years the Kinghornes were in residence.[63]

Raineville and St Boswells would become increasingly Alexander Jnr's demesne, as Alexander Snr's focus of land acquisition shifted elsewhere. He felt that his sons, except for his second son William, were now secured with landholdings, and that his grand plan was partly complete. The final piece of Alexander's pastoral jigsaw required land on the south coast of New South Wales, which would be a base for the transport of his products and livestock by sea to the Sydney markets. Captain William Kinghorne was soon to return to New South Wales from Van Diemen's Land, and *he* was intent on settling by the sea.

A Romance, a Shipwreck and a Marriage

Helen Kinghorne continued writing to her brother Andrew Seton in Galashiels, with little response. She was not happy living at Liverpool, with only the company of her sister Isabella and her father. She disliked the locals and found no-one worthy of friendship. It seemed like 'every man for himself'...

> Altho' we personally, have been much more fortunate than ever we could expect, I cannot reconcile myself to this country at all, it is so different from Scotland. Our society is very limited, excepting the members of our own families, I may almost say that we know of none

that deserves the name of friend. There seems to exist a sort of jealousy amongst the inhabitants of all ranks, every one seems guarding against his neighbours betraying or taking advantage of him in some way or other. I am very sure that you can have a very faint idea as to what an extent sin and wickedness of every description is practised here, even amongst those in whom you would least expect it. I am sometimes afraid that if we must remain long in this colony, we too, will get so hardened that we would be able to hear of and see all sorts of wickedness, which formerly would have affected us much, with little or no uneasiness.[64]

Helen was desperately homesick and decided to return to Scotland to see her friends and relatives, to make better acquaintance with her sister-in-law and new niece, and to exchange family information.

There is almost no information on the record about Helen's travel to Scotland and the time she spent there. It was an unusually brave and adventurous journey for a 37-year-old unaccompanied single lady, an indication of her determined strength of character. Was Helen's trip part of Alexander's plan to try to convince Andrew Seton and his family to emigrate to New South Wales? Given the tone of her previous correspondence, Helen was unlikely to have given Seton a good report of the colony. Nevertheless, Alexander would have ensured his daughter travelled with a reliable and experienced ship's captain and made all the appropriate arrangements for her wellbeing and safety during the voyage.

On reaching Scotland, the family reunion would have been joyous. Seton had married a miller's daughter in Galashiels and was busily engaged in the mechanisation of the rapidly expanding Scottish Borders textile manufacture. They had a young daughter and no intention or need of emigration. Helen found that 'many changes [had] taken place about Lessudden [St Boswells] since [they] left now going on thirteen years'.[65] The economic situation in the Borders was much improved compared with the post-Napoleonic depression when she left, and her millwright brother was well-placed to take advantage of the mechanical developments of the industrial revolution.

Helen returned to Sydney via Hobart on the 338-ton merchant ship *Wallace*, on her maiden voyage. She carried sixteen passengers and a cargo of merchandise. Nearing journey's end, as she was coming up the D'Entrecasteaux channel at 10 am on Tuesday 26 August 1835, the *Wallace* ran aground on the barren rock of Sterile Island. The weather was fine and the channel calm. Apparently oblivious of a nearby whaleboat attempting to head her off the perilous course she had set towards the hidden reef, the ship sailed on and hit the rock. According to the *Hobart Town Courier*, there were 'a great many whale boats close to the spot, by which persons on board were saved.'[66] Helen's brother Ker took up the story in a letter to Andrew Seton in June 1836:

> I received your letter by Helen. I dare say you have seen by the newspaper that the Wallace was totally wrecked at the entrance of the river Derwent, Van Diemen's Land. Fortunately all the passengers and crew were saved and landed on a small island near. When the Government heard the melancholy news they dispatched a vessel to take them to Hobart Town. It is said the wether was very fine the day it happened. If it had been the day before or the day after some of them would have been sent to a watery grave. The sea was so rough that no boat could have approached the wreck. The Harbour Master at Hobart town, a Mr Moriarty, an intimate friend of William's paid Helen [his kind] attention. The vessel filled so soon with water they could not save a single article but what they had on their backs before the vessel began to break up. A great many things were washed ashore, amongst them several things belonging to Helen. It was lucky for her William lives at Hobart Town. He provided everything she stood in need of and a passage up to Sydney.[67]

Helen's brother William was able to quickly arrange lodgings and passage for Helen back to Sydney. On 26 September, she departed on the merchant ship *John*, which docked in Hobart on its way from London, arriving in Sydney on 1 October 1835.

It had been a pleasant end to a romantic but dangerous adventure. However, the trip out from Leith had not been a complete disaster. On the long voyage, she met fellow passenger William Moir, travelling to Sydney to take up his position as an assistant to the Colonial Architect.[68] Although Moir was seven years Helen's junior in age, romance was in the air. Moir was a Scottish Presbyterian, an educated and gentle man, unexposed to the 'sin and wickedness of every description' so prevalent in the colony. He was a very suitable match. After the passage of the appropriate time, they were married by the Rev'd J. McGarvie, at Liverpool, on Monday 20 June 1836.[69] William and Helen lived at Wooloomooloo and Darlinghurst, and remained happily married until his death in 1850, aged 45; Helen died in 1858 aged 60.[70] They had no children.[71]

The Return of Captain Kinghorne

Since 1822, when he parted with his brother James in Hobart, William Kinghorne had commanded four vessels: the schooner *Waterloo*, and the Brigs *Prince Leopold*, *Cyprus*, and *Isabella*. He had largely been employed transporting recidivist convicts from Hobart to their places of incarceration, first to Sarah Island in Macquarie Harbour on the west coast, and later to Port Arthur. He developed skill as a mariner, conquering the terrors of the Southern Ocean and the treacherous 'Hells Gates' entrance to Macquarie Harbour. While in the west of the colony, he participated in the first exploration of the Gordon River and its tributary, the Kinghorne River, which was named after him. In addition to the transportation of convicts, his duties included the carriage of aborigines, the latter arranged by the so-called 'protector of aborigines', George Augustus Robinson. William had been granted land on Bruny Island from which the aboriginal peoples had been dispossessed. These issues are explored in the authors' previous book, *The Master of Hell's Gates*.[72]

It had been a solitary life for William in Van Diemen's Land, but one that suited his character as an independent mariner. After sixteen years in the Colonial Marine, serving two Lieutenant Governors and four superintendents, including James Kelly and William Moriarty who were his closest colleagues and friends, William resigned and, in November 1836, returned to the bosom of his family in New South Wales. His future in that part of the colony was to share with his brothers the management of his father's estates, and to take a key role in Alexander's 'vision splendid'. His responsibility was to be the south coast properties in the County of St Vincent.

The Tribulations of Alexander Kinghorne Jnr

Sadly, the married life of Alexander Jnr and Jane Kinghorne was short-lived. On 14 September 1837, Jane died during the stillbirth of their second child.[73] Their grandson, Charles Kerr Kinghorne, thought Alexander Jnr was so affected by Jane's death that he immediately left the Bathurst district, but his business there continued for several years. His behaviour became increasingly erratic, and he was involved in several

256

lawsuits and a criminal charge.[74] He then went to live on the south coast of New South Wales, as William Kinghorne later recalled; 'I remember my brother living at Jervis Bay, I think in '41…my impression is that he had given up Raineville…' Meanwhile, his young son Alexander III was left increasingly in the care of his grandparents, the Lamberts.[75]

Perhaps as an escape from grief, Alexander Jnr involved himself in several private adventures. He joined the race to open the unexplored inland beyond the limits of settlement in Gippsland and Port Phillip, and 'discovered' new transport routes in south-eastern parts of the colony. He became increasingly indebted with Edward Lord, the financier of his adventures, and William Abercrombie, his major creditors. By 1841 he was insolvent, a matter that caused distress and embarrassment to the rest of the Kinghorne family. As Raineville and St Boswells were in his father's name, they remained with the family, but all his other assets, along with his milling business, were lost. John Ker eventually took over management of the Bathurst properties in 1843. Between 1842 and 1847, Alexander Jnr became superintendent of the Barrier Island copper mine in New Zealand, owned by his creditor William Abercrombie. He made several return trips to Sydney, probably to see his son in Bathurst. Sadly, in July 1847, on a return voyage to New Zealand via Twofold Bay, the ship in which he was travelling was lost, presumably shipwrecked, and all on board perished.[76]

The Fate of Cardross, Maxton and Cardross Grange

The claims that Alexander Kinghorne had made for three separate land grants in the County of Argyle, remained in the records of the New South Wales Surveyor-General. In 1854, when James Kinghorne was preparing to offer parts of the property for sale, these records were released to the Colonial Secretary by the then Surveyor-General, Sir Thomas Mitchell. Mitchell confirmed Alexander's original understanding of the situation, as it had been in 1827:

> The late Mr Alexander Kinghorne has had order for land to the following extent:
>
> 2000 acres Grant, order sated 4 Nov 1825
> 2000 acres Reserve for purchase, order dated 18 Nov 1825
> 1000 acres Reserve for purchase, order dated 31 Dec 1827.[77]

Mitchell went on to explain that no deed appeared to have been issued for the original two thousand-acre Cardross grant and, after consulting the commissioner of claims, rectified this by supplying the necessary details for insertion in the records. However, he accepted Alexander MacLeay's opinion, outlined in his letter of 1827, that 'the order for the 2000 acres Reserve for purchase merged in an authority to purchase 1000 acres, which Mr Kinghorne was to select and of course to pay for' (Cardross Grange). However, Mitchell believed that Alexander had not completed the purchase, nor paid the required quit rent. Moreover, Mitchell wrote, Alexander's name was missing from the official return of individuals 'who had been authorised by Sir Thomas Brisbane and Governor Darling to purchase Crown Lands furnished by the Collector of Internal Revenue in September 1833'. Nevertheless, Alexander's name had been somehow allowed to remain on the survey maps in Mitchell's office.[78]

Based on this opinion, James Kinghorne's claim was referred to the commissioner of claims for investigation in 1854. No decision was reached before James died in 1859, and his nephew Alick, Andrew Seton Kinghorne's son, took the matter to the court of claims in 1880. The claim was lost but, after Alick's accidental death in 1882, it was taken up again by the Chisholm family who finally lost an appeal in the Supreme Court in 1887. Between 1881 and 1887 several people, including John Cole, had conditionally purchased parts of Cardross Grange, even before it was officially returned to the crown, creating an ownership by possession that would have been very difficult to reverse.[79]

In 1882, James Chisholm Jnr's son, Andrew Seton Chisholm, purchased the remnant of Henry Howie's Strathern, together with the whole of Cardross and Maxton.[80] Thus, the core properties in the Kinghorne estate eventually passed to the Chisholm family.

Jervis Bay: Letter from an Australian Settler

Alexander Kinghorne Snr set about obtaining land at Jervis Bay soon after William returned from Van Diemen's Land. He planned to consolidate his sons' positions in the colony, according to his grand plan, by obtaining a large property on Jervis Bay, and he still retained the romantic hope of reuniting the entire family around it.

The largest of the Kinghornes' South Coast properties, to be named

Mount Jervis, was first promised to Alexander Jnr's father-in-law, Robert Lambert, on 16 February 1838.[81] At about the same time, Alexander Snr made an offer on a similar sized block of land in St Vincent, called Comberton Grange, located across on the northwest side of Jervis Bay, which had been granted to Sydney Stephen. The sale of the latter property fell through in May 1839, as recorded in a letter from Stephen to the editor of the *Sydney Gazette*.[82] Lambert's grant, however, was formally transferred to Alexander Snr on 10 September 1841, the documents recording his possession from 1 January 1839.[83] The family connection with Lambert makes it possible that William Kinghorne was on site from as early as July 1837.[84]

Mount Jervis was located on the northern shores of Jervis Bay (Figure 35). The western boundary lay along a line from Montagu Point (Figure 36) through Cabbage Tree (now Green) Point, Scroggy (now Hare) Point, northwards along Cararma Creek and up the eastern shore of Lake Wollumboola to a point just south of Culburra. The eastern boundary started at a point east of Montagu Point and ran north to Crookhaven Bight, covering approximately fifteen miles of ocean beach along this Bight to the north-eastern shore of Lake Wollumboola.[85]

While having a magnificent seascape and access to the harbour, the northern part of Mount Jervis was not productive agricultural land as evidenced by its coverage, mainly, with the sclerophyll forest typical of the land immediately adjacent to Jervis Bay. There were more fertile soils in the less sandy areas around Montagu Point. Once cleared, much of the southern portion of the Kinghorne land would have been suitable for grazing.[86] Nevertheless, one suspects Mount Jervis was chosen more for its strategic and maritime importance, than for the productivity of its soil.

On 5 July 1839 Alexander Kinghorne Snr wrote of his plans to his son, Andrew Seton, and the letter appeared in the *Chambers' Edinburgh Journal* the following January. The letter represented a last attempt by Alexander to attract his son and family to emigrate, and it reflected the flights of fantasy that were now occupying his mind:

> We have been striving very hard for the last twelve years, and vesting what money we could realise in the purchase of land and live stock. We have now as much stock as is required for the foundation of a splendid fortune for those I leave behind; and in regard to land, we have

abundance, and I only wish to obtain 850 acres more, to render my establishment on the seacoast one of the most perfect in the colony ... Mount Jervis, on Jervis's Bay, twelve hours' sail from Sydney, contains 2560 acres; just commenced improvements ... I intend making Mount Jervis my principal residence. James and the Captain [William] have been there since February, busy in clearing and inclosing a fine park and policy of 150 acres with vineyards and orangery of 5 acres, paddocks for tobacco, maize, hops, &c. &c., and laying the foundation of an observatory on the exact parallel of 33 degrees south latitude, and 150 degrees 50 minutes of longitude east from Greenwich. This estate commands thirty miles of sea-coast, namely, fifteen miles on the Pacific Ocean, and fifteen miles on Jervis's Bay, which is perhaps the finest harbour in Her Majesty's dominions, where the whole British navy may find anchorage and ride in safety from every wind. The site of the mansion cannot be excelled in grandeur by any place I ever saw. There is a natural port, called Bunda by the natives, just under my windows, at a quarter of a mile's distance, where vessels of 200 tons anchor within a cable's length of the shore. The Bay and coast abound with fish of every delicacy and variety – oysters, both rock and mud, schnapper, mullet, bream, whiting, and a thousand other varieties. You may often see half a dozen whales spouting about in the bay in the calving season. Part of my northern boundary is formed by an extensive and picturesque lagoon or lake, two and a half by one and a half miles in extent, which abounds with wild geese, ducks, black swans, pelicans, &c. &c, swimming about in vast numbers, also plenty of mullet, perch, and bream ...[87]

It was in Alexander's interests to make Mount Jervis sound as attractive as possible to his son back in Galashiels. The beach along Crookhaven Bight and the migratory birdlife that abounds on Wollumboola Lake are indeed still beautiful today (2022). Most of Portion 1 in the Parish of Beecroft, as Kinghorne's land is marked on the Parish Map, is now either a nature reserve or part of the Commonwealth land used as the Beecroft weapons range (Figure 35). The southern part, that includes this Australian government reserve, is in a natural bushland state, with a remnant of littoral rainforest adjacent to Green Point, the only evidence of what the Kinghornes might have tried to clear in the late 1830s.

That Andrew Seton was to publish this letter was also part of the plan. It was Alexander's announcement to anybody who mattered in Scotland that he had 'made it', that he was a gentleman of considerable property, and wealth, even if much exaggerated. Alexander was almost seventy years of age, and turning his mind to returning to Scotland, particularly as Andrew Seton was not interested in leaving Galashiels. One of the reasons Scots went to the colonies was to make a fortune and return home to take a position in society as a person of means. It is unclear whether this was always Alexander's intention, but it was the public import of this letter.

Some of the details expounded by Alexander have faded into obscurity. It is unlikely that the observatory, for which foundations were being prepared, was ever built and the 'site of the mansion' was probably no more than a hut, of which nothing remains. Doubtful is the planting of 'vineyards and orangery of 5 acres' but tobacco, maize, cattle and dairy are mentioned in a letter of William's that October.[88] How many cattle were on Mount Jervis is also open to question. The Quaker missionary, Rev'd James Backhouse, visited Jervis Bay in 1837 and reported seeing 'large herds of horned cattle that are fed in the wilds of this part of N.S. Wales, from which beef is extensively exported.'[89] Therefore, if the Kinghornes ran cattle on the property, it would have been rangeland grazing at low stocking rates. According to local historian Peter Crabb, rangeland grazing of cattle on the Bay in the 1830s was accompanied by regular burning of the vegetation to improve the cattle feed, and only very small areas of land were cleared.[90]

The only real memorials to Alexander's early dreams for Mount Jervis are in the local place names: the area north of Point Perpendicular from Currarong to Culburra is today called 'Kinghorne'; the rocky outcrop just to the south of Wollumboola Lake, 'Kinghorne Point'; and the main thoroughfare of Nowra is Kinghorne Street.

'King Wagamy'

An inclusion in Alexander's letter to his son in Scotland, is a description of his interaction with the aboriginal people at Jervis Bay:

> Whatever we want for breakfast and dinner is brought by the blackfellows absolutely in loads. We have the chief, or king (Wagamy) and his two black queens, or jins always with us, who have their camp just beside us; he can command us the service of a dozen more of his tribe when they are wanted to shoot fish, strip bark, or go in their canoes messages for many miles by sea. They are the most faithful, gentle and useful blacks I ever met with.

261

King Wagamy has been whaling in New Zealand, Hobart Town and other places, and speaks English very correctly. They have their slops and rations of flour, tobacco, tea and sugar served out to them by us every day and the Government serves a blanket each to everyone of them every winter. Their value to us in catering and fishing is worth double their rations. Their accuracy in shooting and throwing the spear cannot be surpassed. They bring us a kangaroo for soup when wanted.

Wagamy is a most portable figure as he walks about, armed with his double barrel musket, shot belt, and powder flask, with two noble kangaroo dogs, Camp and Tweedo, and the two jins carrying his tomahawk, boomerang, fishing lines and spears. He generally has a bark canoe ready for launching in every creek and inlet.[91]

The authors have been unable to find any other reference to Alexander's indigenous friend 'Wagamy' or 'Wogamai'. There are remains of an aboriginal camp and middens at the southern boundary of Mount Jervis, at Montagu Point, below the possible site of Alexander's house.[92]

Wagamy's command of English, his reputation for whaling in New Zealand, Van Diemen's Land and elsewhere, and his prowess at shooting, suggest that he had worked with white settlers for many years. Indigenous people were often employed as crew on whaling ships and based on his experience, Wagamy might have assisted William Kinghorne in the establishment of one of his enterprises, bay whaling, at Jervis Bay in 1839.[93]

The title of 'King' was a commonplace during this period. It was given to an elder of a group of aborigines by the Europeans, to make them representative of their people in 'negotiations', and their people responsible for what was 'agreed' on their behalf. It was often accompanied by a metal plaque the 'King' could wear around his neck (there are photographs of this type in the Nowra Museum). It was a specious device employed by the colonial government to justify whatever they did to the aboriginal people, short of actual murder. The authors do not wish to express any disrespect to those elders, who were placed in this situation and needed to protect their people from increasing waves of predatory European settlement. Where mentioned, they are generally referred to in the newspapers in amiable terms, but this hides a situation of effective hopelessness.

Wagamy's reputation seems to have died with him. His name, however, or possibly the name of the people he represented, lives on in the Wogamai sandstone formations along the Shoalhaven coast, and as the district of Wogamia, at Longreach west of Nowra, where further land was about to be acquired by William Kinghorne.

Aboriginal people have occupied the area of Jervis Bay for at least twenty thousand years. The Jerringa people, a sub-group of the Wandandian, still live in the area encompassing present-day Orient Point, Crookhaven Head and Culburra.[94] While Alexander's description of Wagamy and his people is good-humoured and accepting, it reflects the patronising attitudes common among European settlers. For every land grant the Kinghornes received, on the Goulburn Plains, at Bathurst, and in the Shoalhaven... aboriginal people were present, dispossessed of their lands, and there were doubtless many kinds of interaction. Yet only twice have they appeared in the records for this history, in James Kinghorne's period in the Wellington Valley (Chapter 21), and here at Mount Jervis, described with Alexander's bonhomie, to be happily reported back 'home'.

This must represent a lack of self-questioning as to the morality of what was being done, and how it fitted with the teachings of Christ. These issues were being addressed in the Supreme Court at the very time Alexander was writing, where those responsible for the massacre at Myall Creek in 1838 were on trial for murder before his mentor, Justice Dowling. Alexander, as a Court officer and reader of newspapers, was well aware of this.

Saltwater Creek

In addition to Mount Jervis, Alexander wished to obtain '850 acres' more in the Shoalhaven district that would be suitable as a home base for William. He also wanted to complete his circle of properties, conveniently spaced apart for the droving and spelling of cattle, starting at Raineville and St Boswells in the Bathurst area, centred on Cardross in the Goulburn area, and ending on Jervis Bay, whence they could be shipped to market.

On 20 September 1839, the Colonial Secretary, Edward Deas Thomson, informed Alexander by letter that Lot 24, a block of 666 acres of land he had requested at the junction of Calymea (or Saltwater)[95] Creek and the Shoalhaven River, upstream from the present town of Nowra, was 'identical to a portion already applied for'. Under these circumstances the land would have to be advertised and there would be an opportunity to bid for it at auction.[96] In a letter to his son-in-law William Moir, Alexander suggested that William Kinghorne wanted to purchase this land, but he seemed more bent on acquiring it as part of his own plans. He asked Moir to attend the auction and bid on his behalf:

> … as my son William is most anxious to purchase it, as it forms a good half way resting place for our cattle etc. going to or returning from Jervis Bay.[97]

Moir was successful in securing the property, named in the original documents as 'Saltwater Creek', for £242.10s. The grant was formalised by Governor Gipps on 29 Feb 1840 at quit rent of 'one farthing forever'.[98]

The land was well located, fertile and productive. It had frontages to both the Shoalhaven River as the north boundary and the Calymea Creek as the eastern boundary, with easterly views towards Pulpit Rock. William Kinghorne was to remain living there, also operating a seasonal whaling and fishing operation on Jervis Bay, until 1857, when he moved to Goulburn to take over the management of all the Kinghorne rural estates.[99]

Alexander Kinghorne in Goulburn

From 1838, Alexander Kinghorne began regular visits to his family in Goulburn. He attended meetings in the town, and addressed his letters from 'Cardross', suggesting that he was spending considerable time in the district. As there was little more than a couple of bark huts on his property, he and Isabella might have stayed with his daughter and son-in-law at Kippilaw. However, an extract from one of the letters of David Waugh, Ker's Scottish friend and the tenant at James Chisholm's Gatton Park, written in July 1838, suggests otherwise…

> Mr [John Ker] Kinghorn told me that the year after he got his father and all the family living with him, he was £50 in pocket; compared with the year before when living alone.[100]

The Chisholm's Georgian mansion at Kippilaw was unusual for its time, and that family was seen by the locals as 'grand Sydney coves'. Most early settlers lived in slab huts, as David Waugh wrote to his family in Scotland…

> The people of Sydney know no more about all this than you do. If any

person wishes to get real information about the country, never ask a Sydney 'cove.'... I would not exchange my present circumstances, rough and solitary as they are, for any thing...But nobody thinks anything of a house here, if it only keeps off the rain, and some times not that even; the bark of most of the trees here is an inch thick, and comes off in one sheet if properly cut. I have seen one of ten feet long and six broad; of this the houses are often made, and always roofed, in the bush. I have seen a man with 1000 sheep, living in a house made of sheets of bark put up like the letter A, and the fire outside.[101]

It is probable Alexander and Isabella stayed in the small two-room cottage that Henry Howie had built on Strathern, the 960-acre property that Alexander had added to Cardross in 1837. It was comfortable enough, with two log fires to keep them warm in the winter.

On 9 March 1838, Alexander attended a meeting of the Presbyterian inhabitants of the Goulburn district, called by the Rev'd William Hamilton. The purpose was to 'take steps for the immediate erection of a Church connected with the Established Church of Scotland.' A subscription of £324 was collected for the building and a request made to the government for the allocation of land in the town. Alexander and James Chisholm Jnr were among the five interim trustees and committee, appointed for the raising of funds and building the church. The *Sydney Herald* reporter was gratified 'to witness the efforts made by private enterprise to effect the great objects of moral reformation and religious instruction in districts not already enjoying facilities for these objects.'[102]

William Hamilton arrived in Goulburn on 14 October 1837. [He] was to labour faithfully for nine years in Goulburn and the surrounding districts...[and] was the motivating force in having the first Presbyterian church built in Goulburn. That he was a man of vision and faith can be seen from an extract from the 'First Resolution' placed before the building committee: *'That the church ... be adequate to accommodate in its area 200 persons ... and shall admit of easy enlargement if needful some time in the future'.* [103]

The Scots church, on the corner of Verner and Sloane Street, Goulburn, was finally opened on the 30 May 1841, but in Alexander's absence.[104]

Alexander's appointment as Acting Police Magistrate in Goulburn coincided with a period of intense bushranger activity in the district. On 28 May 1838, he issued a warrant for the arrest of the absconded convict robber Abraham Kelly [or Atkins] of Gunning.[105] Early the following year Alexander was, himself, 'robbed about two miles from Marulan, on the Goulburn road, by an armed man, who threatened to blow out his brains unless he handed over all his money'. He must have been shaken by this experience, which was only briefly reported in the Sydney papers.[106] But he was back in the Sydney Supreme Court in September 1839, sitting as a magistrate with the Chief Justice in a civil case. [107]

The year 1840 saw further bushranger activity, even though the era of convict bushrangers was about to fade, with the decline in penal transportations to Australia, before peaking again during the later gold rushes. In January 1840 Alexander contributed £5 to a subscription fund for Oliver Fry, for his spirited conduct 'in resisting and repelling the daring attacks made upon him by a ruthless Banditti, he having on one occasion captured one of three notorious armed Bushrangers; and, on a more recent occasion, having shot the leader of four, and beat off the other three, that have so long infested these Southern Districts.'[108] Not long after this, on 1 February, a group of men working for both James Chisholm and the Kinghornes absconded to the bush, formed a gang and started marauding the inhabitants of the Goulburn district, who were 'in a state of alarm, expecting the bushrangers to attack them at any moment.'[109]

But all this was beyond Alexander's care in February 1840. He was not in Goulburn, and his mind was no longer in the colony, as he prepared to leave his estates in the care of his sons and daughters, to return to his native Scotland.

PART III

SCOTLAND

Chapter 24

A Return to the Stronghold: Scotland and the Last Years of Alexander Kinghorne (1840–1847)

Return to your stronghold, O prisoners of hope.
Zechariah 9:12 (English Standard Version)

Just two months after the publication of Alexander's 'Letter of an Australian Settler' from Jervis Bay, he was boarding a ship to return to his native land.

Alexander's departure from New South Wales might seem a snap decision, but this was not the case. While the record gives only a few indications of his plans to return to Scotland, there were signs. From a personal perspective, his altercation with the Wesleyan minister at Liverpool Courthouse had created adverse publicity in 1837. The encounter with the bushranger on the Goulburn Road in 1839 had shocked him. He was approaching the age of seventy, suffering from gout and a general debilitation in his health.[1]

But it was always there. In his tearful letter to Andrew Seton as he was leaving Scotland in March 1824, he had spoken of 'Exile',[2] and there is always in Exile the promise of return. And what is the purpose of going to the colonies to make your fortune, to become a landed gentleman, and to restore your family's lost esteem, if you did not return and take your place of honour?

From a family perspective, his sons James, William, John Ker, and Alexander Jnr were well-established as pastoralists, with significant landholdings to support them and the generations of potential descendants. Alexander's eldest daughters, Helen and Elizabeth, were happily married to prominent and prosperous colonial citizens. Isabella, the youngest, had decided to live with her brothers, James and John Ker, at Maxton, near Goulburn.

Alexander's own dreams of becoming a landed gentleman had come to fruition, but there were other dreams of high office that were only briefly fulfilled through his short appointment as colonial Civil Engineer. He had been in the colony for just sixteen years. His one son remaining in Scotland, Andrew Seton, was at that time a successful millwright in Galashiels. Alexander had nurtured high expectations that Seton and his wife Helen would, in time, emigrate with their children. He wrote, encouraging him to do so, using stronger and more romantic descriptions of the new colony as time went on.

In a desperate last attempt as late as July 1839, he urged Seton to send out his eldest daughter, Eliza, known affectionately as Betty by the family. 'There is no Joke. I am serious', he wrote, sensing his son's disbelief of the hyperbole in his previous correspondence. 'Betty can never do so well at home as her prospects here where her fortune w^d be made' he implored, offering to pay all his granddaughter's expenses. [3] But this, too, was a dream not to be fulfilled in Alexander's lifetime. Andrew Seton had prospered in Galashiels, his wife had just given birth to a son, his daughters Eliza 'Betty' (11) and Jane (14) were attending a school for young ladies at Upper Wooden in Ekford; and they were certainly not interested in emigration. [4]

Given his health issues, Alexander might have decided to fulfil one final ambition: to be laid to rest with his beloved wife Betty in the grounds of Dryburgh Abbey, alongside the remains of the great men who had been his closest mentors: Sir Walter Scott and Lord Buchan – buried as a gentleman among gentlefolk. His heart was yearning for his beloved Vale of Tweed, with its antiquities, soft light and gentle ways.

Whatever other reasons there might have been, Alexander had chosen his time for a return to the stronghold, with the chance of seeing his son Andrew and grandchildren before he died. The planning had been in train for at least a year. In January 1839, he arranged for his house and the associated block of land at the corner of Macquarie and Elizabeth Streets, Liverpool to be sold, [5] and moved in with his daughter and son-in-law, Elizabeth and James Chisholm Jnr, at Gledswood, near Campbelltown. [6] He then placed all his estates, as leases 'at a small annual rent', in the hands of his sons James, William and John Ker. He wrote that these lands formed 'the foundation of a splendid fortune for those I leave behind'.[7] A surviving document shows amounts of £242 in debts, which it is assumed Alexander intended to clear prior to his departure.[8]

After these careful preparations, with the future of his family in New South Wales secure, he was ready, by the beginning of 1840, to return to Scotland.

Alexander Returns on the Trusty

Alexander departed Sydney as a cabin passenger on the *Trusty*, Captain Alexander Jamieson, on 21 March 1840, bound for London.[9]

The *Trusty* was a 366-ton cargo and emigrant ship that had travelled from The Downs, Gravesend, Falmouth, Cape of Good Hope, Launceston, and Port Adelaide to Sydney. She could carry up to 130 passengers.[10] Jamieson had been captain of the convict ship *Mary* until 1833, and so was experienced in sailing the route to New South Wales via the Cape, taking *Trusty* there on her maiden voyage.[11] This time she was on the reverse route, picking up the Roaring Forties, and rounding Cape Horn in late autumn. She took on supplies at Bahia, in Brazil, before sailing for London on 15 July. The *Trusty* arrived at the Port of Deal, Kent, on 28 August 1840, after a five-month voyage from Sydney.[12]

No record has been found of Alexander's travel from England to Scotland. He likely took passage on one of the many Smacks, or one of the new Steam Packets, plying the east coast route from London to Leith.[13] He was in Edinburgh by November, lodging with his brother-in-law, William Brockie and wife Elizabeth. Brockie, a successful baker, lived at 18 Greenside Street, Edinburgh, a short walk north-east on Leith Street from Princes Street.[14] At this stage, the Brockies had five children, aged from a newborn daughter to a six-year-old son, including twin four-year-old girls, so the household must have been crowded.[15] The Brockies were to have a further four children by 1851 and later moved to a larger residence at 12 Broughton Street, Edinburgh.[16] Here, their unmarried children remained living after the deaths of William and Elizabeth.[17]

Hard Times in Galashiels

By 6 June 1841, the census day, Alexander had moved to Galashiels, presumably to be closer to his family. Here he lived, possibly as a lone tenant or guest, in the house of William and Isabella Brown on Paton Street, only a short walk from the home of Andrew Seton in the 'Oald Town'.[18] He would have been comfortable there.

William Brown was a successful but elderly millwright, part of a compact association of Galashiels mill owners of which Andrew Seton was a member. Alexander might have been advising him on the expansion of his milling operations and staying with him in quieter circumstances than Andrew Seton's house afforded. William Brown's descendants would continue to expand the business and do well for the remainder of that century. Although Alexander was not staying with Andrew Seton and family, there is no suggestion of difficulty between father and son, or wife Helen. Such correspondence as survives appears cordial and matter-of-fact, without preciousness about feelings.

How long Alexander remained in Galashiels is unknown – he probably came initially to celebrate baby Alick's first birthday – but he was there in February 1842, when he wrote to his sons in New South Wales, and possibly in January 1843, when he received a letter from William, written while on a brief visit to Cardross in July 1842.[19] By this time, Alexander was clearly in dire straits. He had run out of money and was receiving no income in Scotland apart from what he could glean from advising his old contacts.[20] Neither was he receiving income from his estates in New South Wales, which were now in the hands of his sons, who should have been remitting rent and interest to him. However, the Australian family were also suffering impecunious circumstances from the debt left by Alexander Jnr's catastrophic insolvency, 'exceptionally bad' livestock prices and the failure of Alexander's Liverpool property sale.[21] To make matters worse, Andrew Seton was also in financial difficulty and laying off workers from his Galashiels millwright business.

William seems to have been unaware of his father's plight before visiting Cardross and finding his letter, unanswered. But now he was in a quandary about how to help him. The problem was compounded by the five to six-month delay in communication imposed by the long sea voyage between Britain and Australia. When letters were read, economic circumstances could have changed in the interim, for better or worse. A surviving bank draft for £200 was sent to Alexander dated 14 August 1841 but he had not received it at the time of writing his letter of 6 February

272

1842 – it also took a long time for money orders to be sent from the colony, even by the fastest ships (see this Chapter, Bank Failures). [22]

The Hungry Forties

What was happening in rural New South Wales, the Scottish Borders, and Galashiels in particular, to cause this financial stress? A series of Whig governments under Earl Grey and Viscount Melbourne had ruled Britain between 1830 and 1834, and again from 1835–41. Their non-interventionist policies of laissez-faire capitalism and free trade allowed the so-called recession of the 'hungry forties' to grow unchecked. Like the recession that followed the Napoleonic wars, it disproportionately affected Ireland and Scotland, where unusually wet and cold conditions caused several bad harvests and the proliferation of potato blight. The Corn Laws inhibited the importation of food for the starving people and, from 1845, Irish immigrants began flooding into Scotland, compounding local famine and exacerbating unemployment. [23]

When Britain sneezed, the Empire suffered from the ensuing cold. The Australian colonies, then taking thirty-eight percent of Britain's exports, was second only to India in its dependency on the mother country. [24] As a result, the 'hungry forties' were also experienced there, causing a significant slowing of the colonial economy. The main contributors to the recession in New South Wales were low wool prices in the London market, the collapse of markets for grain and livestock and the downturn of British capital investment. The last inhibited new pastoral development and severely restricted bank credit. Goods piled up in shops as lower earning power led to reduced spending.

By 1843, bankruptcies were increasing in New South Wales. These no longer involved mainly small retail traders and merchants but also extended to the landed interests. Alexander Jnr's insolvency had been a significant drain on the Kinghorne family resources, but this was only the beginning.

A Change in Fashion

Meanwhile in Galashiels the prosperity of the preceding decade had come to an end. From 1843 onwards, there was a gradual decline in handicraft spinning and manual weaving; the old Weavers' Corporation of Galashiels was on its last legs. Crippled by the march of improvement, the advent of the power-loom completed its downfall and swept away the oldest and principal industry of the town. Blankets and cloth of home-grown wool, with knitting yarns and flannels in the grey, blue, and 'drab' colours had ruled wool fashion for years. But these textiles started to lose their popularity, and serious suffering for both woollen manufacturers and their employees was the result. A change of fashion was coming, and it inflicted a check on the prosperity of Galashiels.[25]

This change can be largely attributed to the powerful influence of Sir Walter Scott on the popularity of Scottish culture in Britain. His novels made young girls thrill to the thought of gallant knights, loyal Chieftains and faithful lovers. He spurred young men on to make romantic gestures and to complete dashing deeds. Following the 'splendid novelty' of the visit of King George IV to Edinburgh in 1822, when Scott dressed him in tartans and a kilt, there was a nation-wide outbreak of 'Highlandism' based on Scott's notion of Gaelic culture.[26] Scott became one of the most influential men in Britain, not only through his literature but also as a driver of culture in general, and fashion in particular. By the 1840s, London society wanted to emulate the regal fashion preferences, now led by the young Queen Victoria and her consort Prince Albert, who were promoters of the Caledonian garb.

Andrew Seton's Business Suffers

Andrew Seton Kinghorne operated an engineering millwright business in Galashiels. During Alexander Snr's declining years, his son's formerly booming business entered the doldrums. The business income depended on the building and servicing of woollen mills and the updating of weaving equipment, which the conservative doyens of the Manufacturers, Weavers, and Dyers Corporations, were loath to adopt. Moreover, the dangerous practice of using child labour in the older woollen mills was under scrutiny by the government, adding pressure on millers to update their technology.[27]

Unfortunately, Andrew Seton appeared to be part of the problem, rather than the solution. In May 1844, he and Robert Gill constructed a 'model' waulk-mill (or fulling mill) 'upon a new and improved plan' at the mill of Gill, Sims and Company in Galashiels.[28] *The Caledonian Mercury* reported that 'all who have seen it concur in the opinion, that it is one of the greatest improvements ever introduced into the process of woollen manufacture'. The new machinery was characterised by an economy of power, requiring a third that of existing equipment. [29] Sadly, Seton's initiative, rather than contributing to the required technology change, was an example of the persistence of old technology in Galashiels. The process of fulling was soon to be made obsolete by better methods of wool processing and the mechanisation of weaving machines.[30]

According to the Galashiels historian Robert Hall, the failure to adjust to the 'change in public taste...regarding the style of cloth produced in the town' caused a 'crisis in the trade' which prevailed for many years, so affecting the locals that many of them were 'reduced to the necessity of purchasing the bread and meal sold by the beggars to Johnny Stewart who kept a public lodging house...and which, under ordinary conditions, were used for feeding pigs'. Charity balls were organised to raise funds for the poor and there 'was an extraordinary exodus from the town and district' as people emigrated to the colonies in 'reckless despair'.[31] Andrew Seton explained the predicament in a letter to his brother William, back at Cardross. 'When manufacturing gets bad our trade is done as our sole dependence is on them; any machinery that has been made of late has been taken for too low to allow any profit,' he wrote. 'I speak of ourselves. I may safely say we have not made a penny but lost for the last year.' Seton expressed the hope of improved times when the proposed Edinburgh to Carlisle Railway reached Galashiels. [32]

The recession in Galashiels went beyond 1846, the year of Alexander Kinghorne's death. Within ten years, however, the manufacturers adapted themselves to circumstances, and introduced new fabrics, of which the chief were tartans and mixed trouserings in tweed, and steam started to replace water-power for driving woollen machinery.[33] The railway between Galashiels and Edinburgh finally opened on 1 February 1849, providing a ready supply-line for the coal that fuelled Galashiels' tweed boom.[34] But this was to be preceded by ongoing financial stress for Galashiels in general, and Alexander Kinghorne in particular.

Bank Failures

The Edinburgh and Leith Banking Company failed in 1842. The insolvency of this bank also drove the Savings Bank of Galashiels, which had all its capital in the Leith Bank, into bankruptcy.[35] These failures contributed significantly to Alexander Kinghorne's financial embarrassment, which was averted at the last minute by the arrival of the long-expected bank draft from New South Wales, as Andrew Seton reported in a letter to his sister Helen. 'My father duly received [Mr Moir's] kind letter of date 27 Aug[st] with its enclosures, and wrote in return to him & my brother William on the 20th of March last.' Seton added that the 'remittance just arrived in time to enable him to pay every farthing he owed to Mr Craig's Trustees and the poor unfortunate man [Craig] died of a broken heart just four days after the date of my father's letter.'[36]

The long-awaited bank draft for £200 came, not from Alexander's sons, but from his son-in-law William Moir, presumably as a gift from him and Helen.[37] And it arrived just in time for Alexander. He had been surviving on credit provided by George Craig, the agent for the Leith Bank and treasurer of the Savings Bank of Galashiels. Craig had been appointed treasurer of the first Savings Bank in 1815, but it had come to an 'untimely and disastrous end' when the Leith Bank collapsed. The governor and directors of the Savings Bank disclaimed all responsibility, but by the beginning of 1844 had paid out ten shillings and threepence in the pound to all depositors.[38] Being a shareholder in both banks, George Craig was financially ruined. This 'proved his death-blow, his spirit was broken, and an attack of bronchitis cut him off in 1843, in the sixtieth year of his age.' The arrival of Alexander's bank draft enabled him to pay off Craig's Trustees, but it was too late for the highly respected banker.[39]

Meanwhile, back in New South Wales, two major Australian banks also failed. One of them, the Bank of Australia, directly affected the fortunes of the Kinghorne family. Launched with much fanfare in 1826, Alexander had bought 10 shares, a relatively modest holding, over which he had given James and William power of attorney.

In November 1843, the bank began to spiral into insolvency, making the first of several calls for funds from its shareholders. These eventually left the Kinghornes with a total liability of £720, covered by a mortgage on William Kinghorne's Saltwater Creek property. The family in Goulburn

276

shielded Alexander Snr from any liability for, and probably knowledge of, the consequences of his investment. They eventually survived the crisis through William's good management, but they had harboured ongoing uncertainty, well into the 1850s, as to their likely final liability, as the insolvent bank continued to hold debts exceeding £400,000.[40]

Declining Health

On 6 November 1843 Alexander, recently back in Edinburgh, was living at 4 St Patrick's Square.[41] His reason for returning to Edinburgh is unclear but might have been to make financial arrangements. His grandson in Galashiels had been unwell when he left that place, and Alexander himself was not in the best of health, as he wrote to Andrew Seton: 'I had a most disagreeable day for my journey here, one of the horses broke down and we did not reach Edin^r till ½ past 7 o'clock. I have got a bad cold and have not left the house since I arrived.'[42]

Alexander wrote to his son again on 3 December, pleased to hear that his grandson 'has got the turn and is going on favourably'. Still very concerned about his and Seton's financial embarrassment, he continued... 'if I get a remittance which I expect soon in the ensuing year we surely cannot all starve, even if the shop were shut...[if] you can spare room for me I probably may come out for a week or two.'[43] Alexander headed back to Galashiels by the Prince Blucher[44] coach on 17 December, hoping the family would 'put yourselves to no inconvenience on my acco^t as I could get lodging at John Thorburn's whilst I remain at Galashiels.' Seton met his father on his arrival at Buckholmside. As they walked home together in the late evening, it was clear from Alexander's appearance that he was far from well.[45]

It is likely that Alexander remained at Galashiels for the remaining two years of his life. Andrew Seton expanded on his father's medical condition in 1844, writing to his sister, Helen Moir, in Sydney. Alexander had been 'labouring under very bad health'. He had consulted doctors and visited 'the Wells' for treatment. One such treatment had taken him eighty miles north-west of Galashiels to try 'the waters at Bridge of Allan', near Stirling. The journey could have ended in disaster, if it had not been for the serendipitous assistance of yet another member of the Moir family. Alexander took seriously ill at Alloa, eight miles east of the spa town, probably suffering a stroke. Being unable to walk, he was taken to a hotel by some kind but unknown person. There he was found by William Moir's brother, James Moir, who looked after him. Moir, a WS and banker, lived in Bank Street Alloa, and was well able to provide for Alexander until he recovered sufficiently to return to Galashiels. [46]

Unaware of the extreme financial crisis in New South Wales, Seton's letter berated his brothers for not sending financial assistance...

> None of my brothers or sisters (excepting William) have ever written him a scrape, or sent him a farthing but what he rec[d] through Mr Moir, and it took most of it to clear all his encumbrances and his expenses since at the Wells & Doctors fees have left him very poor indeed, but he shall not want whilst I or my family can afford him support, I know there are many of his old friends who would contribute to his relief but this cannot be brought to ask when he has so valuable a property in Australia and all kept from him by his family who will neither remit him nor write him even a letter to account for their ungrateful conduct. [47]

The money William Moir had sent to Alexander, also covered most of his medical and spa expenses. Seton added in a post-script to his thank-you letter: 'My dear Helen pray endeavour to urge your brothers to make my father a remittance without delay, from all appearance he will not long be a burden to them.' No evidence has been found of further remittances from New South Wales to Alexander, but Seton's correspondence with his brother William, after the death of their father, suggests that William had sent funds. [48]

Ramsay's Ghost

Little is known of the last two years of Alexander Kinghorne's life in Galashiels. A single piece of his correspondence survives from March 1844. It indicates that he was undertaking some service for the next generation of the family of Thomas Williamson Ramsay – for whom he had undertaken the land survey and renovation of the Maxton kirk in 1812. [49] In return for services to the new laird in 1812, aside from any monetary remuneration, Ramsay had arranged for William Kinghorne's entry to the Royal Navy as a trainee Midshipman. Alexander would have retained an affection for Ramsay, who died in 1836 and was survived by his three daughters, who remained living on the Maxton Estate.

This time, Alexander was providing a service to Sir Henry Fairfax, the husband of Ramsay's third daughter Archibald Montgomerie. Through his wife, Fairfax had inherited part of the Maxton Estate, where they lived at Crossflat, the home previously occupied by the Kinghorne family from 1813 to 1823, now renamed 'St Boswells Bank'.[50] The letter from Fairfax to Alexander dated 26 March 1844 concerned this service…

> I have just received the letter of Mr James, with the copy of your reply which is so clear and satisfactory…We will feel much indebted to you for the kind part you have taken in this business.
>
> I must say, that I think the Duke has been ill advised – in pushing a claim, which cannot be supported…[51]

This letter reveals a disagreement between Fairfax and the Duke of Roxburghe, related to the disputed accession of the Dukedom, finalised in the House of Lords in 1812.[52] The Duke's lands surrounded those of the Maxton estate,[53] for which Alexander had prepared the plans for Thomas William Ramsay's purchase in 1812. The letter indicates that Alexander provided some useful information to Fairfax in this respect.

The Death and Will of Alexander Kinghorne

Alexander died at Galashiels, probably at the home of Andrew Seton, on 16 February 1846. There is no death record extant and there was no formal obituary in the British or Australian newspapers. Only the following small family notice appeared, once, in *The Sydney Morning Herald*, *The Melbourne Argus* and *Bell's Life in Sydney and Sporting Reviewer*:

> On the 15th of February last, at Galashiels, Scotland, Alexander Kinghorne, Esq., long well known and respected as a colonist, and active magistrate in New South Wales, deeply regretted by his numerous family and friends.[54]

His estate in Scotland was valued at £341.19.5. Andrew Seton assumed 'possession and management' of this meagre estate, as he had been granted 'Factory and Commission' under Scottish law by his brothers, James, William and John Ker. According to the terms of the will, they inherited the lands and estates in New South Wales, shared between them, after payments of £300 to Helen Moir, £200 to each of Elizabeth Chisholm, and £100 to her second son William Alexander Chisholm,

279

'named after me'. Alexander also left to his youngest daughter Isabella £200, 'and for the unwearied kindness which [she] has at all times paid to me in my old age…Three hundred young breeding Ewes to be depastured with the flocks which I bequest to her brothers…' Alexander left a small sum to his grandson Alexander III, son of Alexander Kinghorne Jnr of Bathurst. However, he left nothing to Alexander Jnr himself, who had 'often expressed to me that he was quite independent in circumstances, and that he wished to have nothing from me, I consider that I have done my duty towards him…'.[55] He left Andrew Seton £300, by codicil dated 25 November 1844, which he paid him 'by cheque' before his death.[56]

A year after Alexander's death, Andrew Seton was winding up the estate. To do this, he sought details of the lands and financial affairs from his brother James back in New South Wales…

> I have just received your very welcome and kind letter, with all the papers connected our father's affairs. I have got them put into the hands of Messrs Haldane & Lees and am now in possession of the property.
>
> I have drawn upon you for £150 – through the National Bank date of the Bills March 1847 – I do assure you your letter made me extremely happy after a whole year's suspence and Father's affairs lying in an unsettled state, as nothing could be done until hearing from you – I have given Haldane & Lees instructions to get the business wound up and settled as speedily as possible.[57]

It had taken the death of their father to unite the Kinghorne brothers in the common purpose of ensuring that, with no expense spared, his last wishes were met. Andrew Seton had employed the most experienced and able legal team in Galashiels to deal with Alexander's estate: Robert Haldane WS and Hugh Lees WS.[58]

But what of Alexander's burial in the grounds of Dryburgh Abbey? He would have ensured that Andrew Seton was aware of this, his most anticipated resting place. Here, Lord Buchan had promised he could be buried, alongside his wife Betty. Lord Buchan was no longer present to keep his promise, and it is unlikely he left any records of the various promises he had made to all and sundry in his declining years. There are no burial instructions specified in Alexander's will. He had personally laid Betty to rest in the Abbey, 'amongst these splendid ruins', as was her right as the daughter of a Bemersyde tenant, 'on Monday 23rd Augt 1819'.[59]

However, there is no record of a surviving grave for Betty or Alexander, either at Dryburgh Abbey or anywhere else in the Scottish Borders. Many of the old headstones at Dryburgh Abbey have been destroyed or lost over the years, making identification impossible.[60]

It can only be wondered if he rests in that tranquil location, surrounded by the antiquities he loved, close to the River Tweed and his old home near St Boswells; nearer still to his mentors Lord Buchan and Sir Walter Scott, and overlooked by the tourists who take in the 'vision splendid' from Scott's View.

Chapter 25

The Legacy of Alexander Kinghorne

*...I pledge myself shall be so Managed and Cultivated, as to do credit to myself,
and add honor to the district of 'Tweedside'*

Alexander Kinghorne. October 1825

A Passion for Improvement

The over-riding theme in Alexander Kinghorne's life was self-advancement driven by scientific improvement. In this he was in keeping with the thinking of the Scottish Enlightenment and the philosophies developed by David Hume and his many followers, emphasizing improvement and utility. Alexander received this not so much as a formal philosophy, but through his social interactions.

For him, this was more than an eagerness for his chosen professions: teaching, surveying, architecture, engineering and agricultural science; it was fed by a deeper hunger: to break away from the social status of his birth and a certainty that his talents deserved better. To rise above his trade background, and to gain traction in his profession, Alexander recognised that he needed patronage. He sought it and made his way by it. His coincident attendance at school with the young Walter Scott, and his later employment as factor to the Scottish aristocrat and lawyer, John Seton Karr, were the genesis of a web of connections that Alexander went on to cultivate.

Romantic Formation

Like many young Scots of his time Alexander was an incurable romantic. Despite his trade roots, Alexander created a romantic notion of his destiny, believing his family had a noble past which had been lost, and developing an ambition to restore them to the landed gentry. At Kelso Grammar, he rubbed shoulders with the sons of the nobility, and met his first and most revered mentor, Walter Scott, who became a means of support and patronage until he left Scotland. Scott changed the face of literature, inventing new genres of the historical novel and the short story,[1] which romanticized the medieval and early modern past.

Alexander Kinghorne embraced this romanticism. He was captivated by the antiquities and history of his surroundings in the Scottish Borders. This informed some of his early work as a surveyor, his involvement in the Bowden Statistical Account (1795), and with the antiquarian George Chalmers (1802).

But it also inflamed his romantic pretentions and ambitions. The coat-of-arms in his Kinghorne Family Bible,[2] was a product of the imagination with little foundation in reality, in contrast with the scientific methods which characterized his chosen professions. Ironically, Alexander did have illustrious ancestors, of whom he was completely unaware. He went to Alexander Deuchar, the armorial expert, in the sincere hope that he could unpick an ancestry he was sure was there somewhere. Instead, what Deuchar delivered was a pastiche, a fake.

Sir Walter Scott was the friend and advisor who encouraged him to take his family to the colonies to improve their prospects. His plans and reveries for his properties in New South Wales, which were in fact realised, though coloured by the straitened circumstances of his final years, became 'the foundation of a splendid fortune for those I leave behind.'

Character

The *Seton Karr of Kippilaw Papers*, which have been a major source for the first half of this history, contain many letters that reflect Alexander's character. One of the positive aspects was loyalty: his persistent support for the cause of John Bellenden Ker, John Seton Karr's preferred candidate for the Dukedom of Roxburghe, in the face of opposition from many of his neighbours and close friends. The letters reveal his faithfulness, affection and high regard for John Seton Karr, the mentor who had given him so many opportunities. He was to show this characteristic again in his loyalty to New South Wales Governor Sir Thomas Brisbane, and to his friend James Chisholm.

Alexander's flowery writing style, typical of the educated and literary classes of the time, and quite familiar from Walter Scott's novels, would have been mirrored in his manner of speech. Alexander enjoyed a gossip and had a dry sense of humour.[3] His letters also reflected his tendency towards romantic hyperbole. This was particularly the case when it came to covering his mistakes or trying to convince his employer of the benefits of his grand schemes. This character flaw persisted into his years in New South Wales, where he dreamed of a grand and imaginative future for his family, particularly expressed in his letters to his son Andrew Seton Kinghorne back in Scotland, whom he was trying to persuade to join the rest of the family in New South Wales. His flights of fancy, as in the *Letter from an Australian Settler*,[4] contrast with the more realistic, and quite negative letter from his daughter Helen, written to her brother from Liverpool in 1828.[5]

As factor at Kippilaw, Scotland, Alexander's interaction with subordinate staff revealed both positive and negative character traits. He was a considerate and kind master, and no fool when it came to handling problems involving individual farm staff. For example, his elegant solution to the laying off of 'Old Tom' the ploughman, provided a 'win-win': both shelter and new employment for Tom's younger family, and rental income for the estate.[6] His caring nature was also extended to the tenants of the grass parks at Kippilaw, who were given indulgence with their rental payments during the terrible winters of 1800–1801.[7] He was generally effective at recruitment, training and retention of farm staff, particularly when dealing with individuals. They responded to him positively and, in some cases, with loyalty. He demonstrated considerable persistence, patience and diplomatic flair, in his dealings with Kippilaw's long-term tenants, and with neighbours over boundary disputes. These were areas where his knowledge gave him confidence – he was a skilled surveyor and understood the legal complexities of land tenure and inheritance.[8]

However, John Seton Karr believed Alexander lacked the strength of character to discipline and control staff because he tended to avoid conflict. Karr recognised that Alexander was unable to cope with the servants at the mansion house and considered him too lenient in dealing with the farm labour, particularly of the annually hired hynds. True, Alexander was unable to supervise his staff closely enough to really know what they were up to; as in the case of the hynd Thomas Scott, an inveterate poacher, who was able to get away with his nightly crimes unobserved for eight months!

Alexander seemed able to retain the confidence and trust of many people at the same or at a higher social status than himself. However, his relationship with those below him suggests that he was kind and supportive of good workers but reluctant to confront those who were lazy and dishonest, or with whom he was at odds, such as the Kippilaw housekeeper, Molly Wilson, regarding whom the lines of responsibility were unclear.

Later, when Superintendent at Emu Plains in NSW, Alexander experienced few, if any problems with staff or convicts. Emu Plains was a significant responsibility for a man with an equivocal track record in the management of farm workers in Scotland. However, his style was clearly suited to the colonial management structure. The key to Alexander's success was his efficient Assistant Superintendent and convict overseer, who converted his orders and leadership style into effective action. This was fortuitous. It might well have been otherwise.

The convicts were required to attend church parades and services, reflecting both government policy and the importance which Alexander placed on their spiritual salvation. Their neat dress and good health were the consequence of Alexander's care for the physical man as well as the reform of his character. Hyacinthe de Bougainville's glowing report, certainly reflecting Governor Brisbane and Alexander's words, nevertheless provides an independent picture of 'comfort, regularity and discipline' that characterised the year of Alexander's superintendence.

Lorraine Stacker described Alexander Kinghorne as 'a kindly, proud man who was respected by his peers as well as the convicts with whom he dealt. He was neither a harsh disciplinarian nor a brutal man and showed considerable compassion and understanding for the convicts and their circumstances'. Under Alexander Kinghorne's light and even-handed management, Emu Plains never waned in Governor Brisbane's esteem as one of the most valuable assets within the colonial service. The character of his regime would be continued by his son, James, and both influenced many convicts to emerge from their sentences and make their lives and families in New South Wales. Of all, this might be Alexander's finest achievement.

Alexander's egalitarian attitude towards convicts extended beyond Emu Plains. He gave court evidence in support of the many convicts he knew or who had been under his superintendence. He emphasised their good points, even when they were obviously guilty of crime, as in the case of Alexander Dick and the Colonial Secretary's silver spoons. Unlike the colonial 'exclusives', he harboured no prejudice against ex-convicts. He did everything in his power to encourage those with promising talent or ability, such as Théodore Constantini and Joseph Peters. In the latter case, his support was well placed and rewarded with loyal service.

Alexander's court service in New South Wales revealed some unique aspects of his character. Mentored by Justice Dowling in the Supreme Court, and Thomas Moore in the Magistrates' Court, he was encouraged to exhibit generosity and compassion towards the poor and oppressed defendants and plaintiffs.[9] Along with Moore, he was a regular and diligent magistrate on the Liverpool bench. Alexander had an ethic of service, and this was clearly a service that he enjoyed and at which he excelled.

An adverse aspect of his character was that he was at key points uncritical of the broader terms of his commissions and the motives of those in authority. Thus, he willingly delivered to Lieutenant-Governor Arthur the required report and plans as to how New Brighton could be made the new capital of Van Diemen's Land. However, he failed to appreciate that it was not viable for the seat of government to be other than in Hobart, and that he was being used by Arthur for petty political ends. Similarly, he completely misread his relationship with Governor Darling, to the point where he was again used, and then summarily dismissed with contempt.

The aboriginal people of the continent had been dispossessed and marginalised by British colonisation, with continuous crimes committed against them. Alexander was a beneficiary of this in the land grants he received, and he accepted the situation as he found it upon his arrival. His and James Kinghorne' contacts with aboriginal people surface only twice in this history, and their interactions were both friendly and patronising. Nevertheless, there was a lack of self-questioning about what had happened, and how this sat with his faith in Jesus Christ.

The Patriarchal Legacy

Alexander's romanticism was also reflected in his plans for, and control of his family's destiny, particularly that of his sons. These ambitions were patrician: his first-born, James, was to follow in his father's footsteps as a surveyor and engineer; and his second, William, was to go into military service, becoming an accomplished mariner. Thereafter, his son's careers tended more towards Alexander's trade origins, as the third son, Andrew Seton, had no vocation for the church. He, and the next son, Alexander Jnr, were apprenticed to learn the millwright trade, with their father's ambition that they would embrace the new scientific developments of the industrial revolution. Helen, the eldest daughter, was destined to care for her mother, Betty, in her declining years, her younger sisters during her mother's illness, and might have remained a spinster. This was not to be, and it was the youngest daughter, Isabella, who remained unmarried.

Whether intentionally or by inclination, Alexander was very much the patriarch, and his children were expected to fit in with his wishes. This would have been seen in their day-to-day lives but was most marked in the major things: their paths in life as seen above, his finding patrons for the boys' careers, or not so in case of the girls, and most particularly in the decision to emigrate to New South Wales.

Alexander's sons inherited, or absorbed through nurture, both his skills and faults to differing degrees. John Ker emulated his father's overstated writing style when describing Cardross to his brother in Scotland.[10] However, both James (in Australia) and Andrew Seton (in Scotland) were reluctant letter writers – no correspondence survives written by James Kinghorne. The few letters extant from Andrew Seton reveal that his reluctance to write was not due to any lack of ability, as his letters are full of grace and care for his father and family. However, he remained in Scotland until his death, maintaining obdurate resistance to his father's ambitions for his career.

James and William were different from their father. Both were fiercely independent, self-reliant and reserved. James initially a disciplinarian towards convicts at Emu Plains, fell in with his father's regime. He became the stalwart of the family business in New South Wales until his death, when William took over the reins, ensuring the family ploughed through the waves of financial uncertainty that engulfed them after their father's death.

Alexander Jnr was stable as a young man, skilled and diligent in his trade, with an apparent good business head, until his wife died. After that, he lost his senses, both in behaviour and business, abandoning his family and his trade, his life ending in tragic loss at sea. Helen, who disliked the rough and uncouth people in Liverpool married late, but happily, living out her life in Sydney.

Elizabeth was always steady, stern and sensible. She absorbed and maintained her father's love of the romanticism of the Scottish Borders. She fulfilled his dreams through her marriage to James Chisholm Jnr, and perpetuated his memory through the names she gave to her family homes. She became the matriarch of a large family of Chisholm boys, all of whom she steeped in Scottish folklore and admiration for their paternal and maternal grandfathers.

Isabella was perhaps the saddest, not so much that she did not marry and find a life partner, but that she felt most keenly the 'Exile' from Scotland, without having the means to return there. She lived out her days at Maxton, New South Wales, cared for by her family with periods of 'mental instability'.[11]

Chosen Vocations

Teacher

Alexander was by all indications a fine teacher. A skill apparent from his engagement with school children and others. His teaching ability is supported by his selection and appointment as schoolmaster at the Bowden parochial school, where he served effectively for ten years. He taught his sons surveying and land management, James becoming a competent surveyor and William an accomplished maritime navigator.

There were other clues to this ability: the two boys who spoke to him as he erected his theodolite in Peebles in October 1809, who experienced an 'awakening in our minds a reverence for the instruments of exact science, and indelibly impressing upon us a pleasing recollection of the kind demonstrator himself'.[12] Alexander was an enthusiastic promoter of his 'science' and, like all good teachers, his enthusiasm was contagious.

His construction of the Male Orphan School at Bonnyrigg was ably assisted by boys who were considered by Rev'd Cartwright to be 'the most troublesome and expensive'. However, 'to their credit and that of their overseer…they are now doing as well as boys under such circumstances can be expected to do.' It seems that Alexander had a flair for engaging the boys in their work and in teaching them useful skills. This reflects not only his teaching skill but also his natural charisma – he had the same effect on the convicts at Emu plains, encouraging them in their theatrical pursuits.

Alexander clearly had highly developed social skills, with a natural affinity for people from all walks of life. His self-promotion, using his patrons, publicity and writing skills were mustered to achieve his personal goals.

Estate Factor

Beyond his romantic view of the world, Alexander was an intelligent and skilled man. He was bright, quick-witted and imaginative, and possessed from a young age an enquiring and absorbent mind. This can be seen from his academic achievements and selection and appointment as a parochial schoolmaster, his love of science, knowledge of surveying, architecture and engineering, and ready adoption of improved methods in agriculture.

Alexander's intelligence and learning, which had led him to the profession of teaching at the Bowden school, also facilitated connections with local landowners, such as the eccentric yet innovative Andrew Blaikie and the antiquarian agricultural improver Lord Buchan of Dryburgh Abbey. Encouraged by his interest in the developing science of land surveying, he changed his profession, when the opportunity arose, to take up a position as estate factor at Kippilaw. Thus, his first employer in the agricultural sphere, and his second most important mentor, was John Seton Karr of Kippilaw. Seton Karr had a high opinion of Alexander's intellect when he employed him; but within a few years developed concerns about his control over staff and finances.

Much of Alexander's working life in Scotland was set against the background of the wars with France of 1793–1815, when Britain was in almost permanent conflict. This posed particular challenges to the agricultural economy of the Scottish Borders. In response, at Kippilaw, Alexander joined the ranks of reformers bent on agrarian improvement as a means of buffering against the ups and downs in supply and demand. In this he was initially encouraged by John Seton Karr, until the costs of these improvements began to mount without any signs of the estate turning a profit. One of these projects, the draining of the Marle Moss, despite its expense, was a significant engineering achievement, celebrated in verse and widely acclaimed.[13] Typically, Alexander's original estimates for the cost and timeframe were wildly optimistic, but its benefits for the productivity of Kippilaw were long-term.

Another area was his small-scale livestock breeding (mainly cattle) at Kippilaw. This limited opportunity, and the associated connections he was able to make with livestock breeders, were to prove valuable for his formation as a landed gentleman and future 'grazier' in New South Wales. His experience with the 'Teeswater' cattle breed – later renamed the Shorthorn – was significant, as this became the principal beef breed later imported to Australia, which formed the backbone of the Kinghornes' pastoral empire. This happened long after Alexander left New South Wales but was one of his legacies to his family.

Alexander's apparent profligacy at Kippilaw was based on three elements: Seton Karr's own indulgence, Alexander's determination to achieve the perfection he believed his employer's status deserved, and his consistent underestimation of the costs of improvements. Alexander championed the new enlightenment idea of raising long-term productivity by investing in improvements, whereas Seton Karr favoured the pre-enlightenment value of stewardship and a conservative approach to maintaining his inheritance. For Alexander, Kippilaw was a place where he lived out his dreams of being an up-to-date agricultural scientist and landed gent, advised by the leading lights and ideas of the day. The Seton Karrs, on the other hand, expected a lavish lifestyle and beautiful scenery, for themselves and their guests, when they were in residence. Seton Karr was never able to realise the profits from Alexander's investment in buildings and farm improvements, as the estate could never be sold under the prevailing laws of inheritance.

This is not to absolve Alexander of responsibility for the finances of the estate. A different person might have displayed the hardness of economy and acumen in trade required to achieve a different result. But, with reservations, it was a relationship with which both John Seton Karr and Alexander were comfortable, being the persons they were.

The eventual parting of Alexander and Seton Karr was amicable. The various commissions and contacts the laird had put his way established Alexander with a formidable reputation as a local surveyor and engineer.

When Alexander moved on from Kippilaw, the Seton Karr family was left with a magnificent new Georgian manor house and a productive estate.

Surveyor, Architect and Civil Engineer

Alexander chose early to branch out into surveying, and soon into architecture and civil engineering. These were initially part of his work as a factor, became external commissions with the encouragement of John Seton Karr, and eventually his independent professions. Underpinning these was the scientific approach to improvement he had espoused from his early period in Bowden. His work is discussed further under 'Main achievements'.

Religion

Alexander was a reformed evangelical Christian of the Presbyterian persuasion, as had been several generations his family, except for his grandfather, who was either a dissenter or worse.[14] But Alexander was a strong supporter of the National Church of Scotland. This can be seen in his church attendance throughout his life, his giving,[15] his continuing support of the Presbyterian congregation at Liverpool and his involvement as a trustee of the first Scots church in Goulburn.

His ancestors had attended kirks in Greenlaw and East Gordon, and his father the kirk that met in the ruins of Kelso Abbey before a new church was built nearby in 1773. Alexander also attended the Kelso kirk, as a child. That Presbytery would have been involved in recommending him for appointment as schoolmaster in Bowden Parish, where he was also a parishioner, and likely the Maxton kirk when living at Crossflat farm. In New South Wales, he and his daughters attended the Presbyterian services at Liverpool and Goulburn. He led prayers each day at Emu Plains convict establishment, supporting his belief in the reform and spiritual salvation of convicts, rather than their punishment.

Most of Alexander's closest friends in Scotland were Presbyterians. In New South Wales they were generally evangelical Christians, such as James Chisholm, and Thomas Moore who mentored him in his duties as a Liverpool Magistrate. He strongly supported general Protestant movements in the colony, such as (Church of England) Bishop Broughton's

291

opposition to the interdiction of Holy Scripture, trinitarian doctrine and prayers, when government sponsored general education was proposed by Governor Bourke in the 1830s. Alexander was a committee member for Liverpool representing Broughton's petition to the Governor.[16] However, his Protestantism was not always bipartisan: the incident at Liverpool involving the visiting Wesleyan minister cannot be taken as typical, but does provide evidence of his sectarian prejudice.[17]

Politics

Alexander was intensely interested in public affairs. Although essentially conservative in outlook, at Kippilaw, under the influence of John Seton Karr, he became an avid reader of the weekly *Political Register* newspaper, founded by William Cobbett in 1802. This originally Tory journal gradually became more radically Whig, and formative in Alexander's outlook. Like Cobbett, Alexander had a strong social conscience, and felt some sympathy for the reformist aspects of Cobbett's agenda. There would be signs of this in his treatment of employees at Kippilaw in Scotland, and convicts and orphans in New South Wales.

It has been noted that Edward Smith Hall, the outspoken editor of *The Sydney Monitor*, modelled himself on William Cobbett. Yet Alexander was no friend of Hall, who used his dismissal as colonial Civil Engineer as part of his published evidence against Governor Darling; he criticised Alexander's judgements as a Liverpool magistrate, and supported the malcontent Robison in the Sudds Thompson case, whose testimony was proved false by the evidence of Alexander's sons, James and Alexander Jnr.

Despite this, Alexander was not very active in the politics of the colony. This was surprising given his close friendship with James Chisholm, who was a strong supporter of William Charles Wentworth's reformist agenda. Alexander had thrived under the laissez-faire policies of Thomas Brisbane and was much favoured by him. He appeared to be the victim of a gross injustice when dismissed by the conservative and controlling Ralph Darling. Yet he made no official complaint, rather being relieved to be rid of the political pressure and desk-bound confinement of the position.

Alexander's participation, along with James Chisholm, in the movement for the introduction of a legislative assembly,[18] finally placed him in the reformist camp in 1833. This was not a matter of expedience under the liberal governorship of Richard Bourke – Alexander did not have the same political drive as James Chisholm. Rather, it was the inevitable conclusion of his early political formation, and his social conscience. Bourke was unsuccessful in changing the system of government in New South Wales, but it was not long before both the legislature and the legal systems were reformed, with the help and support of the descendants of James Chisholm and Alexander Kinghorne.

So, the evidence suggests that Alexander's politics were strongly at the social conscience end of Toryism. Together with his evangelical Christianity, this is one important aspect of his character that could have put him at odds with his principal mentor, Sir Walter Scott. The bard was an arch Tory and, although he started life as a Presbyterian, adhered to the more liberal Scottish Episcopal church in adult life. Be that as it may, Alexander never wavered in his admiration for the author of Waverley.

Main Achievements

Alexander's romantic flair combined with his love of Georgian symmetry in his architectural projects. He was an excellent project manager but a poor quantity surveyor and cost estimator. The Kippilaw mansion house had a significant budget overrun, but the renovation itself was carefully planned and promptly completed. Alexander was between a rock and a hard place in balancing work on the new mansion house at Kippilaw with Seton Karr's reluctance to overspend because of his own growing financial troubles in London. The final result was a substantial architectural achievement that remains a district icon to this day (2022).

Alexander's architectural and building projects combined beauty and functionality. While the design of the mansion house at Kippilaw had a considerable input from its owner, the beautiful coach house was all Alexander's. His architectural flair as exhibited in Gledswood house, Berwickshire, has been praised in recent times as an example of the classical regency villa, and the house was much loved at the time by Walter Scott because of its style and location. No doubt Alexander was aware of Scott's admiration and retained pride in this building, as well as its location, as an epergne of Scott's View.

Alexander's rescue and improvement of the Kippilaw Estate also must be counted among his main achievements. This had been in ruins when he arrived, but he returned it to productivity through scientific improvements.

Considering Alexander's projects in Scotland as a whole, the one that involved the most trust on Seton Karr's part, and the most benefit on Alexander's part, was the survey of the Berwick to Glasgow railway. It was also reflective of Thomas Telford's high opinion of Alexander's ability and work ethic.[19]

Alexander progressed significantly in his skills as a surveyor and cartographer with time and experience. A comparison of his plan of Netherton and Muirside (1806) with that of the Linthill Estate (1820), is a clear indication of changed competence, sophistication, detail and artistry. The county maps of Roxburghshire and Selkirkshire remain his finest cartographical achievements.[20] Alexander's plan of the Emu Plains convict establishment represents a significant document in Australian history.[21]

The humanity of his management of Emu Plains should be reiterated. He encouraged cultural pursuits and morality, without relaxing discipline, a careful balance he managed through the characters and abilities of his support staff. This set a course for the convicts to seek to return to society and make happier lives for themselves. This represented perhaps his finest achievement.

His period as Civil Engineer for New South Wales was short-lived. Among the projects that did not get off the ground was his plan for the gas lighting of Sydney. This demonstrates that he had a vision for an illuminated city, and a civil society, being more than a dark prison at the opposite end of the world. His dismissal left this for others to take on, to their credit.

Like Alexander's problems with the Kippilaw mansion, there were budgetary issues with the construction of the Male Orphan School in New South Wales. The surviving building, Bonnyrigg House, although completed by others to his design, has been described by the Heritage Council of New South Wales as a unique example of early colonial Georgian architecture, and 'the only surviving example of the Civil Engineer Alexander Kinghorne's work'.[22]

Of course, there are many fine examples of Alexander's architectural and engineering work in Scotland. His legacy in Australia would be the prerogative of his children and their descendants.

Personal Goals

One of Alexander's character traits was ambition: for himself and his family. His personal ambition was to attain the status of a landed gentleman. He was unable to achieve this in Scotland through obstacles of class and circumstances. So, he hoped to achieve gentrification through the acquisition of land in the colonies.

To aid his progress towards his goals, he recognised that he needed patronage, marshalling a formidable group of connections initially in support of his work in Scotland, and then of his bid to emigrate with his family as free settlers to New South Wales.

In that colony, land was the key to status, and he was able to obtain his first grant, with some effort, after only one year in government service. His appointment as Superintendent at Emu Plains led to other senior roles: first the disastrous short-term appointment as Civil Engineer of the colony and then as engineer of the Clergy and School Lands Corporation. Alexander finessed the latter role for himself, but it only offered him a twelve-month appointment before his profligacy led to the termination of that employment.

Despite these disappointments, Alexander's land acquisition qualified him for further roles in the legal system of the colony, first as Justice of the Peace and local magistrate at Liverpool. Later, in the Supreme Court, his appointment as special juror and Assessor confirmed that he had gained significant recognition and could certainly consider himself a 'gentleman' in the colonial context. His status as a magistrate gained him invitations to important civic and vice regal events. Without doubt, by the time Alexander Kinghorne returned to Scotland, he had *arrived* in New South Wales Society.

Conclusion

Alexander Kinghorne, from obscurity in the Scottish Borders, had cultivated connections that led him to be befriended by the high and mighty, including the senior aristocracy of the Scottish Borders, praised in poetry as an agricultural improver, taken on as an associate by the greatest civil engineer of the Georgian age and lauded by the governor of an American state. Then, at the age of 54, Alexander was to leave his native Scotland, travel half-way round the world with his family, and settle them in the British Colony of New South Wales.

Alexander's departure from Scotland in the 1820s was the result of economic necessity. The journey was courageous no less; in modern parlance akin to travelling in a spaceship to another galaxy. But Alexander was not looking for another galaxy. Spurred on by his romanticism, he imagined finding a new Caledonia where his family could settle themselves into an idyllic environment, on the beautiful banks of a new Tweed overlooking the rural splendour of their own estate, like one of those they had left behind in the Scottish Borders. He was an idealistic dreamer who, although eventually acquiring much land in New South Wales, tended to imagine it in the guise of his homeland. It would be left to his sons and daughters to adapt these dreams into practical realities.

Unlike his engineering mentors Telford and Rennie, Alexander Kinghorne left no mighty structural work by which he would be remembered. His main legacy to Australia was his descendants, who helped build the pastoral industry that became its backbone throughout the 19th and 20th century. However, his own life was also fascinating, as much for its failures as for its successes. It is remarkable that, despite Alexander's unrealistic expectations, the family eventually settled in an area of southern New South Wales that was not unlike their native Scotland.

After he had achieved all he could in New South Wales, and the ravages of age began to affect his health, he returned to Scotland. He had been recognised for his achievements in the colony, prepared a legacy for his family and there were no more social mountains to climb. He had expected to return to a comfortable retirement in the Scottish Borders, supported by regular remittances from his estates in New South Wales, perhaps to be lauded in Scottish society, like many returning with wealth and power from the Americas. None of this was to be the case, as he arrived at the beginning of an economic recession that kept him, and his family, impoverished. The society he had known had changed, and his principal patrons were dead.

The last years of Alexander's life were marred with illness, financial uncertainty, and disappointment. In Scotland he was again a nobody, but his final romantic ambition was to be buried in the grounds of Dryburgh

Abbey with his wife and near his mentors, Lord Buchan and Sir Walter Scott. As he gradually succumbed to illness, he might have been comforted by his recollections of the bard's early poetic works, such as this extract from Scott's *Marmion*.

Stay yet, illusion, stay a while,
My wildered fancy still beguile!
From this high theme how can I part,
Ere half unloaded is my heart!
For all the tears e'er sorrow drew,
And all the raptures fancy knew,
And all the keener rush of blood,
That throbs through bard in bardlike mood,
Were here a tribute mean and low,
Though all their mingled streams could flow—
Woe, wonder, and sensation high,
In one spring-tide of ecstasy!
It will not be—it may not last—
The vision of enchantment's past:
Like frostwork in the morning ray
The fancied fabric melts away;
Each Gothic arch, memorial-stone,
And long, dim, lofty aisle, are gone;
And lingering last, deception dear,
The choir's high sounds die on my ear.[23]

Appendix 1

Alexander Kinghorne's Key Contacts (1770 ff)

A summary of Alexander Kinghorne's known family, social and business contacts in the period from 1770ff is given in the table below. The entries are in order of when he first met, or mentioned, them in his correspondence. An attempt has been made to indicate who introduced Alexander to each contact.

[A to F indicates social class;[1] AK = Alexander Kinghorne; JSK = John Seton Karr]

Year	Name	Title	Social Class	Introduction	Comments
1770	Cornelius Lundie	Rev.	C	James and Margaret Kinghorn, baptism of AK	(1716–1800), clergy, incumbency from 1750 Kelso
1783	Sir Walter Scott	Baronet of Abbotsford	B	At Kelso Grammar school, according to AK	Fellow student at Kelso Grammar School[2,3]
1783	James Ballantyne	Mr	C	At Kelso Grammar school, according to AK	Fellow student at Kelso Grammar School[1,2]
1783 of before	Lancelot Whale	Mr	C	At Kelso Grammar school, according to AK	Rector of Kelso Grammar School[1,2]

Year	Name	Title	Social Class	Introduction	Comments
1784	Sir William Scott	Baronet of Raeburn & Maxpoffle	B	At Kelso Grammar School	(1773–1855) 6th Scott of Raeburn (Lessudden) and Maxpoffle. Married Susan Horsburgh. On Kelso-Berwick Rail Commission. Frequent visitor to and friend of AK.[2]
1784	Sir Walter Scott	Baronet of Raeburn	B	William Scott (Raeburn's son)	5th Scott of Raeburn (Lessudden). Father of William Scott, above.
1784–1788	Robert Lundie	Rev.	C	At Kelso Grammar school	(1774–1832), incumbency from 1807 at Kelso. Son of Rev. Cornelius Lundie.[2]
1784–1788	Robert Scott	Mr	C	At Kelso Grammar school	Brother of William Scott of Raeburn, above.[2]
1784–1788	Hugh Scott	Mr	C	At Kelso Grammar school	Brother of William Scott of Raeburn, above.[2]
1791 or earlier	John Ker	His Grace the 3rd Duke of Roxburghe	A	Rev. James Hume	(1740–1804). AK recommended to him by Hume as new schoolmaster at Bowden Parochial School.
1791 or earlier	David Ramsay Karr	of Kippilaw	B	At Bowden kirk, but mainly absent	Laird of Kippilaw from ca 1746 to 1794. Uncle of JSK

Year	Name	Title	Social Class	Introduction	Comments
1791 or earlier	John Seton Karr	of Kippilaw	B	At Bowden kirk AK mentions in 1807 that their correspondence commenced earlier than 1798. AK was at Bowden in 1791 or earlier.	Nephew of two former lairds by his mother, their sister, Jean Ramsay. Jean married (1740) Daniel Seton of Powder Hall and d. 1766. Born Edinburgh 5 November 1744, d. 5 May 1815.
1791 or earlier	Elizabeth Seton Karr	Mrs	B	JSK	Wife of JSK (b.1752, d. 9 January 1815)
1791 or earlier	James Hume	Rev.	C	At Kelso or Bowden kirks.	(1712–1792), clergy, incumbency from 1742 Bowden. His death in 1792 places AK at Bowden kirk in the summer of 1791 or earlier.
1791 or before	Elizabeth (Betty) Brockie	Miss	D	Possibly at church: currently unknown.	Future spouse. They married in 1793
1791 or before	Andrew Blaikie	Mr 'Old Blaikie'	C	At Bowden kirk	Feu tenant at Holydean & Riddleton Hill. Kippilaw neighbour. Friend and mentor to AK. Agricultural innovator who met King George III.
1792	Thomas Kirkpatrick	Rev.	C	At Bowden kirk	(1758–1797), clergy, incumbency at Bowden from 1792

Year	Name	Title	Social Class	Introduction	Comments
1793 or before	James Duncan	Rev	C	At Mertoun kirk	(1763–1845), clergy, incumbency at Mertoun from 1790. Conducted marriage of AK and Betty Brockie
1793	Helen Brockie	Miss	D	Betty Brockie	Sister of Betty Brockie
1793	Nancy (Agnes) Brockie	Miss	D	Betty Brockie	Sister of Betty Brockie
1793	William Brockie	Mr	D	Betty Brockie	Feu tenant at Maidenhall, and later of Lauder. Father of Betty Brockie. Park renter at Kippilaw.
1793	John Brockie	Mr	D	Betty Brockie	Feu tenant at Bemersyde, brother of William Brockie. Park renter at Kippilaw
1793	George Brockie	Mr	D	Betty Brockie	Brother of Betty Brockie, of Lochside, Blainslie
1793	John Brockie	Mr	D	Betty Brockie	Brother of Betty Brockie
1793	William Brockie	Mr	D	Betty Brockie	Brother of Betty Brockie, Baker of Edinburgh. Married Elizabeth.
1793	Alexander Brockie	Mr	D	Betty Brockie	Of Bemersyde and later Maidenhall, brother of Betty Brockie

301

Year	Name	Title	Social Class	Introduction	Comments
1793	Thomas Brockie	Mr	D	Betty Brockie	Brother of William Brockie, of Barnhills, Ancrum, and Prieston. Renter of Kippilaw Parks
1793	Thomas Brockie	Mr	D	Betty Brockie	Oldest brother of Betty Brockie of Southfield near Port Seton
1794	Andrew Ramsay Karr	of Kippilaw	B	Bowden Kirk	Laird of Kippilaw from 1794 to 1799. Uncle of JSK
1795	John Carre	Mr	C	According to AK. At church?	(1744–1798) of Cavers and Hundalee.
1795	William Balfour	Rev.	C	At church	(1767–1829), assistant minister at Bowden kirk from 1795. Incumbency from 1797
1799	Francis Napier	WS	C	JSK (Edinburgh friend of William Jerdan, Sir Walter Scott and JSK)	Edinburgh solicitor. Handled local estate matters for JSK after death of Andrew Ramsay Karr in 1799.
1799	John Murray	Mr	D	AK	Tenant at Clarilaw and Faughill
1800 or earlier	David Steuart Erskine	Lord Buchan Earl Cardross	A	1800 first mention by AK in correspondence with JSK	Then on personal speaking terms, buying seed potatoes. Important patron of AK
1800	Richard Edgar Hunter	Lieutenant Colonel	C	AK	Of Linthill

Year	Name	Title	Social Class	Introduction	Comments
1800	William Riddell	Mr	C	AK	Of Camieston. Purchased Lin-thill on death of Col. Hunter
1800	Charles Erskine	WS	C	JSK	Trust lawyer at Melrose
1800	Graham	Mr	D	AK	A friend of AK. The agent in Berwick who ar-ranges transport of goods arriving by sea
1800	Sandy Arm-strong	Mr	E	AK	Hynd at Kippilaw
1800	Minto	Mr	E	AK	Hynd at Kippilaw
1800	Goodfallow	Mr	E	AK	Hynd at Kippilaw
1800	John Spiden	Mr	F	AK	Farm worker at Kippilaw
1800	John Bichet	Mr	F	AK	Farm worker at Kippilaw
1800	Walter Lith-head	Mr	F	AK	Farm worker at Kippilaw
1800	George Lith-head	Mr	F	AK	Farm worker/gar-dener at Kippilaw
1800	A. Cessford	Mr	F	AK	Farm worker at Kippilaw
1800	Molly Wil-son	Mrs	F	JSK	Housekeeper/ cook, Kippilaw Mansion House
1800	Mary Wilson	Miss	F	JSK	House ser-vant, Kippilaw Mansion House. Daughter of Molly. Died of consumption 1811
1800	John Shiel	Mr	F	AK	Tenant of Bowden Muir, Kippilaw

Year	Name	Title	Social Class	Introduction	Comments
1800	Thomas Best	Mr	F	AK	Miller. Tenant of Bowden Mill, Kippilaw
1800	Brown	Mr	F	AK	Tenant of Bowden Mill Farm, Kippilaw
1801	Charles William Henry Montagu Scott	His Grace the 4th Duke of Buccleuch	A	JSK	(1772–1819) Patron of AK
1801	Sir Hugh Scott	Baronet	B	Currently unknown. Possibilities: Sir Walter Scott, JSK, Brockie family.	(1758–1841) of Harden. Later 6th Lord Polwarth. Married Anne, daughter of George Baillie-Hamilton. On Kelso-Berwick Rail Commission. AK's encourager/ patron.
1801	George Baillie-Hamilton	Mr	B	JSK; possibly earlier by Kinghorn relatives in Gordon	(1763–1841) of Jerviswood and Mellerstein. Son of same (1723–1797). Father of same, 10th Earl of Haddington
1801	Sir John Buchanan Riddell	Baronet	B	JSK or at church	(1768–1819), of Riddell Estate and Lilliesleaf (South of Bowden). On Kelso-Berwick Rail Commission
1801	Sir George Douglas	Baronet	B	JSK or AK himself	(1754–1821) 2nd Baronet of the lands of Friarshaw in the parishes of Bowden and Lilliesleaf. On Kelso-Berwick Rail Commission

Year	Name	Title	Social Class	Introduction	Comments
1801	George Chalmers	Mr	C	JSK	(1742–1825), antiquarian, Chief Clerk to the Trade Committee of Privy Council. Author of *Caledonia*
1801	Alexander Carre	Mr	C	JSK	(1746–1817) of Cavers and Hundalee. Brother of John Carre
1801	John Rennie Jnr	Mr	C	JSK	Civil Engineer. He was at that time more famous than Thomas Telford. Took over from Telford as AK's supervising Engineer on Kelso to Berwick Railway
1801	John Campbell	WS	C	JSK	Solicitor in Edinburgh. Former colleague of JSK
1801	John Spottiswoode	WS	C	JSK	(1780–1866) Solicitor of London. Colleague of JSK
1801	Andrew Riddell	Mr	D	AK	Newcastle carrier
1801	James Gordon	Mr	D	AK	Local carrier
1801	Paxton & Laurie,	Messrs	D	AK	Leith & Berwick, transport agents
1801	Archibald Dickson	Mr	D	AK	Seedsman and plant nurseryman of Hawick

Year	Name	Title	Social Class	Introduction	Comments
1801	John Smith	Mr	D	AK	(1783–1864) Stonemason. Consultant on Marle Moss & Kippilaw mansion house. Later, builder/architect of Abbotsford and many bridges.
1802	Jean Seton	Miss	B	JSK	Sister of JSK. Widow of Daniel Seton of Powder Hall d. April 1803.
1802	Mainai Seton	Miss	B	JSK	Daughter of Daniel & Jean Seton
	Daniel Briggs Seton	Master	B	JSK	Son of Daniel & Jean Seton
1802	Robert Shortreed	Mr	D	AK	Feu tenant of Newhall
1802	John Dickson	Mr	D	AK	Feu tenant of Camieston
1802	John Harvie	Mr	D	AK	Feu tenant of Linthill
1802	James Haldane	Mr	D	JSK or the Duke of Roxburghe	Steward and later factor to the Duke of Roxburghe at Fleurs
1802	William Gardner	Mr	D	JSK or AK	Road-maker and Contractor, Crinan Canal & Marle Moss
1802	William Swantson	Mr	D	Andrew Blaikie	Miller to the Duke of Roxburghe.
1802	Clement Mistry	Mr	F	JSK	Servant to Mr and Mrs Seton Karr. Travelled with them to Kippilaw from London.

Year	Name	Title	Social Class	Introduction	Comments
1802	Mary	?	F	JSK	Servant to Mr and Mrs Seton Karr. Travelled with them to Kippilaw from London.
1803	William Bellenden-Ker	His Grace the 4th Duke of Roxburghe	A	JSK	(1728–1805). Duke from 1804–1805.
1803	Nicol Milne	Mr	C	JSK	First Laird of Faldonside (also an 'advocate'). Son of Thomas Milne.
1803	William Sibbald	Leith Merchant	C	JSK or AK	(1748–1817) of Gledswood/ Gladswood and merchant in Leith – AK built his house at Gledswood, Berwickshire
1803	Archibald Dunlop	Mr	C	AK (re. Marle Moss)	(1770–1838), Whitmuirhall, Selkirk
1803	Henderson	Mr	D	AK	Sherriff's clerk at Jedburgh
1803	Thomas Milne	Mr	D	AK	Father of Nicole Milne. Feu tenant of Lindean.
1803	John Sibbald	Mr	D	AK	Feu tenant at Whitelaw
1804	James Zerubabel Haig	Mr	B	Lord Buchan or Brockie family	(1758–1840), 24th Laird of Bemersyde from 1790
1804	White	Mr	C	JSK or AK	Owner of Eastfield. Kippilaw neighbour.
1804	Knox	Mr	F	AK	Sub-tenant at Belchers
1804	Scott	Mr	F	AK	Sub-tenant at Kirkhope

Year	Name	Title	Social Class	Introduction	Comments
1804	John Rutherford	Mr	F	AK	Sub-tenant at Sandystones
1804	James Brunton	Mr	F	AK	Sub-tenant at Camieston
1804	Redford	Mr	F	AK	Sub-tenant at Sinton Mill
1804	George White	Mr	F	AK	Sub-tenant at Elliestown
1804	Tom Hogg	Mr	F	AK	Groom at Kippilaw
1805	Lyel	Major/Baronet	B	Unknown, possibly AK directly	Landowner of Prieston, and Mersington Tower near Greenlaw
1805	James Stalker	Rev.	C	AK	Clergy, incumbency from 1805 at Lilliesleaf until 1816
1805	John Rutherfurd	Major	C	AK	Landowner of Mossburnford
1805	James Murray	Mr	C-D	James Haldane	JP at Jedburgh
1805	Alexander Leadbetter	Mr	C-D	James Haldane	JP at Kelso
1805	Walter Riddell	Mr	C-D	AK	Clerk of Supply, Jedburgh
1805	John Corse Scott	Mr	D	Sir Walter Scott or AK himself	Feu tenant of Sinton. 'Scott of Sinton'. Justice of the Peace and millwright. Assisted in production of AK's map of Selkirkshire, 1824.
1805	Andrew Maither	Mr	D	AK	New sub-tenant of Bowden Mill Farm
1805	Peter Brodie	Mr	D	AK	New tenant of Clarilaw

Year	Name	Title	Social Class	Introduction	Comments
1805	Thomas Nisbet	Mr	E	AK	Langley nr Galashiels, hired as hynd stock-man at Kippilaw (1805–1810)
1805	William Fowler	Mr	E	AK	From Craig Douglas in the parish of Yarrow, hired as plough-man hynd at Kippilaw. Later (1811) he trains James Kinghorne in ploughing and sowing of crops.
1805	Johnny Marr	Mr	E	AK	Roof slater
1805	William Hume	Mr	E	Andrew Blaikie	Hired as a hedger hynd
1805	Tom Henderson	Mr	F	AK	Kippilaw farm-worker
1805	Robin Wright	Mr	F	AK	Kippilaw farm-worker
1806	Sir Gilbert Elliot-Murray-Kynynmound	1st Earl of Minto	A	JSK or, earlier, Thomas Brockie	MP for Rox-burghshire 1777–1784
1806	John Rutherfurd	Mr	C	Lord Minto	(1748–1834) of Edgerston. MP for Roxburgh-shire 1802–1812. Married to daughter of Lord Minto. On Kel-so-Berwick Rail Committee
1806	John Campbell	Rev.	C	AK at church	(1778–1857), clergy, incumbency from 1806 at Selkirk

Year	Name	Title	Social Class	Introduction	Comments
1806	John Cockrane	Mr	D	JSK or AK	Feu tenant at Lilliesleaf
1806	Peter Mather	Mr	D	AK	Local trade or businessman
1806	James Dove	Mr	D	AK	Local trade or businessman
1806	William Fairburn	Mr	F	AK	Kippilaw farm-worker
1807	Anthony Maitland	10th Earl of Lauderdale	A	William Brockie	(1785–1863). William Brockie became his feu tenant and *de facto* factor. Seat Thirlestaine Castle near Lauder.
1807	Usher	Mr	C	AK	Landowner of Totfield
1807	William Laidlaw	Mr	C	AK	(1779–1845) of Philiphaugh. Poet James Hogg's maternal uncle. Friend of Sir Walter Scott
1807	Archibald Swinton	WS	C	JSK or James Haldane	Factor to the Duke William of Roxburghe
1807	'Old' Spence	Dr	C	AK	Doctor in Melrose.[4] First consulted by AK re. Betty's illness.
1807	James Hood	Mr	D	AK	Builder of Kippilaw Mansion House – 1810 renovation
1807	Adam Hood	Mr	D	AK	Builder of Kippilaw Mansion House – 1810 renovation

Year	Name	Title	Social Class	Introduction	Comments
1807	John Wilson	Mr	E	AK	Hynd at Kippilaw
1807	John Hogg	Mr	E	AK	Hynd at Kippilaw
1807	Willie Hume	Mr	F	AK	Farmworker at Kippilaw
1807	Jamie Thomson	Mr	F	AK	Farmworker at Kippilaw
1808	William Kerr	6th Marquess of Lothian	A	JSK	(1763–1824) of Mont Teviot Estate, Newbigging near Jedburgh
1808	Edward Lapidge	Mr	C	JSK	(1779–1860) Critique of AK's design for the renovation of the Kippilaw Mansion House
1808	John Park	Mr	D	AK	Feu tenant at Woodhead. Park renter at Kippilaw. Brother of the African explorer, Mungo Park
1808	Thomas Jamieson	Mr	E	AK	Hynd at Kippilaw
1809	William Ker	Mr	C	AK	Laird of Abbotrule (near Peebles). Cess tax assessor
1809	Thomas Telford	Mr	C-D	JSK	Civil Engineer
1809	Douglas Ainslie	Mr	C	Thomas Telford	(1771–1850) of Cairbank near Duns. On Committee for the Glasgow to Berwick Raiway
1809	William Curruthers	Mr	E	AK	Hynd at Kippllaw

Year	Name	Title	Social Class	Introduction	Comments
1809	John Wilson	Mr	F	AK	Kippilaw farmworker
1810	James Kyd	Mr	C	Unknown	Prospective purchaser of Wester Eccles Estate, Berwickshire, from Nicholas Brown. AK conducted survey of Estate 1810.
1810	Andrew Douglas	Dr	C	AK	Of Timpandead (1774–1827). Physician to the Forces, in Jedburgh. Consulted by AK re. Betty's illness. On Kelso-Berwick Railway Commission
1810	Clarkson	Dr	C-D	AK	Physician in Selkirk. Consulted by AK re. Betty's illness
1811	Walker	Mr	C	AK	Landowner of Wooden. Well-known breeder of working horses. On Kelso-Berwick Rail Commission
1811	Thomas Williamson Ramsay	Mr	C	AK	Merchant of Leith. Purchased Maxton Estate 1811 from Walter Ker of Littledean. Obtained placement in RN for William Kinghorne
1811	Elizabeth Ramsay	Mrs	C	Thomas Williamson Ramsay	Wife of Thomas Williamson Ramsay

Year	Name	Title	Social Class	Introduction	Comments
1811	David Wilson	Mr	D	AK	Takes over as feu tenant of Riddletonhill
1811	Alexander Mein	Mr	D	JSK	b. 1761. Kelso suppliers of Manchester, upholstery, wallpaper and furnishings – renovation of Kippilaw Mansion House
1811	Thomas Scott	Mr	E	AK	Hynd at Kippilaw
1811	Nanny Archibald	Miss	F	Molly Wilson	New house servant at Kippilaw
1812	Sir Alexander McDonald Lockhart	Baronet	B	Unknown	(1776–1816) of Lee in the County of Lockhart. Made 1st Baronet of Lee (1806). MP for Berwick-upon-Tweed. Considerably in debt when he died in 1816 (£4,000). Owed AK £200 in 1812, stayed at Kippilaw Mains
1812	Gowdie	Major-General	C	AK	Landowner of Prior Bank, Melrose
1812	Matthew Buckle	Captain (later Admiral) RN	C	Thomas Williamson Ramsay	(1770–1855). Advisor to AK on getting his son William into the Royal Navy. Flag Captain at Leith
1812	Christopher Nixon	Commander RN	C	Thomas Williamson Ramsay	Captain of William Kinghorne's first ship, *Nightingale*, as first class boy and Midshipman

Year	Name	Title	Social Class	Introduction	Comments
1812	William Foggo	Mr	D	George Baillie-Hamilton	Former Estate Steward at Mellerstain. Hired as replacement for AK at Kippilaw
1812	Robert Oliver	Mr	E	AK	New hynd at Kippilaw
1812	Thomas Watson	Mr	E	AK	New hynd at Kippilaw
1812	John Edgar	Mr	F	AK	Hay cutter at Kippilaw
1813	James Pringle	Mr	C	William Scott of Maxpoffle or Sir Walter Scott	9th Laird of Torwoodlee (1759–1840). Sheriff of Selkirkshire. Strong supporter of Berwick to Kelso railway.
1814	Sir John Owen	Baronet	B	JSK	MP for Pembrokeshire. Owner of Crickmarrin Estate.
1814	John Dunn	Mr	C	JSK or John Seton Karr	Tenant on Crickmarrin, Estate. Employed James Kinghorne as land steward.
1814	William Eliott Lockhart	Lieutenant-Colonel	C	Sir Walter Scott. AK introduced Lockhart to JSK	(1764–1832) Landowner of Borthwickbrae. MP for Selkirkshire 1806–1830
1815	William Robert Kerr	7th Marquess of Lothian	A	Not known	(1794–1841), Earl of Ancrum. Commissioned AK to survey the Estate of Newbigging
1820	John Aimers	Mr	D	Not known	Miller of Galashiels to whom Andrew Seton was apprenticed.

Year	Name	Title	Social Class	Introduction	Comments
1820	Helen Aimers	Miss	D	John Aimers (her great uncle)	Married Andrew Seton Kinghorne
1821	Sir Herbert Taylor	Major-General	C to A	AK wrote to him seeking patronage from The Duke of York	Military Secretary to His Royal Highness The Duke of York
1822 or earlier	James Innes-Ker	His Grace the 5th Duke of Roxburghe	A	AK	(1736–1823). Patron of AK's map of Roxburghshire.
1823	George Cranston	Mr	C-D	AK	Road Surveyor. Collaborated with AK and James Kinghorne on the production of the map of Selkirkshire
1823	John Clark	Mr	C-D	AK	Land Surveyor. Collaborated with AK and James Kinghorne on the production of the map of Selkirkshire
1823	Sir Thomas Livingstone Mitchell	Lieu-tenant-Colonel	C-D	AK and his son James Kinghorne	(1792–1855) A road surveyor in 1823. Collaborated with AK and James Kinghorne on the production of the map of Selkirkshire. Later Surveyor-General of NSW.

Year	Name	Title	Social Class	Introduction	Comments
1824	Right Honourable William John Napier	9th Lord Napier	A	Colonel William Elliot Lockhart, via John Seton Karr or Sir Walter Scott	(1786–1834) Patron of map of Selkirkshire. First Administrator in Canton, recommended British settlement at Hong Kong.
1824	Sir Henry Hay Makdougall	Baronet	B	Sir Walter Scott	(1752–1825), 4th Baronet of Mackerston. Daughter married to Sir Thomas Brisbane. Patron of AK
1824	William Snell	Captain	C	AK	Captain of Australian Company's migrant ship *Portland*.
1824	Sir Thomas Brisbane	Major-General	B	Lord Buchan and Sir Henry Hay Macdougall	(1773–1860) Governor of NSW 1821–1825. Later Sir Thomas Makdougall Brisbane 1st Baronet
1824	George Arthur	Colonel	C	Letters from Patrons and William Kinghorne	(1784–1854) Lieut. Governor Van Diemen's Land 1824–1836. Later Sir George Arthur 1st Baronet.
1824	Frederick Goulburn	Major	C	Sir Thomas Brisbane	(1788–1837) Colonial Secretary of NSW
1824	Family Pitcairn	Messrs	C	AK	Passengers on the *Portland*. Robert became William Kinghorne's solicitor in Hobart.
1824	James Chisholm Snr	Mr	C	Chance meeting in George Street Sydney	Friend & future co-father-in law

Year	Name	Title	Social Class	Introduction	Comments
1824	James Chisholm Jnr	Mr	C	James Chisholm Snr	Future son-in-law
1824	Alexander Dick	Mr	D	AK	Silversmith. Passenger on the *Portland*.
1825	Hyacinthe Yves Philippe Potentien	Baron de Bougain-ville	A	AK	(1781–1846) French naval explorer. Visited Emu Plains.
1825	William Stewart	Colonel	C	Sir Thomas Brisbane	(1769–1854) Lieut Governor of New South Wales (1825–7).
1825	Saxe Ban-nister	Captain	C	Sir Thomas Brisbane	(1790–1877) At-torney General of NSW. Committee CSLC.
1825	John Stephen	Mr (Justice)	C	Sir Thomas Brisbane	(1771–1833) Solicitor General of NSW. Supreme Court Judge.
1825	Francis Forbes	Chief Jus-tice (Sir)	C	Sir Thomas Brisbane	(1784–1841) Chief Justice of · NSW.
1825	William Cowper	Rev. (Arch-deacon)	C	Sir Thomas Brisbane	(1778–1858) Senior Assistant Chaplain of NSW
1825	John Ovens	Major	C	Sir Thomas Brisbane	(1788–1825) Chief Engineer of NSW
1825	Thomas Iceley	Mr	C	James King-horne	(1797–1874) landowner and stockbreeder of Bathurst region
1825	William Bowman	Mr	C	Unknown; possibly James Chisholm Snr	First cousin of James Chisholm's 2nd wife Mary. Client of Alex-ander Kinghorne Jnr.

Year	Name	Title	Social Class	Introduction	Comments
1825	Henry Fulton	Rev.	C	James Kinghorne	(1761–1840) Chaplain at Castlereagh and Evan, also magistrate
1825	Henry Grattan Douglass	Dr	C	James Kinghorne	(1790–1865) Medical Superintendent, Female Factory Parramatta, magistrate
1825	Peter Murdoch	Lieutenant	D	Sir Thomas Brisbane	(1795–1871) Superintendent Emu Plains (1822–1824)
1825	Gregory Blaxland	Mr & Mrs	C	AK	(1778–1853) Explorer & grazier of South Creek, Evan. Local to Emu Plains.
1825	George Cox	Mr & Mrs	C	AK	(1795–1868) Grazier of Mulgoa. Local to Emu Plains.
1825	Henry Cox	Mr	C	AK	Infant son of George Cox
1825	John McHenry	Mr	C	AK	Grazier of Lambridge, Castleragh. Local to Emu Plains.
1825	John Jamieson	Sir	C	AK	(1766–1850) Grazier of Regentville. Local to Emu Plains.
1825	John Stewart	Mr	D	Sir Thomas Brisbane	Assistant Superintendent at Emu Plains
1825	Joseph Peters	Mr	E	James Kinghorne	Overseer of convicts at Emu Plains. Later, overseer at Cardross.

Year	Name	Title	Social Class	Introduction	Comments
1825	Mary Peters (née Robinson)	Mrs	E	Joseph Peters	Convict wife of Joseph Peters. Came to Cardross with Peters.
1825	James Scott	Mr	E	AK	Storekeeper and commissariat officer at Emu Plains
1825	Christopher Dodding	Mr	E	AK	Overseer of tobacco gangs at Emu Plains
1825	Théodore Constantini	Mr	E	AK	Convict artist at Emu Plains
1826	Ralph Darling	Lieutenant General (Sir)	C	AK	(1772–1858) Governor of NSW
1826	Eliza Darling (née Dumaresq)	Mrs	C	AK	Wife of Governor Darling & sister of Henry, William & Edward Dumaresq.
1826	William John Dumaresq	Captain	C	AK	(1793–1868) Inspector of roads and bridges and Civil Engineer of NSW. Brother-in-law of Governor Darling
1826	Henry Dumaresq	Lieutenant Colonel	C	AK	(1792–1838) Private secretary & brother-in-law of Governor Darling
1826	Alexander MacLeay	Mr	C	AK	(1767–1848) Colonial Secretary of NSW
1826	William Lithgow	Mr	C	AK	(1784–1864) Fellow member of the land board. Auditor-general of NSW

Year	Name	Title	Social Class	Introduction	Comments
1826	John Thomas Campbell	Mr	C	AK	(1770–1830) Replaced AK on land board.
1826	Edward Smith Hall	Mr	C	Unknown; possibly James Chisholm Snr	(1786–1860) Newspaper proprietor.
1826	Robert Cartwright	Rev.	C	AK as Civil Engineer	(1771–1856) Master of male orphan school. Incumbent St Luke's Liverpool. Trustee CSLC.
1826	Samuel Marsden	Rev.	C	Clergy & School Lands Corporation (CSLC)	(1765–1838) Senior Chaplain. Trustee CSLC.
1826	Thomas Hobbs Scott	Archdeacon	C	CSLC	(1783–1860) Vice President CSLC. Chair of CSLC Committee.
1826	Robert Campbell	Hon.	C	CSLC	(1764–1846) MLC. Committee CSLC.
1826	James Holland	Mr	C	CSLC	Solicitor General (temp). Committee CSLC.
1826	Charles Cowper	Mr (Sir)	C	CSLC	(1807–1875) Clerk/secretary of CSLC Committee.
1826	John Macarthur	Hon	C	CSLC	(1767–1834) MLC. Committee CSLC.
1826	James Busby	Mr	C	Male Orphan School	(1801–1871) Male Orphan School farm manager.
1826	Charles Throsby	Mr	C	Male Orphan School	(1777–1828) MLC representative. Fellow magistrate at Liverpool.

Year	Name	Title	Social Class	Introduction	Comments
1826	Benjamin Wilson	Mr	E	Male Orphan School	Convict carpenter Male Orphan School, employed by AK.
1827	Ann Drummond	Mrs	E	James Chisholm Snr	Kinghornes' land lady at Drummond Farm, Liverpool.
1827	Patrick Thompson	Mr	E	James Kinghorne	Prisoner transiting through Emu Plains, wearing Joseph Sudds' irons.
1827	George Ranken	Mr	C	James Kinghorne	At Emu Plains establishment en route from the Bathurst district to Sydney. Examined Sudds' irons.
1827	William Lawson	Mr			
1827	Vachell	Lieutenant			
1827	Robert Robison	Captain			
1827	Christie	Lieutenant			
1827	John Oxley	Lieutenant	C	Alexander MacLeay	(1784–1828) Surveyor General of NSW

Year	Name	Title	Social Class	Introduction	Comments
1827	John Bingle	Mr	C	Windsor Quarter Sessions	(1796–1882) of Puen Buen. Grand jury member.
1827	George Bowman	Mr	C		(1795–1878) of Archerfield. Grand jury member.
1827	William Faithful	Mr	C		(1774–1847) of Richmond & Goulburn. Grand jury member
1827	Thomas Arndell Jnr	Mr	C		(1799–1865) of Cattai. Grand Jury member.
1827	Richard Rouse	Mr	C		(1774–1852) of Rouse Hill. Grand jury member.
1827	Cornelius, Delowry	Mr	C	Liverpool Courthouse	Clerk of Magistrate's Court.
1827	Thomas Moore	Mr	C	Liverpool Courthouse	(1762–1840) Fellow magistrate & mentor.
1827	Patrick Hill	Surgeon	C	Liverpool Courthouse	(1794–1852) Colonial Surgeon & Fellow Liverpool Magistrate.
1827	Richard Brooks	Captain	C	Liverpool Courthouse	(1765–1833) Grazier of Denham Court. Fellow Magistrate.
1829	John Dunmore Lang	Rev.	C	AK At marriage of his daughter to James Chisholm Jnr.	(1799–1878) Presbyterian Chaplain at Liverpool.

Year	Name	Title	Social Class	Introduction	Comments
1829	Edward Deas Thomson	Mr (Sir)	C	AK	(1800–1879) Clerk of Executive & Legislative Councils. Colonial Secretary (from 1837).
1830	Robert Lambert	Mr	C	James Kinghorne	Free settler of Bathurst
1830	Jane Kinghorne (née Lambert)	Mrs	C	Alexander Kinghorne Jnr	Daughter of Robert & Grace Lambert of Bathurst. Married Alexander Kinghorne Jnr, 20 Dec 1834.
1830	James Dowling	Justice Sir	C	Supreme Court of NSW	Supreme Court Judge
1830	Donohoe	Constable	E	Liverpool Courthouse	Liverpool police under Alexander Kinghorne JP
1830	Young	Constable	E		
1830	Perry	Constable	E		
1833	John Campbell	Mr	C	NSW Supreme Court	(1802–1886) Prominent merchant. Fellow Supreme Court Assessor
1833	William Charles Wentworth	Mr	C	NSW Supreme Court	(1790–1872) Barrister.
1833	Robert Wardell	Mr	C	NSW Supreme Court	(1793–1834) Barrister
1834	John Edye Manning	Mr	C	NSW Supreme Court	(1783–1870) Court Registrar & fellow Assessor.
1835	William Moir	Mr	C	Helen Kinghorne	(1805–1850) Clerk of works, Colonial Architect, Sydney. Married Helen Kinghorne 20 June 1836.

Year	Name	Title	Social Class	Introduction	Comments
1836	John McGarvie	Rev	C	AK	(1795–1853) Presbyterian minister at Sydney & Liverpool.
1836	Richard Bourke	Sir	B	AK	(1777–1855) Governor of NSW.
1836	David Waugh	Mr	C	John Ker Kinghorne	Tenant at Gatton Park, Goulburn Plains.
1837	Daniel Draper	Rev.	C	AK	Wesleyan minister, Parramatta.
1837	James Allan	Rev.	C	AK	Presbyterian minister, Parramatta.
1837	Thomas Inglis	Mr	C	AK	(1791–1874) Agent of the Australian Company of Edinburgh.
1838	George Gipps	Major Sir	B	AK	(1791–1847) Governor of NSW
1838	William Hamilton	Rev.	C	AK	Presbyterian minister Goulburn, NSW (1837–1864).
1840	Alexander Jamieson	Captain	C	AK	Captain of the cargo and emigrant ship *Trusty*.
1840	Jane Kinghorne	Miss	D	Andrew Seton Kinghorne	Daughters of Andrew Seton and Helen Kinghorne, Galashiels
1840	Eliza (Betty) Kinghorne	Miss	D		
1840	Alexander ('Alick') Kinghorne	Master	D	Andrew Seton Kinghorne	Son of Andrew Seton and Helen Kinghorne, Galashiels
1841	William Brown	Mr ('the Baron')	D	Andrew Seton Kinghorne	Mill owner of Galashiels and Alexander's landlord.

Year	Name	Title	Social Class	Introduction	Comments
1841	Robert Gill	Mr	D	Andrew Seton Kinghorne	Mill owner of Galashiels. Business partner of Andrew Seton Kinghorne.
1841	Robert Haldane WS	Mr	D	Andrew Seton Kinghorne	Solicitor of Galashiels, of Haldane and Lees.
1842	George Craig	Mr	D	Andrew Seton Kinghorne	Banker of Galashiels.
1844	James Moir	Mr	D	AK	Banker of Alloa, Scotland. Brother of William Moir.
1844	Henry Fairfax	Sir	B	AK	Husband of Archibald Montgomery Ramsay, of St Boswells Bank, Maxton.

Appendix 2

Select List of Alexander Kinghorne's Surveying, Architectural and Engineering Works

Year	Project	Patron	Type of Work
1799	Inventory of Estate at Kippilaw	John Seton Karr of Kippilaw or his representative	Inventory and perhaps survey. See Chapter 3 above
1800	'Measuring land' at Jedburgh	Unknown	Survey[1]
1800	Entrance, gate-lodge, tree-lined avenue at Kippilaw	John Seton Karr of Kippilaw	Plan & building works[2]
1800	Stables and Coach House at Kippilaw	John Seton Karr of Kippilaw	Architecture & building[3]
1801ff	Draining of the Marl Moss	John Seton Karr of Kippilaw	Engineering[4]
1801–1805	Kippilaw Mains House	John Seton Karr of Kippilaw	Architecture & building works[5]
1802	Survey of antiquities of Roxburgh	George Chalmers	Survey & MS report[6]
1802	'measuring job'	William Scott of Harden	Survey[7]
1803	Survey of Gled-swood Estate	William Sibbald of Gledswood	Survey, plan & recommendations for improvement[8]
Ca 1805	Gledswood House	William Sibbald of Gledswood	Architecture & building[9]
1805	Surveying a march dyke at Ormiston	James Haldane, factor to 3rd Duke of Roxburghe	Survey[10]

Year	Project	Patron	Type of Work
1806	Survey of Melgrund Estates, the lands of Nethertown and Muirside in Angus	Gilbert Elliot-Murray-Kynynmound (1751–1814), 1st Earl of Minto	Survey & plan[11]
1806	Crookedshaws Farm, Kelso	John Seton Karr as Trustee for 4th Duke of Roxburghe	Survey & plan[12]
1807–1811	Renovation and expansion of the Kippilaw Mansion House	John Seton Karr of Kippilaw	Architecture & building[13]
1808	Plan of Mount Tiviot Estate, Newbigging	William Kerr, 6th Marquess of Lothian	Survey & plan[14]
1808	Boundary between the lands of J. E. Johnstone of Lewinshope and John Boyd of Broadmeadows	Sir Walter Scott as Sheriff-Depute of Selkirk	Survey[15]
1809	Glasgow to Berwick Railway	Thomas Telford	Survey & engineering[16]
1810	Building of William Evans, Selkirk	Sir Walter Scott as Sheriff-Depute of Selkirk	Survey[17]
1810	Wester Eccles Estate, Berwickshire	Mr James Kyd	Survey & plan[18]
1810	Berwick to Kelso Railway	John Rennie	Survey & Engineering[19]
1813	Plan of Faughill	James Haldane, factor to 5th Duke of Roxburghe	Survey & plan[20]
1815	Unnamed farm near Selkirk	Sir Walter Scott as Sheriff-Depute of Selkirk	Survey[21]
1819–1821 (dates of work uncertain)	Plan of Roxburghshire	5th Duke of Roxburghe (not confirmed)	Survey & plan (1822), published map (1824)[22]

Year	Project	Patron	Type of Work
1819	New Road from 'confines of Selkirkshire to St Boswells Green'	Unknown	Survey & plan[23]
1819	New Road from St Boswells Green to Selkirk	Unknown	Survey & plan[24]
1820	Plan of Linthill	William Riddell Carre	Survey & plan[25]
1821	Compendium of weights and measures	James Veitch of Inchbonny	Measuring standards[26]
1821–1824 (dates of work uncertain)	Plan of Selkirkshire	9th Lord Napier	Survey & plan published 1824[27]
1824	Survey of New Brighton, Van Diemen's Land	Lieut. Governor William Sorell	Survey & report
1825 (dated 1826)	Map of Emu Plains, NSW	Governor Sir Thomas Brisbane	Survey & plan[28]
1826	The Colonial Secretary's residence, Sydney	Governor Sir Ralph Darling	Architectural plan[29]
1826	Plan for Gas Lighting of Sydney, NSW	Governor Sir Ralph Darling	Survey & report[30]
1826	Alternations to Female Orphan School, Parramatta	Governor Sir Ralph Darling	Survey & plan[31]
1826	The Male Orphan School, Bonnyrigg, NSW	The Clergy and School Lands Corporation	Architecture & building[32]

Appendix 3

The Ancestry of Alexander Kinghorne

This may be found at the URL: *chismaxwell.com/s/Appendix–3.pdf*

Appendix 4

The Origins of the Duke of Buccleuch (1663–1731)

This may be found at the URL: *chismaxwell.com/s/Appendix–4.pdf*

Appendix 5

The Origins of the Scotts of Harden and Raeburn (1501–1800)

This may be found at the URL: *chismaxwell.com/s/Appendix–5.pdf*

Appendix 6

A Brief History of the Kers of Cessford and Kippilaw

This may be found at the URL: *chismaxwell.com/s/Appendix–6.pdf*

Appendix 7

Kinghorne Land Grants and Pastoral Properties

This may be found at the URL: *chismaxwell.com/s/Appendix–7.pdf*

Notes

Chapter 1: Origins and Prospects (1700–1770)

1 Captain Stawarth Bolton to Sir Piercie Shafton in relation to the exaggerated nobility of the latter's parentage: Scott, *The Monastery*, 407–408.

2 Lord David Cecil, Inaugural Lecture as Goldsmiths' Professor, Oxford University 1949. Cecil's friend, L.P. Hartley, used it as the opening sentence of his novel The Go-Between, 1953. https://en.wikipedia.org/wiki/The_Go-Between.

3 Fleming, *The Reformation in Scotland*, Appendix B: offspring of celibate clergy legitimated, 1529–1559, LIST I, 561.

4 Registers of Gordon and Greenlaw: FamilySearch.

5 ScotlandsPeople 742/00 0010 0262.

6 ScotlandsPeople 742/00 0010 0313.

7 ScotlandsPeople 742/00 0030 0087.

8 27 Jul 1746, SP–1746, Gordon, Berwickshire: FamilySearch.

9 Douglas, Parish of Kelso, 519.

10 No Kinghornes are listed in official records for Edinburgh, Berwick or Roxburgh, 1761–1841: Boog Watson, Edinburgh Burgesses.

11 https://en.wikipedia.org/wiki/Social_class_in_the_United_Kingdom.

12 NLA MS 6207, B 4, S 3, F 30: Kinghorne Bible.

13 1769-07-06 Bans James Kinghorn and Margaret Idington: FamilySearch.

14 1769-07-16, Mar James Kinghorn and Margaret Eddington, FamilySearch.

15 Rev'd Cornelius Lundie was parish minister at Kelso from 1749 to 1801. With the previous minister, James Ramsay, these two ministers spanned the entire 18th century: Moffat, *Kelsae*, 140, 148. Lundie's son, Robert, attended Kelso Grammar School with Alexander Kinghorne (Appendix 1).

16 NLA MS 6207, Box 4, Series 3, Folder 30: Kinghorne Bible; Kelso Baptisms ScotlandsPeople 793/00 0030 0318.

17 Scott's novel *The Monastery* was set in the fictional Kennaquhair Abbey, which was based on Melrose Abbey. Alexander Kinghorne's notes in his copy of *The Monastery* identify the places and people in the novel associated with Melrose. (Kinghorne's Scott, *Monastery*) Scott was doubtless aware of the legend that the heart of King Robert the Bruce was buried at Melrose. He does not mention it in *The Monastery*, due to the fictional identity of the Abbey. He does include an account of a visit by a Benedictine monk to retrieve a relic from the ruins, the buried heart of the sixteenth-century Abbot Ambrose. (*The Monastery*, Introductory Epistle).

18 See details of this story in Appendix 3, 'Noble ancestors?'.

19 There are frequent references to Melrose in Alexander's correspondence with John Seton Karr. In 1822, with financial assistance from the Duke of Buccleuch, Sir Walter supervised the extensive repair work to preserve the ruins. https://en.wikipedia.org/wiki/Melrose_Abbey.

20 Sinclair, *Statistical Account of Scotland,* Vol. X, 1794, No. 37, Parish of Kelso, Christopher Douglas, 587. McCulloch, *Parish of Kelso,* 314–315, 321, 340.

21 Moffat, *Kelsae,* 148–155.

22 Sinclair, *Statistical Account of Scotland,* Vol. X, 1794, 314–315, 321, 340.

23 Sinclair, *Statistical Account of Scotland,* Vol. X, 1794, 587–588.

24 Wood, *Plan of the Town of Kelso,* 1823.

25 NAUK (TNA): Board of Stamps: Apprenticeship Books, 1710–1811: ancestry. com. List of his apprentices Appendix 3, Table 1, 1.1.3.4.

Original data: NAUK (TNA): *Board of Stamps: Apprenticeship Books,* Series IR 1, Piece 58 (p. 90 of.

26 Muirhead, *Dissertations Foederal,* 680.

27 Ship Tax Rolls for Kelso, 1785–1789: ScotlandsPlaces.

28 Sinclair, *Statistical Account of Scotland,* Vol. X, 1794, 586–587, 590. Moffat, *Kelsae,* 106, 151.

29 Sinclair, *Statistical Account of Scotland,* Vol. X, 1794, 593.

30 McCulloch, *Parish of Kelso,* 314–315, 321, 340. Sinclair, *Statistical Account of Scotland,* Vol. III, 189–190.

31 Kinghorne Bible.

32 Isabella Kinghorn (bap Kelso 17/09/1779), Andrew Kinghorn (bap Kelso 20/09/1780; died at Jamaica in June 1808), Margaret Kinghorn (bap Kelso 11/12/1781), James Kinghorn (bap Kelso 19/01/1784; died at London in June 1821), John Kinghorn (bap Kelso 10/02/1787), William Kinghorn (bap Kelso 13/08/1788; died at Kelso 29 April 1813), Anne Kinghorn (bap Kelso 24/05/1790), and Jane Kinghorn (bap Kelso 15/08/1792): ScotlandsPeople, FamilySearch, Kinghorne Bible.

33 Kinghorne Bible.

34 Kinghorne Bible. Alexander's brothers and sisters are discussed in more detail in Chapter 8, Alexander's step-family.

Chapter 2: The Early Life of Alexander Kinghorne (1770–1799)

1 Lazarus, *Town of Kelso,* 21.

2 Kinghorne Family Bible.

3 Lazarus, *Town of Kelso,* 60–63. Haig, *Kelso,* 100–102.

4 https://www.kelsohighschool.org.uk/the-history-of-kelso-high-school/.

5 Kinghorne's Scott, *Monastery,* 27.

6 House of Lords, Sessional Papers.

7 Smith, *History of Kelso Grammar School,* 45.

8 Heritors' Minute (31 Jan 1781) and Minutes of Merchant Company (20 Jan 1781), cited by Smith, *History of Kelso Grammar School,* 36–40.

9 Sinclair, *Statistical Account of Scotland,* Vol. XI, 235.

10 See Chapter 18, The Emu Theatre.

11 Smith, *History of Kelso Grammar School,* 40–41. Lockhart, *Scott,* 26–27. Kinghorne's Scott, *Monastery.* Henderson, *John Ballantyne.* Jerdan, *Men I have Known,* 395.

12 Kinghorne's Scott, *Monastery*, 27.

13 Henderson, *John Ballantyne*. Lockhart, *Scott*, 25–26.

14 Kilpatrick, *Walter Scott's Kelso*, 3–4, 12, 16, 22.

15 Lockhart, *Scott*, 12–19.

16 See also Appendix 5; https://en.wikipedia.org/wiki/Border_Reivers.

17 Lockhart, *Scott*, 12–19.

18 Lockhart, *Scott*, 27.

19 The birthdays of Kinghorne and Scott were 15 May 1770 and 15 August 1771, respectively.

20 The grammar school leaving age was usually 12, and the University entrance age 15: http://en.wikipedia.org/wiki/History_of_education_in_Scotland.

21 Kelso Grammar, 1784–1788.

22 Kelso Grammar, 1784–1788. See also Appendix 1.

23 Lockhart, *Scott*, 26.

24 Lockhart, *Scott*, 26.

25 Crockett, *The Scott Country*, 25–27.

26 Lockhart, *Scott*, 29–30.

27 Scott only kept a written Journal from 1825, after the Kinghornes had left Scotland: Scott, *The Journal of Sir Walter Scott*.

28 See Chapter 19, Death of the Mentors.

29 Grierson, *Scott*, 19.

30 Lockhart, *Scott*, 29–30.

31 See Chapter 10, Employment by Sir Walter Scott; Chapter 14, The Cultivation of Patronage; and Chapter 16, A New Life in the Colonies.

32 'Practical mathematics' was taught at a number of parochial schools, comprising 'measurement of [surfaces] and solids, trigonometry and land-surveying': House of Lords, Sessional Papers.

33 The authors have searched available NRAS Kirk Session Records. There are significant gaps in the mid-late 18th century. No record has been found of Alexander employed by a parochial school in Roxburghshire or Berwickshire, between 1783 and 1791.

34 Kinghorne to Seton Karr, 15 Apr 1806: NRAS2970, B 102.

35 See Appendix 3.

36 Blaikie Lang, *A Scottish Farmer's Ride*.

37 Smith, *History of Kelso Grammar School*, 36.

38 Moffat, *Kelsae*, 137.

39 Scott, Walter, *Letters*. http://www.walterscott.lib.ed.ac.uk/etexts/etexts/letters.html 1790 Sep 3 Kippilaw (Ramsay) I.13; Scott was a frequent visitor to his relatives at Mertoun House, although the earliest documented in his letters are from 1797 onwards.

40 James Hume and Thomas Kirkpatrick: Scott, *Fasti ecclesiae scoticanae*, 172.

41 https://electricscotland.com/webclans/statistical_accounts.htm.

42 https://en.wikipedia.org/wiki/Sir_John_Sinclair,_1st_Baronet; https://en.wikipedia.org/wiki/Statistical_Accounts_of_Scotland.

43 James Hume and Thomas Kirkpatrick: Scott, *Fasti ecclesiae scoticanae*, 172.

44 Sinclair, *Statistical Account of Scotland*, 1795, Vol. XI, 230.

45 See Chapter 3, An Aspiration to Agricultural Improvement.

46 Sinclair, *Statistical Account of Scotland*, 1795, Vol. XI, 243, 637.

47 The 'friend' might have been a 'Statistical Missionary', sent by Sinclair and his editorial board to those Parishes who did not, or could not, immediately, reply to the initial questionnaire; Sinclair, History of the origin and progress of the Statistical Account of Scotland, 1798, xii-xviii.

48 Sinclair, *Statistical Account of Scotland*, 1795, Vol. XI, 240. See also Chapter 4, Antiquities.

49 See Chapter 3, An Aspiration to Agricultural Improvement: Blaikie's encounter with King George III at Windsor.

50 http://en.wikipedia.org/wiki/Thomas_the_Rhymer.

51 Scott, *Fasti ecclesiae scoticanae*, 159–60 (Mertoun), 172 (Bowden). Betty Brockie, b. 14 Jun 1769; Alexander Kinghorne & Betty Brockie, bans 18 Dec 1793 (Bowden), 14 Dec 1793 (Mertoun), marriage 31 Dec 1793 (Mertoun): ScotlandsPeople, FamilySearch & Kinghorne Family Bible.

52 Hallmark: 1790, Edinburgh, David Marshall silversmith: 7 tablespoons retained by Alexander's descendants.

53 Scottish feudal land tenure, property rights granted (= feued) by a superior to a vassal in exchange for rent.

54 Berwickshire OD Name Books, 1856–1858, Vol. 33, OS1/5/33/27, Parish of Merton Sheet 30.12: ScotlandsPlaces.

55 Farm Horse Tax Rolls 1797–1798, Vol. 02, E326/10/2/29–30, ScotlandsPlaces.

56 Kinghorne's Scott, *The Monastery*. The authors visited Dryburgh Abbey in 2014 and 2016 and confirmed the presence of many Brockie graves but could not locate those of Betty Brockie nor of Alexander Kinghorne.

57 Kinghorne to Seton Karr, 20 Jan 1806: NRAS2970, B 102.

58 James Hogg to 'the Editor', June 30 1801, in: Scott, *The Poetical Works*, 49.

59 Moffat, *The Borders*, 305.

60 Child, *English and Scottish Popular Ballads*, 448. Scott, *The Poetical Works*.

61 Symonds, *Weep Not for Me*, 254. Wilkie, *Manuscript Notebook*, 58–59.

62 Agnes Brockie, b. 1780, Mertoun, Berwickshire: FamilySearch.

63 Child, *English and Scottish Popular Ballads*, 448. Symonds, *Weep Not for Me*, 254. Wilkie, *Manuscript Notebook*, 58–59.

64 The authors searched reports of Kirk Session at Mertoun and Presbytery sessions at Earlston. The NRAS catalogue quotes 1741–1849, but in practice CH2/484/2 has a gap from 1766 to 1845. Earlston Presbytery records were available and searched up to 1788, after which there is a considerable gap.

65 See Chapter 14, Lord Buchan and the Kinghornes.

66 See Appendix 3.

67 See Maxwell & Pugh, *The Master of Hell's Gates*, 6–7, for a description of Bowden.

68 Sinclair, *Statistical Account of Scotland*, 235.

69 Jollie, *Parish of Bowden*, 35–44.

70 http://en.wikipedia.org/wiki/Parochial_school.

71 Sinclair, *Statistical Account of Scotland*, 238. Jollie, *Bowden*, 49–50.

72 James Kinghorne b. 8 Nov 1794, Bowden: ScolandsPeople.

73 William Kinghorne b. 12 Aug 1796, Bowden: ScotlandsPeople.

74 Helen (Nellie) Kinghorne b. 12 Aug 1798, Bowden: ScotlandsPeople.

Chapter 3: The Factor of Kippilaw (1799)

1 Mollie Seton Karr to Miriam Chisholm, 4 Aug 1954: NLA MS 6207 B4, S3, F30.

2 Tancred, *Annals of a Border Club*, 448. Farm Horse Tax Rolls, 1797–1798: Scot-landsPlace. Jeffrey, *History and Antiquities of Roxburghshire*, 145, 160–1, 163–71. NRAS2970, various letters.

3 Scott, *Waverley*, General Preface, Appendix No. 1, Fragment of a Romance which was to have been Entitled, Thomas the Rhymer, xliii-xliv. This is an echo of the witch scenes in Shakespeare's Scottish play. It relates an encounter the legendary sage Thomas the Rhymer, not part of his published prophecies, and either newly collected or invented by Scott. It was not published in the original 1814 edition of *Waverley*, but in the General Preface to the 1821 edition, where he wrote that it was from an earlier unpublished work.

4 Scott, *Waverley*, General Preface, Appendix No. 1, Fragment of a Romance which was to have been Entitled, Thomas the Rhymer, xliii-xliv. Again a literary allusion by Scott, this time to the Arthurian legend in Malory's *Morte d'Arthur*. The story of the sword in the stone first appeared Robert de Boron's Merlin, c. 1200, but it's most famous telling was in Malory.

5 Author inspection of site, April 2014. RCAHMS, *Kippilaw Mains*. Christison, *The Forts*, 145.

6 OS Galashiels, Selkirk, Melrose, St Boswells & Lauder. See Chapter 4, Antiquities.

7 Tancred, *Annals of a Border Club*, 308. RCAHMS, *Kippilaw Mains*.

8 Jerdan, *Autobiography*, 11. Will of Andrew Ramsay Karr.

9 Lockhart, *Scott*, 49. http://www.scottisharchitects.org.uk/architect_full. php?id=408137.

10 Lockhart, *Scott*, 101.

11 http://www2.thesetonfamily.com:8080/directory/Descents/parbroath_descent. htm; http://www.saxonlodge.net/getperson.php?personID=I1116&tree=Tatham.

12 Letters regarding the inheritance of Kippilaw July 1802: NRAS2970 B 68.

13 See Appendix 6.

14 University of St Andrews Biographical Register; https://arts.st-andrews.ac.uk/ biographical-register/data/documents/1409540900.

15 http://en.wikipedia.org/wiki/Parliamentary_agents.

16 Marrriage John Seton and Elizabeth Tucker, 17 Mar 1783: ScotlandsPeople.

17 Kinghorne to Seton Karr, 9 Feb 1805, NRAS2970, B 14 & 10 1805: NRAS2970, B 43.

18 House of Commons, *Crinan Canal Company*, 1804, Appendix No. 17, 211. Seton Karr to Walter Logan, 6 Aug 1802, NRAS2970, B 151. Seton Karr to James Hill,

6 Aug 1802, NRAS2970, B 151. Seton Karr to John Anderson, 27 Aug 1802: NRAS2970, B 151.

19 Kinghorne to Seton Karr, 27 Apr 1807, NRAS2970 B 15. Two important points are clear from this statement: 1. These letters should still be in the possession of the family (not found) and 2. Alexander Kinghorne was in correspondence with Seton Karr before 1798.

20 Alternatively, it is possible Rev'd William Balfour recommended Alexander for the survey.

21 Francis Napier to Seton Karr, 22 Feb 1800, NRAS2970, B 65.

22 Contents of the Estate of Kippilaw Belonging to John Seton Karr, 1799: NRAS2970/Bundle 151.

23 Maps of Kippilaw and nearby estates supplied by Mrs Caroline Ridley. State of Accounts Respecting the Estate of Kippilaw from 14 Nov 1798 to 15 Mar 1799 by Alexander Kinghorne: NRAS2970, B 151. Inventory of the Furniture Etc. in Kippilaw House Taken by F. Napier in Mar 1799: NRAS2970, B 151.

24 Plans for furniture and fittings at Kippilaw, 1799: NRAS2970, B 65.

25 Kinghorne to Seton Karr, 9 May 1799: NRAS2970, B 67.

26 Alexander Kinghorne held the position of 'County Fiscal and Road Surveyor for Roxburghshire' in 1800, appointment date unknown. Kinghorne to Seton Karr, 2 March 1800: NRAS2970, B 67. & 30 Jun 1805: NRAS2970, B 14.

27 Whitsunday (1 Jun 1800): the day of Pentecost, observed 7 weeks after Easter.

28 Kinghorne to Seton Karr, 29 Jan 1800: NRAS2970, B 67.

29 John Karr Kinghorne, b. 25 Jul 1800, Bowden, ScotlandsPeople.

30 Hume, *An Enquiry Concerning the Principles of Morals*, 1751, 'In all determinations of morality, this circumstance of public utility is ever principally in view; and wherever disputes arise, either in philosophy or common life, concerning the bounds of duty, the question cannot, by any means, be decided with greater certainty, than by ascertaining, on any side, the true interests of mankind.'

31 Withers, *A Nation Transformed*, 13–14.

32 See Chapter 14, The Earl of Buchan.

33 Boase, *Modern English Biography*, 301.

34 Blaikie, *A Scottish Farmer's Ride through England*, his observations on the King p. 21.

35 Blaikie to Jean Currer (wife): Blaikie, *A Scottish Farmer's Ride through England*, 48–49.

36 Kinghorne to Seton Karr, 21 May 1802: NRAS2970, B 68.

37 Andrew Blaikie to James Haldane 15 Dec 1802: NRAS2970, B 68. Kinghorne to Seton Karr, 18 Dec 1802: NRAS2970, B & 25 Mar 1805: NRAS2970, B 14. See also Chapter 5, The Excambion between Bowden Mill and Holydean.

38 NRAS2970.

39 Scott, *The Monastery*, 69.

40 Kinghorne to Seton Karr, 17 Jan 1806: NRAS2970, B 102.

41 Karr, *A Genealogical tree of the race of the house of Yair*.

42 Kinghorne to Seton Karr, 12 Feb 1803: NRAS2970, B 11.

43 Kinghorne to Seton Karr, 11 Jun 1802: NRAS2970, B 68.

44 Kinghorne to Seton Karr, 1 Jun 1803: NRAS2970, B 11.

45 Kinghorne to Seton Karr, 4 May 1808: NRAS2970, B104.

46 John Seton Karr (Kippilaw) 'Instructions for Mr Kinghorne', 29 Nov 1802: NRAS2970, B. 151.

47 Kinghorne to Seton Karr, 9 Jan 1803: NRAS2970, B 11.

48 Kinghorne to Seton Karr, 4 Jan 1806: NRAS2970, B 102.

49 Kinghorne to Seton Karr, 12 Feb & 26 Jun 1803: NRAS2970, B 11.

50 For example, Kinghorne to Seton Karr, 10 Jun1805: NRAS2970, B 14.

51 For example, Mary Wilson to Seton Karr, 20 Feb 1806: NRAS2970, B 102.

52 Mary Wilson to Seton Karr, 20 Feb 1806: NRAS2970, B 102.

53 Kinghorne to Seton Karr, 7 Apr 1811: NRAS2970, B 105.

54 Kinghorne to Seton Karr, 16 Jul 1806: NRAS2970, B 102.

55 Kinghorne to Seton Karr, 9 Jan 1803: NRAS2970, B 11.

Chapter 4: Improvement (1799–1805)

1 See Appendix 6.

2 Manly, *The mean temperature of central England, 1698*–1952 and http://booty.org.uk/booty.weather/climate/1750_1799.htm. See also Alexander's regular 'Journal of the weather' from February 1800: e.g. Kinghorne to Seton Karr, 29 Jan 1800: NRAS2970, B 67.

3 Maver, *Everyday Life, Industrial Revolution*.

4 Journal of work at Kippilaw, 23 Apr–18 May 1800: NRAS2970, B 65.

5 Tancred, *Annals of a Border Club*, 99–100. Wilson, *A Sketch of the History of Hawick*, 346. List of Trees at Kippilaw by Mr Archibald Dickson (Hawick), 29 Nov 1803; NRAS2970, B 16.

6 RCAHMS, *Kippilaw House*.

7 Sighted by the authors in 2014, this remains one of the most substantial and intact buildings surviving from Alexander Kinghorne's time at Kippilaw.

8 Plan of the Stables at Kippilaw 1800: NRAS2970, B 65. Kinghorne to Seton Karr, 10 Jan, 14 Feb, 2 Mar 1800: NRAS2970, B 67; 16 Mar, plus diagram of the coach house: NRAS2970, B 67. Journal of work at Kippilaw, 17 Mar–16 Apr 1800: NRAS2970, B 65. Sketch of a Lodge and front gate for Kippilaw, 18 May 1800: NRAS2970, B 65.

9 See Chapter 4, Thou Man of Wond'rous ken. Notice of boring in the Moss Park for Marle, Kippilaw 18 Aug 1800: NRAS2970, B 65.

10 Kinghorne to Seton Karr, 9 Jul 1809: NRAS2970, B 17.

11 Moffat, *The Borders*, 305.

12 Kinghorne to Seton Karr, 22 Jun 1800: NRAS2970, B 65.

13 Kinghorne to Seton Karr, 9 Mar 1803: NRAS2970, B 11.

14 Kinghorne to Seton Karr, 14 Feb 1800: NRAS2970, B 67.

15 Kinghorne to Seton Karr, 10 Jan 1800: NRAS2970, B 67.

16 Kinghorne to Seton Karr, 14 Feb 1800: NRAS2970, B 67.

17 Kinghorne to Seton Karr, 2 Mar 1800: NRAS2970, B 67.

18 Kinghorne to Seton Karr, 15 Mar 1801: NRAS2970, B 10.

19 Kinghorne to Seton Karr, 16 Feb 1807: NRAS2970, B 15.

20 Kinghorne to Seton Karr, 16 April 1800: NRAS2970, B 65.

21 Kinghorne to Seton Karr, 22 May 1801: NRAS2970, B 10.

22 Kinghorne to Seton Karr, 7 Jun 1801: NRAS2970, B 10.

23 Kinghorne to Seton Karr, 7 Jun 1801: NRAS2970, B 10. Mary Wilson to Seton Karr, 20 Jun 1801: NRAS2970, B 10.

24 Kinghorne to Seton Karr, 20 Apr 1802: NRAS2970, B 68.

25 Kinghorne to Seton Karr, 18 Dec 1802: NRAS2970, B 68 & 9 Jan 1803: NRAS2970, B 11.

26 Mary Wilson to Seton Karr, 9 Jan 1803: NRAS2970, B 11.

27 Kinghorne to Seton Karr, 3 Apr 1808: NRAS2970, B 104. Mary Wilson to Seton Karr, 4 Apr 1808: NRAS2970, B 104. Mary Wilson to Seton Karr, 21 Jun 1808: NRAS2970, B 104.

28 ScotlandPlaces Farm Horse Tax Rolls 1797–1798, Volume 05, E326/10/5/79.

29 Kinghorne to Seton Karr, 18 Jan 1806: NRAS2970, B 102.

30 Kinghorne to Seton Karr, 2 Jan 1807: NRAS2970, B 15.

31 Kinghorne to Seton Karr, 6 Jan, 21 Apr, 26 May, 5 Jun & 16 Jun 1811,: NRAS2970, B 105.

32 Thornton, *Red Rubies*, 20–25. MacDonald et al., *History of Hereford Cattle*, 3.

33 Kinghorne to Seton Karr, 25 Mar 1805: NRAS2970, B 14.

34 Sanders, *Shorthorn Cattle*, 25, 27.

35 Lewis, *History and Social Anthropology*, 177.

36 Kinghorne to Seton Karr, 5 Apr 1805: NRAS2970, B 14.

37 Kinghorne to Seton Karr, 10 & 30 Jun 1805: NRAS2970, B 14.

38 Kinghorne to Seton Karr, 28 July 1805: NRAS2970, B 14.

39 Kinghorne to Seton Karr, 24 Sep 1805: NRAS2970, B 43.

40 Kinghorne to Seton Karr, 17 Feb, 22 Apr, 15 May & 1 Jul 1806: NRAS2970, B 102.

41 Kinghorne to Seton Karr, 16 Jul 1806: NRAS2970, B 102 & 16 Mar 1807: NRAS2970, B 15.

42 Kinghorne to Seton Karr, 9 Jul 1808: NRAS2970, B 104. 'God bless the Duke of Argyll,': see Ayer, Jean, 'Department of Amplification', *The New Yorker*, October 8, 1955, 134.

43 Kinghorne to Seton Karr, 27 Jan 1811: NRAS2970, B 105.

44 Kinghorne to Seton Karr, 27 Feb & 3 Apr 1809: NRAS2970, B 17.

45 Prices for Cattle in Scotland, 16th to 19th century (in £ sterling): from £5 per head (Hebrides early 19th century) and £7 per head (Argyll late 18th century and Falkirk 1805), to maxima of £20–25 per head (Aberdeenshire 1811); Koufopoulos, *The Cattle Trades of Scotland, 1603–1745*, Table 21, 235.

46 Kinghorne to Seton Karr, 22 Jun 1800: NRAS2970, B 65.

47 Kinghorne to Seton Karr, 20 Jul 1800: NRAS2970, B 67.

48 Jameson, *A Trip to London*, 13, 200.

49 Karr, *A Genealogical tree of the race of the house of Yair*. Seton Karr to the Executors of Andrew Ramsay Karr and response from James Seton, 10 Jul 1801: NRAS2970, B 10. Letters regarding the inheritance of Kippilaw July 1802: NRAS2970, B 68.

50 Kinghorne to Seton Karr, 20 Jul 1800: NRAS2970, B 67.

51 Kinghorne to Seton Karr, 22 Jul 1801: NRAS2970, B 149.

52 Kinghorne to Seton Karr, 12 Feb 1801: NRAS2970, B 10.

53 Kinghorne to Seton Karr, 12 Feb & 15 Mar 1801: NRAS2970, B 10.

54 Kinghorne to Seton Karr, 1 May 1802: NRAS2970, B 68.

55 Hueckel, *English Agriculture during the Napoleonic Wars*, 401–414; particularly Figure 3, 406, and discussion, 405.

56 Kinghorne to Seton Karr, 22 May 1801: NRAS2970, B 10.

57 Kinghorne to Seton Karr, 23 Apr 1803: NRAS2970, B 11.

58 Kinghorne to Seton Karr, 4 & 15 May 1803: NRAS2970, B 11.

59 Kinghorne to Seton Karr, 22 May & 11 Jun 1803: NRAS2970, B 11.

60 Kinghorne to Seton Karr, 10 Jul 1805: NRAS2970, B 14.

61 Kinghorne to Seton Karr, 22 May 1801: NRAS2970, B 10.

62 Kinghorne to Seton Karr, 22 May 1801: NRAS2970, B 10.

63 Kinghorne to Seton Karr, 7 Jun 1801: NRAS2970, B 10.

64 Bowden entry in Sinclair, *Statistical Account of Scotland*.

65 See Chapter 2 – Marriage – The Brockies of Dryburgh.

66 Described by his brother's biographer as 'anti-democratic': Henderson, *John Ballantyne*.

67 http://www.walterscott.lib.ed.ac.uk/works/poetry/apology/home.html.

68 Scott, *Minstrelsy of the Scottish Border*. Henderson, *John Ballantyne*.

69 In 1803, at Scott's urging and with his financial backing, James Ballantyne moved to Edinburgh to expand his printing business, later partnering his brother John and Sir Walter Scott in the firm John Ballantyne and Co: Liukkonen & Pesonen, *James Ballantyne*. The Ballantyne Brothers: http://www.walterscott.lib.ed.ac.uk/biography/ballant.html.

70 Smellie, *An historical account of the Society of Antiquaries*, 402–410. Buchan, *Discourse*, 23.

71 RCAHMS, *Dere Street*.

72 The idea for *Caledonia* probably came from William Camden's great work, *Britannia*, published 1586. Chalmers, *Caledonia*.

73 Grierson, *Scott*, 76.

74 Note: no association between Alexander Kinghorne and Walter Scott can be found in Scott's Journal: commenced 1824 after Alexander left Scotland. There is no mention of Alexander in his earlier letters, but there are associations in other sources.

75 Chalmers to Seton Karr, 23 Sep 1801: NRAS2970, B 114. Author's emphasis.

76 Kinghorne to Seton Karr, 9 Jan 1803: NRAS2970, B 11.

77 Kinghorne to Seton Karr, 12 Feb 1803: NRAS2970, B 11.

78 Chalmers to Seton Karr, 4 Oct 1803: NRAS2970, B 48.

79 Chalmers to Seton Karr, 4 Oct 1803: NRAS2970, B 48.

80 Chalmers, *Caledonia*, 91.

81 Milne, *Parish of Melrose*.

82 Chalmers, *Caledonia* 141. http://en.wikipedia.org/wiki/William_Roy.

83 The OS quotes its sources as 'Chalmers Caledonia, Jeffrey's History of Roxburghshire, Mr Robert Blaikie of Holydean, Mr John Scott Teacher Bowden and
Kinghorns MS Survey.'

84 Septimus Severus, who arrived in Britain in AD 208, conducted exploratory
campaigns into Scotland, reaching the Moray Firth and reoccupying Newstead
(Melrose): http://lost.islesofdarkness.com/index.php?title=Timeline_of_Scot-
land. Moffat, *The Borders*, 97.

85 Ordnance Survey Name Book for Roxburghshire (1858–1860), Vol. 4:
OS1/29/4/40: ScotlandsPlaces.

86 Berwickshire OS Namebooks, 1856–1858, Vol. 6, OS1/5/6/5 and OS1/5/6/35,
Channelkirk Parish, Vol. 5, OS1/5/5/26B, Stoneshiel Hill, Vol. 28, OS1/5/28/108,
Blackchester; Roxburghshire OS Namebooks, 1858–1860, Vol. 4, OS1/29/4/51,
Bowden Parish; Selkirkshire OS Namebooks, 1858, Vol. 13, OS1/30/13/53, Par-
ish of Stow, The Catrail or Pictsworkditch: ScotlandsPlaces.

87 Moffat, *The Borders*, 55, 82, 84.

88 OS Namebook for Roxburghshire, 1858–1860, Vol. 4, OS1/29/13/413: ScotlandsPlaces.

89 RCAHMS, *Kippilaw Mains*.

90 RCAHMS, *Dere Street*. http://www.oldroadsofscotland.com/roman_roads_
known.htm.

91 Crawford, *Defensive Frontier-Dyke near Melrose*. National Library of Scotland,
Ordnance Survey 1979.

92 RCAHMS, *Dere Street*.

93 See Chapter 16, A New Life in the Colonies.

94 Marle, the mudstone layer underlying the moss bog: http://en.wikipedia.org/
wiki/Marl.

95 Kinghorne to Seton Karr, 22 May 1801: NRAS2970, B 10.

96 Water of Ayle, or Ale Water, or Allen Water: a tributary of the Teviot River.

97 Dodgshon, *Land Improvement in Scottish Farming*, 2.

98 Dodgshon, *Land Improvement in Scottish Farming*, 1–3.

99 Jollie, *Bowden*, 44.

100 http://www.welcometoscotland.com/about-scotland/wildlife-around-scotland/
special-places/bogs. http://www.snh.gov.uk/about-scotlands-nature/habi-
tats-and-ecosystems/mountains-heaths-and-bogs/peat-bogs/.

101 Kinghorne to Seton Karr, 15 & 22 Mar 1801: NRAS2970, B 10.

102 http://www.scottisharchitects.org.uk/architect_full.php?id=205589. Kinghorne
to Seton Karr, 22 Mar & 6 Apr 1801: NRAS2970, B 10.

103 Kinghorne to Seton Karr, 17 Jan1802: NRAS2970, B 68.

104 Kinghorne to Seton Karr, 14 Feb 1802: NRAS2970, B 68.

105 Kinghorne to Seton Karr, 1 & 10 Mar 1802: NRAS2970, B 68.

106 Kinghorne to Seton Karr, 4 Apr 1802: NRAS2970, B 68.

107 Kinghorne to Seton Karr, 1 May 1802: NRAS2970, B 68.

108 Kinghorne to Seton Karr, 18 Dec 1802: NRAS2970, B 68.

109 Kinghorne to Seton Karr, 11 Jun 1802: NRAS2970, B 68.

110 Kinghorne to Seton Karr, 12 Feb & 20 Mar 1803: NRAS2970, B 11.

111 Kinghorne to Seton Karr, 23 Apr 1803: NRAS2970, B 11.

112 Kinghorne to Seton Karr, 22 May 1803: NRAS2970, B 11.

113 Dodgshon, *Land Improvement in Scottish Farming*, 4–5.

114 Kinghorne to Seton Karr, 15 Jul 1805: NRAS2970, B 14.

115 Kinghorne to Seton Karr, 10 Nov 1805: NRAS2970, B 43 & 11 Dec 1806: NRAS2970, B 15.

116 Kinghorne to Seton Karr, 18 May 1808: NRAS2970, B 104.

117 Kinghorne to Seton Karr, 23 Feb 1812: NRAS2970, B 106.

118 http://familysearch.org/learn/wiki/en/Bowden,_Roxburghshire,_Scotland.

119 It is ironic that the name Kinghorn is thought by some to derive from the Gaelic *ceann gronn*, meaning 'head of the bog' – there may be a play on these words in 'thou man of wond'rous ken'.

120 Scott, *The Cotter's Moss-Day*.

Chapter 5: Tenancies and Inheritance (1800–1807)

1 'The park No. 7 contains jimply [*sic*, old scots= scant; barely sufficient] 20 Acres, and No. 6 contains nearly 26 Acres, and both the two North parks are considerably worse land than the Dam head park': Kinghorne to Seton Karr, 14 May 1809: NRAS2970, B 17.

2 Kinghorne to Seton Karr, 20 Apr 1802: NRAS2970, B 68.

3 Kinghorne to Seton Karr, 29 Jan 1800: NRAS2970, B 67.

4 Kinghorne to Seton Karr, 14 Feb 1800: NRAS2970, B 67.

5 Kinghorne to Seton Karr, 2 Mar 1800: NRAS2970, B 67; 18 May 1800: NRAS2970, B 65; 16 Feb, 3 & 15 Mar 1801: NRAS2970, B 10; 11 & 28 Jun 1802: NRAS2970, B 68.

6 Kinghorne to Seton Karr, 1 July 1807: NRAS2970, B 15.

7 Kinghorne to Seton Karr 23 April–18 May 1800: NRAS2970, B 65. Thomas Milne was the Laird of Faldonside and His son, Nicol, an 'advocate': Lockhart, *Scott*, 236.

8 Kinghorne to Seton Karr, 3 Mar 1801: NRAS2970, B 10.

9 Kinghorne to Seton Karr, 6 May 1807: NRAS2970, B 15.

10 Kinghorne to Seton Karr, 1 July 1807: NRAS2970, B 15.

11 Kinghorne to Seton Karr, 11 Jun 1802: NRAS2970. B 68; and 9 Jan, 12 Feb, 9 & 20 Mar, 10 Jul 1803: NRAS2970, B 11.

12 James Haldane, of Broomlands, Ednam, was initially sub-factor and later Estate Manager for the Duke of Roxburghe.

13 Andrew Blaikie to James Haldane, 15 Dec 1802: NRAS2970, B 68.

14 Kinghorne to Seton Karr, 10 Jan 1805: NRAS2970, B 14.

15 Kinghorne to Seton Karr, 10 Jan 1805: NRAS2970, B 14.

16 Kinghorne to Seton Karr, 25 Feb 1805: NRAS2970, B 14.

17 See Chapter 10, The Roxburghe Succession Dispute.

18 Barry & Hall, *Spottiswoode*, xvi, 3, 31, 57, 156–157.

19 A decree made by arbitrators chosen by the parties; http://legal-dictionary.the-freedictionary.com/Decree+arbitral.

20 John Spottiswoode to Seton Karr, 5 & 10 Feb 1801, & response 19 Feb 1801: NRAS2970, B 10.
21 Seton Karr to John Spottiswoode, 5 July 1801: NRAS2970, B 10.
22 Seton Karr to the Executors of Andrew Ramsay Karr and response from James Seton, 10 Jul 1801: NRAS2970, B 10.
23 http://en.wikipedia.org/wiki/John_Campbell,_1st_Baron_Campbell.
24 Seton Karr to James Seton, Jul 1802: NRAS2970, B 68.
25 Letters regarding the inheritance of Kippilaw, Jul 1802: NRAS2970, B 68.
26 Kinghorne to Seton Karr, 1 Mar 1802: NRAS2970, B 68.
27 Kinghorne to Seton Karr, 24 Mar 1802: NRAS2970, B 68.
28 Death of John Seton Karr, 5 May 1815, burial records in the Parish of St James: ancestry.com.

Chapter 6: War and politics in the 'Land of Cakes' (1805)

1 Mostert, *The Line upon a Wind*, 63–278.
2 Chalmers to Seton Karr, 4 & 22 Oct 1803: NRAS2970, B 48.
3 Kinghorne to Seton Karr, 17 Jan 1806, NRAS2970, B 102.
4 Lockhart, *Scott*, 61.
5 Lockhart, *Scott*, 79.
6 Scott, *The Antiquary*, 602–605. Kinghorne to Seton Karr, 9 Jan 1805: NRAS2970, B 14.
7 http://en.wikipedia.org/wiki/Napoleon's_planned_invasion_of_the_United_Kingdom.
8 Kinghorne to Seton Karr, 18 Jan 1806: NRAS2970, B 102.
9 Kinghorne to Seton Karr, 18 Jan 1807: NRAS2970, B 15.
10 Kinghorne to Seton Karr, 8 Feb 1808: NRAS2970, B104.
11 Dyck, *Cobbett*.
12 Mostert, *The Line upon a Wind*, 119. Mostert also claimed that Dundas upheld the slave trade, whereas others have argued that he was largely responsible for the final passage of the abolition bill in 1807: for example, Furber, *Dundas*, 302. See also https://en.wikipedia.org/wiki/Henry_Dundas,_1st_Viscount_Melville.
13 Kinghorne to Seton Karr, 14 & 23 Apr 1805: NRAS2970, B 14.
14 http://hansard.millbanksystems.com/commons/1805/apr/29/proceedings-respecting-lord-melville-and. HC Debate 10 October 1805, Vol. 4, cc327–71; http://en.wikipedia.org/wiki/Henry_Dundas,_1st_Viscount_Melville.
15 Burns, *The Poetical Works*, 220–222: 'On The Late Captain Grose's Peregrinations Thro' Scotland, Collecting The Antiquities Of That Kingdom [1789].
16 Fergusson, Robert, *The King's Birth-day in Edinburgh*, 1772; in, Ross, *The Book of Scottish Poems*, 603. http://www.robertburns.org/encyclopedia/LandoCakes-The.504.shtml.
17 Kinghorne to Seton Karr, 15 Jul 1805: NRAS2970, B 14.
18 Kinghorne to Seton Karr, 20 Jan 1806: NRAS2970, B 102.
19 Kinghorne to Seton Karr, 2 May 1805: NRAS2970, B 14.

20 Kinghorne to Seton Karr, 18 May 1807: NRAS2970, B 15.
21 Kinghorne to Seton Karr, 6 April 1807: NRAS2970, B 15.
22 See Chapter 15, Plan of the Estate of Linthill.

Chapter 7: The End of the Beginning at Kippilaw (1805)

1 *Now this is not the end. It is not even the beginning of the end. But it is, perhaps, the end of the beginning,* Winston Churchill, 1942.
2 Kinghorne to Seton Karr, 10 Jan 1805: NRAS2970, B 14.
3 Kinghorne to Seton Karr, 3 Mar 1805: NRAS2970, B 14.
4 Kinghorne to Seton Karr, 3 Mar 1805: NRAS2970, B 14.
5 Kinghorne to Seton Karr, 3 Mar 1805: NRAS2970, B 14.
6 Kinghorne to Seton Karr, 5, 13 Mar & 14 Apr 1805: NRAS2970, B 14.
7 Moffat, *The Borders*, 55, 82, 84. 'hind': Ministry of Labour, *A dictionary of Scottish Terms.*
8 Kinghorne to Seton Karr, 10 Jun 1805: NRAS2970, B 14.
9 Kinghorne to Seton Karr, 21 Mar 1808: NRAS2970, B 104.
10 Kinghorne to Seton Karr, 5 Jun 1811: NRAS2970, B 105.
11 Kinghorne to Seton Karr, 8 Mar 1812: NRAS2970, B 106.
12 Kinghorne to Seton Karr, 28 Aug 1805: NRAS2970, B 43.

Chapter 8: Kinghorne Family Matters (1805–1812)

1 OPR Marriages 793/60197, Kelso, 197 of 444: ScotlandsPeople.
2 Bridge Street Kelso, 1825, U.K. and U.S. Directories, 1680–1830: ancestry.com.
3 ScotlandsPeople: 793/00 0030 0384. Kinghorne Family Bible.
4 ScotlandsPeople: 793/00 0030 0412.
5 Kinghorne to Seton Karr, 22 May 1801: NRAS2970, B 10.
6 Kinghorne Family Bible.
7 ScotlandsPeople 793/00 0030 0426.
8 Courtesy Val Kinghorne.
9 ScotlandsPeople 793/00 0030 0474.
10 Kinghorne to Seton Karr, 13 May 1805: NRAS2970, B 14.
11 FamilySearch. Kinghorne Family Bible. Further Mark Kinghorn, see Appendix 3.
12 ScotlandsPeople: 793/00 0040 0065.
13 Findmypast. ScotlandsPeople: 793/00 0060 0401.
14 ScotlandsPeople: 793/00 0040 0160.
15 Kinghorne to Seton Karr, 9 Mar 1806: NRAS2970, B 102.
16 FamilySearch. Kinghorne Family Bible.
17 Kinghorne Family Bible.
18 ScotlandsPeople: 793/00 0040 0126.
19 ScotlandsPeople: 808/00 0020 0277.
20 ScotlandsPeople: 793/00 0040 0156.
21 ScotlandsPeople: 793/00 0060 0418.
22 NLA MS 6207, B 5, S 3, F 40.

23 Kinghorne to Seton Karr, 22 & 28 Nov 1805: NRAS2970, B 43.

24 Burial Parish of Mertoun in Berwickshire, 25 Jan 1805: ScotlandsPeople. Kinghorne to Seton Karr, 17 Feb & 2 Mar 1806: NRAS2970, B 102.

25 ScotlandsPeople. Kinghorne Family Bible.

26 Kinghorne to Seton Karr, 21 Apr 1807: NRAS2970, B 15.

27 Kinghorne to Seton Karr, 27 Apr 1807: NRAS2970, B 15.

28 Kinghorne to Seton Karr, 6 May 1807: NRAS2970, B 15.

29 Woods, *Infant Mortality in Britain*, 74–88.

30 Kinghorne to Seton Karr, 28 May 1807: NRAS2970, B 15.

31 https://en.wikipedia.org/wiki/Peritonsillar_abscess.

32 Kinghorne to Seton Karr, 9 & 19 Jun, 1 & 12 Jul 1807: NRAS2970, B 15, and 18
May, 5 Jun & 31 Jul 1808: NRAS2970, B 104.

33 Kinghorne to Seton Karr, 16 Jul 1807: NRAS2970, B 15, and 27 Dec 1807 & 17
Feb 1808: NRAS2970, B 104.

34 OPR Births, Bowden: ScotlandsPeople. Kinghorne Family Bible. Kinghorne to
Seton Karr, 21 Mar 1808: NRAS2970, B 104.

35 Kinghorne to Seton Karr, 27 May 1809: NRAS2970, B 17.

36 Mary Wilson to Seton Karr, 8 Jun 1809: NRAS2970, B 17.

37 Kinghorne to Seton Karr, 18 Jun 1809: NRAS2970, B 17.

38 OPR Births, Bowden, ScotlandsPeople. Kinghorne to Seton Karr, 25 Jun & 9 Jul
1809: NRAS2970, B 17, and 15 Dec 1810: NRAS2970, B 105.

39 Kinghorne to Seton Karr, 1 Jan 1811: NRAS2970, B 105.

40 Kinghorne to Seton Karr, 27 Jan 1811: NRAS2970, B 105.

41 Kinghorne to Seton Karr, 6 Jan 1811: NRAS2970, B 105.

42 Kinghorne to Seton Karr, 17 Feb 1811: NRAS2970, B 105.

43 OPR Births, Bowden, ScotlandsPeople. Kinghorne to Seton Karr, 24 Feb 1811:
NRAS2970, B 105.

44 Kinghorne to Seton Karr, 10 Mar 1811: NRAS2970, B 105.

45 Kinghorne to Seton Karr, 17, 24, 31 Mar, 7 Apr 1811: NRAS2970, B 105.

46 Kinghorne to Seton Karr, 15 Apr 1811: NRAS2970, B 105.

47 Kinghorne to Seton Karr, 3 May & 16 Jun 1811: NRAS2970, B 105.

48 Kinghorne to Seton Karr, 12, 19 May, 5, 27 Jun & 14 Jul 1811: NRAS2970, B 105.
Mary Wilson burial, 23 Sept 1811, St Boswells, ScotlandsPeople OPR 804/10 326.

49 Maxwell & Pugh, *The Master of Hell's Gates*, 13–19, 28, 44–45, 47.

50 Kinghorne to Seton Karr, 9 Apr 1812: NRAS2970, B 106.

51 Kinghorne to Seton Karr, 18 Apr & 28 Jun 1812: NRAS2970, B 106.

52 Kinghorne to Seton Karr, 29 Aug 1812: NRAS2970, B 106.

53 Kinghorne Family Bible.

54 Kinghorne to Seton Karr, 17 Mar 1811: NRAS2970, B 105 and 9 Apr 1812:
NRAS2970, B 106.

55 Kinghorne to Seton Karr, 15 Mar 1812: NRAS2970, B 106.

56 Maxwell & Pugh, *The Master of Hell's Gates*, 57.

Chapter 9: The Renovation of the Mansion House at Kippilaw (1807–1811)

1 See Chapter 10, From Surveyor to Architect.

2 Agreement with builders, 4 Dec 1807: NRAS2970, B 16.

3 RCAHMS: Kippilaw House.

4 Kinghorne to Seton Karr, 24, 31 Mar 1811: NRAS2970, B 105.

5 Kinghorne to Seton Karr, 14 Jul 1811, 3 April 1812: NRAS2970, B 105, 106, respectively.

Chapter 10: Alexander Kinghorne: Private Surveyor (1800–1812)

1 See Appendices 1 & 2.

2 Kinghorne to Seton Karr, 2 Mar 1800: NRAS2970, B 67.

3 Kinghorne to Seton Karr, 10 Jul 1803: NRAS2970, B 11.

4 Kinghorne to Seton Karr, 15 Mar 1801: NRAS2970, B 10.

5 Kinghorne to Seton Karr, 12 Feb 1801: NRAS2970, B 10.

6 Millburn, *Adams of Fleet Street*. http://en.wikipedia.org/wiki/George_Adams_(instrument_maker,_elder).

7 Malaquias, *An Eighteenth Century Travelling Theodolite*.

8 Kinghorne to Seton Karr, Tue 3 Mar 1801: NRAS2970/bundle 10.

9 http://en.wikipedia.org/wiki/John_Rennie_the_Elder.

10 Kinghorne to Seton Karr, 15 Mar 1801: NRAS2970, B 10.

11 See Chapter 12, On the Railway Tracks (1809–1813).

12 Kinghorne to Seton Karr, 9 Mar 1803: NRAS2970, B 11.

13 Cruft et al., *The Buildings of Scotland*, 60, 323–324. The house and barn were sighted by one of the authors (C. Maxwell) in 2016.

14 Scott to Sir John Malcolm, *Letters of Sir Walter Scott*, Jan-Feb 1816, 4–133.

15 Veitch, *Tables*.

16 Veitch, *Tables*. James Veitch of Inchbonny, in: Douglas, *A History of the Border Counties*, 419. http://www.jedburgh.org.uk/famous-people-james-veitch.

17 Kinghorne, *Weights and Measures*. The authors requested access to this document at the Hawick Heritage Hub, Scottish Borders Council, in April 2014, but the archivists were unable to locate it.

18 Kinghorne to Seton Karr, 30 Jun 1805: NRAS2970, B 14.

19 Kinghorne to Seton Karr, 2 Mar 1806: NRAS2970, B 102.

20 http://en.wikipedia.org/wiki/Baillie.

21 Kinghorne to Seton Karr, 17 Feb 1806: NRAS2970, B 102.

22 http://en.wikipedia.org/wiki/Gilbert_Elliot-Murray-Kynynmound,_1st_Earl_of_Minto.

23 Minto to Seton Karr, 10 Aug 1806, 30 Oct 1812: NRAS2970, B 102, B 47, respectively.

24 MacGibbon & Ross, *The castellated and domestic architecture of Scotland*.

25 Kinghorne to Seton Karr, 15 Apr & 5 May 1806: NRAS2970, B 102.

26 Buchan, *Lord Minto*. Lever, *Lessudden House*, 77–78. Countess of Minto, *Lord Minto in India*, 232, 256; Scott's unrelated correspondence with Lady Minto 1808, *Letters of Sir Walter Scott* Vol. II pp. 1, 17, 130.
27 Kinghorne to Seton Karr, 2 Jun 1806: NRAS2970/, B 102.
28 Kinghorne, *Plan of Netherton and Muirside*, description.
29 Kinghorne, *Plan of Netherton and Muirside*, cartography.
30 MacGibbon & Ross, *The castellated and domestic architecture of Scotland*.
31 See Chapter 19, The Map of Emu Plains.
32 See Chapter 15, The Plans of Selkirkshire and Roxburghshire.
33 Kinghorne to Seton Karr, 9 Feb 1805: NRAS2970, B 14.
34 Kinghorne to Seton Karr, 5 May 1806: NRAS2970, B 102.
35 Kinghorne to Seton Karr, 9 May 1806: NRAS2970, B 102.
36 RCAHMS: *Crookedshaws Farm*. See Chapter 3, An aspiration to Agricultural Improvement.
37 http://newspaperarchive.com/uk/middlesex/london/charter/1839/10–13/page–11.
38 Kinghorne, *Plan of Newbigging*.
39 Kinghorne to Seton Karr, 13 Mar 1808: NRAS2970, B 104.
40 https://www.gracesguide.co.uk/William_Blackadder.
41 The supreme civil court of Scotland.
42 Kinghorne, *Plan of Wester Eccles*. Hume, *Decisions of the Court of Session*, Nicholas Brown vs. James Kyd, 700–1, 717.
43 The plan is not extant. Kinghorne to Seton Karr, 15 Dec 1810 & 1 Jan 1811: NRAS2970, B 105. Maxwell & Pugh, *The Master of Hell's Gates*, 17.
44 Cruft et al., *The Buildings of Scotland*, 528.
45 Maxwell & Pugh, *The Master of Hell's Gates*, 16–17.
46 Chisholm, *Sir Walter Scott as Judge,* 126–127.
47 Chisholm, *Sir Walter Scott as Judge,* 126–127.
48 Chisholm, *Sir Walter Scott as Judge,* 134–135 & 195.
49 William Bellenden-Ker, 4th Duke of Roxburghe: Mosley, *Burke's Peerage*, Vol. 3, 3425.
50 In this case, and as it turned out, the male primogeniture was difficult to determine.
51 John Bellenden-Ker (1765–1842) was the first cousin once removed of William Bellenden-Ker 4th Duke of Roxburghe. He was the son of Caroline Bellenden (1728–1802), the Duke's first cousin and daughter of John Bellenden 3rd Lord Bellenden (1685–1744), the Duke's Uncle: determined from Burke, *Peerage*, person pages 68726 & 12948.
52 General Ker vs. John Bellenden Ker, Case No. 581, Nov 27 1805: In Hume, *Decisions of the Court of Sessions*, 769–770. Case of Appellants in the Three Appeals, In the House of Lords, 1806, Court Record HAR04207.
53 Duke of Roxburghe vs. Archibald Swinton: Shaw & Dunlop, *Cases Decided in the House of Lords 1824*, 21.
54 James, Duke of Roxburghe, Appellant vs. A. Swinton, W.S., Respondent, 2 March 1824; Shaw & Dunlop, *Cases Decided in the House of Lords 1824*, 18–25.

55 Kinghorne to Seton Karr, 2 Jan 1807: NRAS2970, B 15.

56 Kinghorne to Seton Karr, 18 Jan 1807: NRAS2970, B 15.

57 Kinghorne to Seton Karr, 25 Jan 1807: NRAS2970, B 15.

58 Kinghorne to Seton Karr, 8 Feb 1807: NRAS2970, B 15.

59 Kinghorne to Seton Karr, 3 Apr 1808: NRAS2970, B 104.

60 Kinghorne to Seton Karr, 18 May 1808: NRAS2970, B 104.

61 Kinghorne to Seton Karr, 27 Jun 1811: NRAS2970, B 105.

62 Kinghorne to Seton Karr, 15 Mar 1812; NRAS2970, B 106.

Chapter 11: The Beginning of the End at Kippilaw (1806–1812)

1 https://premium.weatherweb.net/weather-in-history-1800-to-1849-ad/.

2 Adapted from Kinghorne to Seton Karr, 22 Apr 1806: NRAS2970, B 102; 27 & 21
   Apr 1807: NRAS2970, B 15; 2 May 1809: NRAS2970, B 17; 3, 19 May & 14 Jul
   1811: NRAS2970, B 105; data not found for 1810.

3 Rounded to the nearest pound.

4 Kinghorne to Seton Karr, 13 May 1805: NRAS2970, B 14.

5 Hogg, *Tales of the Wars of Montrose*, 232.

6 Kinghorne to Seton Karr, 22 Apr 1806: NRAS2970, B 102; 21 Apr 1807:
   NRAS2970, B 15; 2 May 1809: NRAS2970, B 17. Historical Tax Rolls,
   E326/10/12/34: ScotlandPlaces. Refer also to Appendix 1.

7 Kinghorne to Seton Karr, 25 Mar 1805: NRAS2970, B 14.

8 Kinghorne to Seton Karr, 16 Mar 1806: NRAS2970, B 102.

9 Kinghorne to Seton Karr, 22 April 1806: NRAS2970, B 102.

10 Kinghorne to Seton Karr, 8 Feb 1807: NRAS2970, B 15.

11 Kinghorne to Seton Karr, 23 Mar 1807: NRAS2970, B 15.

12 Kinghorne to Seton Karr, 21 Apr 1807: NRAS2970, B 15.

13 Kinghorne to Seton Karr, 19 Apr 1809: NRAS2970, B 17.

14 Kinghorne to Seton Karr, 2 May 1809: NRAS2970, B 17.

15 Kinghorne to Seton Karr, 14 May 1809: NRAS2970, B 17.

16 Kinghorne to Seton Karr, 8 Jun 1809: NRAS2970, B 17.

17 Kinghorne to Seton Karr, 31 Mar 1811: NRAS2970, B 105.

18 Kinghorne to Seton Karr, 3, 19 May & 14 Jul 1811: NRAS2970, B 105.

19 Kinghorne to Seton Karr, 18 Apr 1812: NRAS2970, B 106.

20 Kinghorne to Seton Karr, 8 Jan 1809: NRAS2970, B 17.

21 Kinghorne to Seton Karr, 15 Jan 1809: NRAS2970, B 17. Mary Wilson to Seton
   Karr, 20 Jan 1809: NRAS2970, B 17.

22 Kinghorne to Seton Karr, 6 Mar 1809: NRAS2970, B 17.

23 Kinghorne to Seton Karr, 6 Mar 1809: NRAS2970, B 17.

Chapter 12: On the Railway Tracks (1809–1813)

1 Telford to Andrew Little, 23 Jul 1784. Smiles, *The Life of Thomas Telford*, 225–378,
   404–461. House of Commons, *Crinan Canal Company*, 1804, Appendix No. 17,
   211. Seton Karr to Walter Logan, 6 Aug 1802: NRAS2970, B 151. Seton Karr to

James Hill, 6 Aug 1802: NRAS2970, B 151. Example of friendly correspondence: Telford to Seton Karr, 29 Aug 1809: NRAS2970, B 45. Glover, *Telford*, 55, 128, 141, 298–99.

2 Robertson, *Origins of the Scottish Railway*, 32, 40.

3 Glover, *Telford*, 259–61.

4 Glover, *Telford*, 246–50.

5 Robertson, *Origins of the Scottish Railway*, 2–15, 22.

6 Telford to Seton Karr, 29 Aug 1809: NRAS2970, B 45.

7 Glover, *Telford*, 53, 71, 92–93, 104.

8 Telford to Seton Karr, 22 Sep 1809: NRAS2970, B 45.

9 Kinghorne to Seton Karr, 21 & 28 Sep 1809: NRAS2970, B 45.

10 http://www.ainslie.org.uk/genealogy/ainslie/dat8.htm.

11 Kinghorne to Seton Karr, 21 Oct 1809: NRAS2970, B 45.

12 Kinghorne, *Letter of an Australian Settler*.

13 Robertson, *Origins of the Scottish Railway*, 41.

14 Telford, *Report by Mr Telford*, 1–19.

15 Glover, *Telford*, 110–116.

16 Telford, *Report by Mr Telford*, 37. http://en.wikipedia.org/wiki/William_Jessop.

17 Kinghorne & Telford, *Plan of Glasgow to Berwick Railway*.

18 General Meeting of the Glasgow and Berwick Rail Road, Edinburgh, 19 May 1810: Caledonian Mercury, Sat 19 May 1810, 1; gale.com.

19 http://en.wikipedia.org/wiki/John_Rennie_the_Elder.

20 Glover, *Telford*, 316.

21 Robertson, *Origins of the Scottish Railway*, 40.

22 Kinghorne to Seton Karr, 6 Jan 1811: NRAS2970, B 105.

23 Kinghorne & Rennie, Plan of the Kelso to Berwick Railway.

24 Robertson, *Origins of the Scottish Railway*, 41.

25 Kinghorne & Rennie, Plan of the Kelso to Berwick Railway.

26 Rennie, *Report Respecting Proposed Rail-Way from Kelso to Berwick, 1810*.

27 Kinghorne to Seton Karr, 20 Jan & 3 Feb 1811: NRAS2970, B 105.

28 Kinghorne to Seton Karr, 3 Feb 1811: NRAS2970, B 105.

29 Kinghorne to Seton Karr, 5 Jun 1811: NRAS2970, B 105.

30 Kinghorne to Seton Karr, 27 Jun 1811: NRAS2970, B 105.

31 51 George III, Cap133, Royal Assent 31st May, 1811.

32 Robertson, *Origins of the Scottish Railway*, 34.

33 See Chapter 2, The Early Life of Alexander Kinghorne (1770–1799) and Appendix 4, The Origins of the Scotts of Harden and Raeburn, 1501–1800.

34 Kinghorne to Seton Karr, 19 May 1811: NRAS2970, B 105.

35 Cross-Rudkin, *James Hollinsworth*, 332.

36 Cross-Rudkin, *John Rennie*, 562.

37 See Appendix 5.

38 Tancred, *Annals of a Border Club*. Lockhart was a close friend of both John Seton Karr and Sir Walter Scott: Lockhart, *Scott*, Chapter VIII, 296, Chapter VIII 1831, 279, 284, 289.

39 http://en.wikipedia.org/wiki/Robert_Stephenson; not to be confused with Robert Stevenson (1772–1850), the Glaswegian grandfather of Robert Louis Stevenson.

40 https://wikivisually.com/wiki/Berwickshire_Railway.

41 Attestation on Alexander Kinghorne's published works after 1813.

42 Glover, *Telford*, 71.

43 Bendall, *Dictionary of land surveyors*.

44 Information provided by Carol Morgan, Archivist, Institution of Civil Engineers, One Great George Street, Westminster, London SW1P 3AA, email 9 May 2014.

Chapter 13: The Kinghornes Leave Kippilaw (1812–1813)

1 Kinghorne to Seton Karr, 31 Apr 1812: NRAS2970, B 106.

2 Kinghorne to Seton Karr, 29 Aug 1812: NRAS2970, B 106.

3 Kinghorne to Seton Karr, 14 Jun 1812: NRAS2970, B 106.

4 Seton Karr to Kinghorne, 20 Apr 1812: NRAS2970, B 106.

5 Kinghorne to Seton Karr, 31 Apr 1812: NRAS2970, B 106.

6 Kinghorne to Seton Karr, 29 Aug 1812: NRAS2970, B 106.

7 Kinghorne to Seton Karr, 14 Jun 1812: NRAS2970/, B 106.

8 Maxwell and Pugh, *The Master of Hell's Gates*, 17.

9 Kinghorne to Seton Karr, 31 Apr & 14 Jun 1812: NRAS2970, B 106.

10 Collinge, *Lockhart*. Shaw & Dunlop, *Cases decided in the Court of Sessions from Nov 13 1827 to July 1828*, 862.

11 Kinghorne to Seton Karr, 22 Jul 1812: NRAS2970, B106.

12 Foggo to Seton Karr, 11 Jun 1814: NRAS2970, B 108.

13 Kinghorne to Seton Karr, 3 Jan 1813: NRAS2970, B 107.

14 Foggo to Seton Karr, 12 Dec 1812: NRAS2970, B 107.

15 Kinghorne to Seton Karr, 19 Mar 1813: NRAS2970, B 46.

16 Kinghorne to Seton Karr, 19 Mar 1813: NRAS2970, B 46.

17 Kinghorne to Seton Karr, 21 Mar 1813: NRAS2970, B 46.

18 Kinghorne to Seton Karr, 1 May 1813: NRAS2970, B 46.

19 Seton Karr to Kinghorne, 7 May 1813: NRAS2970, B 46.

20 Foggo to Seton Karr, 29 May 1813: NRAS2970, B 107.

Chapter 14: The Cultivation of Patronage (1804–1824)

1 See Appendix 1.

2 List of Subscribers: Pace, *Poems on Various Occasions*, 89–95. Henderson, *John Ballantyne*.

3 See this chapter, Lord Buchan and the Kinghornes.

4 Walter Scott to Anne Rutherford Scott, 5 Sep 1788, in Lockhart, *Scott*. http://lordbyron.cath.lib.vt.edu/monograph.php?doc=JoLockh.Scott&select=I.ch5.1. Burke, *A Genealogical and Heraldic History*, 434.

5 https://en.wikipedia.org/wiki/Thomas_Brisbane.

6 Walter Scott (Beardie) (1653–1729) was Sir Walter Scott's great-grandfather, son of Walter Scott first laird of Raeburn. He was a Jacobite who is said to have let

his beard grow in mourning for the demise of the Stuarts: Lever, *Lessudden House*, 34–35.

7 Sir Walter Scott to Thomas Scott, 16 Oct 1819, in Lockhart, *Scott.*

8 See Chapter 17, Superintendent of Emu Plains Prison Farm 1824–1825.

9 Cant, *Buchan*, 1.

10 Cant, *Buchan*, 2.

11 Cant, *Buchan*, 3–8.

12 Dryburgh Abbey: http://www.historic-scotland.gov.uk/index/places/propertyresults/propertyabout.htm?PropID=PL_097&PropName=Dryburgh%20Abbey.

13 Buried in the sacristy in 1829; sighted by authors April 2014.

14 The most prominent of this family, Field Marshall Earl Haig, interred beside Sir Walter Scott in 1928; sighted by authors April 2014.

15 Buried in the north transept of the Abbey, which he called 'St Mary's Aisle', 26 Sep 1832; sighted by authors April 2014.

16 Kinghorne's Scott, *The Monastery.*

17 Cant, *Buchan*, 21, 24.

18 Buchan, *Discourse* 23. See also Chapter 4, Antiquities.

19 Buchan to Erskine, Edinburgh 1782; Scott, *Journal*, 552n.

20 Buchan to Brisbane, 5 Feb 1823: NLA MS6207, S3, F30.

21 Sir Walter Scott to Lord Montague, 1 May 1821: *Letters of Sir Walter Scott*, VI, 428–430. Seton, *A History of the Family of Seton*, 4.

22 See Chapter 4, Agriculture and Farm Structure.

23 Cant, *Buchan*, p. 7.

24 Kinghorne's Scott, *The Monastery.*

25 Cant, *Buchan*, 26.

26 Buchan to the Misses Kinghorne, 10 Aug 1823.

27 Sir Walter Scott to Lord Montague, 1 May 1821: *Letters of Sir Walter Scott*, VI, 428–430.

28 Lockhart, *Scott*, IV, 276–277.

29 Liston, *Sir Thomas Brisbane*, 131. See also Chapter 16, Letters of Introduction.

30 Tammany Hall: The, mainly Irish Catholic, Democratic Party political machine that attempted to control the politics of New York City and State from the 1790s to the 1960s.

31 Koeppel, *Bond of Union*, 7–8, 10–11,14–38, 66ff.

32 *Charleston Times*, n.d., in *Cleaveland Gazette & Commercial Register*, 8 December 1818, cited by Koeppel, *Bond of Union*, 249.

33 Koeppel, *Bond of Union*, 248.

34 *Abstracts Concerning Canals*, Cleaveland Gazette & Commercial Register, 1818, Abstract 124 – CGCR Aug. 18:3/2, 50; Abstract 151 – CGCR Aug. 25:3/2, 63.

35 *Abstracts Concerning Canals*, Cleaveland Gazette & Commercial Register, 1818, Abstract 124 – CGCR Aug. 18:3/2, 50.

Chapter 15: The Kinghornes at St Boswells (1813–1824)

1 See Chapter 10. The Maxton Estate.
2 Kinghorne to Seton Karr, 19 Mar 1813: NRAS2970, B 46.
3 The authors toured the Maxton Estate and examined the Kirk records in 2016. Maxwell and Pugh, *The Master of Hell's Gates*, 16–17, 44–45.
4 Kinghorne, *Selkirk to St Boswell's Green*, 229.
5 Kinghorne, *Plan of the farm of Faugh-hill*.
6 Farm Horse Tax Rolls 1797–1798, Volume 12, E326/10/12/15: ScotlandsPlaces.
7 http://www.bbc.co.uk/history/domesday/dblock/GB–352000–630000/page/8.
8 Westminster Burials, St James Piccadilly: 5 May John Seton Karr GBPRS_WS-MTN_5109365_00517.jpg, 49; 9 Jan 1815 Elizabeth Seton Karr GBPRS_WS-MTN_005620193_00010.jpg, 5.
9 Will of John Seton Karr.
10 Andrew Seton (later Seton-Karr) of Kippilaw: Seton, *A History of the Family of Seton*.
11 Maxwell and Pugh, *The Master of Hell's Gates*, Chapter 3.
12 Kinghorne Family Bible.
13 Kinghorne's Scott, *The Monastery*, 25.
14 See Chapter 14, Lord Buchan and the Kinghornes.
15 Scott, *Rob Roy*, Chap 10, 193.
16 Boutell, *The Handbook to English Heraldry*, 2–3.
17 Alexander Deuchar: http://en.wikipedia.org/wiki/Alexander_Deuchar. http://195.153.34.9/catalogue/person.aspx?code=NA8759&st=1&. George Prince of Wales succeeded as George IV on his father's death 29 January 1820.
18 http://en.wikipedia.org/wiki/Francesco_I_d'Este,_Duke_of_Modena. Mary of Modena: http://en.wikipedia.org/wiki/Mary_of_Modena.
19 Chapter 19, Death of the Mentors.
20 NLA MS 6207, B5, S3, F39: transcription by Miriam Chisholm from Kinghorne Family Bible.
21 *The Quarterly Review,* June and Sep 1826, Vol. 34, No. 67, 272.
22 Kinghorne to Seton Karr, 6 Apr 1807: NRAS2970, B 15. Bower, *Abbey's of Melrose and Old Melrose*, 95. See Chapter 6, Gossip and Dry Humour.
23 Kinghorne to Seton Karr, 18 April 1812: NRAS2970, B 106.
24 Carre, *Border Memories*, 149–150, 201.
25 Carre, *Border Memories*, 225.
26 Kinghorne, *Plan of the Estate of Linthill*.
27 http://farmsandestatessearch.savills.co.uk/property-detail/GBEDRUEDR130040/list.
28 See Chapter 10, From Surveyor to Architect; and Chapter 12, On the Railway Tracks.
29 Kinghorne to Taylor, 28 May 1821.
30 Maxwell & Pugh, *The Master of Hell's Gates*, 57. Kinghorne Family Bible.
31 Kinghorne to Seton Karr, 19 Mar 1813: NRAS2970, B 46.
32 See this Chapter, The Plan if the Estate of Linthill.

33 Thomson, *Atlas of Scotland*, vii.

34 Kinghorne to Taylor, 28 May 1821.

35 Hewitt, *Plan of The County Of Roxburgh*.

36 See Chapter 12, On the Railway Tracks.

37 Thomson, *Atlas of Scotland*, vii.

38 Kinghorne, *Plan of Selkirkshire*.

39 There were earlier maps of Scotland published by John Ainslie (1784–5) and Aaron Arrowsmith (1807) but these relied on earlier surveys. Thomson, *Atlas of Scotland*, iii-iv.

40 Thomson, *Atlas of Scotland*, maps 4 and 5.

41 Hewitt, *Map of a Nation*, xix. Owen & Pilbeam, *Ordnance Survey*.

Chapter 16: A New Life in the Colonies (1819–1824)

1 Kinghorne's Scott, *The Monastery*, note 11 page 61.

2 MacMillan, *Scotland and Australia 1788–1850*, 1.

3 Maxwell & Pugh, *The Master of Hell's Gates*, 46–56.

4 Kinghorne to Taylor, 28 May 1821.

5 https://en.wikipedia.org/wiki/Prince_Frederick,_Duke_of_York_and_Albany.

6 Herbert Taylor: http://en.wikipedia.org/wiki/Herbert_Taylor_(British_Army_officer).

7 Taylor to Kinghorne, 2 Aug 1823.

8 Maxwell & Pugh, *The Master of Hell's Gates*, 66–194.

9 Sydney Gazette, Fri 26 Apr 1822, Trove 2180953.

10 HRA, Series I Vol. XI, 823–825.

11 Brisbane to Buchan, 30 Aug 1822.

12 Buchan to Kinghorne, 28 Dec 1822.

13 Buchan to Brisbane, 5 Feb 1823: NLA MS6207, S3, F30.

14 Buchan to Kinghorne, 28 Dec 1822. Buchan to E Kinghorne, 18 Aug 1823.

15 Buchan to Miss E Kinghorne, 29 Jul 1823.

16 Recommendation to Lord Bathurst in favour Alexander Kinghorne NSW, 24 Jul 1823, SRNSW CS, G039 1 1.

17 See Appendix 3, Table 5, entry A1.1.4.9.2.

18 Proverbs 10:22 (Alexander Kinghorne's remembrance of the King James Version)

19 Kinghorne to AS Kinghorne, Mar 1824.

20 Cf. Proverbs 10: 2, 6, 22.

21 Thomas Williamson married Elizabeth Ramsay, daughter of Robert Ramsay, at South Leith Midlothian, 7 Jun 1785; ancestry.com.

22 Arrived Sydney 16 Oct 1824: Shipping Arrivals & Departures, SN 557.

23 William Snell: O'Byrne, *A Naval Biographical Dictionary*, Vol. 3, 1097.

24 Maxwell & Pugh, *The Master of Hell's Gates*, 90, 195, 219–20, 268.

25 Wool carding was relatively new technology – dating from 1748: Richards, *The Development of the Modern Wool Carding Machine*, 71–3.

26 Kinghorne to AS Kinghorne, 5 Apr 1824.

27 Buchan to AS Kinghorne, 9 Nov 1824.

28 Hobart Town Gazette, Fri 10 Sep 1824, 2,;Trove 1090321. The Australian, Thu 21 Oct 1824, 3; Trove 37072068/4248417. https://www.cocker.id.au/murray/david_murray_1786.php.

29 Hobart Town Gazette, Fri 10 Sep 1824, 2; Trove 1090321.

30 Hobart Town Gazette, Fri 17 Sep 1824, 2; Trove 1090328.

31 Maxwell & Pugh, *The Master of Hell's Gates*, 90–3.

32 Alexander, *The Companion to Tasmanian History*.

33 Sydney Gazette, Thu 16 Jun 1825, 3; Trove 2184144.

34 Sydney Gazette, Thu 16 June 1825, 3; Trove 2184143.

35 Sydney Gazette, Thu 16 Jun 1825, 3; Trove 2184144. Sydney Gazette, Thu 16 June 1825, 3; Trove 2184143.

36 See Chapter 17, The Land Board of Van Diemen's Land and the demise of New Brighton.

37 Hobart Town Gazette, Fri 1 Oct 1824, 4; Trove 1090347.

Chapter 17: Superintendent, Emu Plains Convict Farm (1824–1825)

1 Sydney Gazette, Thu 21 Oct 1824, 2; Trove 2183297; Thu 28 Oct 1824, 2; Trove 2183325. BOM, historical weather statistics.

2 SRNSW, Series 13912, Box 5, Roll 1434, ancestry.com. Sydney Gazette, Mon 28 Nov 1825, 2; Trove 2184768.

3 Liston, *Sir Thomas Brisbane*, 131.

4 Lockhart, *Scott*, Vol. 3, 117.

5 9 September 1824, NSW Australia, Colonial Secretary's Papers, 1788–1825, ancestry.com.

6 Art Gallery of NSW https://www.artgallery.nsw.gov.au/collection/artists/gruner-elioth/.

7 Stacker, *Chained to the Soil*, xi, 9.

8 Chisholm, *Speeches and Reminiscences*, 14.

9 Chisholm, *Speeches and Reminiscences*, 14.

10 Maxwell & Pugh, *The Merchant of Sydney*, 139–40.

11 SRNSW 4/346, 299.

12 Diary of Lachlan Macquarie, cited by Stacker, *Chained to the Soil*, 14.

13 Horatio Walpole to Colonial Secretary, 15 Aug 1829, Colonial Secretary Letters Received 25/6987, SRNSW 4/2043.

14 Rivière, *The Governor's Noble* Guest, 89, 102, 186.

15 Rivière, *The Governor's Noble Guest*, 186.

16 Stacker, *Chained to the Soil*, 1 (map on facing page), 14, 18–19. Rivière, *The Governor's Noble Guest*, 89, 186.

17 Stacker, *Chained to the Soil*, 21.

18 HRA, Vol. XI, 822. Joseph Peters, Register of tickets of leave, NRS 1220, No. 42/1516: ancestry.com. Joseph Peters, Register of Certificates of Freedom, NRS 12208, No. 113/4071; ancestry.com. 1828 Census, Joseph Peters, Goulburn Plains; ancestry.com. See also Chapter 23, Pastoral expansion.

19 Steel, *The History of Carcoar*, 249.

20 Stacker, *Chained to the Soil*, 25.

21 Maxwell & Pugh, *The Master of Hell's Gates*, 237–42.

22 10 Sep 1825, HRA, Vol. XI, 822.

23 10 Sep 1825, HRA, Vol. XI, 819–21.

24 Fulton to Goulburn, May 1823, SRNSW CS, 4/3508, Reel 6010, 242.

25 Sturma, *Eye of the Beholder*, 3–10.

26 10 Sep 1825, HRA, Vol. XI, 813, 815 note 172, 819.

27 10 Sep 1825, HRA, Vol. XI, 813, 815.

28 10 Sep 1825, HRA, Vol. XI, 824–6.

29 Mary Robinson and her daughter appear later in this history: see Chapter 23,
   Pastoral expansion.

30 10 Sep 1825, HRA, Vol. XI, 822–6. Mary Robinson and child, married to Joseph
   Peters: New South Wales 1828 Census TNA; ancestry.com.

31 10 Sep 1825, HRA, Vol. XI, 815.

32 10 Sep 1825, HRA, Vol. XI, 813.

33 10 Sep 1825, HRA, Vol. XI, 817.

34 24 Sep 1825, HRA, Vol. XI, 847.

35 24 Sep 1825, HRA, Vol. XI, 847.

36 Stacker, *Chained to the Soil*, 42–3.

37 Rivière, *The Governor's Noble Guest*, 89–90, 186.

38 Rivière, *The Governor's Noble Guest*, 186.

39 Constantini, *Convict Record*.

40 19 Aug 1825, Theodore Constantine, SRNSW Reel 6015, 4/3515, 163.

41 Rivière, *The Governor's Noble Guest*, 104, 109, 113, 186, 268 n24.

42 Constantini, *Convict Record*.

43 Stillwell, *Costantini*.

44 Maxwell & Pugh, *The Master of Hell's Gates*, Appendix 1, see ship departures for
   January 1828, and for 1831; https://www.chismaxwell.com/resources. Constantini's talent was recognised by Commandant James Butler at Macquarie Harbour,
   who employed him to record images of the settlement: Butler to Colonial
   Secretary.

45 Stillwell, *Costantini*.

46 NSW Australia Returns of the Colony 1825, ancestry.com.

47 Stacker, *Chained to the Soil*, 35–6. Rivière, *The Governor's Noble Guest*, 90.

48 Stacker, *Chained to the Soil*, 38. Brisbane to Bathurst, 8 Feb 1825, HRA, Vol. XI,
   498–511.

49 Brisbane to Horton, 24 March 1824, HRA, Vol. XI, 554.

50 Rivière, *The Governor's Noble Guest*, 90, 187.

51 Stacker, *Chained to the Soil*, 39. Maxwell & Pugh, *The Master of Hell's Gates*, 58.

52 Sydney Gazette, 28 Nov 1825, 1; Trove 2184779.

53 French vs. McHenry, NSW Supreme Court, 9 July 1832: Dowling, Proceedings of
   the Supreme Court of NSW, Vol. 71, SRNSW 2/3254, 59.

54 Thorp, *The Penrith Heritage Study*, 54.

55 Bently & Birmingham, *History of Castlereagh*, 8, 19, 23. Plan of Emu Plains 1826, Alexander Kinghorne, SRNSW map 2661, Crown Plan E–277B.

56 Maxwell & Pugh, *The Master of Hell's Gates*, 197, 226–7, 231–2.

57 Rivière, *The Governor's Noble Guest*, 90, 187, 264 n23.

58 *Barissa or the Hermit Robber*, 1816, a comedy made famous at Sadler's Wells theatre London by the clown, Joseph Grimaldi. Fielding, *The Mock Doctor*. Rhodes, *Bombaster Furioso*.

59 The Australian, Thu 26 May 1825, 4; Trove 37073823/4248541.

60 Sydney Gazette, Thu 21 Jul 1825, 4; Trove 2184252.

61 Garrick, *The Lying Valet*.

62 Sydney Gazette, Thu 21 Jul 1825, 4; Trove 2184252.

63 Rivière, *The Governor's Noble Guest*, 102.

64 Molière, *Le Médecin malgré lui*.

65 Rivière, *The Governor's Noble Guest*, 102–3.

66 Dyer, *The French Explorers in Sydney*, 122, 124, 126. Rivière, *The Governor's Noble Guest*, 34.

67 Dyer, *The French Explorers and Sydney*, 126. Rivière, *The Governor's Noble Guest*, 132–3.

68 Fletcher, *A Governor Maligned*, 177.

69 Fletcher, *A Governor Maligned*, 122, 124.

70 Hobart Town Gazette, 13 May 1825; Trove 2184086.

71 Kinghorne to Brisbane, NLA MS6207.

72 Sydney Gazette, Thu 16 June 1825, 2; Trove 2184149/495176.

73 Sydney Gazette, Thu 16 June 1825, 2; Trove 2184149/495176. Brisbane did not have access to Bigge's recommendations until 1825. The sentiments expressed in this article, presented in parentheses, would have originated from Colonial Secretary Frederick Goulburn.

74 Colonial Times, Fri 10 Nov 1826; Trove 2448847.

75 Kinghorne, *Plan of Emu Plains 1826*, Crown Plan E227a.

76 Kinghorne, *Plan of Emu Plains 1826*, Crown Plan E227b. Stacker, *Chained to the Soil*, 50, note 108.

77 SRNSW letters from J. Kinghorne to CS December 1827-January 1827.

78 Karskens, *Cox's Road*, 48.

79 The Australian, Wed 26 Apr 1826, 2; Trove 37073379.

80 Stacker, *Chained to the Soil*, 42.

81 Brisbane to Bathurst, 24 Sep 1825, HRA, Vol. XI, 847.

Chapter 18: The Colonial Civil Engineer (1825–1828)

1 31 January 1822, SRNSW CS Reel 6039, 4/424, 35. Sydney Gazette, 12 Dec 1825, 3; Trove 2184841.

2 Dunlop, *Ovens*.

3 Colonial Secretary's Papers 1788–1825, 1–2, ancestry.com.

4 Colonial Secretary's Papers 1788–1825, 21 Sep, 22 Oct, and 4 & 12 Nov 1825, 458, 851–855, 858 and Grant Order nos. 281; ancestry.com.

5 Sydney Gazette, Thursday 15 December 1825, 2; Trove 2184859/495509.
6 Sydney Gazette, Thu 16 June 1825, 3; Trove 2184143/495178. Kinghorne to Brisbane, 22 Oct 1825, Colonial Secretary's Papers 1788–1825, 851–4; ancestry.com. Caledonian Mercury, 16 Nov 1815; gale.com.
7 Baker, *Stewart.*
8 Baker, *Stewart.* Colonial Secretary's Papers 1788–1825, 1–2, ancestry.com. Bathurst Free Press and Mining Journal, Sat 15 Apr 1854, 2; Trove 62048048.
9 Fletcher, *A Governor Maligned*, 79.
10 Gray, *Dumaresq.*
11 Darling to Goderich, 31 Dec 1827, HRA XIII, 672–3. Heydon, *Brisbane.* Fletcher, *Darling*, 149–54.
12 Darling to Hay, 23 March 1827, HRA XIII, 181.
13 Darling to Goderich, 31 Dec 1827, HRA XIII, 673.
14 Brisbane to Horton, 16 June 1825, HRA XI, 653. Stewart to Darling, 5 January 1826, SRNSW, 4/1790.
15 Dumaresq to Horton, 10 January 1828, SRNSW CO 201/197, f. 287.
16 How quickly the glory of the world passes away.
17 Captain William Dumeresq, Acting Civil Engineer, appointed 24 December 1825: Returns for the Colony of NSW, 1826; ancestry.com.
18 Returns of the Colony of NSW, 1826, 78a-b79, 86; ancestry.com.
19 For example, A. Kinghorne petition, 22 October 1825, NSW Australia, Colonial Secretary's Papers 1788–1825, 851–858; ancestry.com.
20 Darling to Hay, 2 February 1826, HRA XII, pp. 148–149.
21 Returns of the Colony 1822–1857, 78a-b79, 86, 107a-b108, ancestry.com. Note: the Sydney Gazette article indicates 10 Feb, contrary to the colonial returns.
22 Hobart Town Gazette, Sat 4 Feb 1826, 4; Trove 8791497/679857. Maxwell & Pugh, *The Master of Hell's Gates*, 226.
23 Land Board to MacLeay, 7, 10, Feb 1826 & Land Board to Oxley 9 Feb 1826, NRS906: Colonial Secretary, Special Bundles (1826–1830), Land Board, SRNSW 2/8016.2, 1, 416, 501.
24 Darling to Hay, 2 February 1826, HRA XII, pp. 148–149.
25 Returns of the Colony 1822–1857, 78a-b79, ancestry.com. Sydney Gazette, Sat 18 Feb 1826, 3; Trove 2185249.
26 Heydon, *Brisbane.*
27 *MacLeay.* Gray, *Dumaresq.* Fletcher, *A Governor Maligned*, 229.
28 Bias arising from Col. Dumaresq being Clerk of Executive Council: Forbes to Horton, 5 Sep 1827, Catton Papers, Derby Central Library, reels M791–3, Australian Joint Copying Project, National Library of Australia, 1970. 'The Governor, his Private Secretary and the Colonial Secretary ... the real cabinet of the colony': Forbes to Horton, 22 Mar 1827, Chief Justice Forbes Private Letters to RW Horton, SLNSW A 1819, 117. Fletcher, *A Governor Maligned*, 100–1, 156.
29 Chapter 6, Bonaparte Stirs Invasion Fears.
30 Fletcher, *A Governor Maligned*, 240.
31 Sydney Gazette, Sat 13 May 1826, 3; Trove 37074789 & 4248773.

32 Sydney Gazette, Wed 22 Feb 1826, 2; Trove 2185287.

33 Sydney Gazette, Wed 22 Feb 1826, 2; Trove 2185287.

34 Sydney Gazette, Wed 22 Feb 1826, 1; Trove 2185266.

35 Darling to Bathurst, 5 May 1826, HRA XII, 267–8.

36 Darling to Bathurst, 5 May 1826, HRA XII, 267–8.

37 Darling to Bathurst, 5 May 1826, HRA XII, 267–8; see also Darling's notation to MacLeay, 17 February 1826, SRNSW 4/1915.3 [document enclosed in letter no. 26/7590].

38 Sydney Gazette, Wed 24 May, 1826, 2; Trove 2185861/495885.

39 Government Order (No. 22.) Colonial Secretary's Office, 29 May 29, 1826. Sydney Gazette, Wed 31 May 1826, 1; Trove 2185898/495898.

40 Sydney Gazette, Sat 25 Feb 1826, 1; Trove 2185305/495678.

41 Bathurst to Darling 19 Oct 1826, Darling to Bathurst 7 Aug 1827, HRA XII, 651.

42 McLachlan, *Bathurst at the Colonial Office*.

43 Darling to Hay, 9 May 1826, HRA Vol. XII, 294.

44 Darling to Bathurst, 5 May 1826, 5 Sep 1826, HRA XII, 267–268, 541–542. Dumaresq to Darling, 27 Jul 1827, HRA XIII, 468. Gray, *Dumaresq*.

45 Stacker, *Chained to the soil*, 35ff.

46 Sydney Gazette, Wed 5 Apr 1826, 1; Trove 2185590. Sydney Gazette Sat 15 Apr 1826, 1; Trove 2185653. Kinghorne to MacLeay, 28 Mar 1826, 1826; Kinghorne to MacLeay, 15 May 1826, 819; Dumeresq to MacLeay, 6 Jul 1826, 4008; Dumeresq to MacLeay, 18 Dec 1827, 27/11706: INX–45–274, SRNSW 4/1960.1. Wright to Kinghorne, 7 April 1826, SRNSW 4/346, 66ff. Kinghorne to Scott, 12 April 1826, SRNSW 4/346, 65.

47 Fanny to William MacLeay, 31 Jan 1826: SLNSW ML MSS A4300.

48 Kinghorne to MacLeay, 15 May 1826, 2819: INX–45–274, SRNSW 4/1960.

49 Dumeresq to MacLeay, 18 Dec 1827, 27/11706: INX–45–274, SRNSW 4/1960.

50 Committee on the Australian Gaslight Company Bill, 1837/9, in: Doust, *The Select Committees*, 41. https://en.wikipedia.org/wiki/Australian_Gas_Light_Company. Sydney Mail, Sat 16 April 1898, 803; Trove 163802728/16799451.

51 Sydney Morning Herald, Tue 7 Sep 1937, 10; Trove 17398271.

52 Suttor, *Australian Milestones*, 346.

53 Sydney Herald, Thu 15 Sep 1836, 4; Trove 12864066. Sydney Monitor, Wed 14 Sep 1836, 3; Trove 32152192.

54 The Colonist, Sat 2 June 1838, 2; Trove 31721072.

55 Chapter 17, The Land Board of Van Diemen's Land and the demise of New Brighton.

Chapter 19: The Clergy and School Lands Corporation (1826–1827)

1 Goodin, *Public Education in NSW before 1848*, (4 parts) 82–4.

2 King to Kent, 23 May 1800, HRA, Vol. II, 528–9.

3 Sydney Gazette, 3 Mar 1825, 3; Trove 2183789. Report of Grand Jurors, 28 Sep 1825, HRA, Vol. XI, 861.

4 Jackson and Aird to Kinghorne, 13, 15 Feb, 22, 23, 24 Mar 1826, SRNSW 4/346, 147, 149, 151, 153, 155. Kass et al., *Parramatta: A past revealed*, 99.

5 Macquarie to Bathurst, 24 Mar 1819, HRA, Vol. X, 94.

6 King to Wyndham, 12 Aug 1806, HRA, Vol. V, 763. MacIntosh, Charles, *Report on Church Estates*, 30 March 1824, HRA, Vol. XIV, 778. Sydney Gazette, Tue 10 Apr 1827, 1; 2188017. CSLC Minutes, 22 Aug 1822. Thorp, *Bonnyrigg House*.

7 Appointed May 1825: Cable, *Cartwright*.

8 See Appendix 1.

9 Bathurst to Brisbane, 1 Jan 1825, HRA, Vol. XI, 425. Instructions to Darling, 17 Jul 1825, HRA, Vol. XII, 117. SRNSW AGY–401, Trustees CLSC, 9 Mar 1826–4 Feb 1833, ancestry.com.

10 CSLC Proceedings SRNSW 4/292, 20.

11 The site for the Male Orphan School at Bull Hill is today (2022) in Homestead Park, bounded by Kinghorne Road, Brown Road and Aplin Road, Bonnyrigg Heights NSW 2177. The only remaining building is the Master's House, located at 26 Cartwright Street, Bonnyrigg Heights. Thorp, *Bonnyrigg House*, Plan No. 20. Bubacz, *The Female and Male Orphan Schools*, 258.

12 Busby to Brisbane, 25 Aug 1825, SRNSW 4/346, 19–21. Walsh, *John Busby*. Davidson, *James Busby*. Cowper to MacLeay, 20 Sep 1826, SRNSW NRS 906, Colonial Secretary, Special Bundles, 4/1913.

13 Cartwright to Scott, 15 May 1826, in Male Orphan School Letter Book, SRNSW NRS 775, 3–6.

14 Alexander MacLeay: Colonial Secretary's Office, 29 May 29, 1826, ancestry.com.

15 Replaced by William Dumeresq on 29 May: Returns of the Colony, 1826, 86; ancestry.com.

16 Kinghorne to Scott, 20 May 1826, SRNSW 4/346, 101. 11. CSLC Proceedings SRNSW 4/292, 9 June 1826, 16.

17 Colonial Secretary's Office, 29 May 1826. Sydney Gazette, Wed 31 May 1826, 1; Trove 2185898/495898.

18 Kinghorne to Jackson, Cartwright, Lithgow, 15 Feb & 22–24 Mar: CSLC, Correspondence received from Architects and Mechanics 1825–28, SRNSW 4/346, 147, 149, 151, 153, 155.

19 CSLC Proceedings SRNSW 4/292, 9 June 1826, 16.

20 Bigge, *Report of the Commissioner of Enquiry*, 1823, 71.

21 CSLC Proceedings SRNSW 4/292, 20–1. Kinghorne, *CSLC Journal*, 20–21 Jun 1826, 277.

22 CSLC Proceedings SRNSW 4/292, 77. Kinghorne, *CSLC Journal*, 6 Sep, 280. Kinghorne to Cowper, 28 Jul, 6 Sep & 16 Nov 1826: CSLC Correspondence SRNSW 4/346, 169, 197, 231. Kinghorne's notations indicate he worked a total of 90 days for the CCSL between Jun 1826 and Jan 1827, which he charged at a rate of £3.3.15 per day. Giving a total of £351. He was initially paid £200, and submitted a further claim for £159, which was eventually paid. Kinghorne to Cowper, 1 Apr 1827, 4 Jun 1827: SRNSW 4/346, 275, 285 (salary notations), 299.

23 Parsons, *Throsby*.

24 CSLC Proceedings SRNSW 4/292, 25–6. Kinghorne, *CSLC Journal*, 22–26 Jul 1826, 277.

25 Kinghorne, *CSLC Journal*, 31 Jun–1 Jul 1826, 278.

26 CSLC Proceedings SRNSW 4/292, 30. Kinghorne, *CSLC Journal*, 4–5 Jul 1826, 278.

27 CSLC Proceedings SRNSW 4/292, 43, 63.

28 Thorp, *Bonnyrigg House*, 71–73.

29 Thorp, *Bonnyrigg House*, 91–99.

30 CSLC Proceedings SRNSW 4/292, 34. Kinghorne, *CSLC Journal*, 6–19 Jul 1826, 278–9.

31 Statement of the Corporation, 31 March 1828, HRA, Vol. XIV, 100.

32 CSLC Proceedings SRNSW 4/292, 34–6, 56–7. Davidson, *James Busby*.

33 CSLC Proceedings SRNSW 4/292, 57–8. Kinghorne, *CSLC Journal*, 21–31 August 1826, 280. Cartwright to Scott, 8. Letters received from the Master of the Male Orphan School, NRS–775, No. 96, 5 Aug 1826, 9.

34 CSLC Proceedings SRNSW 4/292, 43–5.

35 CSLC Proceedings SRNSW 4/292, 50–1, 57, 87. Kinghorne, *CSLC Journal*, 1–16 Aug 1826, 279.

36 Scott to Darling, 24 April 1826, SLNSW DLMSQ 608. Kinghorne to Cowper, No. 99, 7 Aug 1826 CSLC Proceedings SRNSW 4/292, 171; Field of Mars, Nos 52, 59, 10 Aug 1826: CSLC Proceedings SRNSW 4/292, 172–175, plus added notes. Benson & Ernest, *The Church on the Hill*, 13–21.

37 Sat 23 Sep: Kinghorne, *CSLC Journal*, 281. CSLC Proceedings SRNSW 4/292, 89. SRNSW NRS–771, Trustees of the Clergy and School Lands, 27 Sep 1826, Item 12, 89.

38 Kinghorne, *CSLC Journal*, 4, 23, 26, 30 & 31 Oct, 282. CSLC Proceedings SRNSW 4/292, 89. Kinghorne to Scott, 12 April 1826, SRNSW 4/346, 65. SRNSW NRS–771, 17 Jan 1827, Item 7, 160.

39 Kinghorne, *CSLC Journal*, Entries for Dec 1826, 283. Statement of Receipts and Disbursements Clergy and School Lands Corporation, SRNSW 4/388.

40 Kinghorne, *CSLC Journal*, 1–17 Jan 1827, 283. NRS–771, 5 April 1827, Item 6, 202.

41 Cartwright to Cowper, 4 Jun 1827, 69; Cartwright to Scott, 23 Jul 1827, 77; Cartwright to Scott, 22 Sep 1827, 93. Letterbook Male Orphan School, 1826–9: SRNSW NRS–775.

42 Thorp, *Bonnyrigg House,* 54–8, 72–3.

43 Kinghorne, *CSLC Journal*, 7 Aug 1826, 279.

44 Thorp, *Bonnyrigg House,* 21.

45 Thorp, *Bonnyrigg House,* 50.

46 Kinghorne to Cowper, 28 Aug 1826: SRNSW 4/346, 183.

47 Kinghorne to Seton Karr, 6 Mar 1809: NRAS2970, B 17.

48 Thorp, *Bonnyrigg House,* 72.

49 Thorp, *Bonnyrigg House,* archaeological descriptions: 91–95; 1831 plans for Master's House and dormitories drawn by the Master, Lieutenant Richard Sadlier, Plans 1 & 2: 148–9.

50 Thorpe, *Bonnyrigg House*, 8.

51 H Kinghorne to AS Kinghorne, 26 Oct 1828.

52 Davidson, *James Busby*. SRNSW NRS–771, 6 Sep 1826, Item 5, 77.

53 Sydney Gazette, Sat 7 Apr, Mon 4 Jun, Fri 21 Dec 1827; Trove 37073644, 2188354, 2189628.

54 Kinghorne to Scott, 13 Jun1826: SRNSW 4/346, 129; Kinghorne to Cowper, 28 Jul 1826: SRNSW 4/346, 165; Kinghorne to Scott, No. 210, 21 Oct 1826: SRNSW 4/346, 219. Chapter 20, The Kinghornes are embroiled.

55 Kinghorne to Cowper, No. 85, 1 Aug 1826: SRNSW 4/346, 169.

56 Kinghorne to Cowper, 4 Jun 1826: SRNSW 4/346, 299.

57 Kinghorne to Cowper, No. 137, 6 Sep 1826: SRNSW 4/346, 197.

58 Kinghorne to Cowper, 16 Nov 1826: SRNSW 4/346, 231. SRNSW NRS–771, 30 Nov 1826, Item 5, 121.

59 Maxwell & Pugh, *The Merchant of Sydney*, 103.

60 Sydney Gazette, Wed 4 July 1827, 2; Trove 2188537. Ann Read, convict record.

61 The Monitor, Tue 3 Jul 1827, 8; Trove 31758546. Sydney Gazette, Wed 4 Jul 1827, 2; Trove 2188537. The Monitor, Sat 11 Oct 1828, 7; Trove 31760801.

62 Sydney Gazette, Wed 1 Aug 1827, 1; Trove 2188687.

63 The Australian, Wed 5 Mar 1828, 1; Trove 37073089.

64 The Gleaner, Sat 21 July 1827, 1; Trove 251535555. The Australian, Wed 19 Sep 1827, 2; Trove 37071517. Op den Brouw, *Town's First Fleet Power Couple*. Maxwell & Pugh, *The Master of Hell's Gates*, 196. The Australian, Wed 5 Mar 1828, 1; Trove 37073089.

65 Chapter 20, The Kinghornes are embroiled.

66 NSW Census for the year 1828, Kinghorne Family, District of Liverpool, Nos 59 & 60, attested by Alexander Kinghorne Snr, Drummond Farm Liverpool, 9 Dec 1828; ancestry.com.

67 H Kinghorne to AS Kinghorne, 26 October 1828.

68 1828 Census Records, Kinghorne family. Op den Brouw, Glen, *Town's First Fleet Power Couple*.

69 Registers of Memorials 1838–40, Memorial No. 295, 14 Jan 1839, Cnr Elizabeth and Macquarie Streets, Liverpool; ancestry.com. Colonial Secretary, Land and Town Purchases and Grants 1839–1840, Town Grant No. 433, 30 Apr 1840, Cnr Elizabeth and Macquarie Streets, Liverpool, St Luke, one rood and 37 perches; ancestry.com.

70 Cant, *Buchan*, 25.

71 Buchan to Erskine, Edinburgh 1782; Scott, *Journal*, 552n.

72 Cant, *Buchan*, 25. Lockhart, *Scott*, Volume 6, 83–5.

73 Hobart Town Courier, Sat 5 Sep 1829, 4; Trove 4214135.

74 Scott, *Journal, from the Original Manuscript*, 453.

75 London Courier, 26 Jun 1826, in Sydney Gazette, Thu 18 Oct 1832, 3; Trove 2209025. Hobart Town Courier, Fri 9 Nov, 1832, 2; Trove 4196117.

76 Glasgow Courier, 16 July 1832, in Sydney Gazette, Sat 17 Nov 1832, 2; Trove 2209482.

77 Perth Gazette, Sat 2 Feb 1833, 18; Trove 642239.

78 The Scotsman, 22 Sep 1832, in Sydney Herald, Thu 7 Feb 1833, 2; Trove 12846210.

79 Launceston Advertiser, Thu 7 Feb 1833, 8; Trove 84774953. Hobart Town Courier, Fri 8 Feb 1833, 4; Trove 4194271. https://www.scotiana.com/dryburgh-abbey-sir-walter-scott's-final-resting-place/.

80 Kinghorne's Scott, *The Monastery*, Introductory Epistle, 20: Footnote to Scott's mention of 'the family of De Haga'.

81 Kinghorne's Scott, *The Monastery*, 277.

Chapter 20: The Death of Private Sudds and its Consequences (1826–1835)

1 NAUK WO 25/424, 57 Foot 1 Battn 1820–1830, ancestry.com.

2 Warre, *Historical Records of the Fifty-Seventh*, 75.

3 Darling, HC 1835, Appendix 2, 151. Clarke, *Old tales of a young country*, Chapter 8, Governor Ralph Darling's Iron Collar.

4 The soldiers of the 57th served 22 years in NSW and India: Warre, *Historical Records of the Fifty-Seventh*, 9, 72–5.

5 Sydney Gazette, Sat 11 Nov 1826, 3; Trove 2186892. Sudds and Thompson were committed by Magistrate Rossi on 19 Sepr: SRNSW 4/640, Reel 85.

6 Sydney Gazette, Sat 25 Nov 1826, 2; Trove 2186983.

7 Sydney Gazette, Sat 11 November 1826, 3; Trove 2186892. Gaol Description and Entrance Books, 1818–1830, ancestry.com.

8 Minute 22 of the Executive Council, 8 Dec 1826, HRA Vol. XII, 744–5. Epidemic with the arrival of the ships *Warspite, Volage* and *Fly*: The Australian, Wed 29 Nov 1826, 2; Trove 37073689.

9 Hall, *Refutation of Lieutenant-General Darling*; front cover of pamphlet.

10 Darling to Bathurst, 4 Dec 1826, HRA Vol. XII, 716–17. General Order, 22 Nov 1826, 721–2. The Monitor, Fri 24 Nov & 1 Dec 1826, 1; Trove 31758029 & 31758003.

11 Executive Council opinion, 12 December 1826, HRA, Series I, Vol. XII, 748–9. Fletcher, *A Governor Maligned*, 245.

12 The Australian, Sat 25 Nov 1826; Trove 4248996.

13 The Australian, Wed 29 Nov 1826, 2–3; Trove 4249000.

14 His secretary Henry Dumeresq. The Monitor, Fri 1 Dec 1826, 5; Trove 31758024/4229695.

15 Darling to Earl Bathurst, 4 Dec 1826, HRA, Vol. XII, 717. The letter also appears in full, dated 1 December 1826, in HC 1831-2, Appendix A, 5 July 1832, Papers Relating to the Punishment of Joseph Sudds, Enclosure No. 2, 39.

16 Connor, *The Politics of Grievance*, 227, 234. Darling to Hay, 4 Dec 1826.

17 Thompson's irons broken 25 Nov 1825: The examination of Patrick Thompson, HC1830, Appendix D Papers, 49.

18 HC 1830, Letter from Mr. Wentworth to Sir G. Murray, Appendix D Papers, 53–55.

360

19 HC 1830, 14 May 1829, Minute No 20, 14. See also Enclosures C, J and K to Minute No. 11, interviews with William Dumeresq, James Kinghorne and George Plumley, 17, 20, 21.

20 The Australian, Sat 9 Dec 1826, 2; Trove 37071800.

21 The Australian, Wed 3 Jan 1827, 2; Trove 37073660.

22 Returns of the Colony of NSW, 1822–1827, 1828, Convict Establishments, 92–93; ancestry.com.

23 Wentworth to Bathurst, 15 Dec 1826, SRNSW CO201/179.

24 Sydney Gazette, Tue 16 Jan 1827, 2; Trove 2187392. The Australian, Wed 31 Jan 1827, 4; Trove 37074497.

25 Darling to Bathurst, 31 January 1827, HRA, Vol. XIII, 50–59. Sydney Gazette, Sat 27 Jan 1827, 2; Trove 2187513. The Australian, Sat 27 Jan, 2 & Wed 31 Jan 1827, 4; Trove 37073368 & 37074497.

26 Darling to Bathurst, 31 Jan 1827, HRA, Vol. XIII, 50–9.

27 The Australian, Fri 20 Mar 1829, 2; Trove 36863881.

28 The chains actually weighed 14lbs 6 oz: HC 1830, 6 May 1829, Minute No 10, 9.

29 HC 1830, No II, Darling to Murray, 28 May 1829, items 13. & 16, 5. Captain Robison was court marshalled in 1828 for opposition to the Governor: NAUK WO 91/15.

30 HC 1833, Robison.

31 Wentworth to Murray, 1 Mar 1829, HRA Vol. XIV, 810–55. HC 1830, Minute No. 7, 30–52, 58.

32 HC 1830, 14 May 1829, Minute No 20, and Enclosure J, 14, 20–1.

33 The minute identifies 'Mr. Kinghorne, jun. millwright': HC 1830, 11 May 1829, Minute No 14, 9, 26.

34 HC 1830, 14 May 1829, Minute No 20, 14.

35 HC 1830, 14 May 1829, Enclosure to Minute No 16, 26.

36 HC 1830, 8 May 1829, Enclosure P to Minute No 12, 24.

37 Darling, HC Select Committee 21 Aug 1835: Cross-examination of Captain R. Robison, paragraphs 310 –370, 17–21; and paragraphs 436–473, 24–27.

38 Darling, HC Select Committee 30 Jul 1835. Final debate and vote in House of Commons: Hansard, HC Debate 30 Jul 1835, Vol. 29, cc1254–75, motion carried 55 to 47.

39 See arguments against Kinghornes' evidence by E.S. Hall in the Monitor, Wed 29 Dec 1830, 3, para 8; Trove 32074728/4294206.

40 Fletcher, A Governor Maligned and Tink, Wentworth, make no mention of this evidence.

Chapter 21: James Kinghorne at Emu Plains and Wellington Valley (1826–1832)

1 Stacker, Chained to the Soil, 44, 48, 50–2, 55–6.

2 James Kinghorne to Colonial Secretary, June 1827, 27/5159, SRNSW 4/1933.

3 Colonial Secretary to Dumeresq, 22 Aug 1827, No. 285, SRNSW Reel 2997, 265.

4 James Kinghorne to MacLeay, 21 Feb 1828, 28/1733, SRNSW 4/1933. 14.

5 Sydney Gazette, Wed 29 March 1826, 2; Trove 2185536.

6 Deposition of Peters, 2 Aug 1826, 26/4685, SRNSW 4/1898.

7 Peters to the Chief Justice, 21 Jun 1826, 26/4685, SRNSW INX–45–1545, 4/1899.
   Fulton to MacLeay, 1 Aug 1826, 26/4685, SRNSW INX–45–1545, 4/1899. James
   Kinghorne to MacLeay, 9 & 10 Aug 1826, 26/44962, SRNSW INX–45–1545,
   4/1899. Peters to Darling (Memorial), 26 Aug 1826, 26/44962, SRNSW INX–
   45–1545, 4/1899.

8 MacLeay to James Kinghorne, 30 December 1826, NRS 962, SRNSW 4/3665–94,
   Reel 1055.

9 Sydney Gazette, Sat 9 Jan 1830, 3; Trove 2194260.

10 Stacker, *Chained to the Soil*, 62.

11 Sydney Gazette, Thu 19 Jan 1832, 3; Trove 2204528.

12 Porter, *History of Wellington*, 2. Sydney Gazette, Thu 19 Jan 1832, 3; Trove
   2204528. Roberts, *The Valley of Swells*, 11.1–11.21. Roberts, *A sort of inland
   Norfolk Island?*, 50–72.

13 James Kinghorne to Alexander MacLeay, 9 Jul 1830: SRNSW 4/2045.

14 Sydney Gazette, Thu 19 Jan 1832, 3; Trove 2204528.

15 Maxwell & Pugh, *The Master of Hell's Gates*, 240–1.

16 Roberts, *The Valley of Swells*, 11.1–11.21.

Chapter 22: Court Service (1827–1840)

1 Temporary until enshrined in the Act of 1828, 4 Geo 4, c.96: http://www.courts.
   justice.nsw.gov.au/Documents/nsw5_doc_1823.pdf. Chief Justice Forbes, 13 Oct
   1823: Curry, *Forbes*.

2 Barker, *Sorely tried*, 54–6.

3 Provided both plaintiff and defendant agreed: Barker, *Sorely tried*, 56.

4 Macarthur, *New South Wales*, 89–90, Appendix 16, 103.

5 HRA, Series 4, Legal Papers. Vol. I, 12. Sydney Gazette, Sat 9 Jan 1830, 1; Trove
   2194262.

6 Colonial Secretary's Papers 1788–1825, 12 Nov 1825, 457–9; ancestry.com. Sydney
   Gazette, Thu 17 Nov 1825, 1; Trove 2184719/495435.

7 List of Individuals who have received Orders for Grants of Land Since 1 May 1825,
   Colonial Secretary's Papers 1788–1825, 93–4: ancestry.com.

8 Sydney Gazette, Fri 15 Jun 1827, 1; Trove 2188423.

9 Alexander and James Kinghorne JPs: Sydney Gazette, Tue 5 Jan 1830, 3, Sat 23
   Apr 1831, 1, Sat 9 Jan 1836, 4 & Tue 11 Dec 1838, 2; Trove 2194233, 2200255,
   2202150 & 2550398, respectively.

10 For example, Sydney Gazette, Thu 2 Apr 1829, 2; Trove 2192135.

11 For example: Sydney Gazette, Thu 30 May 1833, 1; Trove 2212246. In 1827, the
   Liverpool magistrates were Charles Throsby, Thomas Moore, William Browne,
   Patrick Hill, Alexander Kinghorne, and Richard Brooks: The Australian, Wed 18
   Sep 1827, 2; Trove 37071517.

12 Windsor Quarter Sessions: Sydney Gazette, Sat 21 Oct 1826, 3; Trove 2186753.

13 Chapter 21, James Kinghorne at Emu Plains and Wellington Valley.

14 See Chapter 23, Pastoral Expansion.

15 Sydney Gazette, Thu 28 May 1829, 2; Trove 2192535. Australian, Sat 30 May
1829, 3; Trove 36867018.

16 Wade, *Dick*.

17 Bennett, *The establishment of jury trial in New South Wales*, 474–5, 481.

18 Bourke to Goderich, HRA Ser I, Vol. XVI, 564.

19 Sydney Gazette, Sat 25 Sep 1830, 2 & Thu 3 Oct 1833, 1; Trove 2196118 & 2214203.

20 Curry, *Dowling*.

21 Curry, *Stephen*.

22 Sydney Gazette, Sat 25 Sep 1830, 2; Trove 2196118. Sydney Gazette, Thu 3 Sep
1830, 3; Trove 2196147. Monitor, Sat 5 Feb 1831, 2; Trove 32074930. Sydney Gazette, Sat 5 Feb 1831, 2; Trove 2198888. Sydney Gazette, Tue 8 Feb 1831, 3; Trove
2198930. Sydney Herald, Mon 15 Aug 1831, 4; Trove 12843399. Sydney Herald,
Mon 17 Oct 1831, 2; Trove 28654050.

23 Barker, *Sorely tried*, 63–4.

24 Bennett, *The establishment of jury trial in New South Wales*, 619, 482.

25 Faithful, Arndell and Rouse were acquaintances, and Bowman a relative by marriage, of James Chisholm.

26 Sydney Gazette, Fri 12 Jan 1827, 3; Trove 2187366.

27 Australian, Wed 19 Sep 1827, 2; Trove 37071517.

28 Search of trove.nla.gov.au/newspaper articles.

29 This was the same Thomas Moore whose bequest founded Moore Theological
College: Loane, *Moore*.

30 Monitor, Wed 20 Oct 1830, 2; Trove 32074396.

31 Mistaking him for Michael Connolly, who had been a Liverpool constable since
1827: Sydney Herald, Thu 3 Apr 1834, 3; Trove 12849020.

32 Monitor, Sat 30 Oct 1830, 3; Trove 32074435.

33 Monitor, Sat 30 Oct 1830, 3; Trove 32074435.

34 See arguments against Kinghornes' evidence by E.S. Hall in the Monitor, Wed 29
Dec 1830, 3, para 8; Trove 32074728/4294206. See also Chapter 20, The Kinghornes are embroiled.

35 Sydney Gazette, Thu 3 Sep 1830, 3; Trove 2196147.

36 Kenny, *Hall*.

37 Sydney Gazette, Tue 8 Jan 1833, 3; Trove 2210251.

38 The Currency Lad, Sat 23 Feb 1833, 1; Trove 252636548.

39 Australian, Fri 29 Jan 1836, 2; Trove 36853152. The Sydney Herald, Mon 30 May
1836, 2; Trove 12854426. Martens, *Lansdowne Bridge*.

40 Australian, Tue 32 May 1836, 2; Trove 36855488.

41 Sydney Gazette, Tue 31 Jan 1837, 3; Trove 2209118.

42 The Colonist, Thu 5 Oct 1837, 3; Trove 31719914.

43 Sydney Gazette, Sat 7 Oct, 3; Trove 2213310.

44 Sydney Gazette, Sat 7 Oct, 3; Trove 2213310.

45 Draper to Gazette, 10 Oct 1837: Sydney Gazette, Thu 12 Oct 1837, 3; Trove
2213402.

46 For example, Sydney Gazette, Tue 17 Oct 1837, 3; Trove 2213484.

47 Sydney Gazette, Thu 3 Oct 1833, 1; Trove 2214203.

48 Sydney Gazette, Sat 15, 2 & Thu 3 Jun, 3; Trove 2212457 & 12847017, respectively.

49 Sydney Gazette, Sat 7 Jun 1834, 3; Trove 2216322. The Australian, Tue 10 Jun 1834, 3; Trove 42009637. The Australian, Fri 27 Jun 1834, 2; Trove 42009847. The Australian, Fri 19 Sep 1834, 5; Trove 42008535. Sydney Herald, Mon 22 Sep 1834, 1; Trove 12850494. Sydney Herald, Thu 25 Sep 1834, 2; Trove 12850552. Monitor, Wed 1 Oct 1834, 3; Trove 32147269. Australian, Fri 10 Oct 1834, 2; Trove 42009190. Sydney Gazette, Sat 8 Mar 1834, 2; Trove 2215581.

50 Sydney Herald, Thu 25 Sep 1834, 2; Trove 12850552. Manning was then Registrar of the Supreme Court: Newton, *Manning*.

51 For example: Sydney Gazette, Thu 9 Jul 1835, 3; Trove 2199073. Australian, Fri 9 Oct 1835, 3; Trove 42005894. Sydney Gazette, Tue 26 Sep 1837, 2; Trove 2213114. Sydney Gazette, The 5 Oct 1837, 2; Trove 2213284. Sydney Herald, Thu 5 Oct 1837, 2; Trove 12859025.

Chapter 23: The Vision Splendid: Property in New South Wales (1827–1840)

1 Maxwell & Pugh, *The Master of Hell's Gates*, Chapter 14, His Father's Estates, 224–44.

2 Maxwell & Pugh, *The Master of Hell's Gates*, Appendix 3, 275–8.

3 Kinghorne to Brisbane, 22 Oct 1825, Colonial Secretary's Papers 1788–1825, Memorial 443, 851–5: ancestry.com.

4 Kinghorne to Brisbane, 21 Sep 1825, Colonial Secretary's Papers 1788–1825, 855–8: ancestry.com.

5 John Stewart appointed Assistant Superintendent Emu Plains, 16 Feb 1825, New South Wales, Australia, Returns of the Colony 1822–1857, 313; ancestry.com. Grants of 100 & 900 acres to John Stewart, 23 May & 10 Nov 1825, Colonial Secretary's Papers 1788–1856, 20, 27, 110; ancestry.com.

6 1,000 acres promised by Brisbane to James Kinghorne at the Cowpastures 3 May 1824: Land Records 1811–1870, Application 30/343; ancestry.com.

7 Kinghorne to Brisbane, 22 Oct 1825, Colonial Secretary's Papers 1788–1825, Memorial 443, 851–5: ancestry.com.

8 Instructions to Governor Brisbane, 17 July 1825, HRA Vol. I, 12, 107–25. Orders for Grants of Land Since 1 May 1825, Colonial Secretary's Papers 1788–1825, 93–4: ancestry.com.

9 Recommendation to Lord Bathurst in favour Alexander Kinghorne, 24 Jul 1823, Colonial Secretary's Papers 1788–1825, SRNSW G039 1 1. Buchan to Miss E Kinghorne, 29 Jul 1823.

10 Kinghorne to Brisbane, 21 Sep 1825, Colonial Secretary's Papers 1788–1825, 855–8: ancestry.com. Kinghorne to Brisbane, 22 Oct 1825, Colonial Secretary's Papers 1788–1825, Memorial 443, 851–5: ancestry.com.

11 1. Orders for Grants of Land Since 1 May 1825, 4 Nov 1825, Colonial Secretary's Papers 1788–1825, 93–4: ancestry.com. 2. Orders for Grants of Land Since 1 Jan 1825, 18 Nov 1825, Colonial Secretary's Papers 1788–1825, 108–9: ancestry.com.

12 1,000 acres promised by Brisbane to James Kinghorne at the Cowpastures 3 May 1824, converted to 2,000 acres at Argyle: Land Records 1811–1870, Application 30/343; ancestry.com.

13 1,000 acres Argyle, 31 Dec 1826: Land Records 1811–1870, Applications Ordered by Darling; ancestry.com.

14 Sydney Gazette, Sat 20 Feb 1830, 3; Trove 2194542.

15 MacLeay to Kinghorne, 9 June 1827.

16 Tipping, *Hoddle*. Colville, *Hoddle*: 18–21. See Maxwell & Pugh, *The Master of Hell's Gates*, Figures 40 & 41.

17 Maxwell & Pugh, *The Merchant of Sydney*, 139–41, 218–20.

18 Sydney Gazette, Tue 16 Jun 1829, 3; Trove 2192677.

19 NLA MS6207, B2, S2, F23.

20 Grants transferred to James Chisholm on 4 Nov 1834 and 11 Oct 1834: SRNSW NRS 13836, Items 7–506, Reel 2705 & 7–452, Reel 2548, respectively.

21 Sydney Gazette, Thu 5 Aug 1830, 2; Trove 2195699. Transferred to James Chisholm 29 Oct 1834: SRNSW NRS 13836, Item 7–452, Reel 2548 & Items 7–506, Reel 2705.

22 Sydney Gazette, Tue 4 Jun 1839, 4; Trove 2549702. Grantees Rev'd Hugh Gilchrist and Alexander Kinghorne; promised & reserved (Darling) 11 Aug 183; granted & gazetted (Gipps) 21 Apr 1840: Register of Grants & Leases, County of Argyle, 1838–1862, Vol. 2, No. 124, 44–6; ancestry.com.

23 JK Kinghorne to AS Kinghorne, 26 Jun 1836. Maxwell & Pugh, *The Merchant of Sydney*, 143–44, Appendix 1, 232.

24 SRNSW, Various Land Records; ancestry.com. Maxwell & Pugh, *The Merchant of Sydney*, Appendix 1, 232.

25 Maxwell & Pugh, *The Merchant of Sydney*, 141–4. Maxwell & Pugh, *The Master of Hell's Gates*, Figures 40 & 41. Abbott, *Woore*.

26 Maxwell & Pugh, *The Merchant of Sydney*, 137–8.

27 Wyatt, *Goulburn*, 24–5.

28 Chisholm, *Speeches and Reminiscences*, 1. Walsh, *Bradley*. Wyatt, *Goulburn*, 44.

29 See Chapter 21, James Kinghorne at Emu Plains and Wellington Valley.

30 Loss of a 'Certificate of freedom', issued 1834, by the convict George Hewston, who had been assigned to Cardross for his 7-year term; suggesting they had been in occupation with convicts since 1827: Sydney Gazette, Thu 16 Apr 1835, 3; Trove 2197856.

31 Peters died 30 Jan 1872, aged 71, at Bungarby, near Nimmitabel: Sydney Mail, Sat 17 Feb 1872, 19; ancestry.com.

32 NSW 1828 Census (Australian Copy) for Joseph Peters, Mary Robinson and infant Mary, Nos 66, 67 & 68, respectively; ancestry.com.

33 H Kinghorne to AS Kinghorne, 26 Oct 1828.

34 Sydney Gazette, Tue 24 May 1831, 2; Trove 2200703.

35 Transcription from Journal of William Edward Riley (1830–31): NLA MS 6207, B4, S3, F33.

36 JK Kinghorne to Kinghorne, 20 Feb 1832.

37 The Sydney Herald, Mon 9 Jul 1832, 2; Trove 12844836.

38 The claimed weight of 1,600 lbs (726 kg) is higher than that of a modern feed-lot-finished steer (600 kg). The price prevailing at the time for bullocks was between £2–3 per head.

39 Lieut. Robert Futter RN, of Lumley Park, Bungonia.

40 JK Kinghorne to Kinghorne, 20 Feb 1832.

41 Return of Lands Granted 1833, Colonial Secretary's Papers 1822–1857, 209: ancestry.com.

42 SRNSW Reel 1584, Series 12992.

43 Maxwell & Pugh, The Master of Hell's Gates, Figures 40 & 41.

44 Sydney Gazette, Sat 4 Apr 1835, 4; Trove 2197761. The Colonist, Thu 9 Apr 1825, 6; Trove 31716393.

45 Waugh, Letters to Friends, 35.

46 Waugh to his mother, 3 Sep 1834: Sydney Monitor & Commercial Advertiser, Wed 14 Nov 1838, 2; Trove 32161874.

47 JK Kinghorne to AS Kinghorne, 20 Jun 1836.

48 Maxwell & Pugh, The Master of Hell's Gates, 240, & Appendix 3: 275–8.

49 Maxwell & Pugh, The Master of Hell's Gates, 198–200, 275.

50 Barker, A History of Bathurst, 78–79. Sydney Gazette, Mon 28 Nov 1825, 2; Trove 2184768.

51 Long, Ranken.

52 Kinghorne, Plan of Selkirkshire.

53 Sydney Gazette, Thu 19 Jan 1832, 3; Trove 2204528.

54 Porter states 'the caves were discovered about the year 1830, when Mr. [James] Kinghorn was in command of the settlement … [by] Mr Ranken … After several weeks … Mr. Kinghorn, the doctor [Dr Fattarini], and the surveyor [Ranken] … made the first official visit': Porter, History of Wellington, 3.

55 Long, Ranken. Oldroyd, In the Footsteps of Thomas Livingstone Mitchell, 357. Both Mitchell and Lang might have been inspired: Buckland, Reliquiae Diluvianae. Dunkley, The 1830 Cave Diaries of Thomas Livingstone Mitchell, 25.

56 Diary of Thomas Mitchell, 10 Jul 1830, SLNSW, ML MS C42.

57 Maxwell & Pugh, The Master of Hell's Gates, 227. The Alfred, Tue 6 Jan 1835, 3; Trove 252592544.

58 Purchase from James Spicer, 20 Apr 1836, Land Grants 1788–1963, Registers of Memorials, 1820–36; ancestry.com. SRNSW, Reels 1581 & 1582, Series 12992, 7 Sep 1839.

59 JK Kinghorne to AS Kinghorne, 20 Jun 1836.

60 Referred to as Alexander III, to distinguish him from his father and grandfather.

61 Maxwell & Pugh, The Master of Hell's Gates, 227.

62 Monitor, Wed 16 Dec 1835, 4; Trove 32150310. Purchase gazetted 29 March 1836, Return of Land Sold during the Year 1836, Colonial Secretary's Papers 1822–1857, 324–5; and Registers of Land Grants and Leases 1792–1867, 10–11: ancestry.com. Assignment of lease, Raineville.

63 Maxwell & Pugh, The Master of Hell's Gates, 227–8.

64 H Kinghorne to AS Kinghorne, 26 October 1828.

65 JK Kinghorne to AS Kinghorne, 20 June 1836.

66 Hobart Town Courier, Fri 28 Aug 1835, 2; Trove 4179327. Sydney Herald, Thu 10 Sep 1835, 3; Trove 12853027.

67 JK Kinghorne to AS Kinghorne, 20 June 1836.

68 Sydney Gazette, Sat 3 Oct 1835, 2; Trove 2200483. Hobart Town Courier, Fri 4 Sep 1835, 3; Trove 4179121. William Moir appointed on 10 March 1836, under Colonial Architect Mortimer Lewis, as Foreman of Works at Sydney: Returns of the Colony 1822–57, SRNSW Series 1286, Colonial Engineer & Colonial Architect 1836, 96–7 & Colonial Architect 1840, 170–1; ancestry.com.

69 Sydney Gazette, Tue 21 Jun 1836, 3; Trove 2204986.

70 Historical Electoral Rolls, SRNSW CGS 1199, 1842–3 & 1844–45, Sydney Cook No. 154 Wooloomooloo & Sydney Cook, No. 157 Darlinghurst; ancestry.com.

71 Research by Val Kinghorne.

72 Maxwell & Pugh, *The Master of Hell's Gates*, 66–194.

73 Monitor, Mon 18 Sep 1837, 3; Trove 32157390. Sydney Herald, Mon 18 Sep 1837, 2; Trove 12861364.

74 Monitor, Wed 11 Oct 1837, 2; Trove 32157641. Sydney Gazette, Thu 12 Oct 1837, 3; Trove 2213411. Sydney Gazette, Thu 30 Dec 1841, 2; Trove 2555386. Sydney Herald, Mon 28 Mar 1842, 2; Trove 12874396.

75 CK Kinghorne to Miriam Chisholm, 4 March 1935. W Kinghorne to A Cameron, 18 Jul 1853.

76 Maxwell & Pugh, *The Master of Hell's Gates*, 228–32, 236–7.

77 Mitchell to FitzRoy, 15 Sep 1854.

78 Mitchell to FitzRoy, 15 Sep 1854.

79 Mitchell to FitzRoy, 15 Sep 1854. Pennington to Gannon, 26 Jul 1880. NSW Government Gazette Wed 10 Nov 1880, No 437, 5808; Trove 223698241.

80 Maxwell & Pugh, *The Merchant of Sydney*, 269–71.

81 Land Grants and Leases 1792–1867, 89, No. 77, 10 Sep 1841, ancestry.com.

82 Trove 225008596.

83 Register of Land Grants and Leases 1792–1867, Vol. 18, 50, 71/157; ancestry.com.

84 Kinghorne family papers.

85 Land Grants and Leases, Counties of King, Murray and St Vincent, 1839–1867, Vol. 18, 50, Nos. 170, 71, Folio 157, ancestry.com.

86 NSW Environment and Heritage, *Land and Soil Capability mapping of NSW*. NSW Parks and Wildlife, *Jervis Bay National Park*. Thom, *Coastal Geomorphology of the Jervis Bay Area*. Paix, *Field Geology of the Shoalhaven*.

87 Kinghorne, *Letter of an Australian Settler*, 21.

88 W Kinghorne to Kinghorne, 29 Oct 1839.

89 Beale et al., *Backhouse and Walker in Illawarra*, 97.

90 Crabb, *The Jervis Bay Region 1788 to 1939*, 24.

91 Kinghorne, *Letter of an Australian Settler*.

92 Prior, *Topographic map of Beecroft Peninsula*.

93 Staniforth, M., European-Indigenous contact at shore-based whaling sites, In: Veth et al., *Strangers on the Shore*, 126.

94 Zakharov, *Aboriginal Cultural Factors for the Jervis Bay Area*.

95 HLRV, 1873 Parish of Nowra.

96 MacLeay to Kinghorne, 20 Sep 1839.

97 Kinghorne to Moir, 7 Nov 1839.

98 Land Grants and Leases 1792–1867, 22, No. 75, ancestry.com.

99 Maxwell & Pugh, The Master of Hell's Gates, 259–60.

100 David Waugh to his mother, 20 Jul 1838: Sydney Monitor & Commercial Advertiser, Wed 14 Nov 1838, 2; Trove 32161874.

101 David Waugh to his sister Eliza and his mother, May and 15 Jul 1835, respectively: Sydney Monitor and Commercial Advertiser, Wed 14 Nov 1838, 2; Trove 32161874.

102 Sydney Herald, Mon 26 Mar 1838, 2; Trove 28653398.

103 https://www.christianstudylibrary.org/article/william-hamilton-pioneer-missionary-goulburn.

104 Wyatt, *Goulburn*, 412–3. Matheson, *Sowerby*.

105 Australian, Tue 19 Jun 1838, 2; Trove 36858611.

106 Australasian Chronicle, Tue 2 Jun 1840, 3; Trove 31728389.

107 Sydney Herald, Wed 9 Oct 1839, 1; Trove 28653813.

108 Commercial Journal and Advertiser, Sat 22 Feb 1840, 1; Trove 226455821.

109 Sydney Monitor & Commercial Advertiser, Fri 14 Feb 1840, 2; Trove 32167208.

Chapter 24: A Return to the Stronghold: Scotland and the Last Years of Alexander Kinghorne (1840–1847)

1 Kinghorne to Moir, 7 Nov 1839.

2 Kinghorne to AS Kinghorne, Mar 1824.

3 Kinghorne to AS Kinghorne, 5 Jul 1839.

4 Census record 1841, Jane Kinghorne: ScotlandsPeople. Birth of Alexander (Alick) Kinghorne, Galashiels, 4 Sep 1840: ScotlandsPeople.

5 Sale: Memorial No. 295, SRNSW 41492_330035-00251; ancestry.com. Grant: SRNSW 41492_330475-00793; ancestry.com.

6 MacLeay to Kinghorne, 20 Sep 1839.

7 Kinghorne to Moir, 7 Nov 1839. W Kinghorne to Kinghorne, 25 July 1842.

8 Lord to Kinghorne, 25 Dec 1839.

9 Monitor, Mon 3 Mar 1840, 4; Trove 32167599. Australian, Tue 24 March 1840, 2; Trove 36861049.

10 https://www.geni.com/projects/Trusty-Ship-Colonists-to-South-Australia-in–1838/38972. https://www.pioneerssa.org.au/files/MRAS%20Ship%20Voyage%20Data.pdf.

11 https://collections.rmg.co.uk/collections/objects/385632.html. https://www.southaustralianhistory.com.au/geppscross.htm.

12 The Asiatic Journal and Monthly Register for British and Foreign India, China, and Australasia, Vol. 33, New Series, September-December 1840, London: Wm H. Allen and Co, 1840, 169.

13 Leith and London Smacks, London and Leith Steam Packets, several advertise-

ments: Scottish Post Office Directory, 1839–40. It is not possible to determine the exact date or mode of travel, as NAUK holds internal passenger manifests from 1890 only.

14 Kyle to Kinghorne, 12 Nov 1840. Pigot's Directory 1837, 80. Kyle was a land surveyor and partner in Kyle & Frew, Glasgow: http://www.scottisharchitects.org.uk/architect_full.php?id=205764.

15 See The Family Tree of the Brockies of Dryburgh.

16 Scottish Post Office Directory, 1860 indicates 'house, 12 Broughton Street'.

17 I Brockie to W Kinghorne, 19 Dec 1873.

18 Alexander Kinghorne, 1841 census record: ScotlandsPeople 775/2/9, 'Patten Street, Galashiels', 10 of 57. Andrew Seton Kinghorne, 1841 census record: ScotlandsPeople 775/1/3, 'Oald Town Galashiels', 3 of 17. William 'the Baron' Brown: Hall, *History of Galashiels*, 383.

19 W Kinghorne to Kinghorne, 25 July 1842.

20 Fairfax to Kinghorne, 26 Mar 1844.

21 W Kinghorne to Kinghorne, 25 July 1842.

22 Bank draft 4 Aug 1841.

23 https://en.wikipedia.org/wiki/European_Potato_Failure. https://en.wikipedia.org/wiki/Economic_history_of_the_United_Kingdom#19th_century.

24 James, *Rise and Fall of the British Empire*, 172.

25 Hall, *History of Galashiels*, 295, 341.

26 Mudie, *His Majesty's Visit to Scotland*.

27 Gill, Robert, *Deposition of Robert Gill of Galashiels*.

28 Hall, *History of Galashiels*, 564.

29 Caledonian Mercury, Mon 11 Mar 1844, 1; gale.com.

30 Schobert, *Energy and Society*, 92.

31 Hall, *History of Galashiels*, 114–6, 123–4, 355.

32 AS Kinghorne to J Kinghorne, 28 Mar 1847.

33 Hall, *History of Galashiels*, 396–7.

34 Hall, *History of Galashiels*, 100, 121–4, 577.

35 Hall, *History of Galashiels*, 495–6.

36 AS Kinghorne to H Moir, 26 Feb 1844.

37 Bank draft 4 Aug 1841.

38 Hall, *History of Galashiels*, 496.

39 Hall, *History of Galashiels*, 483.

40 Bank of Australia ML MSS 1951/1 Item II fol. 7, 3X, 7; 1951/4 Item 6; & 1951/11 Item 17. Maxwell & Pugh, *The Master of Hell's Gates*, 230–4.

41 RCAHMS, *St Patrick Square, Edinburgh*.

42 Kinghorne to AS Kinghorne, 6 Nov 1843.

43 Kinghorne to AS Kinghorne, 3 Dec 1843.

44 Hall, *History of Galashiels*, 133, 136, 148.

45 Kinghorne to AS Kinghorne, 17 Dec 1843.

46 AS Kinghorne to H Moir, 26 Feb 1844. James Moir WS, Solicitor, Banker, Clerk to the Harbour Trustees, and Factor to the Right Hon. The Earl of Mar & Kellie,

lived in Bank Street Alloa, Clackmannanshire: Slater's Commercial Directory of Scotland, 618. Estate of James Moir, NSW Government Gazette, March-April 1890; ancestry.com.

47 AS Kinghorne to H Moir, 26 Feb 1844.

48 AS Kinghorne to J Kinghorne, 28 Mar 1847.

49 See Chapter 10, The Maxton Estate.

50 Burke, *The Peerage*, 384.

51 Fairfax to Kinghorne, 26 Mar 1844. Sir Henry Fairfax (1790–1860), Bart: Dod, *Peerage, Baronetage, and Knightage*, 239.

52 See Chapter 10, The Roxburghe Succession Dispute.

53 The Duke of Roxburghe owned 'Half of the Lands in Maxton, which [had] belonged to Sir Alexander Don, and part of Torwoodlee's half' of the same. Landrolls for Roxburghshire, Vol. 5, 1813: ScotlandsPlaces E106/29/5/57, 55–56.

54 13, 15 and 21 Aug only: Sydney Morning Herald, Thu 13 Aug 1846, 3; Trove 12889108.

55 Bathurst properties passed to James, William and John Ker Kinghorne on Alexander Jnr's death in 1847.

56 Will of Alexander Kinghorne.

57 AS Kinghorne to J Kinghorne, 28 Mar 1847.

58 Robert Haldane and his brother-in-law Richard Lees, Galashiels legal partnership: Hall, *History of Galashiels*, 483–4, 487.

59 Kinghorne's Scott, *The Monastery*, 20: Footnote to Scott's mention of 'the family of De Haga'.

60 The authors visited Dryburgh Abbey in 2014 and 2016, conducting a careful search of all the surviving graves and graveyard records on both occasions.

Chapter 25: The Legacy of Alexander Kinghorne

1 For a full discussion of Scott and the historical novel, see Duncan, Ian, *Walter Scott and the Historical Novel*, in Garside & O'Brien, *Oxford History of the Novel in English*.

2 Chapter 15, Alexander Kinghorne's Coat of Arms.

3 Chapter 6, Gossip and dry humour.

4 Chapter 23.

5 Chapter 23, A romance, a shipwreck and a marriage.

6 Chapter 4, The Division of Labour on the Estate.

7 Chapter 5, The Park Rents.

8 Chapter 4, Tenancies and Inheritance.

9 Chapter 22, Supreme Court Assessor.

10 Chapter 23, Pastoral Expansion.

11 Maxwell & Pugh, *The Master of Hell's Gates*, 261.

12 Kinghorne, *Letter of an Australian Settler*.

13 Chapter 4, Thou man of wond'rous ken.

14 Chapter 1 The Kinghornes of Greenlaw, Gordon and Kelso.

15 For example, Hibernian Subscription Fund, Minister of Scot's Church Bathurst: Sydney Gazette, Tue 17 Sep 1833, 3; Trove 2213925.

16 Sydney Gazette, Sat 16 Jul 1836, Trove 2205487.

17 Chapter 22, Something Strange.

18 Sydney Gazette, Tue 8 Jan 1833, 3; Trove 2210251.

19 Chapter 12, The Glasgow to Berwick Railway.

20 Chapter 15 The Plans of Roxburghshire and Selkirkshire.

21 Chapter 19, The Map of Emu Plain.

22 Chapter 19, Bonnyrigg House; Thorpe, *Bonnyrigg House*, 8.

23 Scott, *Marmion*, Introduction to Canto First.

Appendix 1: Alexander Kinghorne's Key Contacts (1770 ff)

1 A: Senior aristocracy (Barons, Viscounts, Earls, Marquesses or Dukes); B: Minor aristocracy (baronets or hereditary lairds); C: gentry (parliamentarians, senior public servants, landowners, clergy); C-D: prominent scientists, engineers and professional people; D: feu tenants (inherited tenancies), factors, local business-men and senior tradespeople; E: hynds (skilled farmworkers hired annually by roup); F: sub-tenants, farm workers and servants.

2 Kinghorne's Scott, *The Monastery*.

3 Scholars of Lancelot Whale.

4 Spence, *Autobiography*.

Appendix 2: Select List of Alexander Kinghorne's Surveying, Architectural and Engineering Works

1 Kinghorne to Seton Karr, 2 Mar 1800: NRAS2970, B 67.

2 Journal of work at Kippilaw, 17 Mar – 16 Apr 1800: NRAS2970, B 65. Sketch of a Lodge and front gate for Kippilaw, 18 May 1800: NRAS2970, B 65.

3 Plan of the Stables at Kippilaw, 1800: NRAS2970, B 65. Kinghorne to Seton Karr, 10 Jan, 14 Feb, 2 March 1800: NRAS2970, B 67. Kinghorne to Seton Karr, 16 Mar, plus diagram of the coach house: NRAS2970, B 67.

4 See Chapter 4, Thou Man of Wond'rous ken.

5 Kinghorne to Seton Karr, 23 Apr 1803, NRAS2970, B 11.

6 Chalmers, *Caledonia*. Chalmers to Seton Karr, 23 Sep 1801: NRAS2970, B 114.

7 Kinghorne to Seton Karr, 10 Jul 1803: NRAS2970, B 11.

8 Kinghorne to Seton Karr, 9 Mar 1803: NRAS2970, B 11.

9 Cruft et al., *The Buildings of Scotland*, 60, 323–324.

10 Kinghorne to Seton Karr, 9 Feb 1805: NRAS2970, B 14.

11 Kinghorne, *Plan of Netherton and Muirside*, cartography.

12 Kinghorne to Seton Karr, 9 May 1806: NRAS2970, B 102.

13 See Chapter 9, The Renovation of the Mansion House at Kippilaw (1807–1811).

14 Kinghorne, *Plan of Newbigging*. Kinghorne to Seton Karr 13 Mar 1808, NRAS2970, B 104.

15 Chisholm, *Sir Walter Scott as Judge*, 126–127.

16 Telford to Seton Karr, 29 Aug 1809: NRAS2970, B 45. Kinghorne, *Letter of an Australian Settler*. Telford, *Report by Mr Telford*, 1–19. Kinghorne & Telford, *Plan of Glasgow to Berwick Railway*.

17 Chisholm, *Sir Walter Scott as Judge*, 134–135.

18 Kinghorne, *Plan of the Estate of Wester Eccles*. Hume, *Decisions of the Court of Session*, Nicholas Brown vs. James Kyd, 700–1.

19 Kinghorne to Seton Karr, 6 Jan 1811: NRAS2970, B 105. Rennie, *Plan of a proposed Line of Iron Railway*.

20 Kinghorne, Plan of the farm of Faugh-hill.

21 Chisholm, *Sir Walter Scott as Judge*, 195.

22 Hewitt, *Plan of the County of Roxburgh*. Thomson, *Atlas of Scotland*, vii. Taylor to Kinghorne, 2 Aug 1823.

23 Kinghorne, *Selkirkshire to St Boswells Green*, 229.

24 Kinghorne, *Selkirkshire to St Boswells Green*, 229.

25 Kinghorne, *Plan of the Estate of Linthill*.

26 Kinghorne, *Weights and Measures*.

27 Kinghorne, *Plan of Selkirkshire*. Thomson, *Atlas of Scotland*, vii.

28 Kinghorne, *Plan of Emu Plains 1826*.

29 Kinghorne to MacLeay, 15 May 1826, 2819: INX-45-274, SRNSW 4/1960.

30 The Colonist, Sat 2 Jun 1838, 2; Trove 31721072.

31 Jackson and Aird to Kinghorne, 13, 15 Feb, 22, 23, 24 Mar 1826, SRNSW 4/346, 147, 149, 151, 153, 155.

32 https://fairfieldlocalstudies.wordpress.com/page/3/.

Bibliography

Abbreviations, which appear in the Notes, are shown for the first time here in [bold].

PRIMARY SOURCES

Australian Archives

Archives of the Goulburn & District Historical Society, St Clair

The Author of 'Waverley', *The Monastery, A Romance*, Archibald Constable and John Ballantine: Edinburgh, 1822, R1141-A3 (extensively annotated by Alexander Kinghorne) [**Kinghorne's Scott, Monastery**].

Archives of Tasmania

Shipping arrivals and departures: AOT CUS33/1/3, 199; AOT Microfilm Roll 88, Class and Piece Number HO11/5, 41 (22); AOT Microfilm Roll 89, Class and Piece Number HO11/6, 204.

Théodore Constantini, Convict Record: AOT Microfilm Roll 88, Class and Piece Number HO11/5, 41 (22); https://convictrecords.com.au/convicts/constantine/theodore/114838 [**Constantini, Convict Record**].

Butler to Colonial Secretary, AOT CO Index to Correspondence records 1824–1836 A-H, 5568 [**Butler to Colonial Secretary**].

Author's (Chis Maxwell) Collection of Family Documents

Letters

Alexander Kinghorne to Major General Sir Herbert Taylor, Military Secretary to HRH Duke of York, 28 May 1821, 28 May 1821 [**Kinghorne to Taylor, 28 May 1821**].

Sir Thomas Brisbane to Lord Buchan, 30 Aug 1822, Alexander Kinghorne's original copy; also ML C133, CY 1650 [**Brisbane to Buchan, 30 Aug 1822**].

Lord Buchan to Alexander Kinghorne, 28 Dec 1822, small hand-written note [**Buchan to Kinghorne, 28 Dec 1822**].

Ebenezer Faichney to Miss Elizabeth Margaret Kinghorn, 29 Jul 1823 [**Buchan to Miss E Kinghorne, 29 Jul 1823**].

Major General Sir Herbert Taylor, Military Secretary to HRH Duke of York, to Alexander Kinghorne, 2 Aug 1823 [**Taylor to Kinghorne, 2 Aug 1823**].

Lord Buchan to Miss Elizabeth Margaret Kinghorn, 18 August 1823, small hand-written note [**Buchan to Miss E Kinghorne, 18 August 1823**].

Lord Buchan to the Misses Kinghorne, 10 August 1823 [**Buchan to the Misses Kinghorne, 10 August 1823**].

Alexander Kinghorne to Andrew Seton Kinghorne, Mar 1824 [**Kinghorne to AS Kinghorne, Mar 1824**].

Alexander Kinghorne to Andrew Seton Kinghorne, 5 Apr 1824 [**Kinghorne to AS Kinghorne, 5 Apr 1824**].

Lord Buchan to Andrew Seton Kinghorne, 9 Nov 1824 [**Buchan to A.S. Kinghorne, 9 Nov 1824**].

Alexander MacLeay to Alexander Kinghorne, 9 Jun 1827, No. 5805 [**MacLeay to Kinghorne, 9 Jun 1827**].

Helen Kinghorne to Andrew Seton Kinghorne, 26 Oct 1828 [**H Kinghorne to AS Kinghorne, 26 Oct 1828**].

John Ker Kinghorne to Alexander Kinghorne, 20 Feb 1832 [**JK Kinghorne to Kinghorne, 20 Feb 1832**].

John Ker Kinghorne to Andrew Seton Kinghorne, 26 Jun 1836 [**JK Kinghorne to AS Kinghorne, 26 Jun 1836**].

Alexander Kinghorne to Andrew Seton Kinghorne, 5 Jul 1839 [**Kinghorne to AS Kinghorne, 5 Jul 1839**].

Alexander MacLeay to Alexander Kinghorne, 20 Sep 1939 [**MacLeay to Kinghorne, 20 Sep 1839**].

William Kinghorne to Alexander Kinghorne, 29 Oct 1839 [**W Kinghorne to Kinghorne, 29 Oct 1839**].

Alexander Kinghorne to William Moir, 7 Nov 1839 [**Kinghorne to Moir, 7 Nov 1839**].

Edward Lord to Alexander Kinghorne, 25 Dec 1839 [**Lord to Kinghorne, 25 Dec 1839**].

Thomas Kyle to Alexander Kinghorne, 12 Nov 1840 [**Kyle to Kinghorne, 12 Nov 1840**].

Bank draft from William Moir to Alexander Kinghorne, 4 Aug 1841 [**Bank draft 4 Aug 1841**].

William Kinghorne to Alexander Kinghorne, 25 Jul 1842, 'Rec^d 9 Jan 1843' [**W Kinghorne to Kinghorne, 25 Jul 1842**].

Alexander Kinghorne to Andrew Seton Kinghorne, 6 Nov 1843 [**Kinghorne to AS Kinghorne, 6 Nov 1843**].

Alexander Kinghorne to Andrew Seton Kinghorne, 3 Dec 1843 [**Kinghorne to AS Kinghorne, 3 Dec 1843**].

Alexander Kinghorne to Andrew Seton Kinghorne, 17 Dec 1843 [**Kinghorne to AS Kinghorne, 17 Dec 1843**].

Andrew Seton Kinghorne to Mrs Helen Moir, 26 Feb 1844 [**AS Kinghorne to H Moir, 26 Feb 1844**].

Sir Henry Fairfax to Alexander Kinghorne, 26 Mar 1844 [**Fairfax to Kinghorne, 26 Mar 1844**].

Andrew Seton Kinghorne to James Kinghorne, 28 Mar 1847 [**AS Kinghorne to J Kinghorne, 28 Mar 1847**].

Isabella Brockie to William Kinghorne, 19 Dec 1873 [**I Brockie to W Kinghorne, 19 Dec 1873**].

William Kinghorne to Andrew Cameron, 18 Jul 1853 [**W Kinghorne to A Cameron, 18 Jul 1853**].

Sir Thomas Mitchell to Sir Charles FitzRoy, 15 Sep 1854 Kinghorne Estate papers to Stephen Lawrence & Jacques, Nov 1884, William Alexander Chisholm Papers [**Mitchell to Fitzroy, 15 Sep 1854**].

Pennington to John Gannon, 26 Jul 1880: Kinghorne Estate papers to Stephen Lawrence & Jacques, Nov 1884, William Alexander Chisholm Papers [**Pennington to Gannon, 26 Jul 1880**].

Charles Kerr Kinghorne, *Goonumburrah*, Lydhurst, NSW to Miriam Chisholm, 4 March 1935: [**CK Kinghorne to Miriam Chisholm, 4 March 1935**].

Documents and Maps

Kinghorne, *Plan of the Estate of Linthill*, 1820.

Hewitt, *Plan of Roxburghshire*, 1822.

Kinghorne, *Plan of Selkirkshire*, 1824.

1 January 1838, Thomas Inglis Esquire by direction of the Manager of the

Australian Comp^y of Edinburgh to Alexander Kinghorne Es^q, Assignment of lease of 500 years in an Estate called Raineville [**Assignment of lease, Raineville**].

'Last will and testament of Alexander Kinghorne Senior Esquire a Magistrate of the territory of New South Wales', 1 Mar 1840, Office Copy 19 Mar 1880. Also: Alexander Kinghorne, 12 October 1840, Wills and Testaments: ScotlandsPeople SC63/34/4, Selkirk Sheriff Court, 422–35 [**Will of Alexander Kinghorne**].

Land and Property Information, NSW Office

Land and Property, Parish and historical maps, HLRV, 1873 Parish of Nowra map; http://images.maps.nsw.gov.au/pixel.htm# [**HLRV, 1873 Parish of Nowra**].

Mitchell Library, State Library of NSW

Macleay Papers, SLNSW ML MSS A4300.

Mitchell, TL, *Sir Thomas Mitchell field note and sketchbook*, 21 May 1828–3 Aug 1830: ML C42. [**Diary of Thomas Mitchell, SLNSW, ML MSS C42**]. Bank of Australia ML MSS 1951/1 Item II fol. 7, 3X, 7; 1951/4 Item 6; & 1951/11 Item 17 [**Bank of Australia ML MSS 1951/1**].

National Library of Australia

Miriam Chisholm Papers, NLA MS6207 (Series [**S**] 1 to 8, Folders [**F**] 1–103; 19 document boxes [**B**], 3 Folio boxes [**FB**]) [**NLA MS6207**].

NSW Surveyor General, *Faithfull Family Collection of maps and plans relating to Parish of Quialigo, County of Argyle*, c. 1839–79; https://trove.nla.gov.au/work/158985580?q&versionId=173311807 [**NSW Surveyor General, Faithfull Family Collection of maps**].

State Archives of New South Wales

Apart from those below, citations appear in the Notes as **SRNSW**, *followed by item/serial numbers, reels and images as appropriate. These listings are exclusive of citations to ancestry.com*

Clergy and School Lands Corporation, Minutes of the Accounts of the Orphan School, SRNSW 4/400 [**CSLC Minutes 4/400**].

Clergy and School Lands Corporation, Trustees of the Clergy and School Lands, Proceedings of Committees: NRS–771, 02-05–1826 to 11-08–1830, SRNSW 4/292 [**CSLC Proceedings 4/292**].

Clergy and School Lands Corporation, Correspondence received from Architects and Mechanics 1825–28, SRNSW 4/346 [**CSLC Correspondence 4/346**].

Clergy and School Lands Corporation, Kinghorne, *Journal of Time Devoted to Services of The Corporation of Clergy and School Lands*, 23 June 1826, SRNSW 4/346 [**Kinghorne, CSLC Journal**].

OVERSEAS ARCHIVES

Haverfordwest Archives, Pembrokeshire, Wales

Castlemartin Hundred Land Tax Assessments, 25 March 1816 – 25 March 1819, Haverfordwest Archives, Ref. 23-C-5 [**Castlemartin land tax**].

Institute of Civil Engineers, London

Thomas Telford to Andrew Little, from Portsmouth, 23 Jul 1784 [**Telford to Little, 23 Jul 1784**].

National Archives of the United Kingdom

Cited in the Notes as **NAUK**, followed by the Reference and other details as appropriate.

The National Archives of Scotland

Hewitt, N.T., Plan of The County of Roxburgh, With Pictorial Engravings Of Jedburgh Abbey And Melrose Abbey Church, Edinburgh: John Thomson & Co., 1822; from Records of Strathern and Blair, WS, solicitors, Edinburgh (GD314), The National Records of Scotland RHP93849 [**Hewitt, *Plan of Roxburghshire***]. Original print in the author's collection.

Johnstone, William (drawer), Plan of Selkirkshire, attested by Rt. Hon. Lord Napier, Thomas Mitchell, road surveyor, Alexander Kinghorne, civil engineer and James Kinghorne, land surveyor, Edinburgh: John Thomson and Co., 1824; *National Register of Archives for Scotland,* NRAS2176/3/4, Old Gala Club, Galashiels, 1666–1959; http://maps.nls.uk/view/74400148 Napier, William, 9th Lord Napier: http://en.wikipedia.org/wiki/William_Napier,_9th_Lord_Napier [**Kinghorne, *Plan of Selkirkshire***]. Original print in author's collection.

Josias Jessop to William Scott of Maxpoffle, 12 Nov 1824, National Records of Scotland, Scott of Raeburn Papers 1550–1853: NRAS GD 104/281, Business and Family Letters, Box 7, Bundle 5 [**Jessop to William Scott, 12 Nov 1824**].

Kinghorne, Plan of the Estate of Linthill and Midlem Mill in the County of Roxburgh, 1820, NRAS SC 1524405 [**Kinghorne, *Plan of Linthill***].

Kinghorne, Alexander, Plan of the lands of Netherton and Muirside belonging to the Right Hon[ble]Lord Minto, 1806, Surveyor: Alexander Kinghorne, National Archives of Scotland, NRAS Reference RHP3548 [**Kinghorne, *Plan of Netherton and Muirside***].

Kinghorne, Alexander, Plan of Newbigging, surveyed by Alexander Kinghorne, 1808: National Register of Archives for Scotland, NRAS722.28, Marquess of Lothian (Monteviot), 1771–1959 [**Kinghorne, *Plan of Newbigging***].

Kinghorne, Plan of the farm of Faugh-hill. Photograph of the original plan by Alexander Kinghorne supplied from the Floors Castle Archives by His Grace the 10th Duke of Roxburghe [**Kinghorne, *Plan of the farm of Faugh-hill***].

Kinghorne, Alexander, and Telford, Thomas, *Plans and sections of a proposed cast-iron railway from Glasgow to Berwick-upon-Tweed, 1810*, 'A plan of continuation of the line of the Berwick and Glasgow railway surveyed by A Kinghorne for T Telford' and 'Plan of part of the proposed rail road from Berwick and Glasgow surveyed under the direction of Thomas Telford by Alex[r] Kinghorne', 1810, National Archives of Scotland, NRAS RHP9652 & RHP97762, sighted by the authors April 2014 at Thomas Thomson House, Edinburgh. [**Kinghorne & Telford, *Plan of Glasgow to Berwick Railway***].

Kinghorne, Alexander, Engineer: [John] Rennie; Engraver: J. Barlow, [London] *Plan of a proposed line of iron railway from Kelso to Berwick*, c. 1810: NRAS RHP22529, sighted by the authors April 2014 at Thomas Thomson House, Edinburgh [**Kinghorne & Rennie, *Plan of the Kelso to Berwick Railway***].

Kinghorne, Alexander, *Papers about Weights and Measures*, 1821: Bundle marked 'Papers about Weights and Measures.' Miscellaneous papers, 1820's, including copy report by Mr. Alexander Kinghorne, Civil Engineer, relating to the weights and measures of the Burgh of Selkirk, 1821: Veitch family, of Inchbonny, Jedburgh, 17th century – 19th century, National Register of Archives for Scotland, NRAS337/80 [**Kinghorne, *Weights and Measures***].

Kinghorne, Alexander, Plan of the Estate of (Wester) Eccles, NRAS GB234, RHP3365, sighted by the authors April 2014 at Thomas Thomson House, Edinburgh [**Kinghorne, *Plan of Wester Eccles***].

Notice of Railway Meeting, Melrose, 20th December 1824, National Records of Scotland, Scott of Raeburn Papers 1550–1853: NRAS GD 104/281, Business and Family Letters, Box 7, Bundle 5. [**Notice of Railway Meeting**].

Presbytery and kirk session records for Scotland, NRAS CH2/484 [**NRAS Kirk Session Records**].

Rennie, John, *Report Respecting the Proposed Rail-Way from Kelso to Berwick*, Kelso: Printed by A. Ballantyne, 1810, 3–13; http://books. google.com.au/books?id=l7k5AQAAMAAJ&pg=PA3&lpg=PA3&d-q=Report+on+Berwick+and+Kelso+Railway+Rennie&source=bl&ots=_ QSNSG5cpl&sig=PCXbMHHhB88u7pC90LdpEjQq2-0&hl=en&sa=X-&ei=sDcdVLKZOpbs8AW-koLgBQ&ved=0CDoQ6AEwBA#v=onep-age&q=Kinghorn&f=false [**Rennie, *Report Respecting Proposed Rail-Way from Kelso to Berwick, 1810***].

Ordnance Survey of Galashiels, Selkirk & Melrose, St Boswells & Lauder, 1:25 000 scale, Explorer Map No. 338, Edition A1, revised 2001. Sighted by the authors at Thomas Thomson House, Edinburgh, April 2014 [**OS Galashiels, Selkirk, Melrose, St Boswells & Lauder**].

Pringle, James of Torwoodlee to Scott, William of Maxpoffle, 23 Dec 1824; National Records of Scotland, Scott of Raeburn Papers 1550–1853: NRAS GD 104/281, Business and Family Letters, Box 7, Bundle 5 [**Pringle to Scott, 23 Dec 1824**].

Scholars of Lancelot Whale at Kelso Grammar School 1784–1788; National Records of Scotland, Scott of Raeburn Papers 1550–1853, Business and Family Letters: NRAS GD104/281, Box 7, Bundle 9 [**Kelso Grammar, 1784–1788**].

Seton Karr of Kippilaw Papers, NRAS2970/bundles (Full citations appear in the Notes as **NRAS2970**, followed by the bundle [**B**] numbers).

Scott of Harden, Hugh to William Scott of Maxpoffle, 26 Dec 1824, National Records of Scotland, Scott of Raeburn Papers 1550–1853, Business and Family Letters: NRAS GD104/281, Box 7, Bundle 5. [**Hugh Scott to William Scott, 26 Dec 1824**].

Telford, Thomas, *Report by Mr Telford, relative to the proposed Railway from Glasgow to Berwick-upon-Tweed; with Mr Jessop's opinion thereon; and Minutes of a Meeting of the General and Sub-committees, held 4th April 1810*, Edinburgh: Printed by A. Neill & Co., 1810, pp. 1–19, BR/LIB/S/9/46 [**Telford, *Report by Mr Telford***].

The National Portrait Gallery, London

Doyle, John ('HB'), *Lineal descent of the Crown* (Cartoon of William Cobbett; Joseph Hume; Daniel O'Connell; Charles Grey, 2nd Earl Grey) NPG D41144, lithograph, 28 Jun 1832: https://www.npg.org.uk/collections/search/portrait/mw209674 [**Doyle, *Cobbett, Hume, O'Connell & Grey*, NPG D4114**].

Doyle, John ('HB'), *Incubation Extraordinary* (Cartoon of Joseph Hume; Daniel O'Connell; Sir Robert Peel, 2nd Bt), NPG D41315, lithograph, 17 Mar 1835: https://www.npg.org.uk/collections/search/portrait/mw215015 [**Doyle, *Hume, O'Connell & Peel*, NPG 41315**].

The Welcome Collection, University of London

Doyle, John ('HB'), *Daniel O'Connell and Joseph Hume encourage a dog with the head of Gisborne to leap at a bear with the head of Francis Bruen perching on a pole*, Welcome Library No. 36873i, Coloured lithograph, 30 Mar 1839, https://wellcomecollection.org/works/a679u276 [**Doyle, *O'Connell & Hume*, Welcome #36873i**].

OTHER PRIMARY SOURCES

Newspapers

Citations to Australian newspapers in the Notes are presented as the unique Trove number, which follows the URL identifier: http://trove.nla.gov.au/newspaper/article/. The articles can be accessed by copying this URL followed by the unique number into your search engine.

Australasian Chronicle (Sydney: 1839–1843): http://trove.nla.gov.au

Bathurst Free Press and Mining Journal (Bathurst: 1851–1904): http://trove.nla.gov.au

Bathurst Times (Bathurst: 1905–1925): http://trove.nla.gov.au

Caledonian Mercury (Scotland: 1720–): https://www.britishnewspaperarchive.co.uk/titles/caledonian-mercury

Chambers' Edinburgh Journal (Scotland: 1832–1844, 1854–1910): https://onlinebooks.library.upenn.edu/webbin/serial?id=chambersedinburgh

Colonial Times and Tasmanian Advertiser (Hobart: 1828–1857): http://trove.nla.gov.au

Launceston Advertiser (Tas: 1829–1846): http://trove.nla.gov.au

New South Wales Government Gazette (NSW: 1832–2001): http://trove.nla.gov.au

Tait's Edinburgh Magazine, Edinburgh: William Tait [Scotland: 1832–1861]: http://www.cse.psu.edu/~deh25/post/Timeline_files/Taits-Edinburgh-Magazine.html.

The Alfred (NSW: 1835–1835): http://trove.nla.gov.au

The Asiatic Journal and Monthly Register for British and Foreign India, China, and Australasia (East India Company: 1830–1843): https://www.univie.ac.at/Geschichte/China–Bibliographie/blog/2011/05/28/the–asiatic–journal–and–monthly–register–2nd–series–1830–1843/

The Australian (Sydney: 1824–1848): http://trove.nla.gov.au

The Cleaveland Gazette and Commercial Register (USA: 1818–1818): https://www.loc.gov/item/sn84028765/

The Commercial Journal and Advertiser (NSW: 1835–1840): http://trove.nla.gov.au

The Currency Lad (NSW: 1832–1833): http://trove.nla.gov.au

The Gleaner (NSW: 1827–1827): http://trove.nla.gov.au

The Hobart Town Courier (Tas: 1827–1839): http://trove.nla.gov.au

The Hobart Town Gazette and Van Diemen's Land Advertiser (Tas: 1816–1882): http://trove.nla.gov.au

The New Yorker Magazine (USA: 1925–): https://www.newyorker.com/archive

The Perth Gazette and Western Australian Journal (WA: 1833–1833): http://trove.nla.gov.au

The Scots Magazine (Scotland: 1739–1826): https://www.britishnewspaperarchive.co.uk/titles/the–scots–magazine

The Sydney Gazette and New South Wales Advertiser (NSW: 1803–1842): http://trove.nla.gov.au

The Sydney Mail (NSW: 1860–1871): http://trove.nla.gov.au

The Sydney Monitor (NSW: 1828–1838): http://trove.nla.gov.au

The Sydney Monitor and Commercial Advertiser (NSW: 1838–1838): http://trove.nla.gov.au

The Sydney Morning Herald (NSW: 1842–1854): http://trove.nla.gov.au

On-line Genealogical & Research Resources

Ainslie, Marilyn, genealogical website: www.ainslie.org.uk [**www.ainslie.org.uk**].

Ancestry.com: https://ancestry.co.uk [**ancestry.com**].

BBC Home page: www.bbc.co.uk [**www.bbc.co.uk**].

British Weather from 1700 to 1849: booty.org.uk [**booty.org.uk**].

Bureau of Meteorology, Sydney, historical weather statistics: http://www.bom.gov.au/climate/data-services/station-data.shtml [**BOM, historical weather statistics**].

Canmore, National Record of the Historic Environment, Scotland: canmore. org.uk [**Canmore**].

Chis Maxwell and Alex Pugh website: www.chismaxwell.com [**Authors' website**].

Convict Records of Australia, 1787–1867: convictrecords.com.au [**Convict Records of Australia**].

Dictionary of Scottish Architects: www.scottisharchitects.org.uk [**Dictionary of Scottish Architects**].

Electric Scotland: electricscotland.com [**Electric Scotland**].

Fairfield City Library Heritage blog: fairfieldlocalstudies.wordpress.com [**Fairfield Heritage**].

FamilySearch, Scotland, Births and Baptisms, 1564–1950, Scotland, Marriages, 1561–1910; https://familysearch.org [**FamilySearch**].

Family Tree Maker user trees: familytreemaker.genealogy [**Family Tree Maker**].

Find and Connect website: www.findandconnect.gov.au [**Find and Connect**].

FindMyPast: http://search.findmypast.com.au/search/ [**FindMyPast**].

Gale, Scholarly Resources for Learning and Research, Newspaper Database: gale.com [**gale.com**].

Google Books: books.google.com.au [**Google Books**].

Grace's Guide UK: www.gracesguide.co.uk [**Grace's Guide UK**].

Hansard, 1803–2005: hansard.millbanksystems.com [**Hansard, 1803–2005**].

Hansard, 1803–2005: api.parliament.uk/historic-hansard [**Historic Hansard, 1803–2005**].

Hawick Heritage Hub blog: www.voyageofthevampire.org.uk [**Hawick Heritage Hub**].

Historic Environment Scotland: www.historic-scotland.gov.uk [**Historic Environment Scotland**].

House of Commons Hansard archives (1803–2005): https://www. parliament.uk/business/publications/hansard/commons/ [**House of Commons Hansard archives**].

Savills' property archive: farmsandestatessearch.savills.co.uk [**Savills' UK property archive**].

Legal Dictionary, West's Encyclopedia of American Law: legal-dictionary. thefreedictionary.com [**West's Legal Dictionary**].

Lundy, Daryl, The Peerage, a genealogical survey of the peerage of Britain as well as the royal families of Europe, 2019: www.thepeerage.com [**The Perrage**].

Moffat, Roger, geneaological web site: testing.lisaandroger.com [**Roger Moffat genealogy**].

National Library of Australia Electronic Resources: https://catalogue.nla. gov.au [**NLA Electronic Resources**].

NSW Courts and Tribunals: www.courts.justice.nsw.gov.au [**NSW Courts and Tribunals**].

Newspaper Archive 1607–2020: newspaperarchive.com [**newspaperarchive. com**].

Roberts Burns Country, the Robert Burns works archive: www.robertburns. org [**Robert Burns archive**].

Scotania website: www.scotiana.com [**Scotania**].

ScotlandsPeople, National Archives of Scotland, Old Parish Registers: Births & Baptisms, Banns & Marriages and Deaths & Burials; http://www. scotlandspeople.gov.uk [**ScotlandsPeople OPR**].

ScotlandsPeople, National Archives of Scotland, Wills and Testaments; http://www.scotlandspeople.gov.uk [**ScotlandsPeople Wills**].

ScotlandsPeople, National Archives of Scotland, 1841 Census Records; http://www.scotlandspeople.gov.uk [**ScotlandsPeople 1841 Census**].

ScotlandsPlaces, National Archives of Scotland, Land Tax Rolls for Roxburghshire and Berwickshire; http://www.scotlandsplaces.gov.uk [**ScotlandsPlaces, Call #**].

ScotlandsPlaces, National Archives of Scotland, Valuation Book for the County of Roxburghshire, 1803 & 1811: E106/29/4/41 & E106/29/5/4 [**ScotlandsPlaces, Call #**].

ScotlandPlaces, Roxburghshire Ordinance Survey Name Books, 1858–1860, Volume 38, Parish of St Boswells: OS1/29/38/23 & St Boswellsbank: OS1/29/38/37 [**ScotlandsPlaces, Call #**].

ScotlandPlaces, Royal Commission on the Ancient and Historical Monuments of Scotland (RCAHMS) Archives: https://scotlandsplaces.gov. uk/digital-volumes/rcahms-archives [**RCAHMS**].

Scottish Nature Heritage: www.snh.gov.uk [**Scottish Nature Heritage**].

Scottish Tourist Board: www.welcometoscotland.com [**Scottish Tourist Board**].

Spartacus Educational Encyclopedia: spartacus-educational.com [**Spartacus Encyclopedia**].

The Crocker Family archice: www.cocker.id.au [**Crocker family archive**].

The History of Parliament Online; http://www.historyof parliamentonline.org [**History of Parliament Online**].

The House of Seton family archive: www2.thesetonfamily.com [**Seton Family Archive**].

The Life and Times of Lord Byron, digital archive: lordbyron.cath.lib.vt.edu [**Lord Byron Archive**].

The Lost Isles of Darkness blog: lost.islesofdarkness.com [**Lost Isles**].

The Tatham Family of County Durham website: www.saxonlodge.net [**Tatham Family**].

Trove, National Library of Australia: trove.nla.gov.au [**Trove**].

Walter Scott Digital Archive: www.walterscott.lib.ed.ac.uk [**Walter Scott Archive**].

Wikipedia: https://en.wikipedia.org/wiki & http://www.wikiwand.com/en [**wikipedia, wikiwand**].

WikiVisually: wikivisually.com [**wikivisually**].

Directories

Hume, David, *Decisions of the Court of Sessions 1781–1822, in the Form of a Dictionary*, Edinburgh: William Blackwood, 1839 [**Hume, David, *Decisions of the Court of Sessions***].

Ministry of Labour of Great Britain, *A Dictionary of Occupational Terms Based on the Classification of Occupations used in the Census of Population, 1921*, 024, Agricultural Labourers; http://doot.spub.co.uk/code.php?value=024 [**Ministry of Labour, *A dictionary of Scottish Terms***].

Scottish Post Office Directory, 1839–40; https://digital.nls.uk/directories/browse/archive/85281678?mode=transcription [**Scottish Post Office Directory, 1839–40**].

Scottish Post Office Directory, 1860; https://digital.nls.uk/directories/browse/archive/83581446?mode=transcription [**Scottish Post Office

Directory, 1860].

Pigot's Commercial Directory of Scotland, London: J. Pigot & Co., 1837 [**Pigot's Directory 1837**].

Slater's Royal National Commercial Directory and Topography of Scotland; https://digital.nls.uk/directories/browse/archive/90195760?mode=transcription [**Slater's Commercial Directory**].

Published Papers of the House of Commons

(accessed from Google Books and Hansard)

House of Commons, Accounts and Papers 1830 [**HC 1830**].

House of Commons, Accounts and Papers 1831–2 [**HC 1831–2**].

House of Commons Debate 27 March 1833, Case of Captain Robison, Vol. 16, cc1142-8; https://api.parliament.uk/historic-hansard/commons/1833/mar/27/case-of-captain-robinson#S3V0016P0_18330327_HOC_16 [**HC 1833, Robison**].

House of Commons Select Committee 1835. Final debate and vote in House of Commons: Hansard, HC Debate 30 Jul 1835, Vol 29, cc1254-75, motion carried 55 to 47 151 [**Darling, *HC Select Committee, 30 Jul 1835***].

House of Commons Select Committee 1835, Report from Select Committee on the Conduct of General Darling while Governor of New South Wales, with the Minutes of Evidence, and Appendix, Examination of Captain R. Robison 21 Aug 1835, paragraph 490, 28 [**Darling, *HC Select Committee, 21 Aug 1835***].

House of Commons Select Committee 1835, Report from Select Committee on the Conduct of General Darling while Governor of New South Wales, with the Minutes of Evidence, and Appendix, 1 Sep 1835, Appendix 2, 151 [**Darling, *HC Select Committee, 1 Sep 1835***].

Books, Letters and other Documents

Bentley, Fran and Birmingham, J., *Penrith Lakes Development Scheme Regional Environental Study: History of Castlereagh*; Sydney, June 1982; http://nswaol.library.usyd.edu.au/data/pdfs/12925_ID_Bentley1982PenrithLakesEnvironmentalHrtgRpt.pdf [**Bently & Birmingham, *History of Castlereagh***].

Bigge, J.T., *Report of the Commissioner of Enquiry on the State of Agriculture and Trade in the Colony of NSW* (third report), 13 Mar 1823, SLNSW CO 201 PRO Reel 105; https://nla.gov.au/nla.obj-728220555 [**Bigge, *Report of the Commissioner of Enquiry***].

Blaikie Lang, Jean, *A Scottish Farmer's Ride Through England 100 Years Ago.* Selkirk: George Lewis and Co., 1906; https://scottishfarmer.files.wordpress.com/2016/08/scottish-farmers-ride-complete-scan.pdf [**Blaikie Lang, *A Scottish Farmer's Ride***].

Bower, John Junior, *Description of the Abbey's of Melrose and Old Melrose, with their traditions,* Kelso: Printed by Alexander Leadbetter, for the author, 1813 [**Bower, *Abbey's of Melrose and Old Melrose***].

Buchan, Lord, *Discourse delivered at a meeting for the purpose of promoting the institution of a Society for the investigation of the History of Scotland and its Antiquities,* November 14, 1778, Edinburgh: publisher unidentified, 1780 [**Buchan, *Discourse***], 23; gale.com.

Buchan, John, *Lord Minto, A Memoir,* 1924, Introduction; http://gutenberg.net.au/ebooks05/0500261h.html [**Buchan, *Lord Minto***].

Buckland, W., *Reliquiae Diluvianae, or, Observations on organic remains and on other geological phenomena attesting to the action of a Universal Deluge.* London: John Murray, 1824 [**Buckland, *Reliquiae Diluvianae***].

Burke, John, *Baronetage of Great Britain and Ireland, A Genealogical and Heraldic Dictionary of the Peerage and Baronetage of the British Empire,* 6th Edition, London: Henry Colburn, 1839 [**Burke, *Peerage***].

Burns, Robert, *The Poetical Works of Robert Burns, To Which is Prefixed a Sketch of his Life,* London: Printed for T. Caldwell and other Proprietors, 1822, 'On The Late Captain Grose's Peregrinations Thro' Scotland, Collecting The Antiquities Of That Kingdom [1789]' [**Burns, *The Poetical Works***].

Carre, William Riddell, *Border Memories; or, Sketches of Prominent Men and Women of the Border,* James Tait (ed.), Edinburgh: James Thin, South Bridge, 1876 [**Carre, *Border Memories***].

Chalmers, George, *Caledonia: or, a Historical and Topographical Account of North Britain from the Most Ancient to the Present Times,* Paisley: Alexander Gardner; Vol. 1, The Roman Period, 1887: http://archive.org/stream/caledoniaorhisto01chal#page/140/mode/2up [**Chalmers, *Caledonia*, Vol. 1**]; Vol 3, An Account of North Britain, 1888: http://archive.org/stream/caledoniaorhisto03chal#page/91/mode/1up [**Chalmers, *Caledonia*, Vol. 3**].

Chaterlay of Murray, Extract from Charterlary of Murray – Registium

Moravience, 131; cited in ancestry.co.uk. The authors have been unable to verify the source document referring to the Drybrugh branch of the Brockie family; https://www.ancestry.co.uk/mediaui-viewer/tree/23814725/person/1780056332/media/d7355951-a9fe-47de-9469-2283089ad734 [**Chaterlary of Murray**].

Chisholm, J.K., *Speeches and Reminiscences*, Sydney, Angus and Robertson, 1907 [**Chisholm, *Speeches and Reminiscences***].

Chisholm, John, K.C., *Sir Walter Scott as Judge, His Decisions in the Sheriff Court of Selkirk*, Edinburgh: W. Green and Son, 1918; https://archive.org/details/cu31924013545755 [**Chisholm, *Sir Walter Scott as Judge***].

Clarke, M.A.H., *Old tales of a young country*, Melbourne: Mason, Firth and McCutcheon, 1871, Chapter 8, Governor Ralph Darling's Iron Collar; http://adc.library.usyd.edu.au/data-2/p00069.pdf [**Clarke, *Old tales of a young country***].

Crawford, O. G. S., *Defensive Frontier-Dyke near Melrose, Antiquity,* Vol. 10, 1936, 346. RCAHMS, *An inventory of the ancient and historical monuments of Roxburghshire: with the fourteenth report of the Commission, 2v.* Edinburgh: RCAHMS, 1956, 71–73. National Library of Scotland, Ordnance Survey 1979 [**Crawford, *Defensive Frontier-Dyke near Melrose***].

Douglas, Christopher, *Parish of Kelso (County of Roxburgh)*, 1791–2, in: *The Statistical Account of Scotland*, 1791–1799, Sir John Sinclair (ed.), Vol. III, The Eastern Borders, Edinburgh: EP Publishing Limited, 1979 [**Douglas, Parish of Kelso**].

Doust, R.F. (compiler), Committee on the Australian Gaslight Company Bill, 1837/9, in: *New South Wales Legislative Council, 1824–1856, The Select Committees,* New South Wales Parliamentary Library, 2011 [**Doust, *The Select Committees***].

Douglas, Sir George, *A History of the Border Counties (Roxburgh, Selkirk, Peebles)*, Edinburgh and London: William Blackwood and Sons, 1849 [**Douglas, *A History of the Border Counties***].

Gill, Robert, *Deposition of Robert Gill of Galashiels*, House of Commons Papers, Great Britain. Reports from Commissioners: Sixteen Volumes. Constabulary; Criminal Law; Factories, Session 5 February – 27 August 1839, VOL. XIX., 1839, Factories: [155.] Reports of the Inspectors of Factories to Her Majesty's Principal Secretary of State for the Home Department for Half Year ending 31st December 1838, London: W. Clowes and Sons, 1839; Appendix No. I, Depositions of Witnesses not inserted in Mr. Stuart's Report [**Gill, Robert, *Deposition of Robert Gill of Galashiels***].

Grierson, Herbert, *Sir Walter Scott, Bart*, New York: Haskell House Publishers Ltd, 1938 [**Grierson, *Scott***].

Haig, James, *A Topographical and Historical Account of the Town of Kelso, and of the Town and Castle of Roxburgh*, Edinburgh: John Fairbairn, Waterloo Place, 1825 [**Haig, *Kelso***].

Hall, Edward Smith, Reply in Refutation of the Pamphlets of Lieut.-Gen. R. Darling, Late Governor of New South Wales, and Maj.-Gen. H.C. Darling, His Brother, Addressed by them to J. Hume, Esq. M.P. & Viscount Goderich, (Earl of Ripon,) Late Secretary of State for the Colonies, by Edward Smith Hall, Esq. Editor and Proprietor of the Sydney 'Monitor', London: Published by Benjamin Franklin, No. 378, Strand, 1832 [**Hall, *Refutation of Lieutenant-General Darling***].

Hall, Robert, *The History of Galashiels*, Galashiels: Alexander Walker, 1898 [**Hall, *History of Galashiels***].

House of Commons, Report on Petition from the Crinan Canal Company, 1804, in: Reports from Committees: eight volumes, Vol. 3, Caledonian and Crinan Canals; Church Leases; Fresh Fruits, Session 5 February-2 August 1839, Appendix No. 17, 211; http://books.google.com.au/books?id=5XFbAAAAQAAJ&pg=PA221&lpg=PA221&dq=David+Caldwell+Golden+Square&source=bl&ots=IzVf5Zvpxm&sig=4aYi92hpq9d-nb2zk0ahWh3WMywE&hl=en&sa=X&ei=Yh1DVJOsIcS7mgXuw4Dg-BA&ved=0CCsQ6AEwBA#v=onepage&q=John%20Seton%20Karr&f=false [**House of Commons, *Crinan Canal Company, 1804***].

Hueckel, Glenn, 'Relative Prices and Supply Response in English Agriculture during the Napoleonic Wars', *The Economic History Review*, Vol. 29, Issue 3, August 1976 [**Hueckel, *English Agriculture during the Napoleonic Wars***].

Hume, David, *Decisions of the Court of Session, 1781–1822*, Edinburgh: William Blackwood and Sons, 1839 [**Hume, *Decisions of the Court of Session***].

Hume, Joseph, House of Commons Debate 27 Mar 1833, Hansard, Vol. 16, cc1142-8; https://api.parliament.uk/historic-hansard/commons/1833/mar/27/case-of-captain-robinson#S3V0016P0_18330327_HOC_16 [**Hume, *House of Commons Debate 27 Mar 1833***].

Jeffrey, Alexander, *History and Antiquities of Roxburghshire*, Vol. III, Edinburgh: Thomas C. Jack, 1859; http://booksnow1.scholarsportal.info/ebooks/oca10/39/historyantiquiti03jeff/historyantiquiti03jeff_djvu.txt [**Jeffrey, *History and Antiquities of Roxburghshire***].

Jerdan, William, *Men I have Known*, London: George Routledge and Sons,

1866 [**Jerdan,** *Men I have Known*].

Jerdan, William, *The Autobiography of William Jerdan*, Volume 1, London: Arthur Hall Virtue & Co., 1852; http://lordbyron.cath.lib.vt.edu/monograph.php?doc=WiJerda.1852&select=I-2 [**Jerdan,** *Autobiography*].

Jollie, Rev. Thomas, *Parish of Bowden*, in *The New Statistical Account of Scotland*, No. V, Containing Part of the County of Roxburgh, With Map, and Part of Forfar, Edinburgh: William Blackwood & Sons, 1835 [**Jollie, Bowden**].

Karr, Adam Ramsay, Will of Andrew Ramsay Karr of Kippilaw, Roxburghshire, 19 March 1800: Public Record Office: NAUK PROB 11/1339/193, Image Reference: 473 [**Will of Adam Ramsay Karr**].

Karr, John Seton, *A Genealogical tree of the race of the house of Yair or Zaire from Thomas Karr: who lived prior to the year 1500 and was a lineal descendant of Robert Karr of Yair, second son of the second Ralph Ker of Kersheugh, a lineal descendant of Ralph Ker, the first of Kersheugh (brother of Robert Ker of Altonburn, ancestor of the Kers of Cessford and of Robert first Earl of Roxburghe) and ancestor of Sir Robert Ker of Ferniehirst, whose only daughter and heiress (Margaret) married Thomas Ker of Smelholme, thereafter of Ferniehirst, second son of Andrew Ker of Cessford and ancestor of Robert, Earl of Somerset in England, of the Lords Jedburgh and of Robert Earl of Ancrum, ancestor of the Marquis of Lothian and of Kippilaw from Lieutenant Colonel Andrew Karr (great great grandson of the said Thomas Karr of Yair) who acquired this estate from his kinsman Thomas Karr of Kippilaw, whose ancestors held it for many generations*, Golden Square London: John Seton Karr, 1 January 1812; https://familysearch.org/eng/library/fhlcatalog/supermain-frameset.asp?display=titledetails&titleno=261985 [**Karr,** *A Genealogical tree of the race of the house of Yair*].

Ker, General vs. John Bellenden Ker, Case No. 581, Nov 27 1805: In Hume, David, *Decisions of the Court of Sessions 1781–1822, in the Form of a Dictionary*, Edinburgh: William Blackwood, 1839 [**General Ker vs. John Bellenden Ker**].

Kinghorne, Alexander, *Letter from an Australian Settler*, Chambers' Edinburgh Journal, Vol. 9, No. 417, Saturday January 25 1840, London: WS Orr and Co., Amen Corner, Paternoster Row, 21 [**Kinghorne,** *Letter of an Australian Settler*].

Kinghorne, Alex., Engineer, (1) Plan of a proposed new line of road from the confines of Selkirk to St Boswells Green and (2) Plan of a proposed new road from St. Boswell's Green to Selkirk, House of Lords Record Office (1819. 59 G.3 c. 123. Roxburgh Roads); in Moir, D.G. (ed), *The Early Maps of Scotland To 1850*, By a Committee of the Royal Scottish Geographical Society, 3rd Edition, Volume 2, Edinburgh: The Royal Geographical Society, 1983, 229 [**Kinghorne, *Selkirk to St Boswells Green***].

Lazarus, Ebenezer, *A Particular Description of the Town of Kelso; with a Plain and Undisguised Account of its Admirable and Delightful Situation*, Kelso, printed for the author, 1789, in: Mason, John, *Kelso Records; being Traditions and Recollections of Kelso*, Edinburgh: Peter Brown, St James' Square [**Lazarus, *Town of Kelso***].

Lockhart, J.G., *Memoirs of The Life of Sir Walter Scott, Bart*, Vol. I, Boston: Otis, Broaders, and Company, 1837 [**Lockhart, *Scott***].

McAulay, Karen, *Our Ancient Scottish Song Collection from the Enlightenment to the Romantic Era*, Farnham: Ashgate Publishing Ltd, 2013, Chapter 3; http://books.google.com.au/books?id=N0QJzayWDaUC&pg=PT108&lp-g=PT108&dq=Blaikie+of+Holydean&source=bl&ots=8_nRof5ST2&sig=-fy5OcyOyI7tCAXwx3cOPc7dPLiw&hl=en&sa=X&ei=nEyVU5OAIsy-FlAXnu4E4&ved=0CEYQ6AEwBg#v=onepage&q=Blaikie%20of%20Holydean&f=false [**McAulay, *Our Ancient Scottish Song Collection***].

Malaquias, Isabel, *An Eighteenth Century Travelling Theodolite*, Hist. cienc. saude-Manguinhos, 23 (3) Rio de Janeiro Jul/Sep 2016: http://dx.doi. org/10.1590/S0104-59702016000300004 [**Malaquias, *An Eighteenth Century Travelling Theodolite***].

Manley, Gordon, 'The mean temperature of central England, 1698–1952', *Quarterly Journal of the Royal Meteorological Society*, Vol. 79, 1953; http:// www.rmets.org/sites/default/files/qj53manley.pdf [**Manly, *The mean temperature of central England, 1698–1952***].

Martens, Conrad, *Lansdowne Bridge over Prospect Creek near Liverpool*, 1836, watercolour, NLA PIC Solander Box D1 #R3900; http://nla.gov.au/nla. obj-134387680 [**Martens, *Lansdowne Bridge***].

Macarthur, James, *New South Wales, its present state and future prospects*, London: D Walther, 1837 [**Macarthur, *New South Wales***].

McCulloch, J.M., *Parish of Kelso*, 1838, in: *Statistical Account of Scotland*, Vol. III, Roxburgh-Peebles-Selkirk, Edinburgh and London: William Blackwood and Sons, 1845 [**McCulloch, *Parish of Kelso***].

MacGibbon, D and Ross, T (1887–92), *The castellated and domestic architecture of Scotland from the twelfth to the eighteenth centuries*, 5v Edinburgh, 1887–1892, held at RCAHMS F.5.21.MAC; cited at http://canmore.rcahms. gov.uk/en/site/34798/details/melgund+castle/ [**MacGibbon & Ross, *The castellated and domestic architecture of Scotland***].

Milne, Adam, *A description of the parish of Melrose: in answer to Mr. Mait-*

land's queries, sent to each parish of the Kingdom, Kelso: Printed by James Palmer, for John Martin, and sold by him at Melrose, 1782 [**Milne, *Parish of Melrose***].

Milne, David, *Report of the Committee of the Berwick and Kelso Railway Company, Appointed at a Special General Meeting of the Proprietors, Held at Coldstream on the 5th of October, 1836*, Edinburgh: Printed by Andrew Shortrede, 1837 [**Milne, *Report of the Committee of the Berwick and Kelso Railway Company***].

Minto, The Countess of (editor), *Lord Minto in India: Life and Letters of Gilbert Elliot First Earl of Minto from 1807 to 1814 while Governor-General of India*, London: Longmans, Green, and Co., 1880 [**Countess of Minto, *Lord Minto in India***].

Mosley, Charles (ed.), *Burke's Peerage, Baronetage & Knightage, 107th edition, 3 volumes*, Wilmington, Delaware: Burke's Peerage (Genealogical Books) Ltd, 2003; http://www.thepeerage.com/p12948.htm#i129478 [**Mosley, *Burke's Peerage***].

Mudie, Robert, *Historical Account of His Majesty's Visit to Scotland*, Edinburgh, 1822, ScotlandPages; https://digital.nls.uk/scotlandspages/timeline/18222.html [**Mudie, *His Majesty's Visit to Scotland***].

Muirhead, John, Dissertations on the Foederal Transactions between God and His Church, *Both Before and Since the Canon of Scripture was Completed*, Kelso: James Palmer, 1782 [**Muirhead, *Dissertations Foederal***].

Pace, James (gardener), *Poems on Various Occasions*, Edinburgh: Printed by James Ballantyne for the author, 1804, 89–95; http://books.google.com.au/books?id=iFtDAAAAYAAJ&pg=PP5&lpg=PP5&dq=pace+poems+on+various+occasions&source=bl&ots=d2IYaBSHgB&sig=d8zHY_B3ou8pUnI7n-QbusAtBTRY&hl=en&sa=X&ei=YrxbUvCVHKjsiAfqgYHIAw&ved=0C-CoQ6AEwAA#v=onepage&q=Kinghor&f=false [**Pace, *Poems on Various Occasions***].

Paterson, A.B., *The Works of Banjo Paterson*, London: Wordsworth Poetry Library, 1993 [**Paterson, *The Works of Banjo Paterson***].

Porter, *The History of Wellington*, 2. Sydney Gazette, Thu 19 Jan 1832, 3; https://trove.nla.gov.au/newspaper/article/2204528 [**Porter, *The History of Wellington***].

Priestly, Joseph, *Historical account of the Navigable Rivers, Canals, and Railways of Great Britain, as a reference to Nicols, Priesty and Walker's New Map of Inland Navigation, Derived from Original and Parliamentary Documents*, London: Longman, Rees, Orme, Brown & Green, 1831 [**Priestly, *Historical account of the Navigable Rivers, Canals, and Railways of Great Britain***].

391

Prior, J.H., *Topographic map of Beecroft Peninsula and Currarong Village, Jervis Bay*, New South Wales Department of Lands, compiled by J.H. Prior, Surveyor, 1944 [**Prior, *Topographic map of Beecroft Peninsula***].

Rivière, Marc Serge (translator & Ed.), *The Governor's Noble Guest, Hyacinthe de Bougainville's account of Port Jackson, 1825*, Melbourne: The Miegunyah Press, 1999 [**Rivière, *The Governor's Noble Guest***].

Russell, John, *The Haigs of Bemersyde, A Family History*, Edinburgh & London: William Blackwood and Sons, 1881; https://archive.org/details/haigsofbemersyde00russuoft [**Russell, *The Haigs of Bemersyde***].

Scott, Andrew, 'The Cotter's Moss-Day' in Scott, Andrew, *Poems, chiefly in the Scottish Dialect*, Kelso: Printed by Alexander Leadbetter, 1811, 157–162; https://archive.org/details/poemschieflyinsc00scot. Bowden Free Church, Bowden, Roxburghshire, Scotland, http://familysearch.org/learn/wiki/en/Bowden,_Roxburghshire,_Scotland [**Scott, *The Cotter's Moss-Day***].

Scott, Hew, *Fasti ecclesiae scoticanae; the succession of ministers in the Church of Scotland from the reformation*, Vol. 2, Edinburgh: Oliver and Boyd, 1917 [**Scott, *Fasti ecclesiae scoticanae***].

Scott, John, *Berwick-Upon-Tweed, The History of the Town and Guild*, London: Elliot Stock, 1888 [**Scott, *Berwick-Upon-Tweed***].

Scott, Sir Walter, Bart., *Letters of Sir Walter Scott*; http://www.walterscott.lib.ed.ac.uk/etexts/etexts/letters4.PDF [**Letters of Sir Walter Scott**].

Scott, Sir Walter, Bart., *Marmion*, The Poetical Works of Sir Walter Scott, Bart., Vol. VII, Edinburgh: Ballantine and Co., 1830 [**Scott, *Marmion***].

Scott, Sir Walter, Bart, *Rob Roy*, An Electronic Classic Series, Jim Manis (ed.), Hazleton: University of Pennsylvania State University, Chapter Tenth, 193; http://www2.hn.psu.edu/faculty/jmanis/w-scott/RobRoy6x9.pdf [**Scott, *Rob Roy***].

Scott, Sir Walter, Bart., *The Antiquary*, London: Macmillan and Co., Limited, 1905 [**Scott, *The Antiquary***].

Scott, Sir Walter, Bart., *The Monastery*, London: Macmillan and Co., Limited, 1905 [**Scott, *The Monastery***].

Scott, Sir Walter, Bart., *The Poetical Works of Sir Walter Scott*; First Edition, Containing Minstrelsy of the Scottish Border, Sir Tristrem, and Dramatic Pieces, Paris: Baudry's European Library, 1838 [**Scott, *The Poetical Works***].

Scott, Sir Walter, Bart., *The Journal of Sir Walter Scott from the Original*

Manuscript at Abbotsford, New York: Harper and Brothers, 1891 [**Scott, *The Journal of Sir Walter Scott***].

Sessional Papers printed by order of the House of Lords, Or presented by Royal Command, 1841, Vol VII, various parishes in the Counties of Roxburgh and Berwick. NLA Electronic Resources: https://catalogue.nla.gov.au/Record/7203636/Offsite?url=http%3A%2F%2Fparlipapers.proquest.com%2Fparlipapers%2Fdocview%2Ft70.d75.1867-044857 [**House of Lords, Sessional Papers**].

Seton, George, *A History of the Family of Seton during Eight Centuries*, Vol II, Edinburgh: Privately Printed by T. and A. Constable, 1896, [**Seton, *A History of the Family of Seton***].

Seton Karr, John, Will of John Seton Karr of Saint James Westminster, Middlesex, 11 July, 1812; Public Records Office, NAUK PROB 11/1568/181, 13 May 1815, 346–347; http://discovery.nationalarchives.gov.uk/SearchUI/Details?uri=D609323 [**Will of John Seton Karr**].

Shaw, Patrick and Dunlop, Alexander, *Cases decided in the Court of Sessions from Nov 13 1827 to July 1828*, Vol 6, Edinburgh: Printed for William Blackwood, 1828; http://books.google.com.au/books?id=b30DAAAAQA-AJ&pg=PA21&lpg=PA21&dq=Archibald+Swinton+Duke+of+Rox-burghe&source=bl&ots=WRvr6klN76&sig=iF2UkB0ItgWV0QB8zX-w2bBuoa8k&hl=en&sa=X&ei=l1tXVJ_5CIPW8gW-sIKIDQ&ved=0C-B0Q6AEwAA#v=onepage&q=Archibald%20Swinton%20Duke%20of%20Roxburghe&f=false [**Shaw & Dunlop, *Cases Decided in the House of Lords 1824***].

Sinclair, Sir John, Bart, *The Statistical Account of Scotland Drawn up from the Communications of the Ministers of the Different Parishes*, Vol I to XX, 1791–1799, Edinburgh: Printed and Sold by William Creech, 1795 [**Sinclair, *Statistical Account of Scotland***].

Smith, James, *History of Kelso Grammar School*, Kelso: Printed by John Smith, 'Kelso Mail' Office, for Tweedside Physical and Antiquarian Society; and Published by J. & J.H. Rutherford, 1909 [**Smith, *History of Kelso Grammar School***].

Spence, Catherine Helen, An Autobiography, Australian Digital Collections, The University of Sydney, 1910; http://adc.library.usyd.edu.au/view?docId=ozlit/xml-main-texts/p00014.xml;chunk.id=d1189e196;toc.depth=1;toc.id=d1189e196;database=;collection=;brand=default [**Spence, *Autobiography***].

Stillwell, G.T., *Charles Henry Theodore Costantini*, Melbourne: Design and

Art Australia Online, 1992; https://www.daao.org.au/bio/charles-henry-the-odore-costantini/biography/ [**Stillwell,** *Costantini*].

Sturma, Michael, 'Eye of the Beholder: The Stereotype of Women Convicts, 1788–1852', in *Labour History*, No. 34, 1978 [**Sturma,** *Eye of the Beholder*].

Symonds, Deborah A., *Weep Not for Me, Women, Ballads, and Infanticide in Early Modern Scotland*, Philadelphia: Pennsylvania State University Press, 1997 [**Symonds,** *Weep Not for Me*].

Tancred of Weens, George, *The Annals of a Border Club (The Jedforest), and Biographical Notices of the Families Connected Therewith*, Jedburgh: T.S. Smail, 1899 [**Tancred,** *Annals of a Border Club*].

Thomson, John and Johnson, William, *The Atlas of Scotland*, Edinburgh: John Thomson & Co., 1832, Introduction [**Thomson,** *Atlas of Scotland*].

Thorp, W., *Bonnyrigg House: Cultural Resources Report Comprising Archival and Archaeological Investigations of the Former Male Orphan School, Liverpool*, typescript, Heritage Council of New South Wales, Mar 1982, 43, 46; http://dx.doi.org/10.4227/11/50459ED64E1B1 [**Thorpe,** *Bonnyrigg House*].

Thorp, Wendy, *The Penrith Heritage Study, The Historical Archaeological Component*, Camperdown: Wendy Thorp, 1986 [**Thorp, The Penrith Heritage Study**].

Veitch, James of Inchbonny, *Tables for converting the weights and measures, hitherto used in Roxburghshire, into Imperial Standards*, as established by Act 5, Geo IV, Cap. 4, Jedburgh: Printed by Walter Easton, 1826 [**Veitch,** *Tables*].

Warre, H.J., *Historical Records of the Fifty-Seventh, or, West Middlesex Regiment of Foot, 1755 to 1878*, London: W. Mitchell & Co., 1878, 75 [**Warre,** *Historical Records of the Fifty-Seventh*].

Watson, Frederick (ed.), Historical Records of Australia, Series 1, Volumes. I; II; IV; V; X; XI; XII; XIII; XIV; XVI (Sydney, 1921) [Cited with date, **HRA, 1,** followed by volume and page numbers].

Waugh to his father, written from Nonnorah, 10 February 1836: Waugh, D.L., *Three Years Practical Experience of a Settler in New South Wales, being extracts from letters to his friends in Edinburgh, from 1834 to 1837*, 5th Edition, Edinburgh: John Johnstone, Hunter Square, 1838, http://www.nla.gov.au/apps/doview/nla.aus-f2674-p.pdf [**Waugh,** *Letters to Friends*].

Wilkie, Thomas, manuscript notebook incorporated in Walter Scott's *Scotch*

Ballads, Materials for Border Minstrelsy, Ed. J. E. H. Thomson, Stirling, 1909, 58–59, MS. 877, National Library of Edinburgh: Cited by Montgomerie, William, *Sir Walter Scott and Ballad Editor*, The Review of English Studies, 1956; http://www.jstor.org/stable/511839 [**Wilkie, *Manuscript Notebook***].

Wood, John, ca 1780–1847, *Plan of the Town of Kelso*, Edinburgh: T. Brown, 1823, 1 map 543x742mm, EMS.X.009 (formerly EU.31.W), National Library of Scotland [**Wood, *Plan of the Town of Kelso***].

SECONDARY SOURCES

Abbott, G.J., *Woore, Thomas (1804–1878)*, ADB; http://adb.anu.edu.au/ biography/woore-thomas-4888/text8179 [**Abbott, *Woore***].

Anonymous, *Stephen, Sidney (1797–1858)*, Obituaries Australia, http:// oa.anu.edu.au/obituary/stephen-sidney-28378/text36020 [**Anon, *Sidney Stephen***].

Alexander, Alison, *The Companion to Tasmanian History*, Hobart : Centre for Tasmanian Historical Studies, University of Tasmania, 2005 [**Alexander, *The Companion to Tasmanian History***].

Baker, D.W.A., *Mitchell, Sir Thomas Livingstone (1792–1855)*, ADB, http:// adb.anu.edu.au/biography/mitchell-sir-thomas-livingstone-2463/text3297 [**Baker, *Mitchell***].

Barker, Ian, *Sorely tried: democracy and trial by jury in New South Wales*, Series: Francis Forbes Lectures, Francis Forbes Society for Australian Legal History, 2002 [**Barker, *Sorely tried***].

Barker, Theo, *A History of Bathurst*, Vol. 1, The Early Settlement to 1862, Bathurst: Crawford House Press, 1992 [**Barker, *A History of Bathurst***].

Barker, Theo, *Stewart, William (1769–1854)*, ADB, http://adb.anu.edu.au/ biography/stewart-william-2700/text3787 [**Barker, *Stewart***].

Barry, Tom and Hall, Douglas, *Spottiswoode: Life and Labour on a Berwick-shire Estate, 1753–1793*, East Linton, East Lothian: Tuckwell Press Ltd, 1997, xvi, 3, 31, 57, 156–157 [**Barry and Hall, *Spottiswoode***].

Bathurst, Henry (1762–1834), ADB, http://adb.anu.edu.au/biography/ bathurst-henry-1751/text1945 [**Henry Bathurst**].

Beale, E., Mitchell, W. and Organ, M. (eds), *Backhouse and Walker in Illa-warra and Shoalhaven 1836*, Wollongong: Illawarra Historical Society, 1991 [**Beale et al., *Backhouse and Walker in Illawarra***].

Bendall, Sarah, *Dictionary of land surveyors and local mapmakers of Great Britain and Ireland 1530–1830*, 2nd edition in Two Volumes, London: The British Library, 1997 [**Bendall, *Dictionary of land surveyors***].

Bennett, J.M., *The establishment of jury trial in New South Wales*, Sydney: 1961, SLNSW MLMSS 619 [**Bennett, *The establishment of jury trial in New South Wales***].

Benson, Mavis K. and Ernest, J., *The Church on the Hill*, Ryde, N.S.W.: Parish Council of St Anne's Anglican Church, 1992 [**Benson & Ernest, *The Church on the Hill***].

Black, Adam, *Black's Picturesque Tourist Guide of Scotland*, 3rd edition, Edinburgh: Adam and Charles Black, 1843 [**Black, *Black's Picturesque Tourist Guide of Scotland***].

Boase, Frederic, Modern English Biography, Vol 1, Truro: Netherton and Worth, 1892 [**Boase, *Modern English Biography***].

Boog Watson, Charles B. (editor), *Roll of Edinburgh Burgesses and Guild-brethren, 1761–1841*, Edinburgh: Skinner and Company Ltd, 1933 [**Boog Watson, Edinburgh Burgesse**s].

Boutell, Charles, *The Handbook to English Heraldry*, 11th Edition, London: Reeves & Turner, 1914 [**Boutell, *The Handbook to English Heraldry***].

Bubacz, B.M., The Female and Male Orphan Schools in BNSW 1801–1850, PhD Thesis, University of Sydney, 2007 [**Bubacz, *The Female and Male Orphan Schools***].

Burke, John Bernard, *A Genealogical and Heraldic History of the Commoners of Great Britain and Ireland, Enjoying Territorial Possessions of High Official Rank; but Uninvested with Heritable Honours*, Vol. III, London: Published for Henry Colburn, by R. Bentley, 1836, 434; http://books.google.com.au/books?id=qf4GAAAAQAAJ&pg=PA433&lpg=PA433&dq=Mackerston&source=bl&ots=3q6WEYQjBE&sig=j4tnYYTES8o80IA8GXF9vDu37x-M&hl=en&sa=X&ei=_er-UovBHYSlkAXN9oCICg&ved=0CCwQ6A-EwAQ#v=onepage&q=Mackerston&f=false [**Burke, *Genealogical and Heraldic History***].

Cable, K.J., Cartwright, Robert (1771–1856), ADB; http://adb.anu.edu.au/biography/cartwright-robert-1882/text2211 [**Cable, *Cartwright***].

Cant, Ronald G., *David Steuart Erskine, 11th Earl of Buchan: Founder of the Society of Antiquities of Scotland*, in: Bell, A.S. (ed), *The Scottish Antiquarian Tradition, Essays to mark the bicentennery of the Society of Antiquaries of Scotland and its Museum, 1780–1980*, Edinburgh: John Donald Publishers Ltd, 1980 [**Cant, *Buchan***].

Chancellor, E. Beresford, *The History of the Squares of London, Topographical & Historical*, London: Keegan Paul, Trench, Trübner & Co. Ltd, 1907, 137–138; https://archive.org/stream/historysquaresl02changoog#page/n10/mode/2up [**Chancellor, *The History of the Squares of London***].

Child, F.J., *The English and Scottish Popular Ballads*, Boston: Houghton, Mifflin and Company, 1892 [**Child, *English and Scottish Popular Ballads***].

Christison, D. (1895), 'The forts of Selkirk, the Gala Water, the Southern slopes of the Lammermoors, and the north of Roxburgh', *Proc. Soc. Antiq. Scot.*, Vol. 29, 145 [**Christison, *The Forts***].

Collinge, J.M., *Lockhart, Sir Alexander Macdonald, 1ˢᵗ Bt. (?1776–1816), of Largie, Argyll and Lee Castle and Carnwath, Lanark*, in: *The History of Parliament: the House of Commons 1790–1820*, ed. R. Thorne, 1986 [**Collinge, *Lockhart***].

Colville, Berres Hoddle, *Robert Hoddle: pioneer surveyor-artist in Australia*, National Library of Australia News, Vol. 16, No. 10, July 2006: 18–21 [**Colville, *Hoddle***].

Connor, M. C., *The Politics of Grievance: society and political controversies in New South Wales 1819–1827*, PhD thesis, University of Tasmania, Dec 2002 [**Connor, *The Politics of Grievance***].

Crabb, Peter, *The Jervis Bay Region 1788 to 1939, An Emptied Landscape*, Huskisson: Lady Denman Heritage Complex, 2007 [**Crabb, *The Jervis Bay Region 1788 to 1939***].

Crockett, W.S., *The Scott Country*, London: Adam and Charles Black, 1902 [**Crockett, *The Scott Country***].

Cross-Rudkin, P.S.M., *James Hollinsworth (1787–1828)*, in Skempton, A.W. (ed), *A Biographical Dictionary of Civil Engineers in Great Britain and Ireland*, Vol. 1 1500–1830, London: Thomas Telford Publishing on behalf of the Institution of Civil Engineers, 2002, [**Cross-Rudkin, *James Hollinsworth***].

Cross-Rudkin, P.S.M., *John Rennie FRS FRSE (1761–1821)*, in Skempton, A.W. (ed), *A Biographical Dictionary of Civil Engineers in Great Britain and Ireland*, Vol. 1 1500–1830, London: Thomas Telford Publishing on behalf of the Institution of Civil Engineers, 2002 [**Cross-Rudkin, *John Rennie***].

Cruft, Kitty, Dunbar, John and Fawcett, Richard, *The Buildings of Scotland, Borders*, New Haven and London: Yale University Press, 2006 [**Cruft et al., *The Buildings of Scotland***].

Currey, C.H., Forbes, *Sir Francis (1784–1841)*, ADB, https://adb.anu.edu.au/
biography/forbes-sir-francis-2052/text2545 [**Curry, Forbes**].

Curry, C.H., Dowling, *Sir James (1787–1844)*, ADB; http://adb.anu.edu.au/
biography/dowling-sir-james-1989/text2421 [**Currey, Dowling**].

Darling, Sir Ralph (1772–1858), ADB, http://adb.anu.edu.au/biography/dar-
ling-sir-ralph-1956/text2353 [**Darling**].

Davidson, J.W., *Busby, James (1801–1871)*, ADB, http://adb.anu.edu.au/
biography/busby-james-1858/text2161 [**Davidson, James Busby**].

Dod, Charles R., *The Peerage, Baronetage, and Knightage, of Great Britain
and Ireland*, 14th Year, London: Whitaker and Co., 1854, 239; https://pro-
tect-au.mimecast.com/s/xfxKCL7EwMfV035YtB3gS4?domain=archive.org
[**Dod, The Peerage, Baronetage, and Knightage**].

Dodgshon, Robert A., 'Land Improvement in Scottish Farming: Marl and
Lime in Roxburghshire and Berwickshire in the Eighteenth Century', in: *Ag.
Hist. Rev.* 26, 1978, 2; http://www.bahs.org.uk/AGHR/ARTICLES/26n1a1.
pdf [**Dodgshon, Land Improvement in Scottish Farming**].

Duncan, Ian, *Walter Scott and the Historical Novel*, in Garside, Peter and
O'Brien, Karen, *The Oxford History of the Novel in English,* Vol. 2, English
and British Fiction 1750–1820, 2018, Oxford Scholarship Online:
DOI:10.1093/oso/9780199574803.001.0001 [**Duncan, Walter Scott and the
Historical Novel**].

Dunkley, John R., *The 1830 Cave Diaries of Thomas Livingstone Mitchell*,
Helictite, 42, 2016, 21–37; http://helictite.caves.org.au/pdf1/42.Dunkley.pdf
[**Dunkley, The 1830 Cave Diaries of Thomas Livingstone Mitchell**].

Dunlop, E.W., *Oxley, John Joseph (1784–1828)*, ADB, http://adb.anu.edu.au/
biography/oxley-john-joseph-2530/text3431 [**Dunlop, Oxley**].

Dunlop, E.W., *Ovens, John (1788–1825)*, ADB, http://adb.anu.edu.au/biog-
raphy/ovens-john-2529/text3429 [**Dunlop, Ovens**].

Dyck, Ian, *Cobbett, William (1763–1835)*, Oxford Dictionary of National
Biography, Oxford University Press, 2004; http://www.oxforddnb.com/in-
dex/5/101005734/ [**Dyck, Cobbett**].

Dyer, Colin, *The French Explorers and Sydney, 1788–1831*, St Lucia: University of Queensland Press, 2009 [**Dyer, The French Explorers in Sydney**].

Dyster, Barrie (2007), Bungling a Courthouse: a story of convict workplace
reform, *Journal of the Royal Australian Historical Society*, 93, 1 [**Dyster,
Bungling a Courthouse**].

Edith, Lady Haden-Guest, *Scott, Hugh (1758–1841), of Harden, Roxburgh and Mertoun, Berwicks.*, in *The History of Parliament: the House of Commons 1754–1790*, ed. L. Namier, J. Brooke, 1964: http://www.historyofparliamentonline.org/volume/1754-1790/member/scott-hugh-1758-1841 [**Edith, Hugh Scott of Harden**].

Fergusson, Robert, *The King's Birth-day in Edniburgh*, 1772; in Ross, John, *The Book of Scottish Poems: Ancient and Modern*, Edinburgh Publishing Company, 1884 [**Fergusson, Robert, *The King's Birth-day in Edinburgh***].

Fleming, David Hay, *The Reformation in Scotland: causes, characteristics, consequences*; https://babel.hathitrust.org/cgi/pt?id=uc1.$b686510&view=1up&seq=584 [**Fleming, The Reformation in Scotland**].

Fletcher, Brian H., *Ralph Darling, A Governor Maligned*, Melbourne: Oxford University Press, 1984 [**Fletcher, *A Governor Maligned***].

Fletcher, Brian, Ralph Darling, in *The Governors of New South Wales, 1788–2010*, David Clune and Ken Turner (eds), Sydney: The Federation Press, 2009 [**Fletcher, *Darling***].

Frederick Duke of York: http://en.wikipedia.org/wiki/Prince_Frederick,_Duke_of_York_and_Albany [**Frederick Duke of York, wikipedia**].

Glover, Julian, *Man of Iron, Thomas Telford and the Building of Britain*, London: Bloomsbury, 2017 [**Glover, *Telford***].

Goodin, V.W.E., Public Education in NSW before 1848, *J.R.A.H.S.*, 36, 1950, (4 parts) [**Goodin, *Public Education in NSW before 1848***].

Gray, Nancy, *Dumaresq, William John (1793–1868)*, ADB, http://adb.anu.edu.au/biography/dumaresq-william-john-2239/text2447 [**Gray, *Dumaresq***].

Henderson, Thomas Finlayson, *John Ballantyne (1774–1821)*, Dictionary of National Biography 1885–1900, Volume 3; http://en.wikisource.org/wiki/Ballantyne,_John_(1774–1821)_(DNB00). *Walter Scott, School and University*, © Edinburgh University Library; http://www.walterscott.lib.ed.ac.uk/biography/education.html [**Henderson, *John Ballantyne***].

Hewitt, Rachel, *Map of a Nation – A biography of the Ordnance Survey*, London: Granta, 2010 [**Hewitt, *Map of a Nation***].

Heydon, J.D., *Brisbane, Sir Thomas Makdougall (1773–1860)*, ADB, http://adb.anu.edu.au/biography/brisbane-sir-thomas-makdougall-1827/text2097 [**Heydon, *Brisbane***].

Hogg, James, *Tales of the Wars of Montrose*, Edinburgh: Edinburgh University Press, 2002 [**Hogg, *Tales of the Wars of Montrose***].

James, Lawrence, *The Rise and Fall of the British Empire*, New York: Little, Brown & Co., 1994 [**James, *Rise and Fall of the British Empire***].

Jameson, R., *A Trip to London; or, the Humours of a Berwick Smack*, Edinburgh: Printed by Michael Anderson, 1815; http://books.google.com.au/ books?id=9f4HAAAAQAAJ&pg=PA71&lpg=PA71&dq=London+to+Berwick+by+sea&source=bl&ots=NhJ2Sz5XJd&sig=69Q9UTwybbPBsXED-3FIJD-9A88M&hl=en&sa=X&ei=I4p8U8qGCIS-kQWLhICgDQ&ved=0C-GIQ6AEwBjgK#v=onepage&q=London%20to%20Berwick%20by%20 sea&f=false [**Jameson, *A Trip to London***].

Jones, Ronald, *Stephen, Sidney*, An Encyclopedia of New Zealand, A.H. McLintock (ed); http://www.TeAra.bovt.nz/en/1966/stephen-sidney [**Jones, *Sidney Stephen***].

Karskens, Grace, *An historical and archaeological study of Cox's Road and early crossings of the Blue Mountains, New South Wales*, Sydney: Crown Lands Office, Bicentennial Project Unit, 1988 [**Karskens, *Cox's Road***].

Kass, T., Liston, C. and McClymont, J., *Parramatta: A past revealed*, Parramatta NSW: Parramatta Civic Council, 1996 [**Kass et al., *Parramatta: A past revealed***].

Kerr, Joan, Our Great Victorian Architect, Edmund Thomas Blacket (1817–1883), Sydney, N.S.W.: The National Trust of Australia, 1.78, 42 [**Kerr, *Blacket***].

Kenny, M.J.B., Hall, *Edward Smith (1786–1860)*, ADB, http://adb.anu.au/ biography/hall-edward-2143/text2729 [**Kenny, *Hall***].

Kilpatrick, David, *Walter Scott's Kelso*, Kelso: Kelso District Amenity Society, 2005; http://www.walterscott.lib.ed.ac.uk/publications/criticism/ scottandkelsobooklet.pdf. [**Kilpatrick, *Walter Scott's Kelso***].

Koeppel, Gerard T., *Bond of Union: Building the Erie Canal and the American Empire*, Cambridge MA: Da Capo Press, 2009 [**Koeppel, *Bond of Union***].

Koufopoulos, Alexander, *The Cattle Trades of Scotland, 1603–1745*, PhD Thesis, University of Edinburgh, 2004 [**Koufopoulos, *The Cattle Trades of Scotland, 1603–1745***].

Leighton, John M., *History of the County of Fife: From the Earliest Period to the Present Time*, Vol. III, Glasgow: Joseph Swan, 1811, p. 208; http://books. google.com.au/books?id=3YMLAAAAYAAJ&pg=PA208&lpg=PA208&d-q=%22kinghorn%22+AND+%22jointure%22&source=bl&ots=DK4QUw-00F9&sig=Hjuq18S-UzC0J7Yp7nXAXyt3PvU&hl=en&sa=X&ei=XTJZUt-

2DLqj-iAfMioHgCw&ved=0CCoQ6AEwAA#v=onepage&q=%22king-horn%22%20AND%20%22jointure%22&f=false [**Leighton,** *History of the County of Fife*].

Lever, Tresham, *Lessudden House, Sir Walter Scott and the Scotts of Raeburn*, London: The Boydell Press, 1971 [**Lever,** *Lessudden House*].

Lewis, I.M. (ed), *History and Social Anthropology*, Abingdon Oxfordshire: Routledge, 2004 [**Lewis,** *History and Social Anthropology*].

Liston, Carol, Sir Thomas Brisbane, in *The Governors of New South Wales, 1788–2010*, David Clune and Ken Turner (eds), Sydney: The Federation Press, 2009 [**Liston,** *Sir Thomas Brisbane*].

Loane, M.L., Moore, Thomas (1762–1840), ADB; http://adb.anu.au/biography/moore-thomas-2476/text3325 [**Loane,** *Moore*].

Long, Gavin, *Ranken, George (1793–1860)*, ADB, http://adb.anu.edu.au/biography/ranken-george-2572/text3515 [**Long,** *Ranken*].

MacDonald, James and Sinclair, James, *History of Hereford Cattle*, London: Vinton & Company Ltd, 1909 [**MacDonald et al.,** *History of Hereford Cattle*].

McKenzie, Bill, *McKenzie's around the River Ale*, http://freepages.genealogy.rootsweb.ancestry.com/~wemckenzie/bordermckenzies.htm. The Scots of Ashkirk, http://scott-ourrootsinscotland.weebly.com/scotts-of-ashkirk.html [**McKenzie,** *McKenzie's around the River Ale*].

McLachlan, N.D., 'Bathurst at the Colonial Office 1812–1827: A Reconnaissance', in *Historical Studies*, vol. 13 no. 52, 1969 [**McLachlan,** *Bathurst at the Colonial Office*].

MacLeay, Alexander (1767–1848), ADB, http://adb.anu.edu.au/biography/mcleay-alexander-2413/text3197 [*MacLeay*].

MacMillan, David S, *Scotland and Australia 1788–1850: Emigration, Commerce and Investment*, Oxford: Clarendon, 1967 [**McMillan,** *Scotland and Australia 1788–1850*].

Matheson, Ian, *Sowerby, William (1799–1875)*, ADB; http://adb.anu.edu.au/biography/sowerby-william-4625 [**Matheson,** *Sowerby*].

Matoff, Susan, *Conflicted Life: William Jerdan, 1782–1869*, London Editor, Author and Critic, Eastbourne: Sussex Academic Press, 2011 [**Matoff, Jerdan**].

Maver, Irene, *Everyday Life, Industrial Revolution (1770s to 1830s)*, Copyright © 2004 The GlasgowStory; http://www.theglasgowstory.com/story.

php?id=TGSCA [**Maver,** *Everyday Life, Industrial Revolution*].

Maxwell, Chis and Pugh, Alex, *The Merchant of Sydney, James Chisholm (1772–1837)*, Melbourne: Australian Scholarly Publishing, 2015 [**Maxwell & Pugh,** *The Merchant of Sydney*].

Maxwell, Chis and Pugh, Alex, *The Master of Hell's Gates, William Kinghorne (1796–1878)*, Melbourne: Australian Scholarly Publishing, 2017 [**Maxwell & Pugh,** *The Master of Hell's Gates*].

Maxwell-Stewart, Hamish, *Closing Hell's Gates: the Death of a Convict Station*, Crows Nest: Allen & Unwin, 2008 [**Maxwell-Stewart,** *Closing Hell's Gates*].

Millburn, John. R., *Adams of Fleet Street, Instrument Makers to King George III*. Aldershot: Ashgate Publishing Limited, 2000 [**Millburn,** *Adams of Fleet Street*].

Moffat, Alistair, *Kelsae, A History of Kelso from Earliest Times*, Edinburgh: Birlinn, 2006 [**Moffat,** *Kelso*].

Moffat, Alistair, *The Borders, A History of the Borders from Earliest Times*, Edinburgh: Birlinn, 2007 [**Moffat,** *The Borders*].

Mostert, Noel, The Line upon a Wind: The Great War at Sea, 1793–1815, London: Vintage Books, 2008 [**Mostert,** *The Line upon a Wind*].

New South Wales Office of Environment and Heritage, 2013, *Land and Soil Capability mapping of NSW. Bioregional Assessment Source Dataset*; http://data.bioregionalassessments.gov.au/dataset/08cacd00-81e9-4fec-8a68-c9f047bb13c8 [**NSW Environment and Heritage,** *Land and Soil Capability mapping of NSW*].

New South Wales Parks and Wildlife Service, *Jervis Bay National Park and Woollamia Nature Reserve Draft Management Plan*, 2007; http://www.environment.nsw.gov.au/resources/parkmanagement/JervisBay_Woollamia_Draft.pdf [**NSW Parks and Wildlife,** *Jervis Bay National Park*].

Newton, R.J.M., *Manning, John Edye (1783–1870)*, ADB; http://adb.anu.edu.au/biography/manning-john-edye-2428/text3205 [**Newton,** *Manning*].

O'Byrne, William Richard, *A Naval Biographical Dictionary*, Vol. 3, London: John Murray, 1849 [**O'Byrne,** *A Naval Biographical Dictionary*].

Olroyd, D., *In the Footsteps of Thomas Livingstone Mitchell (1792–1855): soldier, surveyor, explorer, geologist, and probably the first person to compile geological maps of Australia*; in Jackson, P.N. Wise, (ed) *Four Centuries of Geological Travel, The Search for Knowledge on Foot, Bicycle, Sledge and Camel*, Geological Society Special Publication No. 287, London: The

Geological Society, 2007 [**Olroyd,** *In the Footsteps of Thomas Livingstone Mitchell*].

Op den Brouw, Glen, *Town's First Fleet Power Couple*, Liverpool City Champion, 1 April 2019; https://www.liverpoolchampion.com.au/story/5986550/towns-first-fleet-power-couple/ [**Op den Brouw,** *Town's First Fleet Power Couple*].

Owen, Tim and Pilbeam, Elaine, *Ordnance Survey – Map Makers to Britain Since 1791*, Southampton: Ordnance Survey, 1992. Southampton: Ordnance Survey: https://www.ordnancesurvey.co.uk/about/overview/history.html [**Owen & Pilbeam,** *Ordnance Survey*].

Paix, John G., *Field Geology of the Shoalhaven District of NSW Australia, 2013*; http://www.aussiesapphire.com/ALF_Storage/Field%20Geology%20of%20the%20Shoalhaven%20District%20John%20Paix%201970.pdf [**Paix,** *Field Geology of the Shoalhaven*].

Parsons, Vivienne, 'Throsby, Charles (1777–1828)', ADB, http://adb.anu.edu.au/biography/throsby-charles-2735/text3861 [**Parsons,** *Throsby*].

Porter, Robert, History of Wellington: a record of the growth of the town and district from the earliest days, Wellington: Wellington Historical Society, 1991 (facsimile reprint) [**Porter,** *History of Wellington*].

Proudfoot, L.J. and Roche, Michael M. (eds), *(Dis)Placing Empire, Renegotiating Colonial Geographies*, Abington, Oxford: Routledge, 2017, Chapter 4, Place and Presbyterian Discourse in Colonial Australia [**Proudfoot & Roche,** *(Dis)Placing Empire*].

Richards, R.T.D., The development of the modern woollen carding machine, in Jenkins, J. Geraint (ed.), *The wool textile industry in Great Britain* (1 ed.), London [u.a.]: Routledge & Kegan, 1972 [**Richards,** *The development of the modern woollen carding machine*].

Roberts, D. A., 2006, 'The Valley of Swells', 'Special' or 'Educated' Convicts on the Wellington Valley Settlement, 1827–1830, *History Australia*, 3:1, 11.1-11.21, DOI: 10.2104/ha060011 [**Roberts,** *The Valley of Swells*].

Roberts, D. A., 'A sort of inland Norfolk Island?' Isolation, Coercion and Resistance on the Wellington Valley Convict Station, 1823–26, *Journal of Colonial Australian History* Vol. 2, No. 1, April 2000, 50–72 [**Roberts,** *A sort of inland Norfolk Island?*].

Robertson, C.J.A., *The Origins of the Scottish Railway System 1722–1844*, Edinburgh: John Donald Publishers Ltd, 1983 [**Robertson,** *Origins of the Scottish Railway*].

Sanders, Alvin, H., *Shorthorn Cattle*, Chicago: Sanders Publishing Company, 1918 [**Sanders, *Shorthorn Cattle***].

Schobert, Harold H., *Energy and Society*, London: Taylor & Francis, 2002 [**Schobert, *Energy and Society***].

Scott, Douglas, *A Hawick Word Book*, Copyright © 2002–2014 Douglas Scott, 121, 183, 227; http://www.astro.ubc.ca/people/scott/book.pdf [**Scott, *A Hawick Word Book***].

Scott, Walter, *The Complete Works of Sir Walter Scott, with a Biography and his last additions and illustrations, Volume I: Lay of the Last Minstrel*, New York: Conner & Cook, 1833 [**Scott, *The Complete Works***].

Skempton, A.W. (ed). *A Biographical Dictionary of Civil Engineers in Great Britain and Ireland*, Vol. 1, 1500–1830, London: Thomas Telford Publishing, 2002, 394; http://books.google.com.au/books?id=jeOMfpYMOtYC&pg=PA394&lpg=PA394&dq=Lapidge+draughtsman&source=bl&ots=aD-7CXZ_e6f&sig=wUdw1qlrfbHOqGRzKWB3n0rJwNQ&hl=en&sa=X-&ei=saIKVJysMMzauQS50oD4BA&ved=0CF8Q6AEwBA#v=onepage&q=Lapidge%20draughtsman&f=false [**Skempton, *Biographical Dictionary of Civil Engineers***].

Smellie, W., 'An historical account of the Society of Antiquaries of Scotland', *Transactions of the Antiquarian Society of Scotland*. I (1792), iv, in: *The Critical Review or Annals of Literature, Extended or Improved by a Society of Gentlemen*, London: A Hamilton, Falcon-Court, Fleet Street, 1792, Vol. 5, 402–410; books.google.com.au [**Smellie, *An historical account of the Society of Antiquaries***].

Smiles, Samuel, *The Life of Thomas Telford civil engineer with an introductory history of roads and travelling in Great Britain*; https://archive.org/stream/thelifeofthomast00939gut/tlfrd10.txt [**Smiles, *The Life of Thomas Telford***].

Stacker, Lorraine, *Chained to the Soil on the Plains of Emu: A History of the Emu Plains Government Agricultural Establishment 1819–1832*, Penrith: Nepean District Historical Society, 2000 [**Stacker, *Chained to the Soil***].

Steege, Joan, *Emu Plains*, 2nd edition, Penrith: Nepean District Historical Society, 1977 [**Steege, *Emu Plains***].

Steel, Watson A., *The History of Carcoar, 1815–1881*, 270, 281; http://www.rahs.org.au/wp-content/uploads/2015/05/04_Article_The-History-of-Carcoar-1815-1881.pdf [**Steel, *The History of Carcoar***].

Suttor, H.M., *Australian Milestones and Stories of the Past, 1770–1914*, Sydney: John Andrew & Co., 1925, 346 [**Suttor,** *Australian Milestones*].

Symonds, Deborah A., *Weep Not for Me, Women, Ballads, and Infanticide in Early Modern Scotland*, Philadelphia: Pennsylvania State University Press, 1997 [**Symonds,** *Infanticide in Early Modern Scotland*].

Thom, B.G., *Coastal Geomorphology of the Jervis Bay Area*, WETLANDS (Australia) 6 (2), 19–21; http://ojs.library.unsw.edu.au/index.php/wetlands/article/viewfile/135/148 [**Thom,** *Coastal Geomorphology of the Jervis Bay Area*].

Thornton, Clive, *Red Rubies: A History of The Devon Breed of Cattle*, Manchester: Devon Cattle Breeder's Society, 1993 [**Thornton,** *Red Rubies*].

Tink, Andrew, *William Charles Wentworth: Australia's Greatest Native Son*, Sydney: Allen & Unwin, 2009 [**Tink,** *Wentworth*].

Tipping, Marjorie J., *Hoddle, Robert (1794–1881)*, ADB; http://adb.anu.edu.au/biography/hoddle-robert-2190/text2823 [**Tipping,** *Hoddle*].

Veth, P., Sutton, P. and Neale, M. (eds), *Strangers on the Shore: Early coastal contacts in Australia*, Canberra: National Museum of Australia Press, 2008 [**Veth et al.,** *Strangers on the Shore*].

Wade, John, *Dick, Alexander (1791–1843)*, ADB, https://adb.anu.edu.au/biography/dick-alexander-12886/text23277 [**Wade,** *Dick*].

Walsh, G.P., Bradley, William (1800–1868), ADB; http://adb.anu.edu.au/biography/bradley-william-3041/text4469 [**Walsh,** *Bradley*].

Walsh, G.P., *Busby, John (1765–1857)*, ADB; http://adb.anu.edu.au/biography/busby-john-1859/text2115 [**Walsh,** *John Busby*].

West, John, *The History of Tasmania*, Launceston: J.S. Waddell, 1852 [**West,** *The History of Tasmania*].

Wilson, Robert, *A Sketch of the History of Hawick: including some account of the manners and character of the inhabitants; with occasional observations, to which is subjoined a short essay, in reply to Dr Chalmers on Pauperism and the Poor Laws*, Hawick: Printed by Robert Armstrong, 1825 [**Wilson,** *A Sketch of the History of Hawick*].

Withers, Charles W.J., 'A Nation Transformed: Scotland's Geography,

1707–1918', in *The Edinburgh History of Scottish Literature*, Volume 2, Enlightenment, Britain and Empire (1707–1918), Susan Manning, Ian Brown, Thomas Owen Clancy and Murray Pittock (eds), Edinburgh: Edinburgh University Press, 2007 [**Withers, *A Nation Transformed***].

Woods, Robert, *Infant Mortality in Britain: A Survey of Current Knowledge on Historical Trends and Variations*, In: *Infant and Child Mortality in the Past*, Alain Bideau, Bertrand Desjardins and Héctor Pérez Brignoli (eds), Oxford: Clarendon Press, 1997 [**Woods, *Infant Mortality in Britain***].

Wyatt, Ransome, T., *The History of Goulburn, NSW*, Sydney: Landsdowne Press, 1972 [**Wyatt, *Goulburn***].

Zakharov, John, 1987, *A Review of Aboriginal Cultural Factors for the Jervis Bay Area New South Wales*, WETLANDS (Australia) 6(2), 9–10 [**Zakharov, *Aboriginal Cultural Factors for the Jervis Bay Area***].

Acknowledgements

The authors acknowledge the mentorship and friendly direction of the late Emeritus Professor Brian Fletcher, to whom we have dedicated this book. We are particularly grateful to the eminent historian and teacher Stuart Braga for his diligent reading of our manuscript and for writing the Foreword to this book. We also thank Val Kinghorne and Paul Hardage for their comments on a draft manuscript; we are particularly grateful to Val for her interest in the book and her detailed assistance with Appendix 3.

The authors do not wish to become involved in the 'history wars', neither are we qualified to do so. Nevertheless, we acknowledge the dispossession of the traditional owners of the lands occupied by the Kinghorne and Chisholm families in southern New South Wales and elsewhere. In our previous two books we specifically acknowledged the first nation groups concerned, where known.

Much valuable source material was gathered from various archives, libraries and private collections. We thank the staff and volunteers of the following institutions for their assistance: the Mitchell Library at the State Library of NSW in Sydney NSW; the State Records of NSW at Kingswood; the National Library of Australia in Canberra ACT; the Oxley Museum of the Wellington Historical Society Inc., Wellington NSW; the National Archives of Scotland at Register House, and at Thomas Thomson House, in Edinburgh; the National Archives of the United Kingdom at Kew; the Pembrokeshire Archives, Prendergast, Haverfordwest, Wales; the Goulburn and District Historical Society at St Clair Museum, Sloane Street, Goulburn NSW; the Nowra Museum, Kinghorne Street, Nowra NSW; and the Bathurst District Historical Society, Russell Street, Bathurst NSW.

We thank Dr Alison Rosie (Registrar) at the National Register of Archives for Scotland in Edinburgh; and very special thanks to Mrs Caroline Ridley for access to the Seton Karr of Kippilaw Papers, which are a private collection held by her family. We are grateful to His Grace, the late Guy David Innes-Kerr, 10th Duke of Roxburghe, for supplying a copy of the plan of Faughill; Carol Morgan, Archivist at the Institution of Civil Engineers, London, for research on Alexander Kinghorne's status as a civil engineer; Lil Grogan for access to the Kippilaw mansion and estate; Margot Shortreed for hosting us at Kippilaw Mains; James and Claire McCorquodale for generously hosting us at Crossflat Farm; Peter Stubbs for permission to use his high resolution image of Leith Pier and Harbour; Douglas Scott for access to the archives at Maxton Kirk, and for searching the archives at Mertoun Kirk on our behalf; and the Milson and Fouracre families for generous access to the Cardross and Maxton Park properties at Goulburn, respectively. Many thanks also to Claudia Bolling, House Collections Officer, The Abbotsford Trust, for the searches conducted in their archives, and advice. We particularly thank Ian McClumpha of Imchad Ancestry for conducting comprehensive searches of kirk session reports on our behalf at the National Archives of Scotland. Our thanks to our friends Barbara and Alister Wright of Melrose, who first organised our introduction to people at Kippilaw, Scotland, and who have continued to provide encouragement and support.

An important source has been the Papers of Miriam Chisholm in the National Library of Australia, covering Chisholm family history in the period from 1791, and for much of the background to the Kinghorne family.

Last but not least we are grateful to Belinda Maxwell for her research, love and perseverance, and to each other for our continuing collaboration and friendship, throughout the long gestation of all three volumes of the Chisholm-Kinghorne family trilogy (2015–2022).

Index

The Index is divided into three sections:

People, Places & General

409

Brockie, Alexander 29, 140, 301

Brockie, Alison 29

Brockie, Betty 27–32, 40, 59, 92–95, 140, 142, 151, 161, 300–302

Brockie, Elizabeth 27, 271

Brockie, George 116, 301

Brockie, Helen 91, 301

Brockie, John 59, 116, 301

Brockie, Nancy 28, 301

Brockie, Thomas 27, 94, 116, 302, 309

Brockie, William 27–28, 51, 102, 118, 140, 142, 143, 151, 271, 301, 302, 310

Brodie, Mr 34, 85

Brodie, Peter 308

Brooks, Richard 234, 322

Broughton, Bishop 291–292

Brown Isabella 272

Brown, Lieutenant 228

Brown, Nicholas 108, 312

Brown, Mr 304

Brown, William 272, 324

Browne, William 234

Bruce, Robert The 10–11, 35, 154

Brunton, James 308

Buccleuch, Earl of 15

Buccleuch, Duke of 15–16, 128, 139, 156, 304

Buchan, Earl of (see Erskine) 25, 29, 139, 140–146, 162–163, 165–166, 170, 173, 214–215, 217, 242–243, 270, 280–281, 289, 297, 307, 316

Buckle, Matthew 313

Bunker, Mrs 246

Burke, Edmund 104

Burns, Robert 81

Busby, James 206, 208, 212, 320

Busby, John 199–200, 205–206

Campbell, George William

Campbell, John 75–76, 82

Campbell, John Thomas 196–197, 320

Campbell, John 238

Campbell, Robert 205, 320

Cant, Ronald 141, 214–215

Carre, Alexander 305

Carre, John 34, 302, 305

Carre, Walter Riddell 154–155

Cartwright, Robert 205–210, 246, 288

Cessford, A. 131, 135, 303

Chadwick, Willm 248

Chalmers, George 26, 62–67, 77, 87, 105, 158, 162–163, 166, 283, 305, 326

Chalmers, Robert 22

Chisholm, James Kinghorne 246

Chisholm, James Jnr 30, 102, 240, 245–249, 258, 264–266, 270, 288, 317, 322

Chisholm, James Snr 175–176, 191, 197, 212–214, 236, 245–246, 283, 291–293, 316–317, 320, 321

Chisholm, John 110

Christie, Lieutenant 222–223, 228, 321

Clark, John 157, 315

Clayton, Samuel 232

Clerk, William 36

Clarkson (or Clerkson), Dr 93, 312

Clinton, DeWitt 145–146

Cobbett, William 61–62, 80, 197, 212

Cockrane, John 310

Cole, John 258

Constantini, Théodore 182–183, 286, 319

Cowper, Charles 205, 207–208, 211, 213, 320

411

414

McGarvie, John 255
McHenry, (John) 186, 220, 318
MacLaurin, Colin 141
MacLeay, Alexander 196, 201, 206–207, 219, 227, 232, 244, 258, 319, 321
MacLeay, Fanny 201
MacMillan, David 161
Macquarie, Lachlan (Governor) 174, 176, 180, 204
Maitland, Anthony 310
Maitland, James 27, 118
Maither, Andrew 74, 308
Marr, Johnny 309
Marsden, Samuel 204–205, 252, 320
Manning, John Edye 239, 323
Mansfield, Ralph 202
Martens, Conrad 201, 236
Mather, Peter 310
Maxwell, John 227–228
Meehan, James 247
Mein, Capt. 78
Melbourne, Viscount (William Lamb) 273
Meldrum, Adam 70
Melville, Viscount (see also Dundas) 81–82
Milne, Nicol 73, 307
Milne, Thomas 72–73, 307
Minto, Lord (see Elliot)
Minto, Mr 303
Mirabeau, Honoré, compte de 104
Mistry, Clement 306
Mitchell, Thomas 158, 228, 251–252, 257–258, 315
Moir, James 278, 325
Moir, William 30, 255, 264, 276, 278, 323, 325

Molière, Jean-Baptiste Poquelin 186
Moore, Thomas 234–235, 286, 291, 322
Moriarty, William 255, 256
Mostert, Noel 81
Muirhead, John 13
Murdoch, Peter 176–180
Murray, James 308
Murray, John 9, 34, 68, 73, 87, 149, 302

Napier, Francis 38, 74–75, 302
Napier, Francis (8th Lord Napier) 156, 158
Napier, William John 158, 316, 328
Naphthali, Michael 218
Nelson, Horatio 77–78
Nisbet, Thomas 86, 309
Nixon, Christopher 313

Oliver, Robert 134, 314
Ovens, Major John 193–196, 317
Owen, John 156, 314
Oxley, John 193, 225, 227–228, 244, 321

Pace, James 140
Park, John 116, 311
Paterson, Banjo 240
Paul, John 212, 246
Paul, George 246
Paxton and Laurie, Messrs 305
Perry, Constable 235, 323
Peters, Joseph 177–180, 226, 231–232, 247–249, 286, 318–319
Peters, Mary (née Robinson) 180, 247, 319
Pitcairn, Robert 169

417

Places

418

419

420

General

430